Reviewer Acclaim
Debugging Applications

"John has combined his debugging experience with the knowledge of the best debugging gurus. This book is a must for anyone who wants to fully understand debugging in the Windows environment."

Steve Munyan (BoundsChecker development manager, Compuware NuMega)

"John Robbins is my idol. I want to be John Robbins."

Chris Sells (coauthor of *Effective COM* and *ATL Internals*)

"John Robbins has unveiled the black art of debugging Windows software and exposed it for all to see! His energy and excitement in pursuing excellence in this frequently misunderstood area of our industry serve as a beacon of hope to us all."

Peter Ierardi (software engineering consultant, Software Evolution, Inc.)

"*Debugging Applications* should be required reading in any computer science program."

Jim Austin (senior software engineer, Compuware NuMega)

"John Robbins has unveiled the real secrets to shipping better software faster. Even if you have been developing software since the first Altairs, and especially if you haven't, *Debugging Applications* will completely change the way you develop software."

John Maver (software engineer, BoundsChecker team, Compuware NuMega)

"If you are a serious Windows developer, John's book belongs on your 'must read' list. It's as simple as that."

Tim Yuhl (independent contractor)

"Our industry has needed a book like this for a long time. New developers, and even those who remember identifying op-codes as a fun party game, will appreciate John's practical and complete approach to wringing the defects from their code."

Kevin C. Kelly (program manager, Microsoft Visual Studio, Microsoft)

Microsoft®

Debugging
Applications

John Robbins

PUBLISHED BY
Microsoft Press
A Division of Microsoft Corporation
One Microsoft Way
Redmond, Washington 98052-6399

Library of Congress Cataloging-in-Publication Data
Robbins, John, 1964-
    Debugging Applications / John Robbins.
        p.   cm.
    ISBN 0-7356-0886-5
    1. Application software--Development. 2. Debugging in computer science. 3. Microsoft Windows (Computer file) I. Title.

    QA76.76.A65 R597   2000
    005.4'469--dc21   99-055180

Printed and bound in the United States of America.

1 2 3 4 5 6 7 8 9 WCWC 5 4 3 2 1 0

Distributed in Canada by Penguin Books Canada Limited.

A CIP catalogue record for this book is available from the British Library.

Microsoft Press books are available through booksellers and distributors worldwide. For further information about international editions, contact your local Microsoft Corporation office or contact Microsoft Press International directly at fax (425) 936-7329. Visit our Web site at mspress.microsoft.com.

Acquisitions Editor: Ben Ryan
Project Editor: Sally Stickney
Technical Editor: Marc Young

To my wife, Pam.
Did I tell you how much I love you yet today?

Contents

Contents

Contents

Part III   Power Tools and Techniques

Contents

Contents

List of Sidebars

Foreword

If this were a normal foreword, I'd begin by relating some alarming stories about bug-filled programs and warning that buggy applications are the root of society's evils. I'd probably then go on to spout statistics from a research report about the average number of bugs per 100 LOC (lines of code). These issues are legitimate, but I figure that if you're reading this book, you know that keeping bugs out of your code is important. As I see it, I have three tasks here:

- Explain who the heck John Robbins is
- Tell you why you want to read *this* book
- Tell some good stories about John Robbins

My first encounter with John was on a CompuServe forum. He was working on a homebrew debugger and had posted a question about the Microsoft Win32 Debugging API. In jest, he added that if he finished his debugger, maybe he could get a job at NuMega. I noticed the message and replied to him. I also mentioned that, incidentally, NuMega was looking for people (debugger nerds being hard to come by).

So began John's roller-coaster ride at NuMega. John showed up for his interview wearing a suit (probably his only one) and carrying a stack of neatly formatted floppies that contained his sample code, which was his completed debugger. During the interview, one of NuMega's owners fell asleep. (Or so John thought. The owner was actually focusing very intently.) John figured his chance at a job was gone right there, but in fact, he impressed everyone. A few months after John had been hired, he noticed that I was using one of his sample code disks as a coffee coaster. The truth was, I knew just from talking to him that John was hardcore about debugging, and I didn't need to check out the code.

In those days, NuMega was pretty small and was completely focused on getting cutting-edge debugging tools into developers' hands. John paid his dues in this crusade. He was so anxious to start work at NuMega that he moved from Virginia to New Hampshire almost immediately and rented one of the first places he found, a small house behind a fire station. Every time the fire station's doors roared open, John's PC lost power. At work, his first assignment was to write BugBench, a utility that demonstrated every error that BoundsChecker could catch. During that time, we rightfully called John the world's buggiest programmer.

A few months later, John's PC began freezing for roughly 10 seconds every hour or so. Despite his sharp words with the network administrator, no solution was forthcoming. Finally, John got his hands on a very early version of SoftICE for Windows NT (NuMega's kernel debugger). It didn't take long for John to figure out that another engineer had placed a Windows NT service on John's machine that counted to 175 million at random intervals using a time-critical thread. Try as he might, John was never able to top that prank.

A big part of NuMega in those days was sending engineers to trade shows. John's outgoing personality made him a natural target for the marketing folks, who were eager to include him in the booth presentations. One of the more, ahem, *lame* concepts involved a skit that had John starring as "a researcher at the Center for Bug Control in Atlanta." John wanted no part of this escapade, so he and another engineer came up with a completely different concept, an idea that became the genesis of the world-famous "Senior Boy and Junior Boy" skit. John was "Senior Boy," which became one of many nicknames John acquired at NuMega. I'll leave the origination of "Sporkie Boy" to your imagination.

As a footnote to that trade show, it was also where John learned what's really inside those stress-relieving balloons seemingly filled with sand. In this particular instance, the filling appeared to be tiny fragments of walnut shells. As John held the balloon over his head, he managed to puncture it, covering both of us—nay, the entire hotel room—in walnut shells. The shells even managed to find their way into the blankets and sheets of the beds.

The first half of John's time at NuMega was spent working on all aspects of BoundsChecker. His duties included developing the debugger loop, writing API validation stubs, fixing symbol table bugs, tweaking with the reference-counting algorithm for COM interfaces, and extending the code for streaming program trace information to disk. All in the same day! Debugging a debugging tool, especially one that takes liberties with the operating system, provides plenty of opportunity to hone your debugging skills.

Often John and I weren't able to use a debugger on the tough problems. One problem in particular I remember was when I ran BoundsChecker on Microsoft Visual SourceSafe the night before an important beta. It seemed to run fine, but a few minutes later, another engineer noticed that the file dates in Visual SourceSafe were something like "@@1?70." Regular backups weren't yet a part of our engineering process, so I ended up nearly completely destroying the version control database that held the only copy of the source code. Needless to say, the entire company was out for my hide, but John and I knuckled down and discovered that Visual SourceSafe was using some legacy MS-DOS code that trashed our file handles.

You might be wondering, "Why all these stories?" My point is that John is no academic or abstract theorist. John has walked the walk (and definitely likes to talk the talk). John and I frequently lament the fact that so many programming books are written by people who have little or no commercial development experience and who don't write programs that exceed 100 lines. John was a lead developer on several award-winning products. When he writes, he's conveying information learned from his hard-won experiences.

When John decides to do something, he does it whole hog. He will wrestle with a subject until he has it completely pinned. "I couldn't figure it out" isn't in John's vocabulary. Before John began his writing career, he offered to help me with a few functions for a *Microsoft Systems Journal* (MSJ) column I was working on. I think he spent more time on the code than I did. Because we both now write columns for MSJ, we regularly swap stories on the horrors we encounter while writing the code that accompanies our columns. On many occasions, his descriptions of how far he went to chase down a problem have left me slack-jawed.

Writing a book requires more than just knowledge of the subject matter. It also requires a desire to communicate this knowledge effectively to the reader. I noticed John's easy way with words in his very first article. I still consider it a treat to read anything by John Robbins. It's a pleasure to read something when I know the author truly understands the subject matter, has a passion for communicating it, and doesn't make it sound more complicated than it needs to.

John's enthusiasm for writing extends beyond just his articles, his columns, and this book. John leaves his stamp in just about any code he writes, as this excerpt from a classic e-mail I received at work shows:

```
What is with all this "DISCUSSION" crap John litters the
core with? Every damn function header is prefaced with a
complete chapter on the sociological implications of using
the routine and how planets may misalign if you use them
improperly - last month's MSJ was nearly a friggin book,
most of it filled with all of this "DISCUSSION" crap - he
wrote almost a book in and of itself for his "Form Load"
handler. Is the man an author or an engineer? Jeez...
```

As you'll see in this book, the answer is both!

Debugging is a subject that's shrouded in mystery, and in many ways it's an oral tradition. Good texts are sorely needed. The few books available focus mostly on sanitized situations and don't get into the swampy details that effective Windows debugging often entails. From time to time, publishers have approached me about writing a book on debugging, and I've always declined. It's not that I don't know enough about debugging. Rather, I find it difficult to quantify my gut-level debugging knowledge into something that can be put on paper. John doesn't have this problem.

From my perspective, effective debugging is pretty simple at a high level. I always come back to two tenets:

- ■ Know what's supposed to be happening
- ■ Know how to use your tools to see what's really happening

If you have these two things nailed, debugging is usually straightforward. The problem is, both of the above items aren't so easy to pull off. When I say "Know what's supposed to be happening," I don't expect your knowledge to stop at your source code. You have to be able to see both the big picture and the microscopic details. What did the compiler mutate your code into? What happens inside that API call? If you can't answer these questions, you're flying blind.

I'm not saying that to debug you need to trace through every instruction. Rather, when the need arises, you should be able to keep breaking the problem into smaller and smaller pieces—something John recommends in Chapter 1 of this book. You might also have to dig into components that you don't control to find the cause of a crash. Eventually, you'll find the answer if you go deep enough into the bits. A lot of tracking down bugs requires you to know the intricacies of your language, operating system, and CPU—another topic John covers in Chapter 1. The chapter on the minimum amount of x86 assembly language you should know (Chapter 6) will be an invaluable resource for you.

Likewise, knowing how to use your tools effectively is critical. Debugging tools have become fairly sophisticated, and many developers never get (or don't take) the opportunity to become familiar with the full range of their tools' capabilities. I'm reminded of a friend who had a brilliant young graphics programmer working for him. When the prodigy's code crashed one day, he had no idea that his debugger could show him a call stack.

Too many developers learn just enough debugging skills to get them out of their current jam. Often, users overlook great features of debugging tools because the situation in which to use them isn't put into the proper context. Reading through documentation, feature by feature, gets boring, and you learn only the most basic information. John's chapters on power debugging in the Microsoft Visual C++ and Microsoft Visual Basic debuggers (chapters 5 through 7) take you far past the tedium of "step, step, step. Inspect. Step, step, step…"

When I say debugging is an oral tradition, I mean that most people learn a new debugging skill or technique only when they hear about someone else using it to solve a problem. When you watch a master at work with good debugging tools, you can learn 10 times as much in 30 minutes as you would in a day of reading the documentation by yourself. John is just such a master of debugging. He knows the strengths and weaknesses of all the tools he uses. He also invests his time up front to write great diagnostic code that more than pays for itself later. You can do the same for yourself by making debugging a skill that you continually enhance rather than a chore. This book is chock full of nuggets of John's debugging gold to help speed you on your way.

Matt Pietrek
Hollis, New Hampshire
December 1999

Acknowledgments

The first set of people I want to thank are the readers of my "Bugslayer" column in *Microsoft Systems Journal* and the people who have come to hear me speak at various development conferences. Not only have you inspired me to write this book, but you've also, through our e-mail exchanges and conversations, taught me a great deal about software development. Additionally, you've contributed to my becoming a much better developer with your attentiveness to my code—trust me, I know how much joy you get out of telling me about bugs in my programs!

Two people whose names deserve to be on the cover of this book are Sally Stickney (project editor) and Marc Young (technical editor) from Microsoft Press. They did a truly outstanding job making this book readable and correct. I can't thank them enough. I promise never to use "this" or "it" without a clear antecedent again.

A group of friends who earned my eternal gratitude is my "Review Crew." Most books are seen by only a couple of people while the author is writing, but this book had the benefit of my entire Review Crew, who read all the chapters, corrected many mistakes, and suggested some of the coolest debugging tricks in the world. Not only are the Review Crew developers the best in the business today, but they are also the ones who taught *me* how to develop and debug. Here's the lineup: Jim Austin, Jim Harris, Peter Ierardi, Kevin Kelly, John Maver, Steve Munyan, Andy Pennell, Matt Pietrek, Jeffrey Richter, Chris Sells, Eric Yanco, and Tim Yuhl. Many of the good tips in the book belong to them; all the mistakes are mine. I also deeply appreciate the wonderful quotes from them at the front of the book.

I'd also like to extend special thanks to the following people:

- Some wonderful folks at NuMega, who taught me many things about developing software and contributed in numerous ways to this book: Dave Angel, Dom Basile, Frank Grossman, Jon Jesse, Berni McCoy, Farokh Morshed, Jim Moskun, Dave Nanian, Bob Newton, Paul Proulx, Barb Rottenberg, Dave Seidel, and Carol Tyler.

- Matt Pietrek, for letting me watch over his shoulder as we debugged many a problem we encountered developing BoundsChecker and for all the fascinating conversations about Microsoft Windows development and life in general. I also owe Matt for getting me to start writing—he convinced me it wasn't as hard as it looks. (I'm still not sure whether I believe him.) Thanks also to Matt for writing such a wonderful Foreword.

Acknowledgments

- Ed Sullivan, for showing me by example what a great product manager is supposed to do and for putting up with me even though I probably drove him crazy at times.

- Bob O'Brien, for showing me the other three-quarters of this business—sales, marketing, and public relations—and for being a great person.

- Joe Flanigan, Joanne Steinhart, and the rest of the crew at *Microsoft Systems Journal*. They took a huge chance letting a guy with no writing experience be their debugging columnist. I've done my best not to let them down.

- Ben Ryan, acquisitions editor at Microsoft Press, and my agent, Claire Horne, for taking care of all the tough details and letting me concentrate on the writing.

- Rob and Doris Robbins, my parents, for a wonderful childhood and for always supporting me no matter what crazy path I took even though I was probably scaring them to death.

- Deborah and Al Matthews, my sister and brother-in-law, and my perfect niece Alison and my perfect nephew Al for the support and for being excited for me even though they had no idea what I was talking about in the book.

- Stan and Lila Bahl, my in-laws, for being fantastic in-laws and actually helping me get started in software development by giving me my first real computer, an AT&T 6300 PC.

- Sergeant Major Frank Knapp and Lori, Ian, and Alex Knapp for taking care of me the whole time I was in the army. You don't know how much that meant to me.

Finally, the biggest thank-you of all goes to my wife, Pam. She believed in me enough to share her life with this book and never complained when I had to work through the evenings and on weekends. She was always there with a hug and a kiss when I needed it most. There's no way you'd be holding this book now if it weren't for her.

Introduction

Bugs suck. Period. Bugs are the reason you are subjected to death-march projects with missed deadlines, late nights, and grouchy coworkers. Bugs can truly make your life miserable because if enough of them creep in to your software, customers will stop using your product and you could lose your job. Bugs are serious business.

Many times, people in our industry portray bugs simply as annoyances. Nothing could be further from the truth. All engineers can point to projects with runaway bug counts and even to companies that have folded because they released software so full of bugs that the product was unusable. As I was writing this book, NASA lost a Mars space probe because of a bug that snuck in during the requirements and design phase. With computers controlling more and more mission-critical systems, medical devices, and superexpensive hardware, bugs can no longer be laughed at or viewed as something that just happens as a part of development.

My hope is that the information in this book will help you learn how to write your applications with fewer bugs in the first place—and that when you are required to debug, you can do it much faster. Without realizing it, most teams spend an average of 50 percent of their development cycle debugging. If you start debugging properly, you can drastically reduce that amount of time, which means you'll ship your products faster. You can't cut corners when it comes to requirements gathering and design, but you can certainly learn to debug much smarter. This book takes a holistic approach to debugging. I don't consider debugging as a separate step but as an integral part of the entire product cycle. I believe you need to start debugging in the requirements phase and continue through to the final release to manufacturing.

Two issues make debugging in the Microsoft Windows environment difficult and time consuming. The first issue is that debugging has always been a self-taught skill—you've basically been on your own to figure it out. Even if you have a computer science degree, I'm willing to bet that you never took a single college class dedicated to debugging. Other than some esoteric subjects, such as devising automatic program verification for languages that no one uses or developing debuggers for wildly optimistic, massively parallel-processing computers, the science of debugging as it applies to commercial software doesn't seem to be popular with the educational establishment. Some professors point out that you shouldn't be writing bugs in the first place.

Although that's an excellent point and an ideal we should all strive for, reality is a little different. Learning systematic, proven techniques for debugging won't save you from ever writing another bug, but following these practices will help you to limit the number of bugs you add to your code and to track down more quickly those inadvertent bugs that do occur.

The second issue is that though many excellent books on specific Windows technologies are available, none of them cover debugging those technologies in enough depth to be useful. To debug any technology effectively, you have to know far more than a book focused on a specific technology provides. It's one thing to know how to write an ActiveX control to plug into Microsoft Internet Explorer, and it's another thing entirely to be able to debug that ActiveX control. To debug an ActiveX control, you have to know the ins and outs of ActiveX and the Component Object Model (COM), how dynamic-link libraries (DLLs) map into memory, and how COM goes about finding and creating controls. Some books make it look easy to implement sophisticated features, such as remote database connections, using the hot technology du jour, but when "db.Connect ("Foo")" fails in your Microsoft Visual Basic program—and it eventually will—you're on your own to find and mend the broken link in the technology chain. Moreover, although a few books on project management do discuss debugging, they tend to focus on managerial and administrative issues rather than developers' concerns. Those books might include fine information about how to plan for debugging, but they don't help much when you're staring at a crash returning from a callback function.

The idea for this book came out of my trials and tribulations as a developer and manager trying to ship high-quality products on time. Over the years, I've learned skills and techniques that I use to deal with each of the two issues that help make developing Windows-based applications a challenge. To address the first issue, the lack of formal debugging training, I wrote the first part of this book to give you a crash course in debugging—with a decided slant toward commercial development. As for the second issue, the need for a book specifically on debugging in the Windows environment, I think I've provided a book that bridges the gap between specific technologies and nitty-gritty, real-world debugging techniques.

I've been extremely fortunate to have had the opportunity to focus on debugging almost exclusively for the last five years. A couple of experiences have helped shape my unique perspective on the subject of debugging. The first experience was at NuMega Technologies (now Compuware NuMega), where I was one of the first engineers. There I was privileged to work on great teams writing automatic error-detection tools (BoundsChecker), performance tools (TrueTime), code-coverage tools (TrueCoverage), and debuggers (SoftICE). Working on products whose customers (you!) scream bloody murder when they find a problem "encourages" you to write and ship the best products possible.

In addition to having worked as a software engineer and manager at NuMega, I have the pleasure of writing the "Bugslayer" column in *Microsoft Systems Journal*. In the column, I focus on debugging, and my constant interaction with engineers developing every type of application imaginable teaches me even more about the issues that engineers face today when shipping products.

WHO SHOULD READ THIS BOOK?

I wrote this book for developers who are tired of spending late nights at work debugging and want to improve the quality of their code and their organizations. I also wrote this book for managers and team leaders who want to develop more efficient and effective teams.

From a technical perspective, the "ideal reader" is someone who has one to three years of experience using Microsoft Visual C++, Microsoft Visual Basic, or both. I also expect the reader to have been a member of a real-world development team and to have shipped at least one product. Although I don't care for the term, the software industry labels developers with this level of experience "intermediate developers."

Advanced developers will probably learn a great deal as well. I was very blessed to have a wonderful group of friends, my "Review Crew," critique the chapters before I submitted them to Microsoft Press. These engineers, who are listed in the Acknowledgments section of this book, are the people who taught *me* how to develop and debug. Indeed, they are some of the best developers in the business. I was extremely pleased that they all told me they had learned a lot from reading my book.

Note to Visual Basic Developers

If you flip through this book, you'll notice that I emphasize the Visual C++ debugger, C and C++, and assembly language. There are two reasons for this emphasis. First, C and C++ offer more opportunities than Visual Basic for developers to shoot themselves in the foot. Second, because the Visual Basic debugger can't debug native compiled binaries, you need to know the Visual C++ debugger to debug your Visual Basic applications. Even though on the basis of a cursory look you might think this book doesn't cover Visual Basic, rest assured that when it comes to real-world development with Visual Basic, you'll find that nearly the entire book applies to you. Debugging is debugging, regardless of the development environment.

HOW SHOULD YOU READ THIS BOOK?

I divided the book into three distinct parts. You should read the first two parts (chapters 1 through 7) in order because I build the information in a logical progression.

In the first part of the book, "The Gestalt of Debugging" (chapters 1 through 3), I define the different types of bugs and develop a process for debugging that all great developers follow. I also discuss the infrastructure requirements necessary for proper team debugging. Finally, because you can (and should) do a tremendous amount of debugging during the coding phase, I cover how you can proactively debug as you're writing your code.

In the second part of the book, "Power Debugging" (chapters 4 through 7), I explain what a debugger is and describe how various debuggers work. The more you understand your tools, the better able you are to use them. I also cover the Visual C++ and Visual Basic debuggers in considerable depth so that you can learn to maximize their usage. One thing I learned working with developers from across the industry—from the inexperienced to the very experienced—was that they were using only a tiny fraction of the power of the Visual C++ and Visual Basic debuggers. Although this sentiment might sound odd coming from an author of a book about debugging, I want to keep you out of the debugger as much as possible. As you read this book, you'll see that much of my goal for you isn't just to learn how to fix crashes but how to avoid them in the first place. But I also want to teach you to use the debuggers to their maximum effectiveness because there will be times when you're forced to use them.

In the third part of the book, "Power Tools and Techniques" (chapters 8 through 15), I offer solutions to common debugging problems you'll encounter when writing Windows-based applications. I cover topics ranging from finding the source file and line number with just a crash address and how to automatically test your user interfaces to tracking down where your multithreaded program deadlocked. Most of the chapters in this section include utility programs and a tremendous amount of source code that you can learn from.

The final part of the book, "Appendixes" (Appendix A and Appendix B), provides additional information you'll find useful in your debugging adventures. In Appendix A, I explain how to read and interpret a Dr. Watson log. In Appendix B, you'll find annotated lists of resources—books, tools, and Web sites—that have helped me hone my skills as a developer/debugger.

Throughout the book, you'll notice that I've sprinkled sidebars that illustrate common debugging questions and debugging war stories. (See page xv for a complete listing.) Although I enjoy answering the common debugging questions I'm asked, the real fun is in hearing about and relating the debugging war stories. I hope that by sharing with you some of the really "good" bugs I've helped solve (and some I've helped write!) you'll see the practical application of the approaches and techniques I recommend. Additionally, I want to help you avoid the mistakes that I've made.

SYSTEM REQUIREMENTS

To use this book, you'll need the following:

- Microsoft Windows 2000, Microsoft Windows NT 4 Service Pack 3 or higher, or Microsoft Windows 98

- Microsoft Visual Studio 6.0 Service Pack 3 or higher

- DBGHELP.DLL (For more information on this file, see the "READ THIS! The DBGHELP.DLL Symbol Engine" section later in the Introduction.)

WHAT'S ON THE COMPANION CD?

I'm pretty sure that you'll get more source code with this book than you've gotten with any other book you've ever purchased. In addition to implementing an example graphical user interface (GUI) debugger using the Microsoft Foundation Class (MFC) library, I include eight complete utilities on the companion CD to help you debug faster and more effectively. In all, there are over 2.5 megabytes of just source files. Most of the code has been battle-tested in over 50 real-world applications, including, of all things, a piano that uses Windows 98 as an embedded operating system!

The README.TXT file on the companion CD covers any special building and execution issues associated with the projects. I developed and tested all the projects with Microsoft Visual Studio 6 Service Pack 3. I also built all the projects using the Windows 2000 RC2 Platform SDK headers to ensure that you could use them.

I tested all the code using Windows 98, Windows NT 4 Service Pack 4, and Windows 2000 RC3 (the latest version available when I was finishing the book). Because Windows 98 has been out for several years, I decided not to support Windows 95. However, I didn't use any operating system features specific to Windows 98, so if you do need to run my code on Windows 95, you shouldn't have too much difficulty.

READ THIS! The DBGHELP.DLL Symbol Engine

In several of the utilities, I use the Windows 2000 DBGHELP.DLL symbol engine. Although the symbol engine used to be in IMAGEHLP.DLL, it was moved to DBGHELP.DLL to get it out of a core operating system DLL. You must have DBGHELP.LIB and DBGHELP.H to build the source code in this book. Included on the companion CD is the latest Platform SDK at the time I wrote the book.

You should install the Platform SDK, not only because it has many wonderful debugging utilities, but also because you can find DBGHELP.LIB and DBGHELP.H as part of it. Before you install, you should double-check your MSDN Universal Subscription CDs or *msdn.microsoft.com/developer/sdk* to get the latest version.

For the symbol engine to work on Windows NT 4 and Windows 98, you must copy DBGHELP.DLL from Windows 2000 or the <Platform SDK>\Redist\DbgHelp directory and place the file in the same directory as the program that uses it. For example, if you want to use the CrashFinder program to look up the source file and line number at which a crash occurred, you need to place DBGHELP.DLL into the same directory as CRASHFINDER.EXE.

For the DBGHELP.DLL symbol engine to find your symbols, either have your PDB files in the same directory as the one in which you built your binaries or place them in the same directory as your binaries. Alternatively, you can tell the symbol engine where the PDB files are with special environment variables. See the MSDN documentation on the *SymInitialize* API function for more details.

Be prepared to spend some time playing around with the DBGHELP.DLL symbol engine getting it to work. The only way you know the DBGHELP.DLL symbol engine isn't working is if you're not getting function information or source file and line number information out of your files compiled with PDB debugging symbols. If you're having trouble getting the DBGHELP.DLL symbol engine to work, you have an excellent opportunity to try out the debugging skills I discuss in this book! I keep the latest and greatest information about the DBGHELP.DLL symbol engine in the Frequently Asked Questions (FAQ) section of my Web site at *www.jprobbins.com*. Between the FAQ and a little debugging, you should get your symbols.

FEEDBACK

I'm very interested in knowing what you think of this book. If you have questions— or your own debugging war stories—I'd love to hear them! You can send them to *www.jprobbins.com*. I try to answer all reasonable questions. I really enjoy getting your questions because I end up learning a lot trying to answer them. Although I've been fortunate enough to do lots of development, I haven't done it all (yet!). Your questions are a great opportunity for me to hear about the victories and defeats you're having with the latest and greatest technologies.

Thanks for reading, and happy debugging!

John Robbins
December 1999
Hollis, New Hampshire
Bob in 2020

Part I

The Gestalt of Debugging

Chapter 1

Bugs: Where They Come From and How You Solve Them

Debugging is a fascinating topic no matter what language or platform you're using. It's the only part of software development in which engineers kick, scream at, or even throw their computers. For a normally reticent, introverted group, this degree of emotion is extraordinary. Debugging is also the part of software development that's famous for causing you to pull all-nighters. I've yet to run into an engineer who has called his or her spouse and said, "Honey, I can't come home because we're doing our UML diagrams." However, I've run into plenty of engineers who have called their spouse with the lament, "Honey, I can't come home because we've run into a whopper of a bug."

BUGS AND DEBUGGING

Bugs are cool! Well, actually, finding bugs is cool. The coolest of all bugs are those that you find before the customer sees your product. Discovering those prerelease bugs means that you're doing your job and producing a higher quality product. Having your customer find the bug is the opposite of cool.

Compared to other engineering fields, software engineering is an anomaly in two ways. First, software engineering is a new and somewhat immature branch of engineering. Second, users have come to accept bugs in our products, particularly in PC software. Although they grudgingly resign themselves to bugs, they're still not happy when they find them.

You need to care about bugs because ultimately they cost your business in two ways. In the short term, customers contact you for help, forcing you to spend your time and money sustaining the current product while your competitors are working on their next version. In the long term, the invisible hand of economics kicks in and customers just start buying alternatives to your buggy product. As software begins to be delivered more as a service than as a capital investment, the pressure for higher quality software will increase. Very soon, your users will be able to switch among software products from various vendors just by moving from one Web site to another. This boon for users will mean less job security for you and I if our products are buggy and more incentive to create high-quality products.

What Are Bugs?

Before you can start debugging, you need a definition of bugs. My definition of a bug is "anything that causes a user pain." I classify bugs into the following categories:

- Inconsistent user interfaces
- Unmet expectations
- Poor performance
- Crashes or data corruption

Inconsistent User Interfaces

Inconsistent user interfaces, though not the most serious type of bug, are annoying. One of the reasons for the success of Microsoft Windows is that all Windows applications generally behave the same way. When an application deviates from the Windows standard, it becomes a burden for the user. A small example of this nonstandard, irksome behavior is the Find accelerators in Microsoft Outlook. In every other English-language Windows application on the planet, Ctrl+F brings up the Find dialog box so that you can find text in the current window. In Outlook, however, Ctrl+F forwards the open message. Even after many years of using Outlook, I can never remember to use the F4 key to find text in the currently open message.

You can solve problems with inconsistent user interfaces by following the recommendations in the book *Microsoft Windows User Experience* (Microsoft Press, 1999). At the time of this writing, a previous version of the book, *The Windows Interface Guidelines for Software Design,* also appeared on the Microsoft Developer Network (MSDN). If either book doesn't address your particular issue, look for another Microsoft application that does something similar to what you're trying to achieve and follow its model.

Unmet Expectations

Not meeting the user's expectations is one of the hardest bugs to solve. This bug usually occurs right at the beginning of a project, when the company doesn't do sufficient research on what the real customer needs. In both types of shops—shrink-wrap (those writing software for sale) and Information Technology (IT) (those writing in-house applications)—the cause of this bug comes down to communication problems.

In general, development teams don't communicate directly with their product's customers, so they aren't learning what the users need. Ideally, all members of the engineering team should be visiting customer sites so that they can see how the customers use their product. Watching over a customer's shoulder as your product is being used can be an eye-opening experience. Additionally, this experience will give you the insight you need to properly interpret what customers are asking your product to do. If you do get to talk to customers, make sure you speak with as many as possible so that you can get input from across a wide spectrum.

In addition to customer visits, another good idea is to have the engineering team review the support call summaries and support e-mails. This feedback will allow the engineering team to see the problems that the users are having, without any filtering applied.

Another aspect of this kind of bug is the situation in which the user's level of expectation has been raised higher than the product can deliver. This inflation of user expectations is the classic result of too much hype, and you must resist misrepresenting your product's capabilities at all costs. When users don't get what they anticipated from a product, they tend to feel that the product is even buggier than it really is. The rule for avoiding this situation is to never promise what you can't deliver and to always deliver what you promise.

Poor Performance

Users are very frustrated by bugs that cause the application to slow down when it encounters real-world data. Invariably, improper testing is the root of all poor performance bugs—however great the application might have looked in development, the team failed to test it with anything approaching real-world volumes. One project I worked on, NuMega's BoundsChecker 3.0, had this bug with its original FinalCheck technology. That version of FinalCheck inserted additional debugging and contextual information directly into the source code so that BoundsChecker could better report errors. Unfortunately, we failed to sufficiently test the FinalCheck code on larger real-world applications before we released BoundsChecker 3.0. As a result, more users than we cared to admit couldn't use that feature. We completely rewrote the FinalCheck feature in subsequent releases, but because of the performance problems in the original version, many users never tried it again, even though it was one of the product's most powerful and useful features.

You tackle poor performance bugs in two ways. First, make sure you determine your application's performance requirements up front. To know whether you have a performance problem, you need a goal to measure against. An important part of performance planning is keeping baseline performance numbers. If your application starts missing those numbers by 10 percent or more, you need to stop and determine why your performance dropped and take steps to correct the problem. Second, make sure you test your applications against as close to real-world scenarios as possible—and that you do this as early in the development cycle as you can.

Crashes or Data Corruption

Crashes and data corruption bugs are what most developers and users think of when they think of a bug. Users might be able to work around the types of bugs just described, but crashes stop them dead—which is why the majority of this book concentrates on solving these extreme problems. In addition, crashes and data corruption bugs are the most common type of bug. As we all know, some of these bugs are easy to solve, and others are almost impossible. The main point to remember about crashes and data corruption bugs is that you should never ship a product if you know it has one of these bugs in it.

Process Bugs and Solutions

Although shipping software without bugs is possible—given enough attention to detail—I've shipped enough products to know that most teams haven't reached that level of software development maturity. Bugs are a fact of life in this business. However, you can minimize the number of bugs your applications have. That is what teams that ship high-quality products—and there are many out there—do. The reasons for bugs generally fall into the following process categories:

- Short or impossible deadlines
- The "code first, think later" approach
- Misunderstood requirements
- Engineer ignorance or improper training
- Lack of commitment to quality

Short or Impossible Deadlines

We've all been part of development teams for which "management" has set a deadline that was determined by either a tarot card reader or, if that was too expensive, a Magic 8-Ball. Although we'd like to believe that managers are responsible for most unrealistic schedules, more often than not, they aren't to blame. Engineers' work estimates are usually the basis of the schedule, and sometimes engineers underestimate how long it will take them to develop a solid product. Whether an unrealistic ship date is the fault of management or engineering or both, the bottom line is that a schedule that's impossible to meet leads to cut corners and a lower quality product.

I've been fortunate enough to work on several teams that have shipped software on time. In all cases, the development team truly owned the schedule, and we were good at determining realistic ship dates. To figure out realistic ship dates, we based our dates on a feature set. If the company found the proposed ship date unacceptable, we cut features to move up the date. In addition, everyone on the development team agreed to the schedule before we presented it to management. That way, the team's credibility was on the line to finish the product on time. Interestingly, besides shipping on time, these products were some of the highest quality products that I've ever worked on.

The "Code First, Think Later" Approach

My friend Peter Ierardi coined the term "code first, think later" to describe the all-too-common situation in which an engineering team starts programming before they start thinking. Every one of us is guilty of this approach to an extent. Playing with compilers, writing code, and debugging is the fun stuff; it's why we got interested in this business in the first place. Very few of us like to sit down and write documents that describe what we're going to do.

If you don't write these documents, however, you'll start to run into bugs. Instead of stopping and thinking about how to avoid bugs in the first place, you'll start tweaking the code as you go to work around the bugs. As you might imagine, this tactic will compound the problem because you'll introduce more and more bugs into an already unstable code base. If you find yourself saying, "We've got too big an investment in this code base to change now," you have a symptom of the "code first, think later" syndrome.

Fortunately, the solution to this problem is simple: plan your projects. Some very good books have been written about requirements gathering and project planning. I cite them in Appendix B, and I highly recommend that you read them. Although it isn't very sexy and is generally a little painful, up-front planning is vital to eliminating bugs.

Misunderstood Requirements

Proper planning also minimizes one of the biggest bug causers in development: feature creep. Feature creep—the tacking on of features not originally planned—is a symptom of poor planning and inadequate requirements gathering. Adding last-minute features, whether in response to competitive pressure, as a developer's pet feature, or on the whim of management, causes more bugs in software than almost anything else.

Software engineering is an extremely detail-oriented business. The more details you hash out and solve before you start coding, the less you leave to chance. The only way to achieve proper attention to detail is to plan your milestones and the implementation for your projects. Of course, this doesn't mean that you need to go completely overboard and generate thousands of pages of documentation describing what you're going to do.

One of the best design documents I ever created for a product was simply a series of paper drawings, or "paper prototypes," of the user interface. Based on research and on the teachings of Jarod Spool and his company, User Interface Engineering, my team drew the user interface and worked through each user scenario completely. In doing so, we had to focus on the requirements for the product and figure out exactly how the users were going to perform their tasks. In the end, we knew exactly what we were going to deliver and, more important, so did everyone else in the company. If a question about what was supposed to happen in a given scenario arose, we pulled out the paper prototypes and worked through the scenario again.

Even though you might do all the planning in the world, you have to really understand your products' requirements to implement them properly. At one company where I worked—mercifully, for less than a year—the requirements for the product seemed very simple and straightforward. As it turned out, however, most of the team members didn't understand the customers' needs well enough to figure out what the product was supposed to do. The company made the classic mistake of drastically increasing engineering head count but failing to train the new engineers sufficiently. Consequently, even though the team planned out everything to extremes, the product shipped several years late and the market rejected it.

There were two large mistakes on this project. The first was that the company wasn't willing to take the time to thoroughly explain the customers' needs to the engineers who were new to the problem domain, even though some of us begged for the training. The second mistake was that many of the engineers, both old and new, didn't care to learn more about the problem domain. As a result, the team kept changing direction each time marketing and sales reexplained the requirements. The code base was so unstable that it took months to get even the simplest user scenarios to work without crashing.

Very few companies train their engineers in their problem domain at all. Although many of us have college degrees in engineering, we generally don't know much about how customers will use our products. If companies would spend adequate time up front helping their engineers understand the problem domain, they could eliminate many bugs caused by misunderstood requirements.

The fault isn't just with the company, though. Engineers must make the commitment to learn the problem domain as well. Some engineers like to think they're building tools that enable a solution so that they can maintain their separation from the problem domain. As engineers, we're responsible for solving the problem, not merely enabling a solution!

An example of enabling a solution is a situation in which you design a user interface that, although it technically works, doesn't match the way the user works. Another example of enabling a solution is building your application in such a way that it solves the user's short-term problem but doesn't move forward to accommodate the user's changing business needs.

When solving the user's problem rather than just enabling a solution, you, the engineer, become as knowledgeable as you can about the problem domain so that your software product becomes an extension of the user. The best engineers are not those who can twiddle bits but those who can solve a user's problem.

Engineer Ignorance or Improper Training

Another significant cause of bugs is that developers don't understand the operating system, the language, or the technology their projects use. Unfortunately, few engineers are willing to admit this deficiency and seek training. Instead, they cover up their lack of knowledge and, unintentionally, introduce avoidable bugs.

In many cases, however, this ignorance isn't a personal failing so much as a fact of life in modern software development. So many layers and interdependencies are involved in developing software these days that no one person can be expected to know the ins and outs of every operating system, language, and technology. There's nothing wrong with admitting that you don't know something. In fact, if a team is healthy, acknowledging the strengths and limitations of each member works to the team's advantage. By cataloging the skills their developers have and don't have, the team can get the maximum advantage from their training dollars. By strengthening every developer's weaknesses, the team will better be able to adjust to unforeseen circumstances and, in turn, broaden the whole team's skill set.

The team can also schedule development time more accurately when team members are willing to admit what they don't know. If a team member needs to learn about a new technology in order to implement some part of the application but isn't given enough time, the schedule will almost certainly slip.

I'll have more to say about what skills and knowledge are critical for developers to know in the section "Prerequisites to Debugging" later in the chapter.

Lack of Commitment to Quality

The final reason that bugs exist in projects is, in my opinion, the most serious. Every company and every engineer I've ever talked to has told me that they are committed to quality. Unfortunately, some companies and engineers lack the real commitment quality takes. If you've ever worked at a company that was committed to quality or with an engineer who was, you certainly know it. They both feel a deep pride in what they are producing and are willing to spend the effort on all parts of development, not just the sexy parts. For example, instead of getting all wrapped up in the minutia of an algorithm, they pick a simpler algorithm and spend their time working on how best to test that algorithm. The customer doesn't buy algorithms, after all; the customer buys high-quality products. Companies and individuals with a real commitment to quality exhibit many of the same characteristics: careful up-front planning, personal accountability, solid quality control, and excellent communication abilities. Many companies and individuals go through the motions of the big software development tasks (that is, scheduling, coding, and so on), but only those who pay attention to the details ship on time with high quality.

A good example of a commitment to quality is when I had my first annual review at NuMega. One of the key parts of the review was to record how many bugs I had logged against the product. I was stunned to discover that NuMega would evaluate this statistic as part of my performance review, however, because even though tracking bugs is a vital part of maintaining a product's quality, no other company I had worked at had ever checked something so obvious. The developers know where the bugs are, but they must be given an incentive to enter those bugs into the bug tracking system. NuMega found the trick. When I learned about the bug count entry part of my review, you'd better believe I logged everything I found, no matter how trivial. With all the technical writers, quality engineers, development engineers, and managers engaged in healthy competition to log the most bugs, few surprise bugs slipped through the cracks. More important, we had a realistic idea of where we stood on a project at any given time.

When I was a development manager, I followed a ritual that I'm sure fostered a commitment to quality: each team member had to agree that the product was ready to go at every milestone. If any person on the team didn't feel that the product was ready, it didn't ship. I'd rather fix a minor bug and suffer through another complete day of testing than send out something the team wasn't proud of. Not only did this ritual ensure that everyone on the team thought that the quality was there, but it also gave everyone on the team a stake in the outcome. An interesting phenomenon that I noticed was that team members never got the chance to stop the release for someone else's bug; the bug's owner always beat them to it.

A company's commitment to quality sets the tone for the entire development effort. That commitment starts with the hiring process and extends through the final quality assurance on the release candidate. Every company says that it wants to hire the best people, but few companies are willing to offer salaries and benefits that will draw them. In addition, some companies aren't willing to provide the tools and equipment that engineers need to produce high-quality products. Unfortunately, too many companies resist spending $500 on a tool that will solve a nasty crash bug in minutes but are willing to blow many thousands of dollars to pay their developers to flounder around for weeks trying to solve that same bug.

If you do find yourself in an organization that suffers from a lack of commitment to quality, you'll find that there's no easy way to turn a company into a quality-conscious organization overnight. If you're a manager, you can set the direction and tone for the engineers working for you and work with upper management to lobby for extending a commitment to quality across the organization. If you're an engineer, you can work to make your code the most robust and extensible on the project so that you set an example for others.

Planning for Debugging

Now that we've gone over the types and origins of bugs and you have some ideas about how to avoid or solve them, it's time to start thinking about the process of debugging. Although many people start thinking about debugging only when they crash during the coding phase, you should think about it right from the beginning, in the requirements phase. The more you plan your projects up front, the less time— and money—you'll spend debugging them later.

As I mentioned earlier in the chapter, feature creep can be a bane to your project. More often than not, unplanned features introduce bugs and wreak havoc on a product. This doesn't mean that your plans must be cast in stone, however. Sometimes you must change or add a feature to a product to be competitive or to better meet the user's needs. The key point to remember is that before you change your code, you need to determine—and plan for—exactly what will change. And keep in mind that adding a feature doesn't affect just the code; it also affects testing, documentation, and sometimes even marketing messages. When revising your production schedule, a general rule to follow is that the time it takes to add or remove a feature grows exponentially the further along the production cycle you are.

In Steve McConnell's excellent book *Code Complete* (Microsoft Press, 1993, pp. 25–26), he refers to the costs of fixing a bug. To fix a bug during the requirements and planning phases costs very little. As the product progresses, however, the cost of fixing a bug rises exponentially, as does the cost of debugging—much the same scenario as if you add or remove features along the way.

Planning for debugging goes together with planning for testing. As you plan, you need to look for different ways to speed up and improve both processes. One of the best precautions you can take is to write file data dumpers and validators for internal data structures as well as for binary files, if appropriate. If your project reads and writes data to a binary file, you should automatically schedule someone to write a testing program that dumps the data in a readable format to a text file. The dumper should also validate the data and check all interdependencies in the binary file. This step will make both your testing and your debugging easier.

By properly planning for debugging, you minimize the time spent in your debugger, and this is your goal. You might think such advice sounds strange coming from a book on debugging, but the idea is to try to avoid bugs in the first place. If you build sufficient debugging code into your applications, that code—not the debugger—should tell you where the bugs are. I'll cover the issues concerning debugging code more in Chapter 3.

PREREQUISITES TO DEBUGGING

Before we get into the meat of debugging, I want to cover what you must know to be a good debugger. The first quality that all expert debuggers have in common is that they're good developers too. You simply can't be a good debugger without being a good developer, and vice versa.

The Skill Set

Good debuggers and, conversely, good developers all have strong problem-solving skills that are particular to software. Fortunately, you can learn and hone those skills. What sets great debuggers/developers apart from good debuggers/developers is that in addition to having basic problem-solving skills, great debuggers/developers understand how all the parts of a project relate to the project as a whole.

The following list contains the areas in which you need to be proficient to become a great—or at least a better—debugger/developer:

- Your project
- Your language
- Your technology
- Your operating system
- Your CPU

Know Your Project

Knowing your project is the first line of defense for user interface, logic, and performance bugs. By knowing how and where features are implemented in the various source files, you can quickly narrow down who is doing what to whom.

Unfortunately, because each project is different, the only way to learn your project is to read the design documents, if they exist, and walk through the code in the debugger. If you're working with C++ source code, you might also find it helpful to look at the browser files. Additionally, several third-party companies produce tools that will turn your existing source code into Unified Modeling Language (UML) diagrams. Even poorly documented source code is better than nothing if it saves you from having to interpret a disassembly listing.

Know Your Language

Knowing the language (or languages) that your project uses is more difficult than it sounds. I'm referring to knowing what your language is doing behind the scenes as well as knowing how to program in it. For example, developers sometimes forget that local variables that are C++ classes or overloaded C++ operators can create temporary items on the stack. Alternatively, an assignment operator might look innocent enough, but it can cause a great deal of code to execute. Microsoft Visual Basic also generates a considerable amount of code behind your back. Many bugs, especially performance problems, are the result of language misuse, so it's well worth the effort to spend some time reading up on the idiosyncrasies of the programming languages you use.

Know Your Technology

Getting a handle on the technologies you're using is the first big step to tackling the harder bugs. For example, if you have an idea of what the Component Object Model (COM) does to instantiate a COM object and return an interface, you'll have a much easier time tracking down why a specific interface request failed. The same goes for something like the Microsoft Foundation Class (MFC) library. If you're having a problem with your document receiving a Windows message, you need to have an idea of how messages flow through the document/view architecture. I'm not saying that you need to quote file and line from the source code or a book. Rather, I'm saying that you should have at least a general understanding of the technologies you're using and, more important, you should know exactly where you can find more detailed information if you should need it.

Know Your Operating System

Knowing the operating system can make the biggest difference between solving a bug and just floundering around. Here are some of the questions you should be able to answer about the operating system you use: What is a dynamic-link library (DLL)? How does an image loader work? How does the registry work? Many of the worst bugs appear when your program calls into the operating system because either you pass invalid data or you aren't aware of the ramifications of making the call.

Imagine that you have a program that's running out of memory and you can't find which module is leaking. Knowing the operating system would help you solve this bug. By knowing the operating system, you would know that all memory allocations eventually resolve down to a call to the *VirtualAlloc* API function. You could then set a breakpoint on *VirtualAlloc* and check the call stack for which of your modules is doing the calling. My friend Matt Pietrek, who taught me a great deal about debugging, maintains that knowing the operating system and the CPU is what separates the debugging gods from mere mortals.

Know Your CPU

Which brings me to the last thing you must know to be a debugging god: the CPU. You must know a little about the CPU to solve most of the nastiest bugs you'll encounter. Although it would be nice if you always crashed where source code was available, the majority of your crashes drop you right into the Disassembly window. It always amazes me how many engineers don't know—and say they have no interest in knowing—assembly language. Assembly language isn't that hard, and three or four hours spent learning it can save countless hours in the debugger. Again, I'm not saying that you need to be able to write your whole program in assembly language. Even I don't think I could do that anymore. The point is that you need to be able to read it. All you need to know about assembly language is in Chapter 6.

Learning the Skill Set

With any job that regularly deals with technology, you have to study continually just to keep up, let alone get better and advance. Although I can't help you learn your specific projects, in Appendix B I list all the resources that have helped me—and can help you—become a better debugger.

Besides reading books and magazines on debugging, you should also write utilities, any kind of utilities. The ultimate way to learn is by doing, and in this business, coding and debugging are what you need to do. Not only will you enhance your hard skills, such as coding and debugging, but if you treat these utilities as real projects (that is, by completing them on time and with high quality), you'll also enhance your soft skills, such as project planning and schedule estimating.

To give you some impetus to complete your utilities, consider this: completed utilities are excellent show-and-tell items to bring to job interviews. Although very few engineers bring their own code to demonstrate their skills to interviewers, companies consider those candidates who do well before those candidates who don't. Bringing a portfolio of work you did on your own time at home shows that you can complete work on your own and that you have a passion for software engineering—and will almost immediately put you in the top 20 percent of engineers.

Another practice that has helped me a great deal, especially when it comes to learning more about languages, technologies, and the operating system, is to look at other engineers' code. As you probably know, a great deal of code that you can look at is floating around on the Internet. By running different programs under the debugger, you can see how someone else tackles bugs. In addition, if you're having trouble coming up with a utility you'd like to write, you can simply add a feature to one of the utilities you find.

Another technique I would recommend to learn more about technologies, the operating system, and the CPU is to do some reverse engineering. It will help get you up to speed with assembly language and the advanced features in the debugger. After reading Chapter 6, you should know enough about assembly language to get started. Although I wouldn't recommend that you start out by completely reverse engineering the operating system loader, you might consider tackling some smaller tasks. For example, I found it very instructive to walk through the implementation of *CoCreateInstanceEx*.

Reading books and magazines, writing utilities, reviewing other engineers' code, and doing reverse engineering are all great ways to improve your debugging skills.

However, your greatest resources are your engineering friends and coworkers. Never be afraid to ask them how they did something or how something works; unless they are in the middle of a deadline crunch, they should be happy to help. I enjoy it when people ask me questions because I end up learning more than the individuals who ask the questions! Programming newsgroups are also excellent places to pose questions. I read them all the time because their responses are so good, especially from those folks who Microsoft has designated MVPs (Most Valuable Professionals).

THE DEBUGGING PROCESS

Finally, let's start talking about hands-on debugging by discussing the debugging process. Determining a process that works for all bugs, even "freak" bugs (bugs that come out of the blue and don't make any sense), was a bit challenging. But by drawing on my own experiences and by talking to my colleagues about their experiences, I eventually came up with a debugging approach that all great developers intuitively follow but that less experienced (or just poorer) developers often don't find obvious.

As you'll see, this debugging process doesn't take a rocket scientist to implement. The hard part is making sure you start with this process every time you debug. Here are the nine steps involved in the debugging approach that I recommend:

■ Step 1: Duplicate the bug

■ Step 2: Describe the bug

■ Step 3: Always assume that the bug is yours

■ Step 4: Divide and conquer

■ Step 5: Think creatively

■ Step 6: Leverage tools

■ Step 7: Start heavy debugging

■ Step 8: Verify that the bug is fixed

■ Step 9: Learn and share

Depending on your bug, you can skip some steps entirely because the problem and the location of the problem are entirely obvious. You must always start with Step 1 and get through Step 2. At any point between Step 3 and Step 7, however, you might figure out the solution and be able to fix the bug. In those cases, after you fix the bug, skip to Step 8 to verify and test the fix. Figure 1-1 illustrates the steps of the debugging process.

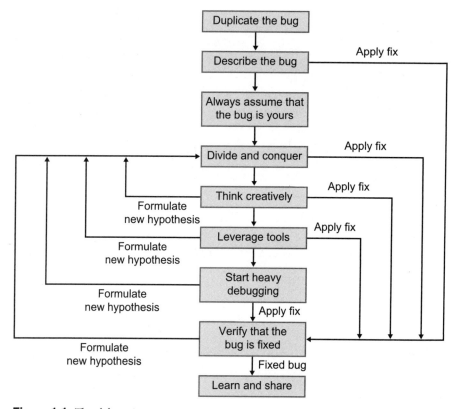

Figure 1-1 *The debugging process*

Step 1: Duplicate the Bug

The most critical step in the process is the first one: duplicating the bug. This is sometimes difficult, or even impossible, but if you can't duplicate a bug, you probably can't eliminate it. When trying to duplicate a bug, you might need to go to extremes. I had one bug in my code that I couldn't duplicate just by running the program. I had an idea of the data conditions that might cause it, however, so I ran the program under the debugger and entered the data I needed to duplicate the bug directly into memory. It worked. If you're dealing with a synchronization problem, you might need to take steps such as loading the same tasks so that you can duplicate the state in which the bug occurred.

Once you've duplicated the bug by using one set of steps, you should evaluate whether you can duplicate the bug through a different set of steps. You can get to some bugs via one code path only, but you can get to other bugs through multiple paths. The idea is to try to see the behavior from all possible angles. By duplicating the bug from multiple paths, you have a much better sense of the data and boundary conditions that are causing the problems. Additionally, as we all know, some bugs can mask other bugs. The more ways you can find to duplicate a bug, the better off you'll be.

Even if you can't duplicate the bug, you should still log it into your bug tracking system. If I have a bug that I can't duplicate, I always log it into the system anyway, but I leave a note that says I couldn't duplicate it. That way, if another engineer is responsible for that section of the code, he or she at least has an idea that something is amiss. When logging a bug that you can't re-create, you need to be as descriptive as possible. If the description is good enough, that information might be sufficient for you or another engineer to solve the problem eventually.

Step 2: Describe the Bug

If you were a typical engineering student in college, you probably concentrated on your math and engineering classes and barely passed your writing classes. In the real world, your writing skills are almost more important than your engineering skills because you need to be able to describe your bugs, both verbally and in writing. When faced with a tough bug, you should always stop right after you duplicate it and describe it. Ideally, you would do this in your bug tracking system, even if it's your responsibility to debug the bug, but talking it out is also useful. The main reason for describing the bug is that it often helps you fix it. I can't remember how many times I've been able to figure out a bug just by describing it to someone.

That "someone" doesn't even have to be a human. My cat, as it turns out, is an excellent debugger, and she has helped me solve a number of nasty bugs when I talked to her about them. For those bugs my cat couldn't solve, describing them to her gave me good practice for when I presented them to my human colleagues.

Of course, your colleagues can help you out only if you're able to describe your bugs so that they can understand them. Hence, the reason having strong communication skills is so important.

Step 3: Always Assume That the Bug Is Yours

In all the years I've been in software development, only a small percentage of the bugs I've seen were the result of the compiler or the operating system. If you have a bug, the odds are excellent that it's your fault, and you should always assume and hope that. If the bug is in your code, at least you can fix it; if it's in your compiler or the operating system, you have bigger problems. You should eliminate any possibility that the bug is in your code before spending time looking for it elsewhere.

Step 4: Divide and Conquer

If you've duplicated your bug and described it well, you have started a hypothesis about the bug and have an idea of where it's hiding. In this step, you start firming and testing your hypothesis. To test the hypothesis, you can sometimes start by doing a little light debugging in the debugger. Light debugging involves checking states and variable values—not slogging through the code groping and guessing for a solution. If your hypothesis doesn't pan out in a few minutes, stop for a moment and reassess the situation. You've learned a little more about the bug, so now you can reevaluate your hypothesis and try again.

Debugging is like a binary search algorithm. You're trying to find where the bug is, and on each iteration through your different hypotheses, you are, hopefully, eliminating the sections of the programs where the bug is not. As you continue to look, you eliminate more and more of the program until you can box the bug into a section of code. As you continue to develop your hypothesis and learn more about the bug, you can update your bug description to reflect the new information.

When I'm in this step, I generally try out three to five solid hypotheses before moving on to the next step. The idea is to have a reason for running the debugger. Ideally, you can test your hypothesis without running the debugger and still prove or disprove it.

Step 5: Think Creatively

If the bug you're trying to eliminate is one of those nasty ones that happens only on certain machines or is hard to duplicate, start looking at the bug from different perspectives. This is the step in which you should start thinking about DLL version mismatches, operating system differences, problems with your program's binaries or its installation, and other external factors.

A technique that sometimes works wonders for me is to walk away from the problem for a day or two. You can sometimes focus so intensely on a problem that you lose sight of the forest for the trees and start missing obvious clues. By walking away from the bug, you give your subconscious a chance to work on the problem for a while.

Step 6: Leverage Tools

I've never understood why some companies let their engineers spend weeks searching for a bug when spending a thousand dollars for error detection, performance, and code-coverage tools would help them find the current bug—and bugs they will encounter in the future—in minutes.

Before I do any heavy debugging, I always run my code through Compuware NuMega's BoundsChecker/SmartCheck (an error detection tool), TrueTime (a performance tool), and TrueCoverage (a code-coverage tool). I have better things to do with my time than play in the debugger, and so do you. Granted, because I helped write each of these products, I'm a little biased toward them; but other companies, such as Rational Software and MuTek Solutions, have products with functionality similar to NuMega's. The point is that if you're not using a third-party tool to help you debug your products, you're spending more time debugging than you need to be.

For those of you who are unfamiliar with these types of tools, let me explain what each of them does. An error detection tool looks for invalid memory accesses, invalid parameters to system APIs and COM interfaces, memory leaks, and resource leaks, among other things. A performance tool helps you track down where your application is slow, which is invariably somewhere other than where you think it is. A code-coverage tool shows you the source lines not executed when you run your program. Code-coverage information is helpful because if you're looking for a bug, you want to look for it only in lines that are executing.

Step 7: Start Heavy Debugging

I differentiate heavy debugging from the light debugging I mentioned in Step 4 by what you're doing in the debugger. When you're doing light debugging, you're just looking at a few states and a couple of variables. In contrast, when you're doing heavy debugging, you're spending a good deal of time exploring your program's operation. It is during the heavy debugging stage that you want to use the debugger's advanced features. Your goal is to let the debugger do as much of the heavy lifting as possible. Chapter 5 discusses the debugger's advanced features.

Just as when you're doing light debugging, when you're doing heavy debugging, you should have an idea of where you think your bug is before you start using the debugger, and then use the debugger to prove or disprove your hypothesis. Never sit in the debugger and just poke around.

Also, when you're doing heavy debugging, remember to regularly review changes you made to fix the bug in the debugger. This double-checking is especially important in the later stages of the project, when you need to be careful not to destabilize the code base.

If you set up your project correctly and follow the debugging steps in this chapter and the recommendations in Chapter 2, you won't have to spend much time doing heavy debugging.

Step 8: Verify That the Bug Is Fixed

When you think you've finally fixed the bug, the next step in the debugging process is to test, test, and retest the fix. Did I also mention that you need to test the fix? If the bug is in an isolated module on a line of code called once, testing the fix is easy. However, if the fix is in a core module, especially one that handles your data structures and the like, you need to be very careful that your fix doesn't cause problems or have side effects in other parts of the project.

When testing your fix, especially in critical code, you should verify that it works with all data conditions, good and bad. Nothing is worse than a fix for one bug that causes two other bugs. If you do make a change in a critical module, you should let the rest of the team know that you made the change. That way, they can be on the lookout for any ripple effects as well.

DEBUGGING WAR STORY

Where Did the Integration Go?

The Battle

One of the developers I worked with at NuMega thought he'd found a great bug in NuMega's Visual C++ Integrated Development Environment (VC IDE) integration because it didn't work on his machine.

For those of you who are unfamiliar with NuMega's VC IDE integration, let me provide a little background information. NuMega's software products integrate with the VC IDE—and have for a number of years. This integration allows NuMega's windows, toolbars, and menus to appear seamlessly inside the VC IDE.

The Outcome

This developer spent a couple of hours using SoftICE, a kernel debugger, exploring the bug. After a while, he had set breakpoints all over the operating system. Finally, he found his "bug." He noticed that when he started the VC IDE, *CreateProcess* was being called with the "\\R2D2\VCommon\MSDev98\Bin\MSDEV.EXE" instead of the "C:\VSCommon\MSDev98\Bin\MSDEV.EXE" he thought it should be. In other words, instead of running the VC IDE from his local machine (C:\VSCommon\MSDev98\Bin\MSDEV.EXE), he was running it from his old machine (\\R2D2\VCommon\MSDev98\Bin\MSDEV.EXE). How did this happen?

The developer had just gotten a new machine and had installed the full NuMega VC IDE integration for the products. To get it set up faster, he had copied his desktop links (LNK files) from his old machine, which were installed without VC IDE integration, to his new machine by dragging them with the mouse. When you drag LNK files, the internal links update to reflect the location of the original link. Therefore, he was always starting the VC IDE from his desktop icon LNK, which had the pointer to the old machine, instead of running the VC IDE from his new machine. He'd been running it from his old machine all along.

The Lesson

The developer went about debugging the problem wrong by just jumping right in with a kernel debugging instead of attempting to duplicate the problem in multiple ways. In Step 1 of the debugging process, "Duplicate the bug," I recommend that you try to duplicate the bug in multiple ways so that you can be assured that you're looking at the right bug, not just multiple bugs masking and compounding each other. If this developer had followed Step 5, "Think creatively," he would have been better off because he would have thought about the problem first instead of plunging right in.

Step 9: Learn and Share

Each time you fix a "good" bug (that is, one that was challenging to find and fix), you should take the time to quickly summarize what you learned. I like to record my good bugs in a journal so that I can later see what I did right in finding and fixing the problem. More important, I also want to learn what I did wrong so that I can learn to avoid dead-ends when debugging and solve bugs faster. You learn the most about development when you're debugging, so you should take every opportunity to learn from it.

One of the most important steps you can take after fixing a good bug is to share the information you learned fixing the bug with your colleagues, especially if the bug is project specific. This information will help your coworkers the next time they need to eliminate a similar bug.

Final Debugging Process Secret

I'd like to share one final debugging secret with you: the debugger can answer all your debugging questions as long as you ask it the right questions. Again, I'm suggesting that you need to have a hypothesis in mind—something you want to prove or disprove—before the debugger can help you. Sometimes I even write out my hypothesis before I ever touch the debugger to ensure that I have a purpose each time I use it.

Remember that the debugger is just a tool, like a screwdriver. It does only what you tell it to do. The real debugger is the software in your hardware cranium.

SUMMARY

This chapter started out by defining bugs and describing process problems that contribute to bugs. Then it discussed what you should know before you start debugging. Finally, it presented a debugging process that you should follow when you debug your code.

The best way to debug is to avoid bugs in the first place. If you plan your projects properly, have a real commitment to quality, and learn about how your products fit with their technologies, the operating system, and the CPU, you can minimize the time you spend debugging.

Chapter 2

Getting Started Debugging

In this chapter, I'll introduce some important infrastructure tools and requirements that will contribute to your debugging success over the lifetime of your application. Some of the tools involve the engineering process, and others are software utilities. What they all have in common is that they allow you to see the progress of your project on a daily basis. I believe this daily monitoring is the key to getting your product out the door on time—with quality. Projects don't slip massively in one day; they slip a little each day along the way.

All the ideas presented here and in Chapter 3 come from my experience shipping real-world software products, and I can't imagine developing without these tools and techniques. I've learned some lessons the hard way, and I hope to save you time and pain by sharing with you what these lessons have taught me. You might think that some of these ideas don't apply to you because you're on a two-person or three-person team. Don't worry, they do. Even when I'm on a team of one, I still approach a project in the same way. I've worked on projects of every size you can think of, so I know the recommendations I make scale from the tiniest to the largest teams.

TRACK CHANGES UNTIL YOU THROW AWAY THE PROJECT

Version control and bug tracking systems are two of the most important infrastructure tools you have because they give you the history of your project. Although the developers might say they can keep everything in their heads, the company needs to have some record of what's been accomplished on the project in case the entire development team wins the lottery and everyone quits the next day. Because most teams don't adequately maintain their requirements and design documents throughout the life of a project, the only real documentation becomes the audit trail in the version control and bug tracking systems.

I hope I'm preaching to the converted. Unfortunately, I keep running into teams that haven't yet started using these tools. As someone interested in history, I feel you have to know where you've been to know where you're going. Putting these two tools to use is the only sure way to learn that lesson. By monitoring the outstanding bugs and bug fix rates in the bug tracking system, you can better predict when your product will be ready to ship. With the version control system, you'll get an idea of your "code churn," the volume of changes, so that you can see how much additional testing needs to be done. Additionally, these tools are the only effective way to judge whether you're getting any results from changes you implement in your development cycle.

When you bring a new developer to your team, these tools can pay for themselves in a single day. When the new developer starts, have her sit down with the version control and bug tracking software and begin working her way through the changes. Good design documents are ideal, but if they aren't available, the version control and bug tracking systems at least provide a record of the code evolution and highlight any trouble areas.

I'm talking about these two tools in the same breath because they are inseparable. The bug tracking system captures all the events that might have driven changes to your master sources. The version control system captures every change. Ideally, you want to maintain the relationship between reported problems and actual changes in the master sources. By correlating the relationship, you can see your cause and effect for bug fixes. If you don't track the relationship, you're left wondering why certain changes to the code occurred. Invariably, in later versions of the product, you have to find the developer who made the change and hope he or she remembers the reason for the change.

Some products are integrated and automatically track the relationship of the master source change to the bug report, but if your current systems don't, you'll need to maintain the relationship manually. You can track the relationship by including the bug number in the comments that describe the fix. When you check the file back into version control, you'll need to identify the bug number you're fixing in the check-in comment for the file.

Version Control Systems

The version control system isn't just for your project's master sources. Anything and everything related to the project—including all test plans, automated tests, the help system, and design documents—needs to go into the version control system. Some companies even include the build tools (that is, the compiler, linker, include files, and libraries), which allows them to completely re-create the shipped version of their product. If you have any question about whether something should go in version control, ask yourself whether maintenance programmers could use the information in a couple of years. If you think they could, that information belongs in the version control system.

Controlling Changes

Tracking change is vital; however, having a good bug tracking system in place doesn't mean that developers should be allowed to make wholesale changes to the master sources whenever they want. Such carte blanche would make all the tracking pointless. The idea is to control the changes during development, restricting certain types of changes to certain stages of the project so that you can have an idea of the state of the master sources on a day-to-day basis. The best scheme I've heard of for controlling changes comes from my friend Steve Munyan, and he calls it "Green, Yellow, and Red Times." In Green Time, anyone can check in anything to the master sources. The earliest parts of the project are usually fully in Green Time because at this point the team is working on new features.

Yellow Time is when the product is in a bug fix phase or nearing a code freeze. The only code changes allowed are for bug fixes—and *only* bug fixes. No new features or other changes are permitted. Before a developer can check in a bug fix, a technical lead or a development manager must approve it. The developer making the bug fix must describe the bug fix he's making and what it affects. In essence, this process is a mini code review for every single bug fix. On some teams I've been on, the product was in Yellow Time from day one because the team liked the code review aspects of this stage. We did loosen the approval requirements so that any other developer could approve changes. The interesting outcome was that because of the constant code reviews the developers caught many bugs before they checked the code into the master sources.

Red Time occurs when you're in a code freeze or near a key milestone and all code changes require the product manager's approval. When I was a product manager, I even went to the extent of changing the permissions in the version control system so that the team had read-only access. I took this step mainly because I understood what the developers were thinking: "This is just a little change; it will fix this bug, and it won't hurt anything else." The developers' intentions were good, but that one little change could mean that the entire team would have to restart the test plan from the beginning.

The product manager must strictly enforce Red Time. If the product has a reproducible crash or data corruption, the decision to make the change is essentially automatic because you just do it. In most cases, however, deciding whether to fix a particular bug is less black and white. To help me decide how critical a bug fix was, I always asked the following questions with the company's needs in mind:

- How many people does this problem affect?

- Is the change in a core or a peripheral part of the product?

- If the change is made, what parts of the application will need to be re-tested?

The answers to these questions provided the criteria I needed to allow or to decide against the change.

The Importance of Labeling

One of the most important commands that you can learn to use in your version control system is its label command. Microsoft Visual SourceSafe calls it a label, MKS Source Integrity calls it a checkpoint, and PVCS Version Manager calls it a version label. Different version control systems might refer to the label command in different ways, but whatever it's called, a label marks a particular set of master sources. A label allows you to retrieve a specific version of your master sources in the future. If you make a labeling mistake, you might never be able to retrieve the exact master sources used for a particular version. That could mean that you might not be able to discover why a particular version is crashing.

When deciding what to label, I've always followed these three hard-and-fast rules:

1. Label all internal milestones.

2. Label any build sent to someone outside the team.

3. Label anytime a daily build occurs.

In all cases, I follow a scheme of "<project name> <Milestone/Reason> <Date>" so that the label names are descriptive. With the first two rules, I'd never release the team from Yellow Time or Red Time until I applied the labels.

The third labeling rule is one that many people forget. Your quality engineers are usually working with the daily build, so when they report a problem, it's against a particular version of the master sources. Because developers can change code quickly, you want to make it simple for them to get back to the exact version of the files they need to reproduce the bug.

COMMON DEBUGGING QUESTION

What do we do if we're having trouble reproducing builds sent to others outside the team?

Every time you do a build for someone outside the team, you should make a complete copy of the project build directory to CD or tape. This copy will include all your source files, the intermediate files, the symbol files, and the final output. Also include the installation kit that you sent the customer. You might even want to consider copying the build tools. CDs and tapes are inexpensive insurance against future problems.

Even when I've done everything possible to preserve a particular build in version control, I've still experienced cases in which a rebuild produced a binary that differed from the original. By having the complete build tree archived, you can debug the user's problem with exactly the same binaries that you sent.

Bug Tracking Systems

In addition to tracking your bugs, the bug tracking system makes an excellent vehicle for jotting down reminders and keeping a to-do list, especially when you're in the process of developing code. Some developers like to keep notes and to-do lists in notebooks, but essential information often gets lost between random hexadecimal number streams from a debugging session and the pages on pages of doodling that you used to keep yourself awake in the last management status meeting. By putting these notes into the bug tracking system and assigning them to yourself, you consolidate them in one place, making them easier to find. Additionally, although you probably like to think that you "own" the code you work on, you really don't—it belongs to the team. With your to-do list in the bug tracking system, other team members who have to interface with your code can check your list to see what you have or haven't done. Another benefit of including to-do lists and notes in the bug tracking system is that fewer details fall through the cracks at the last minute as a result of you forgetting about a problem or another issue. I always find myself running the bug tracking system so that I can quickly jot down important notes and to-dos right when I think about them.

I like to reserve the lowest priority bug code in the system for notes and to-do lists. Flagging notes and to-do lists as lowest priority bugs makes it easier to keep them separate from the real bugs, but at the same time, you can quickly raise their priority if you need to. You should also structure your bug metrics reports so that they don't include the lowest priority bug code, because it will skew your results.

Don't be afraid to peruse the bug tracking data either. All the unvarnished truths about your products are there. When you're planning an update, run through the bug tracking system and find those modules or features that had the most bugs reported against them. Consider adding some time in your schedule to allow team members to go back and strengthen those sections.

When deploying your bug tracking system, make sure that everyone who needs it has it. At a minimum, everyone on the development team and the technical support team needs access to it. If your bug tracking system supports different levels of access, you might also want to think about allowing others, such as sales engineers (technical experts who are part of the sales organization and help the salespeople as needed when they're selling a complicated product) and marketing representatives, to have access as appropriate. For example, you might want to allow certain sales and marketing people to enter bugs and feature requests but not to view existing bugs. These two groups are generally out talking to customers more than your typical engineers are, and the customer feedback they can supply can be invaluable. Having them log their requests and problems in the same system that everyone else uses is efficient and practical. The idea is to have one central place where all problems and feature requests reside. If you store this information in multiple locations, you're more likely to lose track of it.

Choosing the Right Systems for You

Numerous version control systems are available. Some might be easier to use than others or offer more features, but the real issue in choosing the best version control system comes down to your specific requirements. Obviously, if you're in a shop that has high-end requirements, such as multiple platform support, you're going to need to look at one of the more expensive systems. If you're a small team targeting just Microsoft Windows development, however, you can consider some of the less costly alternatives. Make sure you spend some time doing some hard evaluation of the system you're thinking about implementing, especially in trying to predict what you'll need in the future. You're going to be living with your version control system for a while, so make sure it will grow with you. And keep in mind that just as important as choosing the right version control system is using a version control system in the first place: any system is better than no system.

As for bug tracking systems, I've seen many people try to limp along with a homegrown system. Although doing a project with a homemade system is possible,

I'd recommend investing in a commercial product. The information in the bug tracking system is too vital to put into an application that you don't have the time to support and that can't grow to meet your needs six months or a year into the project.

The same criteria apply for choosing a bug tracking system as for choosing a version control system. Once, as a product manager, I decided on a bug tracking system without spending enough time looking at the most important part, reporting bugs. The product was easy enough to set up and use. Unfortunately, its reporting capabilities were so limited that we ended up transferring all our existing bugs over to another product right after we hit our first external code milestone. I was rather embarrassed for not having evaluated the product as thoroughly as I should have.

As I mentioned earlier in the chapter, you should definitely consider a bug tracking product that offers integration with a version control product. In the Windows marketplace, most version control systems support the Microsoft Source-Code Control Interface (SCCI). If your bug tracking system supports SCCI as well, you can coordinate the bug fixes with particular file versions.

Some people have described code as the lifeblood of a development team. If that description is accurate, the version control and bug tracking systems are the arteries. They keep the lifeblood flowing and moving in the right direction. Don't develop without them.

SCHEDULE TIME FOR BUILDING DEBUGGING SYSTEMS

As you're doing the design and initial scheduling for your project, make sure to add in time for building your debugging systems. You need to decide up front how you're going to implement your crash handlers (a topic covered in Chapter 9), file data dumpers, and other tools you'll need to help you reproduce problems reported from the field. I've always liked to treat the error handling systems as if they were a product feature. That way, others in the company can see how you're going to handle bugs proactively when they come up.

As you're planning your debugging systems, you need to establish your preventive debugging policies. The first and most difficult parts of this process involve determining how you're going to return error conditions in the project. Whatever you do, make sure you pick only one way and stick with it. One project I encountered long ago (and fortunately wasn't a part of) had three different ways to return errors: return values, *setjmp/longjmp* exceptions, and through a global error variable similar to the C run-time library's *errno* variable. Those developers had a very difficult time tracking errors across subsystem boundaries.

Unfortunately, I can't make a blanket recommendation for a particular way of returning errors because Windows development involves too many dependencies on technologies and third-party components. Technologies such as the Component Object Model (COM) enforce an error-return standard. In general, across subsystem boundaries, I prefer the COM approach, in which you check a return value instead of throwing objects such as C++ exceptions. I realize that some hardcore C++ developers might disagree with my preference, but I always err on the side of simplicity and understandability, both of which are apparent in the COM approach.

Build All Builds with Debugging Symbols

Some of the debugging system recommendations that I do make aren't that controversial. I've been harping on my first recommendation for years: build all builds, including release builds, with full debugging symbols. Debugging symbols are the data that lets the debugger show you source and line information, variable names, and data type information for your program. I don't relish the task of debugging a release build binary completely at the assembly-language level. If you like challenges, I guess you could do it, but I like to save time.

Of course, debugging release builds with symbols has its drawbacks. For example, the optimized code the compiler produces won't always match the flow of execution in the source code, so you might find that stepping through release code is a little harder than stepping through debug code. Another problem to watch out for in release builds is that sometimes the compiler optimizes the stack registers such that you can't see the complete call stack, as you would in a straight debug build. Also be aware that when you do add debugging symbols to the binary, it will grow a small amount. However, the size increase is negligible when compared to the ease of being able to solve bugs quickly.

Turning on debug symbols for a release build is quite easy. For Microsoft Visual Basic, on the Project Properties dialog box Compile tab, check Create Symbolic Debug Info. For Microsoft Visual C++ projects, two separate steps are required. The first step is to set the compiler, CL.EXE, to put debug symbols into the OBJ files. In the Project Settings dialog box, select Win32 Release in the Settings For combo box to modify your release builds only. On the C/C++ tab, General Category, Debug Info combo box, select Program Database. This setting will add the /Zi switch to your compiles. Make sure you don't select Program Database For Edit And Continue (/ZI)—that option adds all sorts of padding and other information to your binary so that you can edit the source code as you debug.

The second step for Visual C++ projects is to have the linker, LINK.EXE, generate the actual debug symbols. Select Win32 Release in the Settings For combo box, and on the Link tab, General Category, check Generate Debug Info. This setting turns on the /DEBUG switch to the linker, which is fine for debug builds. You also need to type */OPT:REF* in the Project Options edit box on the Link tab. Using the /DEBUG switch with the linker automatically tells it to bring in all functions whether or not they are referenced, which is the default for debug builds. The /OPT:REF switch tells the linker to bring in only functions that your program calls directly. If you forget to add the /OPT:REF switch, your release application will also contain the functions that are never called, making it much larger than it should be.

Although you might be concerned that turning on debugging symbols will make reverse engineering your application easier, it doesn't. When you select the Program Database (PDB) setting in your project, all debugging symbols are stored in the separate PDB files your program generates. Because you don't ship those files to your customers, the extra debugging symbols won't make reverse engineering your application any easier.

After you build your release builds with full PDB files, you need to store the PDB files in a safe place along with any binary files you ship to customers. If you lose your PDB files, you'll be right back to debugging at the assembly-language level. Treat your PDB files as you would your distributed binaries.

Treat Warnings as Errors—Maybe

Because Visual Basic is much more sensitive to compilation errors than C++ is, anything the compiler reports to you is an error. C++, as anyone who has compiled any program larger than "Hello, World!" knows, is a much looser language and lets you get away with murder and mayhem. Like Visual Basic, Visual C++ has some hard errors that will abort the compilation. Errors such as C2037, "left of 'operator' specifies undefined struct/union 'identifier'," mean that the compiler can't continue. What makes Visual C++ different from Visual Basic is that it can also report warnings.

These warnings generally mean that some part of your code is ambiguous, but the compiler will take an educated guess at the correct meaning. A warning such as C4244, "'conversion' conversion from 'type1' to 'type2', possible loss of data," which is always reported on conversions between signed and unsigned types, is an excellent example. Although some people feel that warnings are just that, I feel that any warning is the same as an error and that you need to treat it as such. As soon as I see a compiler warning, I stop and fix my code so that it is unambiguous to the compiler.

If you ever had the opportunity to learn about compiler construction, particularly parsing, you probably walked away with one thought: parsing is very hard, especially with a language as complex as C++. If the Visual C++ compiler writers go to all the trouble to report a warning, they are trying to tell you that something in your code is ambiguous and they will have to guess what you mean. I don't like letting a tool guess for me—it's a perfect way to introduce bugs. When someone asks me to help with a bug, the first thing I do is verify that the code compiles with no warnings. If it doesn't, I tell them that I'll be glad to help, but not until their code compiles cleanly.

The default projects that the Visual C++ wizards create are at warning-level 3, which corresponds to the /W3 switch to CL.EXE. The next step up is warning-level 4, /W4, and you can even have the compiler treat all warnings as errors with /WX. These levels are all easy to set in the Visual C++ integrated development environment (IDE) in the Project Settings dialog box. On the C/C++ tab, General Category, you set the warning level in the Warning Level combo box, and in the check box right below it, Warnings As Errors, you set the /WX switch.

Although I can almost justify making the global statement "All builds should compile with warning-level 4, and you should treat all warnings as errors," reality intrudes to force me to temper this remark. First off, some common header files won't compile with /W4 and /WX set. The compiler itself has a couple of unnecessary information warnings that it treats as real warnings, so using /WX will stop the compile. The Standard Template Library (STL) that comes with Visual C++ has many warning-level 4 issues in it. The compiler also has a few problems with templates. Fortunately, you can work around most of these issues.

You might think that just setting the warning level to 4 and turning off treating warnings as errors would be fine; in fact, that scheme defeats the purpose. I've found that developers quickly become desensitized to warnings in the Build window. If you don't fix all the warnings as they happen, no matter how innocuous a warning seems, you'll start to lose more important warnings because they'll be hidden amid the output stream. The trick is to be more explicit about which warnings you want to handle. Although your goal should be to get rid of most warnings by writing better code, you can also turn off specific errors with the *#pragma warning* directive. Additionally, you can use the *#pragma warning* directive to control the error level around specific headers.

A good example of lowering the error level is when you're including headers that don't compile at warning-level 4. The extended *#pragma warning* directive, first offered in Visual C++ 6, can lower the warning level. In the following code snippet, I set the warning level before including the suspect header and reset it so that my code compiles with warning-level 4:

```
#pragma warning ( push , 3 )
#include "IDoNotCompileAtWarning4.h"
#pragma warning ( pop )
```

You can also disable individual warnings with the *#pragma warning* directive. This directive comes in handy when you're using a nameless structure or union and you get a C4201 error, "nonstandard extension used : nameless struct/union," with warning-level 4. To turn off that warning, you use the *#pragma warning* directive as in the following code. Notice that I commented what I was turning off and explained why I was turning it off. When disabling individual warnings, be sure to restrict the scope of the *#pragma warning* directive to specific sections of code. If you place the directive at too high a level, you can mask other problems in your code.

```
// Turning off "nonstandard extension used : nameless struct/union"
// because I'm not writing portable code
#pragma warning ( disable : 4201 )
struct S
{
    float y;
    struct
    {
        int a ;
        int b ;
        int c ;
    } ;
} *p_s ;
// Turn warning back on.
#pragma warning ( default : 4201 )
```

If you're not using STL, the scheme above works well. If you're using STL, it might work, but it might not. Always try to get the STL headers to compile at warning-level 4 before you lower the error level around them with *#pragma warning (push , 3)*. You might have to turn off some additional individual warnings, but strive to keep the warning level at 4, if possible. On a couple of projects, I never did get the code to compile without warnings no matter what workaround I tried. In those cases, I dropped the global warning level to 3. Even then, however, I still kept the Warnings As Errors option on.

The bottom line is that you should try to compile with the highest warning level possible and treat all warnings as errors from the start of your project. When you first boost the warning level for your project, you'll probably be surprised by the number of warnings you get. Go through and fix each one. You'll probably notice that just fixing the warnings will solve a bug or two. For those of you who think getting your program to compile with /W4 and /WX is impossible, I have proof otherwise: all the sample code on this book's companion CD compiles with both flags set for all configurations.

Know Where Your DLLs Load

If you've ever been hiking in the woods, you know that landmarks can be very important in keeping you from getting lost. When you don't have any landmarks, you can end up going around in circles. When your application crashes, you need a similar kind of landmark to help point you in the right direction so that you're not wandering around in the debugger.

The first big landmark for crashes is the base address of your dynamic-link libraries (DLLs) and ActiveX controls (OCXs), which indicates where they loaded into memory. When a customer gives you a crash address, you should be able to narrow down which DLL it came from quickly by the first two or three numbers. I don't expect you to have all the system DLLs memorized, but you should memorize at least your project's DLL base addresses.

If all your DLLs load at unique addresses, you have some good landmarks to help guide your search for the crash. But what do you think would happen if all your DLLs had the same load address? Obviously, the operating system doesn't map them all into the same place in memory. It has to "relocate" any incoming DLL that wants to occupy memory that's already filled by putting the incoming DLL into a different place. The issue then becomes one of trying to figure out which DLL is loaded where. Unfortunately, you have no way of knowing what the operating system will do on different machines. Consequently, you'd have no idea where the crash came from, and you'd spend days searching through the debugger looking for it.

By default for wizard-created projects, Visual Basic DLLs load at 0x11000000, and Visual C++ DLLs load at 0x10000000. I'm willing to bet that at least half the DLLs in the world today try to load at one of those addresses. Changing the base address for your DLL is called *rebasing,* and it's a simple operation in which you specify a different load address than the default.

Before we jump into rebasing, let's look at an easy way to find out whether you have load conflicts in your DLLs. If you see the following notification in the Visual C++ debugger Output window, you need to stop and fix the load addresses of the conflicting DLLs immediately so that you don't forget to fix them later. Make sure you fix the load addresses for both release and debug builds.

```
LDR: Dll xxx base 10000000 relocated due to collision with yyy
```

The *xxx* and *yyy* in this statement are the names of the DLLs that are conflicting.

In addition to making it difficult to find a crash, when the operating system has to relocate a DLL, your application slows down. When relocating, the operating system needs to read all the relocation information for the DLL, run through each place in the code that accesses an address within the DLL, and change the address because the DLL is no longer at its preferred place in memory. If you have a couple of load address conflicts in your application, startup can sometimes take more than twice as long!

There are two ways to rebase the DLLs in your application. The first method is to use the REBASE.EXE utility that comes with the Platform SDK. REBASE.EXE has many different options, but your best bet is to call it using the /b command-line switch with the starting base address and put the appropriate DLLs on the command line.

Table 2-1 shows a table from the Platform SDK documentation for rebasing your DLLs. As you can see, the recommended format is to use an alphabetical scheme. I generally follow this scheme because it's simple. The operating system DLLs load from 0x70000000 to 0x78000000, so using the range in Table 2-1 will keep you from conflicting with the operating system.

Table 2-1   DLL REBASING SCHEME

DLL First Letter	Starting Address
A–C	0x60000000
D–F	0x61000000
G–I	0x62000000
J–L	0x63000000
M–O	0x64000000
P–R	0x65000000
S–U	0x66000000
V–X	0x67000000
Y–Z	0x68000000

If you have four DLLs in your application, APPLE.DLL, DUMPLING.DLL, GINGER.DLL, and GOOSEBERRIES.DLL, you would run REBASE.EXE three times to get all the DLLs rebased appropriately. The following three commands show how you would run REBASE.EXE with those DLLs:

```
REBASE /b 0x60000000 APPLE.DLL
REBASE /b 0x61000000 DUMPLING.DLL
REBASE /b 0x62000000 GINGER.DLL GOOSEBERRIES.DLL
```

If multiple DLLs are passed on the REBASE.EXE command line, as shown here with GINGER.DLL and GOOSEBERRIES.DLL, REBASE.EXE will rebase the DLLs so that they are loaded back to back starting at the specified starting address.

The other method of rebasing a DLL is to specify the load address when you link the DLL. In Visual Basic, set the address in the DLL Base Address field on the Compile tab of the Project Properties dialog box. In Visual C++, specify the address by selecting the Link tab on the Project Settings dialog box, choosing Output from the Category combo box, and then entering the address in the Base Address edit box. Visual C++ translates the address you enter in the Base Address edit box into the /BASE switch to LINK.EXE.

Although you can use REBASE.EXE to automatically handle setting multiple DLL load addresses at a time, you have to be a little more careful when setting the load address at link time. If you set the load addresses of multiple DLLs too close together, you'll see the loader relocation message in the Ouput window. The trick is to set the load addresses far enough apart that you never have to worry about them after you set them.

Using the same DLLs from the REBASE.EXE example, I'd set their load address to the following:

```
APPLE.DLL           0x60000000
DUMPLING.DLL        0x61000000
GINGER.DLL          0x62000000
GOOSEBERRIES.DLL    0x62100000
```

The important two DLLs are GINGER.DLL and GOOSEBERRIES.DLL because they begin with the same character. When that happens, I use the third-highest digit to differentiate the load addresses. If I were to add another DLL that started with "G," its load address would be 0x62200000.

To see a project in which the load addresses are set manually, look at the WDBG project in the section "WDBG: A Real Debugger" in Chapter 4. The /BASE switch also allows you to specify a text file that contains the load addresses for each DLL in your application. In the WDBG project, I use the text-file scheme.

Either method, using REBASE.EXE or rebasing the DLLs manually, will rebase your DLLs and OCXs, but it might be best to follow the second method and rebase your DLLs manually. I manually rebased all the sample DLLs on this book's companion CD. The main benefit of using this method is that your MAP file will contain the specific address you set. A MAP file is a text file that indicates where the linker put all the symbols and source lines in your program. You should always create MAP files with your release builds because they are the only straight text representation of your symbols that you can get. MAP files are especially handy in the future when you need to find a crash location and your current debugger doesn't read the old symbols. If you use REBASE.EXE to rebase a DLL instead of rebasing it manually, the MAP file created by the linker will contain the original base address, and you'll have to do some arithmetic to convert an address in the MAP file to a rebased address. In Chapter 8, I'll explain MAP files in more detail.

One of the big questions I get when I tell people to rebase their files is, "What files am I supposed to rebase?" The rule of thumb is simple: If you or someone on your team wrote the code, rebase it. Otherwise, leave it alone. If you're using third-party components, your binaries will have to fit around them.

COMMON DEBUGGING QUESTION

What additional compiler and linker options will help me with my proactive debugging?

A number of compiler and linker switches can help you control your application's performance and better debug your application. Additionally, I don't completely agree with the default compiler and linker settings that the Visual C++ project wizards give you, as I mentioned earlier in the chapter. Consequently, I always change some of the settings.

Compiler Switches for CL.EXE

You can type all these compiler switches directly into the Project Options edit control on the bottom of the C/C++ tab of the Project Settings dialog box.

/P (preprocess to a file)

If you're having trouble with a macro, the /P switch will preprocess your source file, expanding all macros and including all include files, and send the ouput to a file with the same name but with an .I extension. You can look in the .I file to see how your macro expanded. Make sure that you have sufficient disk space because the .I files can be several megabytes apiece. If your .I files are too big for the disk, you can use the /EP switch with /P to suppress the *#line* directives output by the preprocessor. The *#line* directives are what the preprocessor uses to coordinate line numbers and source file names in a preprocessed file so that the compiler can report the location of compilation errors.

/X (ignore standard include paths)

Getting a correct build can sometimes be a pain if you have multiple compilers and SDKs installed on your machine. If you don't use this switch, the compiler, when invoked by a MAK file, will use the INCLUDE environment variable. To control exactly which header files are included, the /X switch will cause the compiler to ignore the INCLUDE environment variable and look only for header files in the locations you explicitly specify with the /I switch.

/Zp (structure member alignment)

You should *not* use this flag. Instead of specifying on the command line how structure members should be aligned in memory, you should align structure members by using the *#pragma pack* directive inside specific headers. I've seen some huge bugs in code because the development team originally built by

(continued)

setting /Zp. When they moved to a new build or another team went to use their code, the /Zp switch was forgotten, and structures were slightly different because the default alignment was different. It took a long time to find those bugs.

/GZ (catch release-build errors in debug build)

Visual C++ 6 introduced the outstanding debugging feature in which the compiler automatically initializes a function's local variables and checks the call stack after function calls. This flag is on by default for debug builds, but you can also use it in release builds. If you're having trouble with uninitialized memory reads (wild reads), uninitialized memory writes (wild writes), or memory overwrites, create a new project configuration that is based on your release build and add this switch to the compile options. With all your local variables filled with 0xCC as they're created, you can start looking around to see what changed the values at the wrong time.

Additionally, the /GZ switch will generate code that saves the current stack pointer before an indirect function call (such as a call to a DLL function) and verifies that the stack pointer is unchanged after the call. Validating the stack pointer helps protect you against one of the most insidious bugs around: a mismatched calling convention declaration. This bug occurs when you call a _ _stdcall function but you misdeclare it as a _ _cdecl function. These two calling conventions clean up the stack differently, so you'll crash later in the program if you get the calling convention wrong.

/O1 (minimize size)

By default, a project created by the Microsoft Foundation Class (MFC) library AppWizard uses /O2 (maximize speed) for its release-build configurations. However, Microsoft builds all its commercial applications with /O1, and that's what you should be using. What Microsoft has found is that after picking the best algorithm and writing tight code, avoiding page faults can help speed up your application considerably. As I've heard it said, "Page faults can ruin your day!"

Page faults occur when your executing code moves from one page of memory (4 KB for x86 Intel) to the next. To resolve a page fault, the operating system must stop executing your program and place the new page on the CPU. If the page fault is soft, meaning that the page is already in memory, the overhead isn't too terrible—but it's extra overhead nonetheless. If the page fault is hard, however, the operating system must go out to disk and bring the page into memory. As you can imagine, this little trip will cause hundreds of thousands of instructions to execute, slowing down your application. By minimizing the size of your binary, you decrease the total number of pages your application uses, thereby reducing the number of page faults. Granted, the operating system's loaders and cache management are quite good, but why take more page faults than you have to?

In addition to using /O1, you should look at using the Working Set Tuner (WST) utility from the Platform SDK. WST will help you order your most commonly called functions to the front of your binary so that you minimize your working set, the number of pages kept in memory. With your common functions up front, the operating system can swap out the unneeded pages. Thus, your application runs faster. For more on using WST, see my February 1999 "Bugslayer" column in *Microsoft Systems Journal* on MSDN.

Linker Switches for LINK.EXE

You can type all these compiler switches directly into the Project Options edit control on the bottom of the Link tab of the Project Settings dialog box.

/MAP (generate MAP file)

/MAPINFO:LINES (include line information in the MAP file)

/MAPINFO:EXPORTS (include export information in the MAP file)

These switches build a MAP file for the linked image. (See Chapter 8 for instructions on how to read a MAP file.) You should always create a MAP file because it's the only way to get textual symbolic information. Use all three of these switches to ensure that the MAP file contains the most useful information.

/NODEFAULTLIB (ignore libraries)

Many system header files include *#pragma comment (lib#, XXX)* records to specify what library file to link with, where XXX is the name of the library. /NODEFAULTLIB tells the linker to ignore the pragmas. This switch lets you control which libraries to link with and in what order. You'll need to specify each necessary library on the linker command line so that your application will link, but at least you'll know exactly which libraries you're getting and in which order you're getting them. Controlling the order in which libraries are linked can be important any time the same symbol is included in more than one library, which can lead to very difficult-to-find bugs.

/ORDER (put functions in order)

After you've run WST, the /ORDER switch allows you to specify the file that contains the order for the functions. /ORDER will turn off incremental linking, so use it only on release builds.

(continued)

/PDBTYPE:CON (consolidate PDB files)

You should always turn on /PDBTYPE:CON for all your builds, both release and debug. Visual C++ projects don't have this switch on by default. This switch consolidates all the debugging information for a module into a single PDB file instead of spreading it into multiple files. Having a single PDB file makes it much easier for multiple users to debug the same binaries; it also simplifies the archiving of your debugging information.

/VERBOSE (print progress messages)

/VERBOSE:LIB (print libraries searched only progress messages)

If you're having trouble linking, these messages can show you what symbols the linker is looking for and where it finds them. The output can get voluminous, but it can show you where you're having a build problem. I've used /VERBOSE and /VERBOSE:LIB when I've had an odd crash because a function being called didn't look, at the assembly-language level, anything like I thought it should. It turned out that I had two functions with identical signatures, but different implementations, in two different libraries, and the linker was finding the wrong one.

/WARN:3

Generally, I don't use this switch all the time, but a couple times during the project's life I look to see which libraries I'm actually referencing. Turning on /WARN:3 will tell you whether libraries passed to LINK.EXE are referenced. Personally, I like to control exactly which libraries I link against, and I remove unreferenced libraries from the link list.

Design a Lightweight Diagnostic System for Release Builds

The bugs I hate the most are those that happen only on the machines of one or two users. Every other user is merrily running your product, but one or two users have something unique going on with their machines—something that is almost impossible to figure out. Although you could always have the user ship the misbehaving machine to you, this strategy isn't always practical. If the customer is in the Caribbean, you could volunteer to travel there and debug the problem. For some reason, however, I haven't heard of too many companies that are that quality conscious. Nor have I heard of many developers who would volunteer to go to the Arctic Circle to fix a problem either.

When you do have a problem situation that occurs on only one or two machines, you need a way to see the program's flow of execution on those machines. Many developers already track the flow of execution through logging files and writing to the event log, but I want to stress how important that log is to solving problems. The problem-solving power of flow logging increases dramatically when the whole team approaches tracking the program's flow of execution in an organized fashion.

When logging your information, following a template is especially important. With the information in a consistent format, developers will find it much easier to parse the file and report the interesting highlights. If you log information correctly, you can record tons of information and have Perl scripts pull out the significant items so that you don't need to spend 20 minutes reading a text file just to track down one detail.

What you need to log is mostly project-dependent, but at a minimum, you should definitely log failure and abnormal situations. You also want to try to capture a logical sense of the program operation. For example, if your program is performing file operations, you wouldn't want to log fine-grained details such as "Moving to offset 23 in the file," but you would want to log the opening and closing of the file so that if the last entry in the log is "Preparing to open D:\Foo\BAR.DAT," you know that BAR.DAT is probably corrupt.

The depth of the logging also depends on the performance hit associated with the logging. I generally log everything I could possibly want and keep an eye on the release-build performance when not logging. With today's performance tools, you can quickly see whether your logging code is getting in the way. If it is, you can start to back off on the logging a little bit until you strike enough of a balance that you get sufficient logging without slowing down the application too much.

For C++ code, I like to use a macro such as the following to do the logging. Note that *G_IsLogging* is a global variable that all modules can see. By having the global variable, you can avoid the performance cost of a function call.

```
// Visual C++ macro to do logging
#define LOGGING(x)                    \
    if ( TRUE == G_IsLogging )  \
    {                                 \
        LoggingInfo ( x ) ;    \
    }
```

For Visual Basic code, since there are no macros in the language, I just check the global variable manually. If you were ambitious, you could write a simple Visual Basic IDE add-in that with a button would add everything but the string to pass to the logging function.

```
' Visual Basic example of calling the logging function
If ( 1 = G_IsLogging ) Then
    LoggingInfo ( "Preparing to open " & sFile )
End If
```

You set the global logging flag in one of two ways. If your target audience is experienced computer users, you can set it with an environment variable. Because most of us are targeting ordinary people, however, I recommend making the flag a registry setting. Additionally, I'd create a small utility to set the special registry flag and install it with the application. If users reported problems, your technical support engineers could have them run the utility and ensure that they have the logging turned on. Providing a utility to set the registry flag also relieves your support staff of having to take a novice user on a long and potentially damaging trip through the registry over the phone.

FREQUENT BUILDS AND SMOKE TESTS ARE MANDATORY

Two of the most important pieces of your infrastructure are your build system and your smoke test suite. The build system is what compiles and links your product, and the smoke test suite comprises tests that run your program and verify that it works. Jim McCarthy, in his book *Dynamics of Software Development* (Microsoft Press, 1995), called the daily build and smoke test the heartbeat of the product. If these processes aren't healthy, the project is dead.

Frequent Builds

Ideally, you should build your application once a day. However, I realize that some projects are so large that a daily build wouldn't leave enough time to test the application sufficiently. For those longer and more complex projects, you need to work out a scheme in which you're building as frequently as possible.

When building your product, you should be building both release and debug versions at the same time. As you'll see later in the chapter, the debug builds are critical. Breaking the build must be treated as a sin. If developers check in code that doesn't compile, they need to pay some sort of penalty to right the wrong. A public flogging might be a little harsh (though not by much), but what has always worked on the teams I've been on is penance in the form of supplying donuts to the team and publicly acknowledging the crime. If you're on a team that doesn't have a full-time release engineer, you can punish the build breaker by making him or her responsible for taking care of the build until the next build breaker comes along.

One of the best daily-build practices I've used is to notify the team via e-mail when the build is finished. With an automated nightly build, the first message everyone can look for in the morning is the indication of whether the build failed; if it did, the team can take immediate action to correct it.

To avoid problems with the build, everyone must have the same versions of all build tools and parts. As I mentioned earlier, some teams like to keep the build system in version control to enforce this practice. If you have team members on different versions of the tools, including the service pack levels, you've got room for error in the build. Unless there is a compelling reason to have someone using a different version of the compiler, no developer should be upgrading on his or her own.

Your build system will be pulling the latest master sources from your version control system each time you do a build. Ideally, the developers should be pulling from version control every day as well. Nothing is worse than spending time trying to fix a nasty problem only to find out that the problem is related to an older version of a file on a developer's machine. Another advantage of developers pulling frequently is that it helps enforce the mantra of "no build breaks." By pulling frequently, any problem with the master build automatically becomes a problem with every developer's local build. Whereas managers get annoyed when the daily build breaks, developers go ballistic when you break their local build. With the knowledge that breaking the master build means breaking the build for every individual developer, the pressure is on everyone to check only clean code into the master sources.

COMMON DEBUGGING QUESTION

When should I freeze upgrades to the compiler and other tools?

Once you've hit feature complete, also known as beta 1, you should definitely not upgrade any tools. You can't afford the risk of a new compiler optimization scheme, no matter how well thought out, changing your code. By the time you hit beta 1, you've already done some significant testing, and if you change the tools, you'll need to restart your testing from ground zero.

Smoke Tests

In case you're not familiar with the term, a smoke test is a test that checks your product's basic functionality. The term comes from the electronics industry. At some point in a product's life cycle, electronics engineers would plug in their product to see whether it smoked (literally). If it didn't smoke, or worse, catch fire, they were making progress. In most software situations, a smoke test is simply a run-through of the product to see whether it runs and is therefore good enough to start testing seriously. A smoke test is your gauge of the baseline health of the code.

Your smoke test is just a checklist of items that your program can handle. Initially, start out small: install the application, start it, and shut it down. As you progress through the development cycle, your smoke test needs to grow to exercise new features of the product. The best rule of thumb is that the smoke test should contain at least one test for every feature and major component of the product. If you are in a shrink-wrap company, that means testing each feature that appears in a bullet point for your ads. In an IT shop, that means testing each of the major features you promised the CIO and your client. Keep in mind that your smoke test doesn't need to exhaustively test every code path in your program, but you do want to use it to judge whether you can handle the basics. Once your program passes the smoke test, the quality engineers can start doing the hard work of trying to break the program.

One vital component of your smoke test is some sort of performance benchmark. Many people forget to include these and pay the price later in the development cycle. If you have an established benchmark for an operation (for example, how long the last version of the product took to run), you can define failure as a current run that is 10 percent or more over your benchmark. I'm always amazed by how many times a small change in an innocuous place can have a detrimental impact on performance. By monitoring performance throughout the development cycle, you can fix performance problems before they get out of hand.

The ideal situation for a smoke test is one in which your program is automated so that it can run without requiring any user interaction. The tool you use to automate the input and operations on your application is called a regression-testing tool. Unfortunately, you can't always automate every feature, especially when the user interface is in a state of flux. A number of good regression-testing tools are on the market, and if you're working with a large, complicated application and can afford to have someone assigned to maintaining the smoke tests, you might want to consider purchasing such a tool. I've listed some of these tools in Appendix B. If you can get by with just sending some keystrokes to your application to automate it, however, you can look at the testing system that I put together in Chapter 13.

Breaking the smoke test should be as serious a crime as breaking the build. It takes more effort to create a smoke test, and no developer should treat it lightly. Because the smoke test is what tells your QA team that they have a build that's good enough to work on, keeping the smoke test running is mandatory. If you have an automated smoke test, you should also consider having the smoke test available for the developers so that they can use it to help automate their testing as well. Additionally, with an automated smoke test, you should have the daily build kick it off so that you can immediately gauge the health of the build. As with the daily build, you should notify the team via e-mail to let them know whether the smoke test succeeded or failed.

BUILD THE INSTALLATION PROGRAM IMMEDIATELY

Begin developing the installation program immediately after you start developing your project. The installation program is the first part of your product that your users see. Too many products give a poor first impression, showing that the installation program was left to the last minute. By getting the installation program started as early as possible, you have sufficient time to test and debug it. If the installation program is done early, you can also incorporate it into your smoke test. This way, you're always testing it and your tests will be one step closer to simulating how the users will be running your program.

Earlier in the chapter, I recommended that you should build both release and debug versions of your product. You also need to have an installation program that allows you to install either version. All modern COM software now requires so much stuff in the registry that it's almost impossible to properly use an application without running its installation program. By having a debug build installation program, it becomes trivial for developers to get a debug version on a machine so that they can quickly start debugging a problem. To ensure that no overlap problems between installing debug and release versions occur, you should probably have different registry keys for both your debug and release products.

One extra benefit of having the installation program done as early as possible is that others in your company can start testing your program that much sooner. With the installation program done, the technical support engineers can start using your program and providing you with feedback—early enough in the cycle so that you can actually do something about the problems they find.

QA MUST TEST WITH DEBUG BUILDS

If you follow my recommendations in Chapter 3, you'll have some excellent diagnostics in your code base. The problem is that, generally, only the developers benefit from the diagnostics. To better help debug problems, the quality engineers need to be using the debug builds as well. You'll be amazed at how many problems you'll find and fix when the QA folks do their testing with debug builds.

In the initial stages of the product cycle, the quality engineers should be alternating between debug and release builds. As the product progresses, they should gradually start concentrating more on the release builds. Until you reach the alpha release milestone, at which point you have enough of the features implemented to show customers the product, you should have the quality engineers use the debug build two to three days a week. As you approach beta 1, they should drop to two days a week. After beta 2, when all features and major bugs are fixed, they should drop to one day a week. After the release candidate milestone, they should be on the release build exclusively.

SUMMARY

This chapter covered vital infrastructure requirements necessary to help you minimize your debugging time. They run the gamut from version control and bug tracking systems, to the compiler and linker settings you need, to the benefits of daily builds and smoke tests.

Although you might need additional infrastructure requirements for your unique environment, you'll find the ones covered in this chapter are generic across all environments. And, they are the ones that I've seen make a great deal of difference in real-world development. If you don't have one or more of these infrastructure tools or techniques set up at your development shop, I strongly encourage you to implement them immediately.

Chapter 3

Debugging During Coding

In Chapter 2, I laid the groundwork for the projectwide infrastructure needed to enable engineers to work more efficiently. In this chapter, we'll turn to what you need to do while you're heavy in the coding battles to make debugging easier. Most people refer to this process as defensive programming, but I like to think of it as something broader and deeper: proactive programming, or debugging during coding. To me, defensive programming is the error handling code that tells you an error occurred. Proactive programming tells you why the error occurred.

Coding defensively is only part of the battle of fixing and solving bugs. Engineers generally attempt to make the obvious defensive maneuvers—for example, verifying that a pointer to a string isn't *NULL*—but they often don't take the extra step that proactive programming would require: checking that same parameter to see whether the memory is sufficient to hold the maximum string allowed. Proactive programming also means finding problematic areas as you're writing the code so that you start the debugging process as soon as you type the first line of code.

It's a simple fact: bugs don't just magically appear in code. The "secret" is that you and I put them in as we're writing the code, and those pesky bugs can come from myriad sources. They can be the result of a problem as critical as a design flaw in your application or as simple as a typographical error. Although some bugs are easy to fix, others are nearly impossible to solve without major rewrites. It would be nice to blame the bugs in your code on gremlins, but you need to accept the fact that you and your coworkers are the ones putting the bugs in the code.

Because you and the other developers are responsible for any bugs in the code, the issue becomes one of finding ways to create a system of checks and balances that let you catch bugs as you go. I've always referred to this approach as "trust, but verify," which is Ronald Reagan's famous quote about how the United States was going to enforce one of the nuclear arms limitation treaties with the then Soviet Union. I trust that I and my colleagues will use my code correctly. To avoid bugs, however, I verify everything. I verify the data that others pass into my code, I verify my code's internal manipulations, I verify every assumption I make in my code, I verify data my code passes to others, and I verify data coming back from calls my code makes. If there's something to verify, I verify it. This obsessive verification is nothing personal against my coworkers, and I don't have any psychological problems (to speak of). It's just that I know where the bugs come from; I also know that you can't let anything by without checking it if you want to catch your bugs as early as you can.

Before we go any further, I need to stress one key tenet of my development philosophy: code quality is the sole responsibility of the development engineers, not the test engineers, technical writers, or managers. You and I are the ones implementing and fixing the code, so we're the only ones who can take meaningful measures to ensure the code we write is as bug free as possible.

The bulk of our responsibility for code quality starts with the coding and finishes with the unit testing. When unit testing, you must strive to execute as much of your code as possible and ensure that it doesn't crash. The other team members can help with the systemwide testing, but they won't get very far if the program crashes just trying to handle simple data that should have been part of a unit test. By having strong unit tests, the test engineers can spend their time more effectively looking for integration problems. We'll go over unit testing in detail in the section "Trust Yourself, but Verify (Unit Testing)" near the end of this chapter.

ASSERT, ASSERT, ASSERT, AND ASSERT

I hope that most of you already know what an assertion is, because it's the most important proactive programming tool in your debugging arsenal. For those who are unfamiliar with the term, here's a brief definition: an assertion declares that a certain condition must be true at a specific point in a program. The assertion is said to *fail* if the condition is false. You use assertions in addition to your normal error checking. Traditionally, assertions are functions or macros that execute only in debug builds and bring up a message box telling you what condition failed. I extend the definition of assertions to include conditionally compiled code that checks conditions and assumptions that are too complex for a general assertion function or macro to handle. Assertions are a key component of proactive programming because they help developers and test engineers determine not just that bugs are present but also why the errors are happening.

Even if you've heard of assertions and drop them in your code occasionally, you might not be familiar enough with them to use them effectively. Engineers can never be too rich or too thin—or use too many assertions. The rule of thumb I've always followed to judge whether I've used enough assertions is simple: I have enough assertions when my junior coworkers complain that they get multiple message boxes reporting assertion failures whenever they call into my code with invalid information or assumptions.

If used sufficiently, assertions will tell you most of the information that you need to diagnose a problem at the first sign of trouble. Without assertions, you'll spend considerable time in the debugger working backward from the crash searching for where things started to go wrong. A good assertion will tell you where and why a condition was invalid. A good assertion will also let you get into the debugger after a condition fails so that you can see the complete state of the program at the point of failure.

A side benefit of using plenty of assertions is that they serve as additional documentation in your code. Although assertions will never replace thorough comments, they can serve as reminders to others who are maintaining your code about what you were expecting for function data.

How and What to Assert

My stock answer when asked what to assert is to assert everything. You should assert any condition because it might be the one you need to solve a nasty bug in the future. Don't worry that putting in too many assertions will hamper your program's performance—assertions usually are active only in debug builds, and the bug-finding opportunities created more than outweigh the small performance hit.

Before jumping into examples of how to use assertions and what to assert, I need to point out that assertions should never change any variables or states of a program. Treat all data you check in assertions as read-only. Because assertions are active only in debug builds, if you do change data with an assertion, you'll have different behavior between debug and release builds and tracking down the difference will be extremely difficult.

How to Assert

The first rule to using assertions is to check a single item at a time. If you check multiple conditions with just one assertion, you have no way of knowing which condition caused the failure. In the following example, I show the same function with two assertion checks. Although the assertion in the first function will catch a bad parameter, the assertion won't tell you which condition failed or even which of the three parameters is the offending one.

```
// The wrong way to write an assertion. Which parameter was bad?
BOOL GetPathItem ( int i , LPTSTR szItem , int iLen )
{
    ASSERT ( ( i > 0                                      ) &&
             ( NULL != szItem                             ) &&
             ( ( iLen > 0 ) && ( iLen < MAX_PATH )        ) &&
```

(continued)

49

```
                        ( FALSE == IsBadWriteStringPtr ( szItem , iLen ) ) ) ;
        :
        :

}

// The proper way. Each parameter is checked individually so that you
// can see which one failed.
BOOL GetPathItem ( int i , LPTSTR szItem , int iLen )
{
    ASSERT ( i > 0 ) ;
    ASSERT ( NULL != szItem ) ;
    ASSERT ( ( iLen > 0 ) && ( iLen < MAX_PATH ) ) ;
    ASSERT ( FALSE == IsBadWriteStringPtr ( szItem , iLen ) ) ;
        :
        :

}
```

When you assert a condition, you need to strive to check the condition completely. For example, if your function takes a pointer to a function as a parameter and you simply check that parameter against *NULL*, you're checking only part of the error condition. If you have a stack overrun that overwrites the function parameter and the value changes to 1, an assertion such as the following wouldn't fail but you'd still crash later.

```
// An example of checking only a part of the error condition
BOOL EnumerateListItems ( PFNELCALLBACK pfnCallback )
{
    ASSERT ( NULL != pfnCallback ) ;
        :
        :

}
```

You can check the full condition by using the *IsBadCodePtr* application programming interface (API) function to completely validate the pointer.

```
// An example of completely checking the error condition
BOOL EnumerateListItems ( PFNELCALLBACK pfnCallback )
{
    ASSERT ( FALSE == IsBadCodePtr ( pfnCallback ) ) ;
        :
        :

}
```

Another step I always take is to ensure that I'm asserting against specific values. The following example shows an incorrect way to check for a positive value and then the correct way.

```
' Example of a poorly written assertion:  nCount should be positive,
' but the assertion doesn't fail when nCount is negative.
Function UpdateListEntries(ByVal nCount As Integer) as Integer
    Debug.Assert nCount
    .
    .
    .
End Function

' A proper assertion that explicitly checks against what the value
' is supposed to be
Function UpdateListEntries(ByVal nCount As Integer) as Integer
    Debug.Assert nCount > 0
    .
    .
    .
End Function
```

The incorrect sample essentially checks only whether *nCount* isn't 0, which is only half the information that needs to be asserted. By explicitly checking the acceptable values, you guarantee that your assertion is self-documenting, and you also ensure that your assertion catches corrupted data.

C and C++ have all sorts of functions that can help make your assertions as descriptive as possible. Table 3-1 shows the helper functions that you can use to check exactly the condition needed. You can call these functions from Microsoft Visual Basic, but Visual Basic does a good job of avoiding pointer problems, so you might not need to use them.

Table 3-1 **HELPER FUNCTIONS FOR DESCRIPTIVE C AND C++ ASSERTIONS**

Function	*Description*
GetObjectType	A graphics device interface (GDI) subsystem function that returns the type for a GDI handle
IsBadCodePtr	Checks that the memory pointer can be executed
IsBadReadPtr	Checks that the memory pointer is readable for the specified number of bytes
IsBadStringPtr	Checks that the string pointer is readable up to the string's *NULL* terminator or the maximum number of characters specified
IsBadWritePtr	Checks that the memory pointer is writable for the specified number of bytes
IsWindow	Checks whether the *HWND* parameter is a valid window

IsBadStringPtr and *IsBadWritePtr* are not thread-safe. While one thread calls *IsBadWritePtr* to check the access permissions on a piece of memory, another thread could be changing the access permissions. If you're using either function just to check normal C run-time heap allocated memory, you shouldn't have any problems. However, if your application updates page permissions and does other advanced memory manipulations, you should provide your own thread-safe versions of *IsBadStringPtr* and *IsBadWritePtr*.

Visual Basic has its own set of functions that can help you validate Visual Basic–specific conditions. All those great *Is* functions are listed in Table 3-2. If you follow the good Visual Basic programming practice of not using *Variant*s and explicitly specifying *ByVal* and *ByRef* for all your parameters, you might not need to validate variable types that often; if you do need to, however, at least you have some rich means to do it.

Table 3-2   HELPER FUNCTIONS FOR DESCRIPTIVE VISUAL BASIC ASSERTIONS

Function	Description
IsArray	Checks whether the variable is an *Array* type
IsDate	Checks whether the variable can be converted to a date
IsEmpty	Checks whether the *Variant* variable has been initialized
IsError	Checks whether the variable is an error value
IsMissing	Checks whether the optional *Variant* argument was passed to the procedure
IsNull	Checks whether the *Variant* variable is *Null*
IsNumeric	Checks whether the variable can be converted to a numeric type
IsObject	Checks whether the variable is an object
TypeName	Returns the type name for the variable

The following code shows one of the mistakes that I used to make with my assertions.

```
// Poor assertion usage
BOOL CheckDriveFreeSpace ( LPCTSTR szDrive )
{
    ULARGE_INTEGER ulgAvail ;
    ULARGE_INTEGER ulgNumBytes ;
    ULARGE INTEGER ulgFree ;
    if ( FALSE == GetDiskFreeSpaceEx ( szDrive     ,
                                       &ulgAvail    ,
                                       &ulgNumBytes ,
                                       &ulgFree     ) )
    {
        ASSERT ( FALSE ) ;
        return ( FALSE ) ;
    }
    :
    :
}
```

Although I was using an *ASSERT*, which is good, I wasn't showing the condition that failed. The assertion message box will show just the expression "FALSE," which isn't that helpful. When using an assertion, you want to try to get as much information about the assertion failure in the message box as possible.

My friend Dave Angel pointed out to me that in C and C++ you can just use the logical-NOT operator (!) and use a string as its operand. This combination will give you a much better expression in the assertion message box so that you at least have an idea of what failed without looking at the source code. The following example shows the proper way to assert a false condition. Unfortunately, Dave's trick doesn't work in Visual Basic.

```
// Proper assertion usage
BOOL CheckDriveFreeSpace ( LPCTSTR szDrive )
{
    ULARGE_INTEGER ulgAvail ;
    ULARGE_INTEGER ulgNumBytes ;
    ULARGE INTEGER ulgFree ;
    if ( FALSE == GetDiskFreeSpaceEx ( szDrive      ,
                                       &ulgAvail    ,
                                       &ulgNumBytes ,
                                       &ulgFree     ) )
    {
        ASSERT ( !"GetDiskFreeSpaceEx failed!" ) ;
        return ( FALSE ) ;
    }
    .
    .
    .
}
```

You can also extend Dave's assertion trick by using the logical-AND conditional operator (&&) to perform a normal assertion and still have the message text. The following example shows how.

```
BOOL AddToDataTree ( PTREENODE pNode )
{
  ASSERT ( ( FALSE == IsBadReadPtr ( pNode , sizeof ( TREENODE) ) ) &&
           "Invalid parameter!"                ) ;
    .
    .
    .
}
```

What to Assert

Now that you have an idea of how to use assertions, let's turn to what you need to assert. As you saw in the examples above, you need to assert the parameters coming into a function. Asserting parameters is especially critical with interface functions and public class members that others on your team call. Because those gateway functions are the entry points into your code, you want to make sure that each parameter and assumption is valid.

In Chapter 4, I write an example debugger to give you an idea of how debuggers work. I set up a dynamic-link library (DLL) that contains the debug loop. One of the key functions in that DLL is the *StopDebugging* function. In the following code snippet, I show the assertion for the parameter to the function. Notice that the assertion comes first and that the real error handling immediately follows the assertion. Remember that assertions in no way replace any normal error handling.

```
BOOL DEBUGINTERFACE_DLLINTERFACE __stdcall
    StopDebugging ( LPHANDLE lpDebugSyncEvents )
{
    ASSERT ( FALSE ==
                IsBadWritePtr ( lpDebugSyncEvents ,
                                sizeof ( HANDLE ) * NUM_DEBUGEVENTS ) );
    if ( TRUE == IsBadWritePtr ( lpDebugSyncEvents ,
                                sizeof ( HANDLE ) * NUM_DEBUGEVENTS ) )
    {
        SetLastError ( ERROR_INVALID_PARAMETER ) ;
        return ( FALSE ) ;
    }

    // Signal the debug thread with the event name to close.
    VERIFY ( SetEvent ( lpDebugSyncEvents[ CLOSEDEBUGGER ] ) ) ;
    return ( TRUE ) ;
}
```

As you move inside your module, the parameters of the module's private functions might not require as much checking, mainly depending on where the parameters originated. Much of the decision about which parameters to validate comes down to a judgment call. It doesn't hurt to assert every parameter of every function, but if a parameter comes from outside the module, and if you fully asserted it once, you might not need to again. By asserting each parameter on every function, however, you can possibly catch some errors internal to your module.

I sit right in the middle of the two extremes. Deciding how many parameter assertions are right for you just takes some experience. As you get a feel for how you program and learn where you typically encounter problems in your code, you'll figure out where and when you need to assert parameters internal to your module. One safeguard I've learned to use is to add parameter assertions whenever a bad parameter blows up my code. That way, the mistake won't get repeated because the assertion will catch it.

Another area in which I routinely use assertions is on return values to functions called in the normal processing flow. Asserting the return values alerts you to problems as they're happening. I tend to check almost every return value with an assertion. In Listing 3-1, which is the *StartDebugging* function from the debugger in Chapter 4, I assert various return values that cause me to fail the function.

```
HANDLE DEBUGINTERFACE_DLLINTERFACE __stdcall
    StartDebugging ( LPCTSTR        szDebuggee        ,
                     LPCTSTR        szCmdLine         ,
                     LPDWORD        lpPID             ,
                     CDebugBaseUser * pUserClass      ,
                     LPHANDLE       lpDebugSyncEvents )
{
    // Assert the parameters.
    ASSERT ( FALSE == IsBadStringPtr ( szDebuggee , MAX_PATH ) ) ;
    ASSERT ( FALSE == IsBadStringPtr ( szCmdLine , MAX_PATH ) ) ;
    ASSERT ( FALSE == IsBadWritePtr ( lpPID , sizeof ( DWORD ) ) ) ;
    ASSERT ( FALSE == IsBadReadPtr ( pUserClass ,
                            sizeof ( CDebugBaseUser * ) ) ) ;
    ASSERT ( FALSE == IsBadWritePtr ( lpDebugSyncEvents ,
                            sizeof ( HANDLE ) *
                                NUM_DEBUGEVENTS ) ) ;
    // Check them all for real.
    if ( ( TRUE == IsBadStringPtr ( szDebuggee , MAX_PATH )    ) ||
         ( TRUE == IsBadStringPtr ( szCmdLine , MAX_PATH )     ) ||
         ( TRUE == IsBadWritePtr ( lpPID , sizeof ( DWORD ) )  ) ||
         ( TRUE == IsBadReadPtr ( pUserClass ,
                            sizeof ( CDebugBaseUser * ) ) )     ||
         ( TRUE == IsBadWritePtr ( lpDebugSyncEvents ,
                            sizeof ( HANDLE ) *
                                NUM_DEBUGEVENTS )     )          )
    {
        SetLastError ( ERROR_INVALID_PARAMETER ) ;
        return ( INVALID_HANDLE_VALUE ) ;
    }


    // The handle of the startup acknowledgment that this function
    // will wait on until the debug thread gets started
    HANDLE   hStartAck ;
    // The string used for the startup acknowledgment event
    TCHAR    szStartAck [ MAX_PATH ] ;

    // Load up the string for startup acknowledgment.
    if ( 0 == LoadString ( GetDllHandle ( )    ,
                    IDS_DBGEVENTINIT    ,
                    szStartAck          ,
                    sizeof ( szStartAck ) ) )
    {
        ASSERT ( !"LoadString IDS_DBGEVENTINIT failed!" ) ;
        return ( INVALID_HANDLE_VALUE ) ;
    }
```

Listing 3-1 *Examples of assertions on return values*   *(continued)*

Listing 3-1 *continued*

```
    // Create the startup acknowledgment event.
    hStartAck = CreateEvent ( NULL    ,    // Default security
                              TRUE    ,    // Manual-reset event
                              FALSE   ,    // Initial state=Not signaled
                              szStartAck ) ; // Event name
    ASSERT ( FALSE != hStartAck ) ;
    if ( FALSE == hStartAck )
    {
        TRACE ( "StartDebugging : Unable to create Start Ack event\n" ) ;
        return ( INVALID_HANDLE_VALUE ) ;
    }

    // Bundle up the parameters.
    THREADPARAMS stParams ;
    stParams.lpPID = lpPID ;
    stParams.pUserClass = pUserClass ;
    stParams.szDebuggee = szDebuggee ;
    stParams.szCmdLine  = szCmdLine  ;

    // The handle to the debug thread
    HANDLE hDbgThread ;

    // Try to create the thread.
    hDbgThread = (HANDLE)_beginthread ( DebugThread , 0 , &stParams ) ;
    ASSERT ( NULL != hDbgThread ) ;
    if ( NULL == hDbgThread )
    {
        TRACE ( "StartDebugging : _beginthread failed\n" ) ;
        VERIFY ( CloseHandle ( hStartAck ) ) ;
        return ( INVALID_HANDLE_VALUE ) ;
    }

    // Wait until the debug thread gets good and cranking.
    ::WaitForSingleObject ( hStartAck , INFINITE ) ;

    // Get rid of the acknowledgment handle.
    VERIFY ( CloseHandle ( hStartAck ) ) ;

    // Check that the debug thread is still running. If it isn't,
    // the debuggee probably couldn't get started.
    DWORD dwExitCode = ~STILL_ACTIVE ;
    if ( FALSE == GetExitCodeThread ( hDbgThread , &dwExitCode ) )
    {
        ASSERT ( !"GetExitCodeThread failed!" ) ;
        return ( INVALID_HANDLE_VALUE ) ;
    }
```

```
ASSERT ( STILL_ACTIVE == dwExitCode ) ;
if ( STILL_ACTIVE != dwExitCode )
{
    TRACE ( "StartDebugging : GetExitCodeThread failed\n" ) ;
    return ( INVALID_HANDLE_VALUE ) ;
}

// Create the synchronization events so that the main thread can
// tell the debug loop what to do.
BOOL bCreateDbgSyncEvts =
            CreateDebugSyncEvents ( lpDebugSyncEvents , *lpPID ) ;
ASSERT ( TRUE == bCreateDbgSyncEvts ) ;
if ( FALSE == bCreateDbgSyncEvts )
{
    // This is a serious problem. I got the debug thread going, but
    // I was unable to create the synchronization events that the
    // user interface thread needs to control the debug thread. My
    // only option here is to punt. I'll kill the
    // debug thread and just return. I can't do much else.
    TRACE ( "StartDebugging : CreateDebugSyncEvents failed\n" ) ;
    VERIFY ( TerminateThread ( hDbgThread , (DWORD)-1 ) ) ;
    return ( INVALID_HANDLE_VALUE ) ;
}
// Life is good!
return ( hDbgThread ) ;
}
```

The final time to use assertions is when you need to check an assumption. For example, if the specifications for a function say that it requires 3 MB of disk space, you should check this assumption with an assertion. Here's another example: if your function takes an array of pointers to a specific data structure, you should walk through the data structure and validate that each individual item is valid.

In both these cases, as with most assumption assertions, you can't check the assumption with a general function/macro. In these situations, you need to use the conditional compilation technique that I indicated earlier should be part of your assertion toolkit. Because the code you'll be executing in the conditional compilation will be working on live data, you must take extra precautions to ensure that you don't change the state of the program. In both Microsoft Visual C++ and Visual Basic programs, I prefer to implement these types of assertions in separate functions if possible. That way, you avoid changing any local variables inside the original function. Additionally, the conditionally compiled assertion functions can come in handy in the Watch window, as you'll see in Chapter 5 when we talk about the Visual C++ debugger. The following example shows a conditionally compiled assertion function, *ValidatePointerArray*, which does deep validations on an array of data.

```
#ifdef _DEBUG
void ValidatePointerArray ( STDATA * pData , int iCount )
{
    // Check the array buffer first.
    ASSERT ( FALSE == IsBadReadPtr ( pData ,
                                     iCount * sizeof ( STDATA * ) ) ) ;
    for ( int i = 0 ; i < iCount ; i++ )
    {
        ASSERT ( pData[ i ].bFlags < DF_HIGHVAL ) ;
        ASSERT ( FALSE == IsBadStringPtr ( pData[ i ].pszName ,
                                           MAX_PATH           ) ) ;
    }
}
#endif

void PlotDataItems ( STDATA * pData , int iCount )
{
#ifdef _DEBUG
    ValidatePointerArray ( pData , iCount ) ;
#endif
    :
    :
}
```

The *VERIFY* Macro

Before we get into the various assertion macros and functions you'll encounter in Microsoft Windows development, and some of the problems with them, I want to talk about the *VERIFY* macro that's used in Microsoft Foundation Class (MFC) library development. In a debug build, the *VERIFY* macro behaves the same way as a normal assertion. If the condition evaluates to 0, the *VERIFY* macro triggers the normal assertion message box to warn you. Unlike a normal assertion, however, in a release build, the parameter to the *VERIFY* macro stays in the source code and is evaluated as a normal part of processing.

In essence, the *VERIFY* macro allows you to have normal assertions with side effects, and those side effects stay in release builds as well. Ideally, you should never use conditions to any type of assertion that cause any side effects. However, in one situation the *VERIFY* macro is useful—when you have a function that returns an error value that you wouldn't check otherwise. For example, when you call *ResetEvent* to clear a signaled event handle and the call fails, there's not much you can do, which is why most engineers call *ResetEvent* and never check the return value in either debug or release builds. If you wrap the call with the *VERIFY* macro, at least you'll be notified in your debug builds that something went wrong. Of course, I could achieve the same results by using *ASSERT*, but *VERIFY* saves me the trouble of creating a new variable just to store and verify the return value of the *ResetEvent* call—a variable that would probably be used only in debug builds anyway.

I think most MFC programmers use the *VERIFY* macro for convenience, but you should try to break yourself of the habit. In most cases, when engineers use the *VERIFY* macro, they should be checking the return value instead. A good example of where everyone seems to use *VERIFY* is around the *CString::LoadString* member function, which loads resource strings. Using *VERIFY* this way is fine in a debug build because if *LoadString* fails, the *VERIFY* macro warns you. In a release build, however, if *LoadString* fails, you end up using an uninitialized variable. If you're lucky, you'll just have a blank string, but most of the time, you'll crash in your release build. The moral of this story is to check your return values. If you're about to use a *VERIFY* macro, you need to ask whether ignoring the return value will cause you any problems in release builds.

The Different Types of Visual C++ and Visual Basic Assertions

Even though I define all my C++ assertion macros and functions to just plain *ASSERT*, which I'll talk about in a moment, I want to quickly go over the different types of assertions available in Visual C++ and Visual Basic and provide a little information about their implementation. That way, if you see one of them in someone else's code, you can recognize it. Additionally, I want to alert you to the problems with some of the implementations.

assert, _ASSERT, and _ASSERTE

The first type of assertion is from the C run-time library, the ANSI C standard *assert* macro. This version is portable across all C compilers and platforms and is defined by including ASSERT.H. In the Windows world, if your application is a console application and it fails an assertion, *assert* will send the output to *stderr*. If your application is a Windows graphical user interface (GUI) application, *assert* will show the assertion failure as a message box.

The second type of assertion in the C run-time library is specific to Windows. These assertions are *_ASSERT* and *_ASSERTE,* which are defined in CRTDBG.H. The only difference between the two is that the *_ASSERTE* version also prints the expression passed as its parameter. Because the expression is so important to have, especially when your test engineers are testing, if you're using the C run-time library, you should always use *_ASSERTE*. Both macros are part of the extremely useful debug run-time library code, and the assertions are only one of its many features.

DEBUGGING WAR STORY

Disappearing Files and Threads

The Battle

While working on a version of NuMega's BoundsChecker, we had an incredibly difficult problem with random crashes that were almost impossible to duplicate. The only clues we had were that file handles and thread handles would occasionally become invalid, which meant that files would randomly close and thread synchronization would sometimes break. The user interface (UI) developers were also experiencing occasional crashes, but only when running under the debugger. These problems plagued us throughout development and finally escalated to the point that all the developers on the team stopped what they were doing and started trying to solve these bugs.

The Outcome

The team nearly tarred and feathered me because the problem turned out to be my fault. I was responsible for the debug loop in BoundsChecker. In the debug loop, you use the Windows Debugging API to start and control another process, the debuggee, and to respond to debug events the debuggee generates. Being a conscientious programmer, I saw that the *WaitForDebugEvent* function was returning handle values for some of the debugging event notifications. For example, when a process started under a debugger, the debugger would get a structure that contained a handle to the process and the initial thread for that process.

Because I'm so careful, I knew that if an API gave you a handle to some object and you no longer needed the object, you called *CloseHandle* to free the underlying memory for that object. Therefore, whenever the Debugging API gave me a handle, I closed that handle as soon as I finished using it. That seemed like the reasonable thing to do.

However, much to my chagrin, I hadn't read the fine print in the Debugging API documentation, which says that the Debugging API itself closes any handles it generates. What was happening was that I was holding some of the

---

Although *assert*, *_ASSERT*, and *_ASSERTE* are convenient to use and free of charge, they do have a few drawbacks. The *assert* macro has two problems that can cause you some grief. The first is that the filename display truncates to 60 characters, so you can sometimes end up not having any idea what file triggered an assertion. The second problem with *assert* occurs if you're working on a project that doesn't have a UI, such as a Windows 2000 service or a Component Object Model (COM) out-of-process server. With *assert* sending its output to *stderr* or a message box, you can miss the assertion. And in the case of using a message box, your application will hang because you can't dismiss the message box when your UI isn't displayable.

handles returned by the Debugging API until I needed them. However, I was closing those same handles after I finished using them—after the Debugging API had already closed them.

To understand how this situation led to our problem, you need to know that when you close a handle, the operating system marks that handle value as available. Microsoft Windows NT 4, the operating system we were using at the time, is particularly aggressive about recycling handle values. (Microsoft Windows 2000 exhibits the same aggressive behavior toward handle values.) Our UI portions, which were heavily multithreaded and opened many files, were creating and using new handles all the time. Because the Debugging API was closing my handles and the operating system was recycling them, sometimes the UI portions would get one of the handles that I was saving. As I closed my copies of the handles later, I was actually closing the UI's threads and file handles!

I was barely able to avoid the tar and feathers because I showed that this bug was also in the debug loop of previous versions of BoundsChecker. We'd just gotten lucky before. What had changed was that the version we were working on had a new and improved UI that was doing much more with files and threads, so the conditions were ripe for my bug to do more damage.

The Lesson

I could have avoided this problem if I'd read the fine print in the Debugging API documentation. Additionally, and this is the big lesson, I learned that you always check the return values to *CloseHandle*. Although you can't do much when you close an invalid handle, the operating system does tell you when you're doing something wrong, and you should pay attention.

As a side note, I want to mention that if you attempt to double close a handle or pass a bad value to *CloseHandle* and you're running under a debugger, Windows NT 4 and Windows 2000 will report an *Invalid Handle* exception (0xC0000008). When you see that exception value, you can stop and explore why it occurred.

The other lesson I learned is that it really helps to be able to out-sprint your coworkers when they're chasing you with a pot of tar and bags of feathers.

The C run-time implementation macros, on the other hand, address the issue with defaulting to a message box by allowing you to redirect the assertion to a file or to the *OutputDebugString* API function by calling the *_CrtSetReportMode* function. All the Microsoft-supplied assertions suffer from one fatal flaw, however: they change the state of the system, which is the cardinal rule that assertions can't break. Having your assertion calls suffer from side effects is almost worse than not using assertions at all.

The following code shows an example of how the supplied assertions can change your state between debug and release builds. Can you spot the problem?

```
// Send the message over to the window. If it times out, the other
// thread is hung, so I need to abort the thread. As a reminder, the
// only way to check whether SendMessageTimeout failed is to check
// GetLastError. If the function returned 0 and the last error is
// 0, SendMessageTimeout timed out.
_ASSERTE ( NULL != pDataPacket )
if ( NULL == pDataPacket )
{
    return ( ERR_INVALID_DATA ) ;
}
LRESULT lRes = SendMessageTimeout ( hUIWnd                    ,
                                    WM_USER_NEEDNEXTPACKET    ,
                                    0                         ,
                                    (LPARAM)pDataPacket       ,
                                    SMTO_BLOCK                ,
                                    10000                     ,
                                    &pdwRes                   ) ;
_ASSERTE ( FALSE != lRes ) ;
if ( 0 == lRes )
{
    // Get the last error value.
    DWORD dwLastErr = GetLastError ( ) ;
    if ( 0 == dwLastErr )
    {
        // The UI is hung or not processing data fast enough.
        return ( ERR_UI_IS_HUNG ) ;
    }
    // If the error is anything else, there was a problem
    // with the data sent as a parameter.
    return ( ERR_INVALID_DATA ) ;
}
return ( ERR_SUCCESS ) ;
        :
        :
```

The problem, which is insidious, is that the supplied assertions destroy the last error value. In the case above, the "_ASSERTE (FALSE != lRes)" would execute, show the message box, and change the last error value to 0. Thus in debug builds, the UI thread always appears to hang, whereas in the release build, you would see the cases in which the parameters passed to *SendMessageTimeout* were bad.

The fact that the last error value is destroyed with the system-supplied assertions might never be an issue in the code you write, but my own experience has been different—two bugs that took a great deal of time to track down turned out to be related to this problem. Fortunately, if you use the assertion presented later in this section, I'll take care of this problem for you as well as give you some information that the system-supplied version doesn't.

ASSERT_KINDOF and ASSERT_VALID

If you're doing MFC programming, you'll run into two additional assertion macros that are specific to MFC and are fantastic examples of proactive debugging. If you've declared your classes with *DECLARE_DYNAMIC* or *DECLARE_SERIAL*, you can use the *ASSERT_KINDOF* macro to check whether a pointer to a *CObject*-derived class is a specific class or is derived from a specific class. The *ASSERT_KINDOF* assertion is just a wrapper around the *CObject::IsKindOf* method. The following code snippet first checks the parameter in the *ASSERT_KINDOF* assertion and then does the real parameter error checking.

```
BOOL DoSomeMFCStuffToAFrame ( CWnd * pWnd )
{
    ASSERT ( NULL != pWnd ) ;
    ASSERT_KINDOF ( CFrameWnd , pWnd ) ;
    if ( ( NULL  == pWnd ) ||
        ( FALSE == pWnd->IsKindOf ( RUNTIME_CLASS ( CFrameWnd ) ) ) )
    {
        return ( FALSE ) ;
    :
    :
    :
    // Do some MFC stuff; pWnd is guaranteed to be a CFrameWnd or
    // to be derived from a CFrameWnd.
    :
    :
    :
}
```

The second MFC-specific assertion macro is *ASSERT_VALID*. This assertion resolves down to *AfxAssertValidObject*, which completely validates that the pointer is a proper pointer to a *CObject*-derived class. After validating the pointer, *ASSERT_VALID* calls the object's *AssertValid* method. *AssertValid* is a method that you can override in your derived classes so that you can check each of the internal data structures in your class. This method is a great way to do a deep validation on your classes. You should override *AssertValid* for all your key classes.

Debug.Assert

In some ways, Visual Basic programmers have it easier than C and C++ programmers because Visual Basic doesn't require extensive parameter type and pointer validations as long as you're not using *Variant*s as parameters. In other ways, however, properly employing proactive programming in Visual Basic has been made much more difficult than it should be. Even though it took four versions, Visual Basic finally has a built-in assertion with *Debug.Assert*.

That's the good news. The bad news is that *Debug.Assert* isn't usable when you really need it, which is when you're debugging compiled code. I think that the Visual Basic team made a big mistake in not allowing *Debug.Assert* to compile into native code. *Debug.Assert* is available only when running inside the Visual Basic integrated development environment (IDE), and when an assertion fails when debugging, it drops you into the IDE at the *Debug.Assert* line. Even though *Debug.Assert* is active only in the IDE, you still need to use it as much as possible so that you can proactively check for problems.

I was all set to solve the problems with *Debug.Assert* when I ran across the book *Advanced Visual Basic 6* (2nd ed., Microsoft Press, 1998) by The Mandelbrot Set, a development company based in England. In that book, Mark Pearce wrote a wonderful Visual Basic add-in called Assertion Sourcerer. It alone is worth the price of the book (though I found the rest of the book excellent as well). Assertion Sourcerer automatically hunts down your *Debug.Asserts* and puts a call to a real assertion after *Debug.Assert*. It also calculates the source and line so that you can find out exactly where the problem occurred. In addition to putting the real assertions in your code, Assertion Sourcerer even takes them out when you're done with them!

I found it quite easy to extend Mark's code to look for *Debug.Print* statements as well and to insert real trace statements for those. Additionally, I use my own VBASSERTANDTRACE.BAS file, shown in Listing 3-2, to supply the implementation for the real assertion and trace statements. I wanted to leverage my own *SUPERASSERT* code, discussed in the next section, to handle the assertions.

```
Attribute VB_Name = "VBAssertAndTrace"
'''''''''''''''''''''''''''''''''''''''''''''''''''''''''''''''''''''''''
' "Debugging Applications" (Microsoft Press)
' Copyright (c) 1999-2000 John Robbins -- All rights reserved.
'
' To use this file:
'
' Optional (but highly recommended!):
'    Use Mark Pearce's Assertion Sourcerer Visual Basic add-in from
'    "Advanced Microsoft Visual Basic 6.0" (2nd ed).
'    Mark's add-in will hunt down all the Debug.Assert statements in
'    your program and put a call to BugAssert under each one so that
'    you can have real assertions in compiled Visual Basic.
'    I use Mark's utility all the time, and you should too!
'
' 1.   Compile BUGSLAYERUTIL.DLL because this file uses several of the
'      exported functions.
' 2.   Liberally sprinkle Debug.Assert statements around your code.
' 3.   When you're ready to compile, use Mark's add-in to add the
'      calls to BugAssert.
' 4.   Include this file in your project.
' 5.   Compile your project and have fun watching assertions.
'
' You can also call the various BUGSLAYERUTIL.DLL functions to set
' the options and output handles.
'''''''''''''''''''''''''''''''''''''''''''''''''''''''''''''''''''''''''
```

Listing 3-2 *VBASSERTANDTRACE.BAS*

```
Option Explicit

' Declare all the BUGSLAYERUTIL.DLL functions that this module can use.
Public Declare Sub DiagOutputVB Lib "BugslayerUtil" _
                (ByVal sMsg As String)
Public Declare Function DiagAssertVB Lib "BugslayerUtil" _
                (ByVal dwOverrideOpts As Long, _
                 ByVal bAllowHalts As Long, _
                 ByVal sMsg As String) _
                As Long
Public Declare Function AddDiagAssertModule Lib "BugslayerUtil" _
                (ByVal hMod As Long) _
                As Long
Public Declare Function SetDiagAssertFile Lib "BugslayerUtil" _
                (ByVal hFile As Long) _
                As Long
Public Declare Function SetDiagAssertOptions Lib "BugslayerUtil" _
                (ByVal dwOpts As Long) _
                As Long
Public Declare Function SetDiagOutputFile Lib "BugslayerUtil" _
                (ByVal dwOpts As Long) _
                As Long

Private Declare Function GetModuleFileName Lib "kernel32" _
                Alias "GetModuleFileNameA" _
                (ByVal hModule As Long, _
                 ByVal lpFileName As String, _
                 ByVal nSize As Long) _
                As Long
Public Declare Sub DebugBreak Lib "kernel32" ()


' My TRACE statement. I'm too used to TRACE to be able to use any other
' macro. Additionally, I updated the Assertion Sourcerer to add TRACE
' calls after Debug.Print. You might want to do that as well.
Public Sub TRACE(ByVal sMsg As String)
    DiagOutputVB sMsg
End Sub


' The BugAssert function inserted by Assertion Sourcerer
Public Sub BugAssert(ByVal vntiExpression As Variant, sMsg As String)
    CallAssert vntiExpression, 0, sMsg
End Sub


' Sometimes I know I'm in trouble so I resort to SUPERASSERT.
Public Sub SUPERASSERT(ByVal vntiExpression As Variant, sMsg As String)
    CallAssert vntiExpression, 7, sMsg
End Sub


Private Sub CallAssert(ByVal vntiExpression As Variant, _
                    ByVal iOpt As Long, _
                    sMsg As String)
    If (vntiExpression) Then
        Exit Sub
    Else
        ' The flag used to determine whether I already called InDesign. No
        ' need to call the function repeatedly.
        Static bCheckedDesign As Boolean        ' False, by default.
        ' The allow halts flag I pass to DiagAssertVB.  If this flag is
```

(continued)

```
            ' set to 1, DiagAssertVB will allow you to halt the application.
            ' If this flag is set to 0, the user is running in the VB IDE so
            ' DiagAssertVB won't allow halts. If the user is running inside
            ' the VB IDE, breaking is a little too dangerous. Nothing like
            ' a little lost data to ruin your day!
            Static lAllowHalts As Long

            ' Call InDesign only once.
            If (False = bCheckedDesign) Then
                If (True = InDesign()) Then
                    lAllowHalts = 0
                Else
                    lAllowHalts = 1
                End If
                bCheckedDesign = True
            End If

            Dim lRet As Long
            lRet = DiagAssertVB(iOpt, lAllowHalts, sMsg)
            If (1 = lRet) Then
                ' The user wants to break. However, I won't allow the
                ' break if the user is running inside the VB IDE.
                If (1 = lAllowHalts) Then
                    DebugBreak
                End If
            End If
        End If
End Sub

'.........................................................................
' This wonderful function comes from Peet Morris's excellent chapter
' "On Error GoTo Hell," pages 25 and 26 in "Advanced Microsoft Visual
' Basic 6.0." InDesign allows you to check whether you're running in the
' VB IDE. I greatly appreciate Peet letting me use this function in my
' book!
'.........................................................................
Public Function InDesign() As Boolean
    ' I'll leave Peet's comment alone--he has an excellent point.
    '*****************************************
    ' The only thing Debug.Assert is good for!
    '*****************************************
    Static nCallCount As Integer
    Static bRet As Boolean           ' By default, this flag is False.

    nCallCount = nCallCount + 1

    Select Case nCallCount
        Case 1: ' First time in
            Debug.Assert InDesign()
        Case 2: ' Second time in, so Debug.Assert must have executed
            bRet = True
    End Select

    ' If Debug.Assert was called, return True to prevent the trap.
    InDesign = bRet

    ' Reset for future calls.
    nCallCount = 0
End Function
```

SUPERASSERT

Having told you what the problems are with the supplied assertions, now I want to show you how I was able to fix and extend the assertions to really make them tell you how and why you had a problem. Figure 3-1 shows an example of a *SUPER-ASSERT* message box. The program, file, line, and expression fields are self-explanatory. The interesting fields follow the Last Error field.

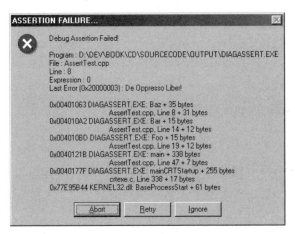

Figure 3-1 *Example* SUPERASSERT *message box*

In *SUPERASSERT*, I translate the last error values into their textual representations. Seeing the error messages written out as text is extremely helpful when an API function fails: you can see why it failed and can start debugging faster. For example, if *GetModuleFileName* fails because the input buffer isn't large enough, *SUPERASSERT* will set the last error value to 122, which is *ERROR_INSUFFICIENT_BUFFER* from WINERROR.H. By immediately seeing the text "The data area passed to a system call is too small," you know exactly what the problem is and how to fix it.

Additionally, if you look at the last error line in Figure 3-1, you see that it certainly isn't a standard Windows error message. If you set your own last error values, which I recommend that you do, you can add your own message resources module into the *SUPERASSERT* last error message translation. For more information on using your own message resources, look up the "Message Compiler" topic in MSDN. An added incentive to using message resources is that they make internationalizing your application much easier.

The part after the last error is where *SUPERASSERT* earns its money. It's a stack trace of how you got into the assertion. I show as much information as possible in an assertion so that I don't have to gather that same information by using the debugger. By showing the stack trace, I know exactly which path leads to the problem.

Another feature of *SUPERASSERT* is that you can choose not to have the assertions pop up a message box. At first, that might seem counterproductive, but I assure you that it isn't! If you followed my recommendations from Chapter 2 and started testing your debug builds with a regression-testing tool, you know that handling those random assertion message boxes is almost impossible. Because of the problems in handling assertion message boxes, your test engineers are much less likely to use the debug build. With my assertion code, you can specify that you want the output to go to *OutputDebugString*, a file handle, or both. This flexibility allows you to run the code and get all the great assertion information but still be able to automate your debug builds. Additionally, in those cases in which your application doesn't have a UI, my assertion will still work for you.

Using my assertions is easy. For C and C++, you just need to include BUG-SLAYERUTIL.H and link against BUGSLAYERUTIL.LIB. Listing 3-3 shows DIAG-ASSERT.H, which contains all the macros and functions (and is included automatically by BUGSLAYERUTIL.H).

```
/*---------------------------------------------------------------------
"Debugging Applications" (Microsoft Press)
Copyright (c) 1999-2000 John Robbins -- All rights reserved.
---------------------------------------------------------------------*/

#ifndef _DIAGASSERT_H
#define _DIAGASSERT_H

#ifdef __cplusplus
extern "C" {
#endif  //__cplusplus

#include <tchar.h>
/*//////////////////////////////////////////////////////////////////////
                            Defines
//////////////////////////////////////////////////////////////////////*/
// Keep the core stuff available in both release and debug builds.
// Uses the global assert flags.
#define DA_USEDEFAULTS        0x0000
// Turns on showing the assert in a message box. This is the default.
#define DA_SHOWMSGBOX         0x0001
// Turns on showing the assert as through OutputDebugString. This is
// the default.
#define DA_SHOWODS            0x0002
// Shows a stack trace in the assert. This is off by default with the
// ASSERT macro and on in the SUPERASSERT macro.
#define DA_SHOWSTACKTRACE     0x0004
```

Listing 3-3 *DIAGASSERT.H (included by BUGSLAYERUTIL.H)*

```
/*-------------------------------------------------------------------
FUNCTION        :   SetDiagAssertOptions
DISCUSSION      :
    Sets the global options for normal ASSERT macros.
PARAMETERS      :
    dwOpts - The new options flags
RETURNS         :
    The previous options
-------------------------------------------------------------------*/
DWORD BUGSUTIL_DLLINTERFACE __stdcall
    SetDiagAssertOptions ( DWORD dwOpts ) ;


/*-------------------------------------------------------------------
FUNCTION        :   SetDiagAssertFile
DISCUSSION      :
    Sets a HANDLE where the data in any assertion will be written. To
turn off logging, call this function with INVALID_HANDLE_VALUE. The
options set in SetDiagAssertOptions still apply; this function just
lets you log the assertion information to a file.
    No error checking is done on the file handle or on any writes to it.
PARAMETERS      :
    hFile - The file handle
RETURNS         :
    The previous file handle
-------------------------------------------------------------------*/
HANDLE BUGSUTIL_DLLINTERFACE __stdcall
    SetDiagAssertFile ( HANDLE hFile ) ;


/*-------------------------------------------------------------------
FUNCTION        :   AddDiagAssertModule
DISCUSSION      :
    Adds the specified module to the list of modules that error strings
will be pulled from
PARAMETERS      :
    hMod - The module to add
RETURNS         :
    TRUE  - The module was added.
    FALSE - The internal table is full.
-------------------------------------------------------------------*/
BOOL BUGSUTIL_DLLINTERFACE __stdcall
    AddDiagAssertModule ( HMODULE hMod ) ;


/*-------------------------------------------------------------------
FUNCTION        :   DiagAssert
DISCUSSION      :
    The assert function for C and C++ programs
```

(continued)

Listing 3-3 *continued*

```
PARAMETERS     :
    dwOverrideOpts - The DA_* options to override the global defaults
                     for this call into DiagAssert
    szMsg          - The message to show
    szFile         - The file that showed the assert
    dwLine         - The line that had the assert
RETURNS        :
    FALSE - Ignore the assert.
    TRUE  - Trigger the DebugBreak.
------------------------------------------------------------------------*/
BOOL BUGSUTIL_DLLINTERFACE __stdcall
    DiagAssertA ( DWORD      dwOverrideOpts  ,
                  LPCSTR     szMsg           ,
                  LPCSTR     szFile          ,
                  DWORD      dwLine          ) ;

BOOL BUGSUTIL_DLLINTERFACE __stdcall
    DiagAssertW ( DWORD      dwOverrideOpts  ,
                  LPCWSTR    szMsg           ,
                  LPCSTR     szFile          ,
                  DWORD      dwLine          ) ;


#ifdef UNICODE
#define DiagAssert  DiagAssertW
#else
#define DiagAssert  DiagAssertA
#endif


/*-----------------------------------------------------------------------
FUNCTION       :  DiagAssertVB
DISCUSSION     :
    The assert function for VB programs.
PARAMETERS     :
    dwOverrideOpts - The DA_* options to override the global defaults
                     for this call into DiagAssert.
    bAllowHalts    - If TRUE, doesn't show Retry and Ignore buttons
    szMsg          - The message to show. The Visual Basic side is
                     responsible for formatting the string.
RETURNS        :
    FALSE - Ignore the assert.
    TRUE  - Trigger DebugBreak.
------------------------------------------------------------------------*/
BOOL BUGSUTIL_DLLINTERFACE __stdcall
    DiagAssertVB ( DWORD    dwOverrideOpts  ,
                   BOOL     bAllowHalts     ,
                   LPCSTR   szMsg           ) ;
```

```
/*-----------------------------------------------------------------
FUNCTION      :    SetDiagOutputFile
DISCUSSION    :
    Sets a HANDLE where the data in any trace statements will optionally
be written. To turn off logging, call this function with
INVALID_HANDLE_VALUE.
    No error checking is done on the file handle or on any writes to it.
PARAMETERS    :
    hFile - The file handle
RETURNS       :
    The previous file handle
-------------------------------------------------------------------*/
HANDLE BUGSUTIL_DLLINTERFACE __stdcall
    SetDiagOutputFile ( HANDLE hFile ) ;


/*-----------------------------------------------------------------
FUNCTION      :    DiagOutput
DISCUSSION    :
    Provides a tracing routine to send strings through
OutputDebugString
PARAMETERS    :
    szFmt - The format string
    ...   - Parameters that will be expanded into szFmt
RETURNS       :
    None.
-------------------------------------------------------------------*/
void BUGSUTIL_DLLINTERFACE
    DiagOutputA ( LPCSTR szFmt , ... ) ;

void BUGSUTIL_DLLINTERFACE
    DiagOutputW ( LPCWSTR szFmt , ... ) ;

#ifdef UNICODE
#define DiagOutput   DiagOutputW
#else
#define DiagOutput   DiagOutputA
#endif

/*-----------------------------------------------------------------
FUNCTION      :    DiagOutputVB
DISCUSSION    :
    Provides a tracing routine to send strings through
OutputDebugString for Visual Basic programs
PARAMETERS    :
    szMsg - The message string
```

(continued)

Listing 3-3 *continued*

```
RETURNS          :
    None.
------------------------------------------------------------------------*/
void BUGSUTIL_DLLINTERFACE __stdcall
    DiagOutputVB ( LPCSTR szMsg ) ;


/*//////////////////////////////////////////////////////////////////////
                            UNDEFINES
//////////////////////////////////////////////////////////////////////*/
#ifdef ASSERT
#undef ASSERT
#endif

#ifdef assert
#undef assert
#endif

#ifdef VERIFY
#undef VERIFY
#endif
#ifdef TRACE
#undef TRACE
#endif

#ifdef TRACE0
#undef TRACE0
#endif
#ifdef TRACE1
#undef TRACE1
#endif
#ifdef TRACE2
#undef TRACE2
#endif
#ifdef TRACE3
#undef TRACE3
#endif



/*//////////////////////////////////////////////////////////////////////
                          _DEBUG Is Defined
//////////////////////////////////////////////////////////////////////*/
#ifdef _DEBUG

/*//////////////////////////////////////////////////////////////////////
                            Defines
//////////////////////////////////////////////////////////////////////*/
```

```
// The different global options that can be set with
// SetDiagAssertOptions. If any of these options are passed to DiagAssert in
// the first parameter, that value will override whatever the
// global settings are.

// The assert macro used by ASSERT and SUPERASSERT.
// Turn off "conditional expression is constant" because of while(0).
// I need to turn this off globally because the compilation error
// occurs on the expansion of the macro.
#pragma warning ( disable : 4127 )
#ifdef PORTABLE_BUGSLAYERUTIL
#define ASSERTMACRO(a,x)                                              \
    do                                                               \
    {                                                                \
        if ( !(x)                                              && \
            DiagAssert ( a , _T ( #x ) , __FILE__ , __LINE__)    )\
        {                                                            \
                DebugBreak ( ) ;                                     \
        }                                                            \
    } while (0)
#else   //!PORTABLE_BUGSLAYERUTIL
#define ASSERTMACRO(a,x)                                              \
    do                                                               \
    {                                                                \
        if ( !(x)                                              && \
            DiagAssert ( a , _T ( #x ) , __FILE__ , __LINE__)    )\
        {                                                            \
                __asm int 3                                         \
        }                                                            \
    } while (0)
#endif  // PORTABLE_BUGSLAYERUTIL

// The normal assert. It just uses the module defaults.
#define ASSERT(x) ASSERTMACRO(DA_USEDEFAULTS,x)

// Do the lowercase one.
#define assert ASSERT

// Trust, but verify.
#define VERIFY(x)    ASSERT(x)

// Full-blown assert with all the trimmings
#define SUPERASSERT(x) ASSERTMACRO ( DA_SHOWSTACKTRACE |    \
                                     DA_SHOWMSGBOX     |    \
                                     DA_SHOWODS        ,    \
                              x                      , )
```

(continued)

Listing 3-3 *continued*

```
// The options macro
#define SETDIAGASSERTOPTIONS(x) SetDiagAssertOptions(x)

// The add module macro
#define ADDDIAGASSERTMODULE(x) AddDiagAssertModule(x)

// The TRACE macros
#ifdef __cplusplus
#define TRACE    ::DiagOutput
#endif

#define TRACE0(sz)             DiagOutput(_T("%s"), _T(sz))
#define TRACE1(sz, p1)         DiagOutput(_T(sz), p1)
#define TRACE2(sz, p1, p2)     DiagOutput(_T(sz), p1, p2)
#define TRACE3(sz, p1, p2, p3) DiagOutput(_T(sz), p1, p2, p3)


#else   // !_DEBUG
/*//////////////////////////////////////////////////////////////////////
                    _DEBUG Is !!NOT!! Defined
//////////////////////////////////////////////////////////////////////*/
#define ASSERTMACRO(a,x)
#define ASSERT(x)
#define VERIFY(x)   ((void)(x))
#define SUPERASSERT(x)
#define SETDIAGASSERTOPTIONS(x)
#define ADDDIAGASSERTMODULE(x)

#ifdef __cplusplus
//inline void TraceOutput(LPCTSTR, ...) { }
#define TRACE   (void)0
#endif

#define TRACE0(fmt)
#define TRACE1(fmt,arg1)
#define TRACE2(fmt,arg1,arg2)
#define TRACE3(fmt,arg1,arg2,arg3)

#endif  // _DEBUG


#ifdef __cplusplus
}
#endif  //__cplusplus

#endif  // _DIAGASSERT_H
```

With *SUPERASSERT*, I automatically redirect all *ASSERT* and *assert* calls to my functions. I don't redirect the *_ASSERT* and *_ASSERTE* macros because you might be doing some advanced work with the debug run-time library and I didn't want to break your existing solutions. I leave *ASSERT_KINDOF* and *ASSERT_VALID* alone as well. For Visual Basic, you just need to include VBASSERTANDTRACE.BAS in your project.

If you use the *SUPERASSERT* macro or function, you'll automatically get the stack trace. By default, the stack tracing is off for *ASSERT*. I didn't want to incur the overhead associated with stack tracing on general assertions. If you want to use stack tracing, however, turning it on is easy: just set the options with the *SETDIAG-ASSERTOPTIONS* macro or the *SetDiagAssertOptions* function and pass in the *DA_SHOWSTACKTRACE* bit flag. I tend to use *SUPERASSERT* where I least expect problems or would be surprised to be executing—for example, in an exception block. For normal assertion situations, *ASSERT* works fine for me. The choice is yours because you can set the defaults.

COMMON DEBUGGING QUESTION

Why do you always put the constants on the left-hand side of conditional statements?

As you look through my code, you'll notice that I always use statements such as "if (INVALID_HANDLE_VALUE == hFile)" instead of "if (hFile == INVALID_HANDLE_VALUE)." The reason I use this style is to avoid bugs. You can easily forget one of the equal signs, and using the former version will yield a compiler error if you do forget. The latter version might not issue a warning—whether or not it does depends on the warning level—and you'll change the variable's value. In both C/C++ and Visual Basic, trying to assign a value to a constant will produce a compiler error. If you've ever had to track down a bug involving an accidental assignment, you know just how difficult this type of bug is to find.

If you pay close attention, you'll notice that I also use constant variables on the left side of the equalities. As with the constant values case, the compilers will report errors when you try to assign a value to a constant variable. I've found that it's a lot easier to fix compiler errors than to fix bugs in the debugger.

Some developers have complained, sometimes vociferously, that the way I write conditional statements makes the code more confusing to read. I don't agree. My conditional statements take only a second longer to read and translate. I'm willing to give up that second to avoid wasting huge amounts of time later.

TRACE, TRACE, TRACE, AND TRACE

Assertions might be the best proactive programming trick you can learn, but trace statements, if used correctly with assertions, will truly allow you to debug your application without the debugger. Like assertions, *TRACE* macros for C and C++, and *Debug.Print* for Visual Basic, go away in release compiles, so you can use as many as you want. For some of you old hands out there, trace statements are essentially *printf*-style debugging. You should never underestimate the power of *printf*-style debugging because that's how most applications were debugged before interactive debuggers were invented.

Deciding how much to trace has always been a problem, especially if you're working on a team of more than one person. If everyone traces just a little, the volume of trace statements can quickly become overwhelming. At a minimum, key data structures and paths through the code should have trace statements associated with them. However, because trace statements are so useful, I've made it easy for you to put as many trace statements in your application as you'd like. The LIMODS (Limit OutputDebugString) program that's the topic of Chapter 14 allows you to limit the trace statements to only the source files you're interested in seeing.

Although trace statements can solve almost all your problems, they have two drawbacks. Neither limitation is serious enough to prevent you from using trace statements, but you do need to keep in mind the issues that can arise when you use them.

The first limitation is that trace statements usually cause your application to serialize execution when you call them. This means that your high-speed multithreaded application can perform in a completely different way when you use trace statements because the threads block and are scheduled around the trace statements. If you properly developed your multithreading code, as I describe in Chapter 12, you shouldn't have any problems. However, I've seen cases in which code that works inside the debugger or with lots of trace statements doesn't run outside the debugger or in release mode.

The second limitation is that, because of the serialization problem, too many trace statements can make your debug build run very slowly. If you encounter this problem, you're trying to trace too much and you need to cut back. For example, always avoid putting trace statements inside tight loops.

When you're planning your tracing strategy, your team should spend some time thinking about how to format trace statements. If everyone uses a similar format, finding information with *grep* or writing simple parsers to analyze the logs is easy. I prefer to follow the format "*function : trace statement.*" By starting with the function name, I can easily *grep* just for the functions I want to see. Be careful not to get too complicated with the format. If you make the format too complex, developers won't remember it and therefore won't use it.

Normally, you see trace statements only in the debugger Output window. However, a must-have free utility, DebugView/Enterprise Edition from Mark Russinovich at *www.sysinternals.com*, allows you to see your trace statements as your application runs outside the debugger. I run DebugView/Enterprise Edition all the time. Because I can see my trace statements, I can see what's happening in my applications. DebugView/Enterprise Edition is especially helpful when you're working on multiprocess COM applications because you can see all the cross-process interaction in one place. Another area in which DebugView/Enterprise Edition is a huge help is with those COM applications that run in contexts that you might not control, such as Microsoft Internet Information Services (IIS).

COMMENT, COMMENT, COMMENT, AND COMMENT

One day, my friend François Poulin, who was working full time on maintaining some code someone else wrote, came in wearing a button that said, "Code as if whoever maintains your code is a violent psychopath who knows where you live." François is by no means a psychopath, but he did have a very good point. Although you might think your code is the model of clarity and completely obvious, without correct comments, your code is as bad as raw assembly language to the maintenance developers. The irony is that the maintenance developer for your code can easily turn out to be you! Remember François's button every time you write a line of code.

Our job as engineers is twofold: develop a solution for the user and make that solution maintainable for the future. The only way to make your code maintainable is to comment it. By "comment it," I don't mean simply writing comments that duplicate what the code is doing; I mean documenting your assumptions, your approach, and your reasons for choosing the approach you did. You also need to keep your comments coordinated with the code. Normally mild-mannered maintenance programmers can turn into raving lunatics when they're trying to update code that does something different from what the comments say it's supposed to do.

I use the following approach to commenting:

■ Each function or method needs a sentence or two that clarifies the following information:

❑ What the routine does

❑ What assumptions the routine makes

❑ What each input parameter is expected to contain

- ❑   What each output parameter is expected to contain on success and failure

- ❑   Each possible return value

■   Each part of the function that isn't completely obvious from the code needs a sentence or two that explains what it's doing.

■   Any interesting algorithm deserves a complete description.

■   Any nontrivial bugs you've fixed in the code need to be commented with the bug number and a description of what you fixed.

■   Well-placed trace statements, assertions, and good naming conventions can also serve as good comments and provide excellent context to the code.

■   Comment as if you were going to be the one maintaining the code in five years.

■   If you find yourself saying, "This is a big hack" or "This is really tricky stuff," you probably need to rewrite the function instead of commenting it.

Proper and complete documentation in the code marks the difference between a serious, professional developer and someone who is playing at it. Donald Knuth once observed that you should be able to read a well-written program just as you read a well-written book. Although I don't see myself curling up by the fire with a copy of the TeX source code, I strongly agree with Dr. Knuth's sentiment.

I recommend that you study "Self-Documenting Code," Chapter 19 of Steve McConnell's phenomenal book *Code Complete* (Microsoft Press, 1993). Reading this chapter is how I learned to write comments. If you comment correctly, even if your maintenance programmer turns out to be a psychopath, you know you'll be safe.

TRUST YOURSELF, BUT VERIFY (UNIT TESTING)

I always thought Andy Grove from Intel had it right when he titled his book *Only the Paranoid Survive*. This notion is especially true for software engineers. I have many good friends who are excellent engineers, but when it comes to having them interface with my code, I verify their data down to the last bit. In fact, I even have a healthy skepticism about myself. Assertions, tracing, and commenting are how I start verifying my fellow developers who are calling my code. Unit testing is how I verify myself. Unit tests are the scaffolding that you put in place to call your code outside the normal program as a whole.

The first way I verify myself is to start writing my unit tests as soon as I start writing my code, developing them in parallel. Once I figure out the interface for a module, I write the stub functions for that module and immediately write a test program, or harness, to call those interfaces. As I add a piece of functionality, I add new test cases to the test harness. Using this approach, I can test each incremental change in isolation and spread out the test harness development over the development cycle. If you do all the regular development after you've implemented the main code, you generally don't have enough time to do a good job on the harness and therefore do a less thorough job implementing an effective test.

The second way I verify myself is to think about how I'm going to test my code before I write it. Try not to fall into the trap of thinking that your entire application has to be written before you can test your code. If you discover that you're a victim of this pitfall, you need to step back and break down your testing. I realize that sometimes you must rely on important functionality from another developer to compile your code. In those cases, your test code should consist of stubs for the interfaces that you can compile against. At a minimum, have the interfaces hard-coded to return appropriate data so that you can compile and run your code.

One side benefit of ensuring that your design is testable is that you quickly find problems that you can fix to make your code more reusable and extensible. Because reusability is the Holy Grail of software, whatever steps you can take to make your code more reusable are worth the effort. A good example of this windfall is when I was working on the crash handler code for Chapter 9. As I was unit testing on Windows 98, I noticed that the *SymInitialize* API function for the DBGHELP.DLL symbol engine didn't automatically load symbols for all the modules in the processes as it did for Windows 2000. I saw that automatically loading all the process modules was going to be something that I needed in other utilities, so I developed the *BSUSym-Initialize* function. My unit test for the crash handler code tested *BSUSymInitialize*, and I came out of the development with a perfectly reusable solution.

While you're coding, you should be running your unit tests all the time. I seem to think in an isolated functionality unit of about 50 lines of code. Each time I add or change a feature, I rerun the unit test to see whether I broke anything. I don't like surprises, so I try to keep them to a minimum. I definitely recommend that you run your unit tests before you check in your code to the master sources. Some organizations have specific tests, called check-in tests, that need to be run before code can be checked in. I've seen these check-in tests drastically reduce the number of build and smoke test breakages.

The key to the most effective unit tests comes down to two words: *code coverage*. If you take nothing else away from this chapter except those two words, I'll consider it a success. Code coverage is simply the percentage of lines you've executed in your module. If 100 lines are in your module and you execute 85, you have 85 percent code coverage. The simple fact is that a line not executed is a line waiting to crash.

You can get code-coverage statistics in two ways. The first way is the hard way and involves using the debugger and setting a breakpoint on every single line in your module. As your module executes a line, clear the breakpoint. Continue running your code until you've cleared all the breakpoints and you have 100 percent coverage. The easy way to get coverage is to use a third-party code-coverage tool such as Compuware NuMega's TrueCoverage or Rational's Visual PureCoverage.

Personally, I don't check in any code to the master sources until I've executed at least 85 to 90 percent of the lines in my code. I know some of you are groaning right now. Yes, getting good code coverage can be time consuming. Sometimes you need to do far more testing than you ever considered, and it can take a while. Getting the best coverage means that you need to run your application in the debugger and change data variables to execute code paths that are hard to hit otherwise. Your job is to write solid code, however, and in my opinion, code coverage is about the only way you'll get it during the unit test phase.

Nothing is worse than having your QA staff sitting on their hands while they're stuck with builds that crash. If you get 90 percent code coverage in the unit test, your QA people can spend their time testing your application on different platforms and ensuring that the interfaces between subsystems work. QA's job is to test the product as a whole and to sign off on the quality as a whole. Your job is to test a unit and to sign off on the quality of that unit. When both sides do their jobs, the result is a high-quality product.

Granted, I don't expect that developers will be able to test on each different Microsoft Win32–based operating system that customers might be using. However, if engineers can get 90 percent coverage on at least one operating system, the team wins 66 percent of the battle for quality. If you're not using one of the third-party code-coverage tools, you're cheating yourself on quality.

In addition to the code coverage, I frequently run third-party error detection and performance tools, as discussed in Chapter 1, on my unit test projects. Those tools help me catch bugs much earlier in the development cycle so that I spend less time debugging overall.

If you follow the recommendations presented in this section, you'll have some effective unit tests at the end of your development—but the work doesn't stop there. If you look at the BUGSLAYERUTIL.DLL code that's on the companion CD, you'll see a directory named Tests under the main source code directory. That directory holds my unit tests. I keep my unit tests as part of the code base so that others can find them easily. In addition, when I make a change to the source code, I can easily test to see whether I broke anything. I highly recommend that you check your tests into your version control system. Finally, although most unit tests are self-explanatory, make sure that you document any key assumptions so that others don't waste their time wrestling with your tests.

SUMMARY

This chapter presented the best proactive programming techniques you can use to debug during coding. The best technique is to use assertions everywhere so that you gain control whenever a problem occurs. The *SUPERASSERT* code presented avoids all the problems associated with the assertions supplied by the Microsoft compilers. In addition to assertions, proper tracing and comments can make maintaining and debugging your code much easier for you and others. Finally, the most important quality gauges for engineers are unit tests. If you can properly test your code before you check it in, you can eliminate many of the bugs and problems that frustrate maintenance engineers later.

The only way to unit test properly is to run a code-coverage tool while you're doing your tests. You need to strive to get at least 85 to 90 percent coverage on your code before you ever check it in to the master sources. The more time you spend debugging your code during development, the less time you'll have to spend debugging it later.

Part II

Power Debugging

Chapter 4

How Do Debuggers Work?

Learning how your tools operate is a crucial part of this business. If you understand the capabilities and limitations of your tools, you can better maximize their return and thus spend less time debugging. Most of the time, debuggers help you out tremendously, but sometimes they can cause subtle problems that will baffle you. In this chapter, I'll explain what a debugger is and demonstrate how various debuggers operate in Microsoft Win32 operating systems.

In describing debuggers in general, I'll go over what special features are turned on when your process is running under a debugger. I'll also explain some ways in which you can leverage certain Win32 features to make your debugging easier. I'll present two debuggers that I wrote and whose source code is on the companion CD. The first, MinDBG, does just enough to call itself a debugger. The second, WDBG, is a real Microsoft Windows debugger sample that does nearly everything a real debugger is supposed to, including manipulating symbol tables, handling breakpoints, generating disassembly, and coordinating with a graphical user interface (GUI). In discussing WDBG, I'll also cover topics such as how breakpoints work and what all the different symbol files are and what they mean.

Before jumping into the chapter, I want to make sure to define two standard terms that I'll be using throughout this book: *debugger* and *debuggee*. Simply put, a debugger is a process that can control another process in a debugging relationship, and a debuggee is a process started under a debugger. Some operating systems refer to the debugger as the *parent process* and the debuggee as the *child process*.

TYPES OF WINDOWS DEBUGGERS

If you've been programming Windows for any length of time, you've probably heard about several different types of debuggers that you can use. Two types of debuggers are available in the Windows world: user-mode debuggers and kernel-mode debuggers.

User-mode debuggers are much more familiar to most developers. Not surprisingly, user-mode debuggers are for debugging user-mode applications. The Microsoft Visual C++ debugger is a prime example of a user-mode debugger. Kernel-mode debuggers, as the names implies, are those that let you debug the operating system kernel. These debuggers are used mostly by device driver writers when they're debugging their device drivers.

User-Mode Debuggers

User-mode debuggers are used to debug any application that runs in user mode, which includes any GUI programs as well as applications you wouldn't expect, such as Windows 2000 services. Generally, user-mode debuggers use GUIs. The main hallmark of user-mode debuggers is that they use the Win32 Debugging application programming interface (API). Because the operating system marks the debuggee as running in a special mode, you can use the *IsDebuggerPresent* API function to find out whether your process is running under a debugger.

The Win32 Debugging API comes with an implied contract: once a process is running under the Debugging API, thus making it a debuggee, the debugger can't detach from that process. This symbiotic relationship means that if the debugger ends, the debuggee will end as well. The debugger is also limited to debugging only the debuggee and any processes spawned by the debuggee (if the debugger supports descendant processes).

For interpreted languages and run times that use a virtual machine approach, the virtual machines themselves provide the complete debugging environment and don't use the Win32 Debugging API. Some examples of those types of environments are the Microsoft or Sun Java Virtual Machines (VMs), the Microsoft scripting environment for Web applications, and the Microsoft Visual Basic p-code interpreter.

We'll get to Visual Basic debugging in Chapter 7, but be aware that the Visual Basic p-code interface is undocumented. I won't go into the Java and scripting debugging interfaces, subjects beyond the scope of this book. For more information on debugging and profiling the Microsoft Java VMs, search for the "Debugging and Profiling Java Applications" topic on MSDN. The interfaces are rich and extensive and allow you to completely control the operation of the Java VM. For information on writing a script debugger, search MSDN for the topic, "Active Script Debugging API Objects."

Like the Java VM, the script debugger objects provide a rich interface for accessing scripts and document-hosted scripts.

A surprising number of programs use the Win32 Debugging API. These include the Visual C++ debugger, which I cover in depth in Chapters 5 and 6; the Windows Debugger (WinDBG), which I discuss in the kernel-mode debugger section that follows; Compuware NuMega's BoundsChecker; the Platform SDK HeapWalker program; the Platform SDK Depends program; the Borland Delphi and C++ Builder debuggers; and the NT Symbolic Debugger (NTSD). I'm sure there are many more.

Kernel-Mode Debuggers

Kernel-mode debuggers sit between the CPU and the operating system. That means that when you stop in a kernel-mode debugger, the operating system also stops completely. As you can imagine, bringing the operating system to an abrupt halt is helpful when you're working on timing and synchronization problems. Except for one kernel-mode debugger that I'll talk about later (in the section "SoftICE" on page 89), however, you can't debug user-mode code with kernel-mode debuggers.

There aren't that many kernel-mode debuggers. A few are the Windows 80386 Debugger (WDEB386), the Kernel Debugger (i386KD), WinDBG, and SoftICE. I'll briefly describe each of these debuggers in the following sections.

WDEB386

WDEB386 is the Windows 98 kernel-mode debugger distributed with the Platform SDK. This debugger is useful only for developers writing Windows 98 virtual device drivers (VxDs). Like most kernel-mode debuggers for Windows operating systems, WDEB386 requires two machines and a null modem cable to work. Two machines are necessary because the kernel-mode portion that runs on the target machine has limited access to the target machine's hardware, so it sends its output to and receives its commands from another machine.

WDEB386 has an interesting history. It started out as a Microsoft internal tool back in the Windows 3.0 days. It's hard to use and doesn't have much support for source-level debugging and other nice features that the Visual C++ and Visual Basic debuggers have spoiled us with.

The "DOT" commands are the most important feature of WDEB386. Through INT 41, you can extend WDEB386 to add more commands to the debugger. This extensibility allows VxD writers to create custom debugger commands that give them easy access to information in their VxDs. The Windows 98 debug version supports a plethora of DOT commands that allow you to observe the exact state of the operating system at any point in the debugging process.

i386KD

Windows 2000 is different from Windows 98 in that the actual kernel-mode debugger portion is part of NTOSKRNL.EXE, the main kernel file of the Windows 2000 operating system. This debugger is available in both the free (release) and checked (debug) builds of the operating system. To turn on kernel-mode debugging, set the /DEBUG boot option in BOOT.INI and, additionally, the /DEBUGPORT boot option if you need to set the communications port for the kernel-mode debugger to a port other than the default (COM1). i386KD runs on its own machine and communicates with the Windows 2000 machine through a null modem cable.

The NTOSKRNL.EXE kernel-mode debugger does just enough to control the CPU so that the operating system can be debugged. The bulk of the debugging work—handling symbols, advanced breakpoints, and disassembly—happens on the i386KD side. At one time, the Windows NT 4 Device Driver Kit (DDK) documented the protocol used across the null modem cable. However, Microsoft no longer documents this protocol.

The power of i386KD is apparent when you see all the commands that it offers for accessing the internal Windows 2000 state. If you've ever wanted to see what happens in the operating system, these commands will show you. Having a working knowledge of how Windows 2000 device drivers work will help you follow much of the command's output. For all its power, i386KD is almost never used because it's a console application, which makes it tedious to use with source-level debugging.

WinDBG

WinDBG is the debugger that comes with the Platform SDK. You can also download it from *http://msdn.microsoft.com/developer/sdk/default.asp*. It's a hybrid debugger in that it can be a kernel-mode debugger as well as a user-mode debugger, but WinDBG won't let you debug both kernel-mode and user-mode programs at the same time. For kernel-mode debugging, WinDBG offers all the same power of i386KD but in an easier to use GUI front end that supports much simpler source-level debugging. With WinDBG, you can debug your device drivers nearly as easily as you would your user-mode applications.

As a user-mode debugger, WinDBG is good, and I strongly recommend that you install it if you haven't already. WinDBG offers more power than the Visual C++ debugger in that WinDBG shows you much more information about your process. However, that power does come at a cost: WinDBG is harder to use than the Visual C++ debugger. Still, I'd advise you to spend some time and effort learning about WinDBG. The investment might pay off by helping you solve a bug much faster than you can with the Visual C++ debugger alone. On average, I find that I spend about 70 percent of my debugging time in the Visual C++ debugger and the rest in WinDBG.

The first time you start WinDBG, you'll see that it has a Command window. Like the Visual C++ debugger, WinDBG does source-level debugging. However, the real power of WinDBG is found in its Command window interface. If you get comfortable with the different commands, you might find that you can debug faster with the Command window than you can with just a GUI.

The importance of the Command window increases when you add your own commands, called WinDBG extensions, to WinDBG. Whereas the Visual C++ debugger is only a little flexible when your process is stopped in the debugger, WinDBG has an entire API that allows you to get at all the debugger functionality, including the disassembler, the symbol engine, and the stack trace engine. For more information about WinDBG extensions, search for the "Debugger Extension" topic on MSDN.

In certain situations, I use WinDBG rather than the Visual C++ debugger because WinDBG supports more powerful breakpoints. Because of the Command window, you can associate commands with a breakpoint. If you stop and think about this capability, you'll realize that it allows you to take your debugging to new levels. For example, when you're tracking down a problem in a module you call many times, it would be nice if you could see the values at each call without stopping the application. With WinDBG, you can create a breakpoint command that dumps the data and then resumes execution of the program. In the Command window, you'll have a stream of all the data values leading up to the problem.

In addition to providing better debugger extensibility than the Visual C++ debugger does, WinDBG has one feature that you should definitely consider if your application runs on Windows 2000 or Windows NT 4: WinDBG can read user-mode dump files created by Dr. Watson. This capability means that you can load the exact state of your program at the time of the crash into the debugger so that you can see exactly where the program was when it crashed. See my December 1999 and January 2000 "Bugslayer" columns in *Microsoft Systems Journal* for more information about what you need to get this feature set up and working on your systems.

WinDBG will never become my full-time debugger because the Visual C++ debugger is so much easier to use. However, I hope that I've piqued your interest in using it. The power and capabilities it offers can help you find some very nasty problems more easily than you can with the Visual C++ debugger alone. A small investment in learning WinDBG can mean saving a huge amount of time when it comes to figuring out that one tough crash.

SoftICE

SoftICE is a commercial kernel-mode debugger from Compuware NuMega and is the only commercial kernel-mode debugger (that I know of) on the market. It's also the only kernel-mode debugger that can operate on a single machine. Unlike the other kernel-mode debuggers, however, SoftICE does an excellent job debugging user-mode programs. As I mentioned earlier, kernel-mode debuggers sit between the CPU and the operating system; SoftICE also sits between the CPU and the operating system when debugging a user-mode program, thereby stopping the entire operating system dead.

At first glance, you might not be impressed by the fact that SoftICE can bring the operating system to a halt. But consider this question: What happens if you have some timing-dependent code you need to debug? If you're using an API function such as *SendMessageTimeout*, you can easily time out as you step through another thread with a typical GUI debugger. With SoftICE, you can step all you want because the timer that *SendMessageTimeout* relies on won't be executing while you're running under SoftICE. SoftICE is the only debugger that allows you to effectively debug multithreaded applications. The fact that SoftICE stops the entire operating system when it's active means that solving timing problems is far easier.

Another benefit of SoftICE sitting between the CPU and the operating system is that debugging cross-process interactions becomes very easy. If you're doing COM programming with multiple out-of-process servers, you can easily set breakpoints in all the processes and step between them. Finally, if you do need to step from user mode to kernel mode and back, SoftICE makes such shifting trivial.

SoftICE really shines when you need to stop the application when it's accessing a particular piece of memory. SoftICE takes advantage of the i386 debug registers, which allow you to specify up to a 4-byte piece of memory to break on. You can break when the memory location is read from, written to, or executed. Because SoftICE can use up to four hardware breakpoints, your application runs at full speed until your memory location is accessed. This feature is invaluable for tracking down memory-corruption problems.

The other major advantage that SoftICE has over all other debuggers is that it has a phenomenal collection of informational commands that let you see virtually everything that's happening in the operating system. Although i386KD and WinDBG have a substantial number of these commands, SoftICE has many more. You can view almost anything in SoftICE, from the state of all synchronization events, to complete *HWND* information, to extended information about any thread in the system. I run SoftICE all the time and can't imagine developing software without it. It's one of the best tools I've ever used. In fact, on Windows 98 I don't use any other debuggers.

As you might expect, all this wonderful raw power has a price tag. SoftICE, like any kernel-mode debugger, has a steep learning curve because it's essentially its own operating system when it's running. However, your return on investment makes learning how to use SoftICE worth the effort.

COMMON DEBUGGING QUESTION

How do I change the default debugger that the operating system will use when a crash occurs?

When an application crashes, Windows 2000 looks in the registry key *HKEY-_LOCAL_MACHINE\SOFTWARE\Microsoft\Windows NT\CurrentVersion\AeDebug*, and Windows 98 looks in the [AeDebug] section of WIN.INI to determine what they should call to debug the application. If no values are in the key, Windows 2000 reports the address of the crash. If an access violation caused the crash, Windows 2000 also reports the memory location that the process couldn't read or write. Windows 98 displays the standard crash dialog box, and if you click the Details button, it will list the module, address, and registers at the time of the crash.

Three possible string values can be placed in the *AeDebug* key or section.

■   Auto

■   Debugger

■   UserDebuggerHotKey

If *Auto* is set to 0 (zero), the operating system will generate the standard crash dialog box and enable the Cancel (Windows 2000) or Debug (Windows 98) button if you want to attach the debugger. If *Auto* is set to 1 (one), the debugger is automatically started. The *Debugger* value specifies the debugger the operating system will start on the crashed application. The only requirement for the debugger is that it supports attaching to a process. The *UserDebuggerHotKey* value identifies the key that will be used to break into the debugger. Refer to the section "Quick Break Keys" later in the chapter to find out how to set this value.

You can set the *AeDebug* key manually, but Dr. Watson (Windows 2000 only), WinDBG, and the Visual C++ debugger allow you to set it through various means. Dr. Watson and WinDBG use the -I command-line switch that will set them as the default debugger. To set the Visual C++ debugger as the debugger the operating system will call, on the Debug tab in the Options dialog box, check Just-In-Time Debugging.

If you do look at the *AeDebug* key, the value that's entered for *Debugger* looks like a string passed to the *wsprintf* API function: "drwtsn32 -p %ld -e %ld -g." That's exactly what it is. The -p is the process ID for the crashing process, and the -e is an event handle value that the debugger needs to signal when its debug loop gets the first thread exit debug event. Signaling the event handle tells the operating system that the debugger attached cleanly.

WINDOWS 2000 OPERATING SYSTEM SUPPORT FOR DEBUGGEES

In addition to defining the API that a debugger must call in order to be a debugger, Windows 2000 provides a few other features that help you find problems with your applications. Some of these features aren't that well known and can be confusing the first time you encounter them.

Windows 2000 Heap Checking

As an application starts under a debugger, Windows 2000 turns on the operating system debug heap checking. This heap isn't the C run-time library debug heap; it's the Windows 2000 heap code for those heaps created with the *HeapCreate* API function. The C run-time library heap is a separate entity, and we'll examine it in Chapter 15. Because processes use the Windows 2000 heaps extensively, you might see information related to heaps in your normal operation, which is why it's important to cover them here. If you attach a debugger to your application rather than start your application under the debugger, you won't activate the Windows 2000 debug heap checking.

With the Windows 2000 debug heap checking turned on, your application will run slightly slower because the Windows 2000 debug heap checking will validate the heap when your application calls *HeapFree*. Listing 4-1 is a sample program that corrupts memory. When you run the code in Listing 4-1 under a debugger, you'll see that it calls *DebugBreak* twice on the first *HeapFree*. Additionally, you'll see output such as the following that shows what was wrong. If you run the program outside the debugger, it runs to completion without reporting any problems.

```
HEAP[Heaper.exe]: Heap block at 00441E98 modified at 00441EAA past
    requested size of a
HEAP[Heaper.exe]: Invalid Address specified to
    RtlFreeHeap( 440000, 441ea0)
```

If you're using your own Windows 2000 heaps, you can turn on some additional flags to receive more diagnostic output. The Platform SDK includes a small utility named GFLAGS.EXE. With it, you can set some of the global flags that Windows 2000 checks when it first starts an application. Figure 4-1 on page 94 shows GFLAGS.EXE set up for HEAPER.EXE, which is the program in Listing 4-1. Many of the System Registry and Kernel Mode options are global, so you need to be careful if you set them because they can have a major impact on system performance. Setting Image File Options, as shown in Figure 4-1, is much safer because the settings are limited to just that one module.

```
void main(void)
{
    // Create an operating system heap.
    HANDLE hHeap = HeapCreate ( 0 , 128 , 0 ) ;

    // Allocate a 10-byte block.
    LPVOID pMem = HeapAlloc ( hHeap , 0 , 10 ) ;

    // Write 12 bytes to a 10-byte block (an overwrite).
    memset ( pMem , 0xAC , 12 ) ;

    // Allocate a new 20-byte block.
    LPVOID pMem2 = HeapAlloc ( hHeap , 0 , 20 ) ;

    // Underwrite 1 byte on the second block.
    char * pUnder = (char *)( (DWORD)pMem2 - 1 ) ;
    *pUnder = 'P' ;

    // Free the first block. This call to HeapFree will trigger a
    // breakpoint from the operating system debug heap code.
    HeapFree ( hHeap , 0 , pMem ) ;

    // Free the second block. Notice that this call won't report
    // a problem.
    HeapFree ( hHeap , 0 , pMem2 ) ;

    // Free a bogus block. Notice that this call won't report a problem.
    HeapFree ( hHeap , 0 , (LPVOID)0x1 ) ;

    HeapDestroy ( hHeap ) ;

}
```

Listing 4-1 *Windows 2000 heap corruption example*

If you set the same flags that I checked in Figure 4-1, you'll see much more output when you run the same program. Fortunately, the explanations of the flags I've checked are obvious. If you do turn on the flags and run the program, you'll get the same breakpoints, but the output, as shown here, is a little more verbose.

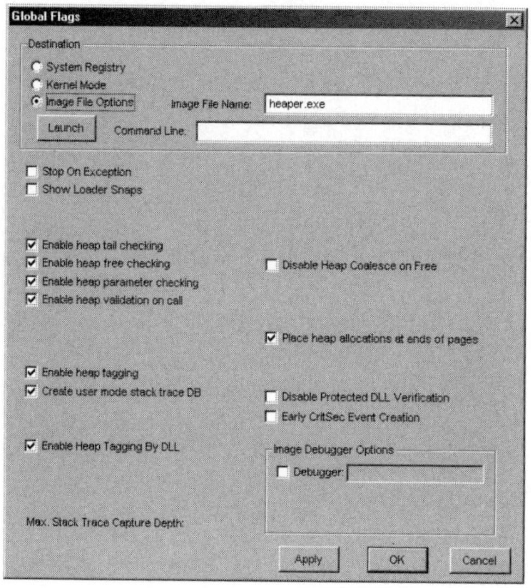

Figure 4-1 *GFLAGS.EXE*

```
PAGEHEAP: process 0x490 created debug heap 00430000
    (flags 0x1, 50, 25, 0, 0)
PAGEHEAP: process 0x490 created debug heap 00CF0000
    (flags 0x1, 50, 25, 0, 0)
PAGEHEAP: process 0x490 created debug heap 01600000
    (flags 0x1, 50, 25, 0, 0)
PAGEHEAP: Tail fill corruption detected:
        Allocation at  0x01606FF0
        Requested size 0x0000000A
        Allocated size 0x00000010
        Corruption at  0x01606FFA
PAGEHEAP: Attempt to reference block which is not allocated
```

Because I'm on the subject of GFLAGS.EXE, I want to take a moment to point out one very useful option, Show Loader Snaps. If you check that box and run your application, you'll see where Windows 2000 is loading the DLLs and how it's going about fixing up the imports, called *snapping*, for your application. If you need to see exactly what the Windows 2000 loader is doing when it loads your application (in case you have a problem), you'll find it helpful to turn this option on. For more information on loader snaps, see Matt Pietrek's "Under the Hood" column in the September 1999 *Microsoft Systems Journal.*

Automatically Starting in a Debugger

Some of the hardest types of applications to debug are those started by another process. Windows 2000 services and COM out-of-process servers fall into this category. In many cases, you can use the *DebugBreak* API function to force a debugger to attach to your process. In two instances, however, using *DebugBreak* won't work. First, in some cases, *DebugBreak* won't work with Windows 2000 services. If you need to debug the service startup, calling *DebugBreak* will get the debugger to attach, but by the time the debugger gets started, the service timeout limit might be reached and Windows 2000 will stop your service. Second, *DebugBreak* won't work when you need to debug a COM out-of-process server. If you call *DebugBreak*, the COM error handling will catch the breakpoint exception and terminate your COM out-of-process server. Fortunately, Windows 2000 lets you specify that your application should start in a debugger. This feature allows you to start debugging right from the first instruction. Before you enable this feature for a Windows 2000 service, however, make sure to configure your service to allow interaction with the desktop.

You can enable the start with debugger feature in two ways. The easiest way is to use GFLAGS.EXE and select the Image File Options radio button after typing just your binary's name in the Image File Name edit box. Check the Debugger check box, and type the complete path to the debugger in the edit box next to the Debugger check box.

The other, more difficult, way is to manually set the option with the registry editor. In the *HKEY_LOCAL_MACHINE\SOFTWARE\Microsoft\Windows NT\Current-Version\Image File Execution Options* key, create a key that is the same as your application's filename. For example, if your application is FOO.EXE, your registry key is *FOO.EXE*. In your application's registry key, create a new string value named *Debugger*. In the debugger value, type the complete path and filename to your debugger of choice. If you were using GFLAGS.EXE and you set some global options, you might notice a *GlobalFlag* string value in your application's key.

Now when you start your application, the debugger automatically starts with your application loaded. If you want to specify any command-line options to the debugger, you can specify them as well in the *Debugger* value. For example, if you want to use WinDBG and automatically initiate debugging as soon as WinDBG starts, you can fill your *Debugger* value with "d:\platform sdk\bin\windbg.exe -g."

Quick Break Keys

At times, you need a way to get into the debugger as fast as possible. If you're debugging a console-based application, pressing Ctrl+C or Ctrl+Break will cause a special exception, *DBG_CONTROL_C*. The *DBG_CONTROL_C* exception will pop you right into the debugger and allow you to start debugging.

A nice feature of both Windows 2000 and Windows NT 4 is that you can also pop into the debugger at any time for your GUI-based applications. When running under a debugger, by default, pressing the F12 key forces a call to *DebugBreak*. An interesting aspect of the F12 key processing is that even if you're using F12 as an accelerator or otherwise processing the keyboard messages for F12, you'll still break into the debugger.

The quick break key defaults to F12 in Windows NT 4, but in Windows 2000, you can specify which key to use. In the *HKEY_LOCAL_MACHINE\SOFTWARE\ Microsoft\Windows NT\CurrentVersion\AeDebug* registry key, you can set the *UserDebuggerHotKey* value to the *VK_** value you want to use. For example, if you want to use the Scroll Lock key to break into the debugger, you'd set the *User-DebuggerHotKey* value to 0x91. After you set a new value, you must reboot the computer for the change to take effect.

MINDBG: A SIMPLE WIN32 DEBUGGER

From a distance, a Win32 debugger is a simple program, with only a couple requirements. The first requirement is that the debugger must pass a special flag in the *dwCreationFlags* parameter to *CreateProcess*: *DEBUG_ONLY_THIS_PROCESS*. This flag tells the operating system that the calling thread will enter a debug loop to control the process it's starting. If the debugger can handle multiple processes spawned by the initial debuggee, it will pass *DEBUG_PROCESS* as the creation flag.

As you can see from the call to *CreateProcess* above, in the Win32 Debugging API, the debugger and debuggee are in separate processes, making the Win32 operating systems much more robust when debugging. Even if the debuggee has wild memory writes, the debuggee won't crash the debugger. (Debuggers in the 16-bit Windows and Macintosh operating systems are susceptible to debuggee mischief because the debugger and the debuggee run in the same process context.)

The second requirement is that after the debuggee starts, the debugger must enter into a loop calling the *WaitForDebugEvent* API function to receive debugging notifications. When it has finished processing a particular debugging event, it calls *ContinueDebugEvent*. Be aware that only the thread that called *CreateProcess* with the special debug creation flags can call the Debugging API functions. The following pseudocode shows just how little code is required to create a Win32 debugger:

```
void main ( void )
{
    CreateProcess ( ..., DEBUG_ONLY_THIS_PROCESS ,.... ) ;
```

```
while ( 1 == WaitForDebugEvent ( ... ) )
{
    if ( EXIT_PROCESS )
    {
        break ;
    }
    ContinueDebugEvent ( ... ) ;
}
}
```

As you can see, a minimal Win32 debugger doesn't require multithreading, a user interface, or much of anything else. Nevertheless, as with most applications in Windows, the difference between minimal and reasonable is considerable. In reality, the Win32 Debugging API almost dictates that the actual debug loop needs to sit in a separate thread. As the name implies, *WaitForDebugEvent* blocks on an internal operating system event until the debuggee performs some operation that makes the operating system stop the debuggee so that it can tell the debugger about the event. If your debugger had a single thread, your user interface would totally hang until the debuggee triggered a debug event.

During the time a debugger sits in the debug loop, it receives various notifications that certain events took place in the debuggee. The following *DEBUG_EVENT* structure, which is filled in by the *WaitForDebugEvent* function, contains all the interesting information about a debug event. Table 4-1 describes each of the individual events.

```
typedef struct _DEBUG_EVENT {
    DWORD dwDebugEventCode;
    DWORD dwProcessId;
    DWORD dwThreadId;
    union {
        EXCEPTION_DEBUG_INFO Exception;
        CREATE_THREAD_DEBUG_INFO CreateThread;
        CREATE_PROCESS_DEBUG_INFO CreateProcessInfo;
        EXIT_THREAD_DEBUG_INFO ExitThread;
        EXIT_PROCESS_DEBUG_INFO ExitProcess;
        LOAD_DLL_DEBUG_INFO LoadDll;
        UNLOAD_DLL_DEBUG_INFO UnloadDll;
        OUTPUT_DEBUG_STRING_INFO DebugString;
        RIP_INFO RipInfo;
    } u;
} DEBUG_EVENT
```

Table 4-1 **Debugging Events**

Debugging Event	Description
CREATE_PROCESS_DEBUG_EVENT	This debugging event is generated whenever a new process is created in a process being debugged or whenever the debugger begins debugging an already active process. The kernel generates this debugging event before the process begins to execute in user mode and before the kernel generates any other debugging events for the new process.
	The DEBUG_EVENT structure contains a CREATE_PROCESS_DEBUG_INFO structure. This structure includes a handle to the new process, a handle to the process's image file, a handle to the process's initial thread, and other information that describes the new process.
	The handle to the process has PROCESS_VM_READ and PROCESS_VM_WRITE access. If a debugger has these types of access to a thread, it can read and write to the process's memory by using the ReadProcessMemory and WriteProcessMemory functions.
	The handle to the process's image file has GENERIC_READ access and is opened for read-sharing.
	The handle to the process's initial thread has THREAD_GET_CONTEXT, THREAD_SET_CONTEXT, and THREAD_SUSPEND_RESUME access to the thread. If a debugger has these types of access to a thread, it can read from and write to the thread's registers by using the GetThreadContext and SetThreadContext functions and can suspend and resume the thread by using the SuspendThread and ResumeThread functions.
CREATE_THREAD_DEBUG_EVENT	This debugging event is generated whenever a new thread is created in a process being debugged or whenever the debugger begins debugging an already active process. This debugging

Debugging Event	*Description*
	cvent is generated before the new thread begins to execute in user mode.
	The *DEBUG_EVENT* structure contains a *CREATE_THREAD_DEBUG_INFO* structure. This structure includes a handle to the new thread and the thread's starting address. The handle has *THREAD_GET_CONTEXT*, *THREAD_SET-_CONTEXT*, and *THREAD_SUSPEND_RESUME* access to the thread. If a debugger has these types of access to a thread, it can read from and write to the thread's registers by using the *GetThreadContext* and *SetThreadContext* functions and can suspend and resume the thread by using the *SuspendThread* and *ResumeThread* functions.
EXCEPTION_DEBUG_EVENT	This debugging event is generated whenever an exception occurs in the process being debugged. Possible exceptions include attempting to access inaccessible memory, executing breakpoint instructions, attempting to divide by 0, or any other exception noted in the Platform SDK topic, "Structured Exception Handling."
	The *DEBUG_EVENT* structure contains an *EXCEPTION_DEBUG_INFO* structure. This structure describes the exception that caused the debugging event.
	Besides the standard exception conditions, an additional exception code can occur during console process debugging. The kernel generates a *DBG_CONTROL_C* exception code when Ctrl+C is input to a console process that handles Ctrl+C signals and is being debugged. This exception code isn't meant to be handled by applications. An application should never use an exception handler to deal with it. It is raised only for the benefit of the debugger and is used only when a debugger is attached to the console process.

(continued)

Table 4-1 *continued*

Debugging Event	*Description*
EXCEPTION_DEBUG_EVENT (cont.)	If a process isn't being debugged or if the debugger passes on the *DBG_CONTROL_C* exception un-handled, the application's list of handler functions is searched. (For more information about console process handler functions, see the MSDN documentation for the *SetConsoleCtrlHandler* function.)
EXIT_PROCESS_DEBUG_EVENT	This debugging event is generated whenever the last thread in a process being debugged exits. It occurs immediately after the kernel unloads the process's DLLs and updates the process's exit code. The *DEBUG_EVENT* structure contains an *EXIT_PROCESS_DEBUG_INFO* structure that specifies the exit code. The debugger deallocates any internal structures associated with the process on receipt of this debugging event. The kernel closes the debugger's handle to the exiting process and all the process's threads.
EXIT_THREAD_DEBUG_EVENT	This debugging event is generated whenever a thread that is part of a process being debugged exits. The kernel generates this debugging event immediately after it updates the thread's exit code. The *DEBUG_EVENT* structure contains an *EXIT_THREAD_DEBUG_INFO* structure that specifies the exit code. The debugger deallocates any internal structures associated with the thread on receipt of this debugging event. The system closes the debugger's handle to the exiting thread. This debugging event doesn't occur if the exiting thread is the last thread of a process. In this case, the *EXIT_PROCESS_DEBUG_EVENT* debugging event occurs instead.
LOAD_DLL_DEBUG_EVENT	This debugging event is generated whenever a process being debugged loads a DLL. This debugging event occurs when the system loader resolves links to a DLL or when the debugged process uses the *LoadLibrary* function. This debugging event is

Debugging Event	Description
	called each time the DLL loads into the address space. If the DLL's reference count falls to 0, the DLL is unloaded. The next time the DLL is loaded, this event will be generated again.
	The *DEBUG_EVENT* structure contains a *LOAD_DLL_DEBUG_INFO* structure. This structure includes a handle to the newly loaded DLL, the base address of the DLL, and other information that describes the DLL.
	Typically, a debugger loads a symbol table associated with the DLL on receipt of this debugging event.
OUTPUT_DEBUG_STRING_EVENT	This debugging event is generated when a process being debugged uses the *OutputDebugString* function.
	The *DEBUG_EVENT* structure contains an *OUTPUT_DEBUG_STRING_INFO* structure. This structure specifies the address, length, and format of the debugging string.
UNLOAD_DLL_DEBUG_EVENT	This debugging event is generated whenever a process being debugged unloads a DLL by using the *FreeLibrary* function. This debugging event occurs only the last time a DLL is unloaded from a process's address space (that is, when the DLL's usage count is 0).
	The *DEBUG_EVENT* structure contains an *UNLOAD_DLL_DEBUG_INFO* structure. This structure specifies the base address of the DLL in the address space of the process that unloads the DLL.
	Typically, a debugger unloads a symbol table associated with the DLL upon receiving this debugging event.
	When a process exits, the kernel automatically unloads the process's DLLs but doesn't generate an *UNLOAD_DLL_DEBUG_EVENT* debugging event.
RIP_INFO	This debugging event is generated only by the Windows 98 checked build and is used to report error conditions such as closing invalid handles.

When the debugger is processing the debug events returned by *WaitForDebugEvent*, it has full control over the debuggee because the operating system stops all the threads in the debuggee and won't reschedule them until *ContinueDebugEvent* is called. If the debugger needs to read from or write to the debuggee's address space, it can use *ReadProcessMemory* and *WriteProcessMemory*. If the memory is marked as read-only, you can use the *VirtualProtect* function to reset the protection levels. If the debugger patches the debuggee's code via a call to *WriteProcessMemory*, it must call *FlushInstructionCache* to clear out the instruction cache for the memory. If you forget to call *FlushInstructionCache*, your changes might work, but if the memory you changed is currently in the CPU cache, it might not. Calling *FlushInstructionCache* is especially important on multiprocessor machines. If the debugger needs to get or set the debuggee's current context or CPU registers, it can call *GetThreadContext* or *SetThreadContext*.

The only Win32 debug event that needs special handling is the loader breakpoint. After the operating system sends initial *CREATE_PROCESS_DEBUG_EVENT* and *LOAD_DLL_DEBUG_EVENT* notifications for the implicitly loaded modules, the debugger receives an *EXCEPTION_DEBUG_EVENT*. This debug event is the loader breakpoint. The debuggee executes this breakpoint because the *CREATE-_PROCESS_DEBUG_EVENT* indicates only that the process was loaded, not that it was executed. The loader breakpoint, which the operating system forces each debuggee to execute, is the first time the debugger knows when the debuggee is truly running. In real-world debuggers, the main data structure initialization, such as for symbol tables, is handled during process creation, and the debugger starts showing code disassembly or doing necessary debuggee patching in the loader breakpoint.

When the loader breakpoint occurs, the debugger should record that it saw the breakpoint so that the debugger can handle subsequent breakpoints accordingly. The only other processing needed for the first breakpoint (and for all breakpoints in general) depends on the CPU. For the Intel Pentium family, the debugger has to continue processing by calling *ContinueDebugEvent* and passing it the *DBG_CONTINUE* flag so that the debuggee resumes execution.

Listing 4-2 shows MinDBG, a minimal debugger. MinDBG processes all the debug events and properly runs a debuggee process. If you run MinDBG, notice that the debug event handlers don't really display any interesting information, such as the executable or DLL names. Taking a minimal debugger and turning it into a real debugger involves quite a bit of work.

```
/*---------------------------------------------------------------
The world's simplest debugger for Win32 programs
----------------------------------------------------------*/


/*//////////////////////////////////////////////////////////////////
                        The Usual Includes
//////////////////////////////////////////////////////////////////*/
#include "stdafx.h"
/*//////////////////////////////////////////////////////////////////
                        Prototypes
//////////////////////////////////////////////////////////////////*/
// Shows the minimal help.
void ShowHelp ( void ) ;

// Display functions
void DisplayCreateProcessEvent ( CREATE_PROCESS_DEBUG_INFO & stCPDI ) ;
void DisplayCreateThreadEvent ( CREATE_THREAD_DEBUG_INFO & stCTDI ) ;
void DisplayExitThreadEvent ( EXIT_THREAD_DEBUG_INFO & stETDI ) ;
void DisplayExitProcessEvent ( EXIT_PROCESS_DEBUG_INFO & stEPDI ) ;
void DisplayDllLoadEvent ( LOAD_DLL_DEBUG_INFO & stLDDI ) ;
void DisplayDllUnLoadEvent ( UNLOAD_DLL_DEBUG_INFO & stULDDI ) ;
void DisplayODSEvent ( HANDLE                      hProcess ,
                       OUTPUT_DEBUG_STRING_INFO & stODSI   ) ;
void DisplayExceptionEvent ( EXCEPTION_DEBUG_INFO & stEDI ) ;


/*//////////////////////////////////////////////////////////////////
                        Entry Point!
//////////////////////////////////////////////////////////////////*/
void main ( int argc , char * argv[ ] )
{
    // Check that there is a command-line argument.
    if ( 1 == argc )
    {
        ShowHelp ( ) ;
        return ;
    }

    // Concatenate the command-line parameters.
    TCHAR szCmdLine[ MAX_PATH ] ;
    szCmdLine[ 0 ] = '\0' ;

    for ( int i = 1 ; i < argc ; i++ )
    {        strcat ( szCmdLine , argv[ i ] ) ;
```

Listing 4-2 *MINDBG.CPP*   *(continued)*

Listing 4-2 *continued*

```
    if ( i < argc )
    {
        strcat ( szCmdLine , " " ) ;
    }
}

// Try to start the debuggee process. The function call looks
// like a normal CreateProcess call except for the special start
// option flag DEBUG_ONLY_THIS_PROCESS.
STARTUPINFO         stStartInfo    ;
PROCESS_INFORMATION stProcessInfo  ;

memset ( &stStartInfo   , NULL , sizeof ( STARTUPINFO         ) ) ;
memset ( &stProcessInfo , NULL , sizeof ( PROCESS_INFORMATION ) ) ;

stStartInfo.cb = sizeof ( STARTUPINFO ) ;

BOOL bRet = CreateProcess ( NULL                          ,
                            szCmdLine                     ,
                            NULL                          ,
                            NULL                          ,
                            FALSE                         ,
                            CREATE_NEW_CONSOLE |
                              DEBUG_ONLY_THIS_PROCESS ,
                            NULL                          ,
                            NULL                          ,
                            &stStartInfo                  ,
                            &stProcessInfo            ) ;

// See whether the debuggee process started.
if ( FALSE == bRet )
{
    printf ( "Unable to start %s\n" , szCmdLine ) ;
    return ;
}

// The debuggee started, so let's enter the debug loop.
DEBUG_EVENT stDE                        ;
BOOL        bSeenInitialBP  = FALSE ;
BOOL        bContinue       = TRUE  ;
HANDLE      hProcess        = INVALID_HANDLE_VALUE ;
DWORD       dwContinueStatus            ;

// Loop until told to stop.
while ( TRUE == bContinue )
```

```
{
        // Pause until a debug event notification happens.
        bContinue = WaitForDebugEvent ( &stDE , INFINITE ) ;

        // Handle the particular debug events. Because MinDBG is only a
        // minimal debugger, it handles only a few events.
        switch ( stDE.dwDebugEventCode )
        {
            case CREATE_PROCESS_DEBUG_EVENT   :
            {
                DisplayCreateProcessEvent ( stDE.u.CreateProcessInfo ) ;
                // Save the handle information needed for later.
                hProcess = stDE.u.CreateProcessInfo.hProcess ;
                dwContinueStatus = DBG_CONTINUE ;
            }
            break ;
            case EXIT_PROCESS_DEBUG_EVENT   :
            {
                DisplayExitProcessEvent ( stDE.u.ExitProcess ) ;
                bContinue = FALSE ;
                dwContinueStatus = DBG_CONTINUE ;
            }
            break ;

            case LOAD_DLL_DEBUG_EVENT     :
            {
                DisplayDllLoadEvent ( stDE.u.LoadDll ) ;
                dwContinueStatus = DBG_CONTINUE ;
            }
            break ;
            case UNLOAD_DLL_DEBUG_EVENT   :
            {
                DisplayDllUnLoadEvent ( stDE.u.UnloadDll ) ;
                dwContinueStatus = DBG_CONTINUE ;
            }
            break ;

            case CREATE_THREAD_DEBUG_EVENT  :
            {
                DisplayCreateThreadEvent ( stDE.u.CreateThread ) ;
                dwContinueStatus = DBG_CONTINUE ;
            }
            break ;
            case EXIT_THREAD_DEBUG_EVENT     :
            {
```

(continued)

Listing 4-2 *continued*

```
            DisplayExitThreadEvent ( stDE.u.ExitThread ) ;
            dwContinueStatus = DBG_CONTINUE ;
    }
    break ;

    case OUTPUT_DEBUG_STRING_EVENT  :
    {
        DisplayODSEvent ( hProcess , stDE.u.DebugString ) ;
        dwContinueStatus = DBG_CONTINUE ;
    }
    break ;
    case RIP_EVENT  :
    {
        dwContinueStatus = DBG_CONTINUE ;
    }
    break ;

    case EXCEPTION_DEBUG_EVENT        :
    {
        DisplayExceptionEvent ( stDE.u.Exception ) ;

        // The only exception that I have to treat specially is
        // the initial breakpoint the loader provides.
        switch ( stDE.u.Exception.ExceptionRecord.ExceptionCode )
        {
            case EXCEPTION_BREAKPOINT :
            {

                // If a breakpoint exception occurs and it's the
                // first seen, I continue on my merry way;
                // otherwise, I pass the exception on to the
                // debuggee.
                if ( FALSE == bSeenInitialBP )
                {
                    bSeenInitialBP = TRUE ;
                    dwContinueStatus = DBG_CONTINUE ;
                }
                else
                {
                    // Houston, we have a problem!
                    dwContinueStatus =
                                    DBG_EXCEPTION_NOT_HANDLED ;
                }
            }
            break ;
```

```
                            // Just pass on any other exceptions to the
                            // debuggee.
                            default :
                            {
                                dwContinueStatus = DBG_EXCEPTION_NOT_HANDLED ;
                            }
                            break ;
                    }
            }
            break ;

            // For any other events, just continue on.
            default :
            {
                dwContinueStatus = DBG_CONTINUE ;
            }
            break ;
    }

    // Pass on to the operating system.
    ContinueDebugEvent ( stDE.dwProcessId ,
                         stDE.dwThreadId  ,
                         dwContinueStatus ) ;

    }
}

/*//////////////////////////////////////////////////////////////////////
////////////////////////////////////////////////////////////////////////*/
void ShowHelp ( void )
{
    printf ( "MinDBG <program to debug> "
             "<program's command-line options>\n" ) ;
}


void DisplayCreateProcessEvent ( CREATE_PROCESS_DEBUG_INFO & stCPDI )
{
    printf ( "Create Process Event     :\n" ) ;
    printf ( "    hFile                 : 0x%08X\n" ,
             stCPDI.hFile                          ) ;
    printf ( "    hProcess              : 0x%08X\n" ,
             stCPDI.hProcess                       ) ;
    printf ( "    hThread               : 0x%08X\n" ,
             stCPDI.hThread                        ) ;
```

(continued)

Listing 4-2 *continued*

```
    printf ( "    lpBaseOfImage          : 0x%08X\n" ,
             stCPDI.lpBaseOfImage                    ) ;
    printf ( "    dwDebugInfoFileOffset  : 0x%08X\n" ,
             stCPDI.dwDebugInfoFileOffset            ) ;
    printf ( "    nDebugInfoSize         : 0x%08X\n" ,
             stCPDI.nDebugInfoSize                   ) ;
    printf ( "    lpThreadLocalBase      : 0x%08X\n" ,
             stCPDI.lpThreadLocalBase                ) ;
    printf ( "    lpStartAddress         : 0x%08X\n" ,
             stCPDI.lpStartAddress                   ) ;
    printf ( "    lpImageName            : 0x%08X\n" ,
             stCPDI.lpImageName                      ) ;
    printf ( "    fUnicode               : 0x%08X\n" ,
             stCPDI.fUnicode                         ) ;
}

void DisplayCreateThreadEvent ( CREATE_THREAD_DEBUG_INFO & stCTDI )
{
    printf ( "Create Thread Event      :\n" ) ;
    printf ( "    hThread               : 0x%08X\n" ,
             stCTDI.hThread                          ) ;
    printf ( "    lpThreadLocalBase     : 0x%08X\n" ,
             stCTDI.lpThreadLocalBase                ) ;
    printf ( "    lpStartAddress        : 0x%08X\n" ,
             stCTDI.lpStartAddress                   ) ;
}

void DisplayExitThreadEvent ( EXIT_THREAD_DEBUG_INFO & stETDI )
{
    printf ( "Exit Thread Event         :\n" ) ;
    printf ( "    dwExitCode            : 0x%08X\n" ,
             stETDI.dwExitCode                       ) ;
}

void DisplayExitProcessEvent ( EXIT_PROCESS_DEBUG_INFO & stEPDI )
{
    printf ( "Exit Process Event       :\n" ) ;
    printf ( "    dwExitCode            : 0x%08X\n" ,
             stEPDI.dwExitCode                       ) ;
}

void DisplayDllLoadEvent ( LOAD_DLL_DEBUG_INFO & stLDDI )
{
    printf ( "DLL Load Event           :\n" ) ;
    printf ( "    hFile                 : 0x%08X\n" ,
```

```
                    stLDDI.hFile                          ) ;
    printf ( "    lpBaseOfDll          : 0x%08X\n" ,
             stLDDI.lpBaseOfDll                           ) ;
    printf ( "    dwDebugInfoFileOffset : 0x%08X\n" ,
             stLDDI.dwDebugInfoFileOffset                 ) ;
    printf ( "    nDebugInfoSize       : 0x%08X\n" ,
             stLDDI.nDebugInfoSize                        ) ;
    printf ( "    lpImageName          : 0x%08X\n" ,
             stLDDI.lpImageName                           ) ;
    printf ( "    fUnicode             : 0x%08X\n" ,
             stLDDI.fUnicode                              ) ;
}

void DisplayDllUnLoadEvent ( UNLOAD_DLL_DEBUG_INFO & stULDDI )
{
    printf ( "DLL Unload Event        :\n" ) ;
    printf ( "    lpBaseOfDll          : 0x%08X\n" ,
             stULDDI.lpBaseOfDll                          ) ;
}

void DisplayODSEvent ( HANDLE                    hProcess ,
                       OUTPUT_DEBUG_STRING_INFO & stODSI    )
{
    printf ( "OutputDebugString Event    :\n" ) ;
    printf ( "    lpDebugStringData    : 0x%08X\n" ,
             stODSI.lpDebugStringData                     ) ;
    printf ( "    fUnicode             : 0x%08X\n" ,
             stODSI.fUnicode                              ) ;
    printf ( "    nDebugStringLength   : 0x%08X\n" ,
             stODSI.nDebugStringLength                    ) ;
    printf ( "    String               :\n" ) ;

    char szBuff[ 512 ] ;
    if ( stODSI.nDebugStringLength > 512 )
    {
        return ;
    }

    DWORD dwRead ;
    BOOL bRet ;
    bRet = ReadProcessMemory ( hProcess                  ,
                               stODSI.lpDebugStringData   ,
                               szBuff                     ,
                               stODSI.nDebugStringLength  ,
                               &dwRead                    ) ;
```

(continued)

Listing 4-2 *continued*

```
    printf ( "%s" , szBuff ) ;
}
void DisplayExceptionEvent ( EXCEPTION_DEBUG_INFO & stEDI )
{
    printf ( "Exception Event                :\n" ) ;
    printf ( "    dwFirstChance             : 0x%08X\n" ,
            stEDI.dwFirstChance                        ) ;
    printf ( "    ExceptionCode             : 0x%08X\n" ,
            stEDI.ExceptionRecord.ExceptionCode        ) ;
    printf ( "    ExceptionFlags            : 0x%08X\n" ,
            stEDI.ExceptionRecord.ExceptionFlags       ) ;
    printf ( "    ExceptionRecord           : 0x%08X\n" ,
            stEDI.ExceptionRecord.ExceptionRecord      ) ;
    printf ( "    ExceptionAddress          : 0x%08X\n" ,
            stEDI.ExceptionRecord.ExceptionAddress     ) ;
    printf ( "    NumberParameters          : 0x%08X\n" ,
            stEDI.ExceptionRecord.NumberParameters     ) ;
}
```

WDBG: A REAL DEBUGGER

I thought the best way to show you how a debugger worked was to write one, so I did. Although WDBG might not replace the Visual C++ debugger any time soon, it certainly does most of the things a debugger is supposed to do. If you look at Figure 4-2, you'll see WDBG debugging Microsoft Word. In the figure, Word is stopped at a breakpoint I set on *GetProcAddress*. The Memory window, the one in the upper right-hand corner, is showing the second parameter that Word passed to this particular instance of *GetProcAddress*, the string *PHevCreateFileInfo*. As you look around Figure 4-2, you'll see that WDBG takes care of the business you'd expect a debugger to tend to, including showing registers, viewing call stacks, disassembling code, and showing the currently loaded modules and the currently running threads. What you don't see in the picture but what will become apparent when you first run WDBG is that WDBG also supports breakpoints, symbol enumeration, and breaking the application to stop in the debugger.

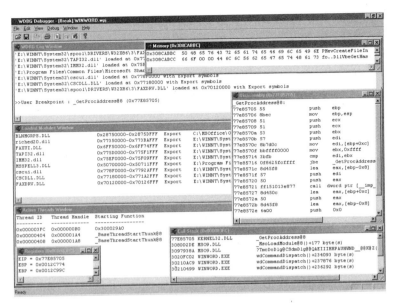

Figure 4-2 *WDBG in action*

Overall, I'm happy with WDBG because it's a good sample. Looking at the WDBG user interface (UI), however, you can see that I didn't spend a great deal of time fiddling with the UI portions. In fact, all the multiple-document interface (MDI) windows in WDBG are edit controls. That was intentional—I kept the UI simple because I didn't want UI details to distract you from the essential debugger code. I wrote the WDBG UI using the Microsoft Foundation Class (MFC) library, so if you're so inclined, you shouldn't have any trouble designing a spiffier UI.

Before moving into the specifics of debugging, let's take a closer look at WDBG. Table 4-2 lists all the main subsystems of WDBG and describes what they do. One of my intentions in creating WDBG was to define a neutral interface between the UI and the debug loop. With a neutral interface, if I wanted to make WDBG.EXE support remote debugging over a network, I'd just have to replace the local debugging DLLs.

Table 4-2   **WDBG MAIN SUBSYSTEMS**

Subsystem	Description
WDBG.EXE	This module contains all the UI code. Additionally, all the breakpoint processing is taken care of here. Most of this debugger's work occurs in WDBGPROJDOC.CPP.
LOCALDEBUG.DLL	This module contains the debug loop. Because I wanted to be able to reuse this debug loop, the user code, WDBG.EXE in this case, passes a C++ class derived from *CDebugBaseUser* (defined in DEBUGINTERFACE.H) to the debug loop. The debug loop will call into that class when any of the debugging events occurs. The user's class is responsible for all synchronization. For WDBG.EXE, WDBGUSER.H and WDBGUSER.CPP contain the coordinating class. WDBG.EXE uses simple *SendMessage* synchronization. In other words, the debug thread sends a message to the UI thread and blocks until the UI thread returns. If the debugging event is one that required user input, the debug thread blocks after the send message on a synchronization event. Once the UI thread processes the Go command, it sets the synchronization event and the debug thread starts running again.
LOCALASSIST.DLL	This simple module is just a wrapper around the API functions for manipulating the debuggee's memory and registers. By using the interface defined in this module, WDBG.EXE and I386CPUHELP.DLL can instantly handle remote debugging just by replacing this module.
I386CPUHELP.DLL	This module is the IA32 (Pentium) helper module. Although this module is specific to Pentium processors, its interface, defined in CPUHELP.H, is CPU-independent. If you wanted to port WDBG to a different processor, this module is the only one you should have to replace. The disassembler in this module came from the Dr. Watson sample code that ships on the Platform SDK. Although the disassembler works, it appears to need updating to support the later Pentium CPU variants.

Reading and Writing Memory

Reading from a debuggee's memory is simple. *ReadProcessMemory* takes care of it for you. A debugger has full access to the debuggee if the debugger started it because the handle to the process returned by the *CREATE_PROCESS_DEBUG_EVENT* debug event has *PROCESS_VM_READ* and *PROCESS_VM_WRITE* access. If your debugger attaches to the process with *DebugActiveProcess*, you must use *OpenProcess* to get a handle to the debuggee, and you need to specify both read and write access.

Before I can talk about writing to the debuggee's memory, I need to briefly explain an important concept: copy-on-write. When Windows loads an executable file, Windows shares as many mapped memory pages of that binary as possible with the different processes using it. If one of those processes is running under a debugger and one of those pages has a breakpoint written to it, the breakpoint obviously can't be present in all the processes sharing that page. As soon as any process running outside the debugger executed that code, it would crash with a breakpoint exception. To avoid that situation, the operating system sees that the page changed for a particular process and makes a copy of that page that is private to the process that had the breakpoint written to it. Thus, as soon as a process writes to a page, the operating system copies the page.

Writing to the debuggee memory is almost as straightforward as reading from it. Because the memory pages you want to write to might be marked as read-only, however, you first need to call *VirtualQueryEx* to get the current page protections. Once you have the protections, you can use the *VirtualProtectEx* API function to set the page to *PAGE_EXECUTE_READWRITE* so that you can write to it and Windows is prepared to do the copy-on-write. After you do the memory write, you'll need to set the page protection back to what it originally was. If you don't, the debuggee might accidentally write to the page and succeed when it should fail. If the original page protections were read-only, the debuggee's accidental write would lead to an access violation. By forgetting to set the page protection back, the accidental write wouldn't generate the exception and you'd have a case in which running under the debugger is different from running outside the debugger.

An interesting detail about the Win32 Debugging API is that the debugger is responsible for getting the string to output when an *OUTPUT_DEBUG_STRING_EVENT* comes through. The information passed to the debugger includes the location and the length of the string. When it receives this message, the debugger goes and reads the memory out of the debuggee. In Chapter 3, I mentioned that trace statements could easily change your application's behavior when running under a debugger. Because all threads in the application stop when the debug loop is processing an event, calling *OutputDebugString* in the debuggee means that all your threads stop. Listing 4-3 shows how WDBG handles the *OUTPUT_DEBUG_STRING_EVENT*. Notice that the *DBG_ReadProcessMemory* function is the wrapper function around *ReadProcessMemory* from LOCALASSIST.DLL.

```
static
DWORD OutputDebugStringEvent ( CDebugBaseUser *            pUserClass   ,
                               LPDEBUGGEEINFO             pData         ,
                               DWORD                      dwProcessId .
                               DWORD                      dwThreadId   ,
                               OUTPUT_DEBUG_STRING_INFO & stODSI       )
{
    TCHAR szBuff[ 512 ] ;

    HANDLE hProc = pData->GetProcessHandle ( ) ;

    DWORD dwRead ;

    // Read the memory.
    BOOL bRet = DBG_ReadProcessMemory( hProc                              ,
                                       stODSI.lpDebugStringData           ,
                                       szBuff ,
                                       min ( sizeof ( szBuff )            ,
                                             stODSI.nDebugStringLength ),
                                       &dwRead                          );
    ASSERT ( TRUE == bRet ) ;
    if ( TRUE == bRet )
    {
        // Always NULL terminate the string.
        szBuff [ dwRead + 1 ] = _T ( '\0' ) ;
        // Convert CR/LFs if I'm supposed to.
        pUserClass->ConvertCRLF ( szBuff , sizeof ( szBuff ) ) ;
        // Send the converted string on to the user class.
        pUserClass->OutputDebugStringEvent ( dwProcessId ,
                                             dwThreadId  ,
                                             szBuff      ) ;
    }

    return ( DBG_CONTINUE ) ;
}
```

Listing 4-3 OutputDebugStringEvent *from PROCESSDEBUGEVENTS.CPP*

Breakpoints and Single Stepping

Most engineers don't realize that debuggers use breakpoints extensively behind the scenes to allow the debugger to control the debuggee. Although you might not directly set any breakpoints, the debugger will set many to allow you to handle tasks such as stepping over a function call. The debugger also uses breakpoints when you choose to run to a specific source file line and stop. Finally, the debugger uses breakpoints to break into the debuggee on command (via the Debug Break menu option in WDBG, for example).

The concept of setting a breakpoint is simple. All you need to do is have a memory address where you want to set a breakpoint, save the opcode (the value) at that location, and write the breakpoint instruction into the address. On the Intel Pentium family, the breakpoint instruction mnemonic is "INT 3" or an opcode of 0xCC, so you need to save only a single byte at the address you're setting the breakpoint. Other CPUs, such as the Intel Merced, have different opcode sizes, so you would need to save more data at the address.

Listing 4-4 shows the code for the *SetBreakpoint* function. As you read through this code, keep in mind that the *DBG_** functions are those that come out of LOCALASSIST.DLL and help isolate the various process manipulation routines, making it easier to add remote debugging to WDBG. The *SetBreakpoint* function illustrates the processing (described earlier in the chapter) necessary for changing memory protection when you're writing to it.

```
int CPUHELP_DLLINTERFACE __stdcall
    SetBreakpoint ( PDEBUGPACKET dp        ,
                    ULONG         ulAddr   ,
                    OPCODE *      pOpCode   )
{
    DWORD dwReadWrite = 0 ;
    BYTE bTempOp = BREAK_OPCODE ;
    BOOL bReadMem ;
    BOOL bWriteMem ;
    BOOL bFlush ;
    MEMORY_BASIC_INFORMATION mbi ;
    DWORD dwOldProtect ;


    ASSERT ( FALSE == IsBadReadPtr ( dp , sizeof ( DEBUGPACKET ) ) ) ;
    ASSERT ( FALSE == IsBadWritePtr ( pOpCode , sizeof ( OPCODE ) ) ) ;
    if ( ( TRUE == IsBadReadPtr ( dp , sizeof ( DEBUGPACKET ) ) ) ||
         ( TRUE == IsBadWritePtr ( pOpCode , sizeof ( OPCODE ) ) )   )
    {
        TRACE0 ( "SetBreakpoint : invalid parameters\n!" ) ;
        return ( FALSE ) ;
    }

    // If the operating system is Windows 98 and the address is above
    // 2 GB, just leave quietly.
```

Listing 4-4 SetBreakpoint *from I386CPUHELP.C*   *(continued)*

Listing 4-4 *continued*

```
    if ( ( FALSE == IsNT ( ) ) && ( ulAddr >= 0x80000000 ) )
    {
        return ( FALSE ) ;
    }
    // Read the opcode at the location.
    bReadMem = DBG_ReadProcessMemory ( dp->hProcess   ,
                                       (LPCVOID)ulAddr ,
                                       &bTempOp        ,
                                       sizeof ( BYTE ) ,
                                       &dwReadWrite    ) ;
    ASSERT ( FALSE != bReadMem ) ;
    ASSERT ( sizeof ( BYTE ) == dwReadWrite ) ;
    if ( ( FALSE == bReadMem                ) ||
         ( sizeof ( BYTE ) != dwReadWrite ) )
    {
        return ( FALSE ) ;
    }

    // Is this new breakpoint about to overwrite an existing
    // breakpoint opcode?
    if ( BREAK_OPCODE == bTempOp )
    {
        return ( -1 ) ;
    }

    // Get the page attributes for the debuggee.
    DBG_VirtualQueryEx ( dp->hProcess
                         (LPCVOID)ulAddr
                         &mbi
                         sizeof ( MEMORY_BASIC_INFORMATION )  ) ;

    // Force the page to copy-on-write in the debuggee.
    if ( FALSE == DBG_VirtualProtectEx ( dp->hProcess
                                         mbi.BaseAddress      ,
                                         mbi.RegionSize       ,
                                         PAGE_EXECUTE_READWRITE ,
                                         &mbi.Protect         ) )
    {
        ASSERT ( !"VirtualProtectEx failed!!" ) ;
        return ( FALSE ) ;
    }
```

```
        // Save the opcode I'm about to whack.
        *pOpCode = (void*)bTempOp ;

        bTempOp = BREAK_OPCODE ;
        dwReadWrite = 0 ;
        // The opcode was saved, so now set the breakpoint.
        bWriteMem = DBG_WriteProcessMemory ( dp->hProcess    ,
                                             (LPVOID)ulAddr   ,
                                             (LPVOID)&bTempOp ,
                                             sizeof ( BYTE )  ,
                                             &dwReadWrite        ) ;
        ASSERT ( FALSE != bWriteMem ) ;
        ASSERT ( sizeof ( BYTE ) == dwReadWrite ) ;


        if ( ( FALSE == bWriteMem              ) ||
             ( sizeof ( BYTE ) != dwReadWrite ) )
        {
            return ( FALSE ) ;
        }

        // Change the protection back to what it was before I blasted the
        // breakpoint in.
        VERIFY ( DBG_VirtualProtectEx ( dp->hProcess     ,
                                        mbi.BaseAddress ,
                                        mbi.RegionSize  ,
                                        mbi.Protect     ,
                                        &dwOldProtect    ) ) ;

        // Flush the instruction cache in case this memory was in the CPU
        // cache.
        bFlush = DBG_FlushInstructionCache ( dp->hProcess    ,
                                             (LPCVOID)ulAddr ,
                                             sizeof ( BYTE ) ) ;

        ASSERT ( TRUE == bFlush ) ;

        return ( TRUE ) ;
}
```

After you set the breakpoint, the CPU will execute it and will tell the debugger that an *EXCEPTION_BREAKPOINT* (0x80000003) occurred—that's where the fun begins. If it's a regular breakpoint, the debugger will locate and display the break-point location to the user. After the user decides to continue execution, the debugger has to do some work to restore the state of the program. Because the breakpoint overwrote a portion of memory, if you, as the debugger writer, were to just let the process continue, you would be executing code out of sequence and the debuggee would probably crash. What you need to do is to move the current instruction pointer back to the breakpoint address and replace the breakpoint with the opcode you saved when you set the breakpoint. After restoring the opcode, you can continue executing.

There's only one small problem: How do you reset the breakpoint so that you can stop at that location again? If the CPU you're working on supports single-step execution, resetting the breakpoint is trivial. In single-step execution, the CPU executes a single instruction and generates another type of exception, *EXCEPTION-_SINGLE_STEP* (0x80000004). Fortunately, all CPUs that Win32 runs on support single-step execution. For the Intel Pentium family, setting single-step execution requires that you set bit 8 on the flags register. The Intel reference manual calls this bit the TF, or Trap Flag. The code in Listing 4-5 shows the *SetSingleStep* function and the work needed to set the TF. After replacing the breakpoint with the original opcode, the debugger marks its internal state to reflect that it's expecting a single-step exception, sets the CPU into single-step execution, and then continues the process.

```
BOOL CPUHELP_DLLIMNTERFACE __stdcall
    SetSingleStep ( PDEBUGPACKET dp )
{
    BOOL bSetContext ;
    ASSERT ( FALSE == IsBadReadPtr ( dp , sizeof ( DEBUGPACKET ) ) ) ;
    if ( TRUE == IsBadReadPtr ( dp , sizeof ( DEBUGPACKET ) ) )
    {
        TRACE0 ( "SetSingleStep : invalid parameters\n!" ) ;
        return ( FALSE ) ;
    }

    // For the i386, just set the TF bit.
    dp->context.EFlags |= TF_BIT ;
    bSetContext = DBG_SetThreadContext ( dp->hThread , &dp->context ) ;
    ASSERT ( FALSE != bSetContext ) ;
    return ( bSetContext ) ;
}
```

Listing 4-5 SetSingleStep *function from I386CPUHELP.C*

After the debugger releases the process by calling *ContinueDebugEvent*, the process immediately generates a single-step exception after the single instruction executes. The debugger checks its internal state to verify that it was expecting a single-step exception. Because the debugger was expecting a single-step exception, it knows that a breakpoint needs to be reset. The single step caused the instruction pointer to move past the original breakpoint location. Therefore, the debugger can set the breakpoint opcode back at the original breakpoint location. The operating system automatically clears the TF each time the *EXCEPTION_SINGLE_STEP* exception occurs, so there's no need for the debugger to clear it. After setting the breakpoint, the debugger releases the debuggee to continue running.

If you want to see all the breakpoint processing in action, look for the *CWDBGProjDoc::HandleBreakpoint* method in the WDBGPROJDOC.CPP file on the companion CD. I defined the breakpoints themselves in BREAKPOINT.H and BREAKPOINT.CPP, and those files contain a couple of classes that handle different styles of breakpoints. I set up the WDBG Breakpoints dialog box so that you could set breakpoints as the debuggee is running, just as you do in the Visual C++ debugger. Being able to set breakpoints on the fly means that you need to keep careful track of the debuggee state and the breakpoint states. See the *CBreakpointsDlg::OnOK* method in BREAKPOINTSDLG.CPP on the companion CD for details on how I handle enabling and disabling breakpoints, depending on what the debuggee state is.

One of the neater features I implemented in WDBG was the Debug Break menu option. This option means that you can break into the debugger at any time while the debuggee is running. Although WDBG uses the breakpoint operations described earlier in the chapter, the breakpoints used to implement the Debug Break option are referred to as *one-shot breakpoints* because the breakpoints are removed just as soon as they trigger. Getting those one-shot breakpoints set is pretty interesting. The full details are in *CWDBGProjDoc::OnDebugBreak* in WDBGPROJDOC.CPP, but I'll go into greater detail here because I think you'll find the explanation enlightening. Listing 4-6 shows the *CWDBGProjDoc::OnDebugBreak* function from WDBGPROJDOC.CPP. (To find out more about one-shot breakpoints, see the section "Step Into, Step Over, and Step Out" later in this chapter.)

```
void CWDBGProjDoc :: OnDebugBreak ( )
{
    // Just for my own peace of mind.
    ASSERT ( m_vDbgThreads.size ( ) > 0 ) ;

    // The idea here is to get all the debuggee's threads suspended and
    // set a breakpoint at the current instruction pointer for each.
```

Listing 4-6 *Debug Break processing in WDBGPROJDOC.CPP*   *(continued)*

Listing 4-6 *continued*

```
// That way, I can guarantee that at least one of the threads
// will trip the one-shot breakpoints.
// One situation in which setting a breakpoint on each thread
// won't work is when an application is hung. Because no
// threads are turning over, the breakpoints never get called.
// To make the deadlock case work, I'd need to use an algorithm such
// as the following:
// 1. Set the breakpoints as this function does.
// 2. Set a state flag indicating that I'm waiting on a Debug Break
//    breakpoint.
// 3. Set a background timer to wait for the breakpoint.
// 4. If one of the breakpoints goes off, clear the timer. Life is
//    good.
// 5. If the timer goes off, the application is hung.
// 6. After the timer, set the instruction pointer of one of the
//    threads to another address and put a breakpoint at that
//    address.
// 7. Restart the thread.
// 8. When this special breakpoint fires, clear the breakpoint and
//    reset the instruction pointer back to the original location.
// To avoid problems, I'll boost the priority of this thread so
// that I get through setting these breakpoints as fast as possible
// and keep any of the debuggee's threads from being scheduled.
HANDLE hThisThread = GetCurrentThread ( ) ;
int iOldPriority = GetThreadPriority ( hThisThread ) ;
SetThreadPriority ( hThisThread , THREAD_BASE_PRIORITY_LOWRT ) ;

HANDLE hProc = GetDebuggeeProcessHandle ( ) ;

DBGTHREADVECT::iterator i ;

for ( i  = m_vDbgThreads.begin ( ) ;
      i != m_vDbgThreads.end ( )   ;
      i++                          )
{
    // Suspend this thread. If it has a suspend count already, I
    // don't really care. That's why I set a breakpoint on each
    // thread in the debuggee. I'll hit an active one eventually.
    DBG_SuspendThread ( i->m_hThread ) ;

    // Now that the thread is suspended, I can get the context.
    CONTEXT ctx ;
    ctx.ContextFlags = CONTEXT_FULL ;
```

```
        // If GetThreadContext fails, I have to handle the error message
        // carefully. Because this thread's priority is set to real-time,
        // if I use an ASSERT, the computer might hang on the message
        // box, so in the else statement, I can indicate the error only
        // with a trace statement.
        if ( FALSE != DBG_GetThreadContext ( i->m_hThread , &ctx ) )
        {
            // Find the address that the instruction pointer is about to
            // execute. That address is where I'll set the breakpoint.
            DWORD dwAddr = ReturnInstructionPointer ( &ctx ) ;

            COneShotBP cBP ;

            // Set the breakpoint.
            cBP.SetBreakpointLocation ( dwAddr ) ;

            // Arm it.
            if ( TRUE == cBP.ArmBreakpoint ( hProc ) )
            {
                // Add this breakpoint to the Debug Break list only if
                // the breakpoint was successfully armed. The debuggee
                // could easily have multiple threads sitting on the
                // same instruction, so I want only one breakpoint set
                // on that address.
                m_aDebugBreakBPs.Add ( cBP ) ;
            }
        }
        else
        {
            TRACE ( "GetThreadContext failed! Last Error = 0x%08X\n" ,
                    GetLastError ( ) ) ;
#ifdef _DEBUG
            // Because GetThreadContext failed, I probably need to take a
            // look at what happened. Therefore, I'll pop into the
            // the debugger debugging the WDBG debugger. Even though
            // the WDBG thread is running at a real-time priority level,
            // calling DebugBreak will immediately pull this thread out
            // of the operating system scheduler, so the priority drops.
            DebugBreak ( ) ;
#endif
        }
    }

    // All the threads have breakpoints set. Now I'll restart them all
```

(continued)

Listing 4-6 *continued*

```
// and post a thread message to each one. The reason for posting
// the thread message is simple. If the debuggee is chugging away
// on messages or other processing, it will break immediately.
// However, if it's just idling in a message loop, I need to give it
// a tickle to force it into action. Because I have the thread ID,
// I'll just send the thread a WM_NULL message. WM_NULL is supposed
// to be a benign message, so it shouldn't screw up the debuggee. If
// the thread doesn't have a message queue, this function just fails
// for that thread with no harm done.

for ( i  = m_vDbgThreads.begin ( ) ;
      i != m_vDbgThreads.end ( )   ;
      i++                          )
{
    // Let this thread resume so that it hits the breakpoint.
    DBG_ResumeThread ( i->m_hThread ) ;
    PostThreadMessage ( i->m_dwTID , WM_NULL , 0 , 0 ) ;
}

// Now drop the priority back down.
SetThreadPriority ( hThisThread , iOldPriority ) ;
}
```

When you want to stop a debuggee that's churning like mad, you need to get a breakpoint jammed into the CPU instruction stream so that you can stop in the debugger. The question is, What do you need to do to get the instruction in there? If a thread is running, the only thing you can do to get it to a known point is to suspend it by using the *SuspendThread* API function. Once the thread is suspended, you can look at it with the *GetThreadContext* API function and determine the current instruction pointer. Once you have the instruction pointer, you're back to setting simple breakpoints. After you set the breakpoint, you need to call the *ResumeThread* API function so that you can let the thread continue execution and have it hit your breakpoint.

Although breaking into the debugger is fairly simple, you still need to think about a couple of issues. The first issue is that your breakpoint might not trigger. If the debuggee is processing a message or doing some other work, it will break. If the debuggee is sitting there waiting for a message to arrive, however, the breakpoint won't trigger until the debuggee receives a message. Although you could require the user to move the mouse over the debuggee to generate a *WM_MOUSEMOVE* message, the user might not be too happy about this requirement.

To ensure that the debuggee reaches your breakpoint, you need to send a message to the debuggee. If all you have is a thread handle given to you by the Debugging API, how do you turn the handle into the appropriate *HWND*? Unfortunately, you can't. However, because you have the thread handle, you can always call *PostThreadMessage*, which will post a message to the thread message queue. Because the *HWND* message processing layers on top of the thread message queue, calling *PostThreadMessage* does exactly what you need it to do.

The only question then becomes, What message do I post? You don't want to post a message that could cause the debuggee to do any real processing, thus allowing the debugger to change the behavior of the debuggee. For example, posting a *WM_CREATE* message probably wouldn't be a good idea. Fortunately, the *WM_NULL* message is supposed to be a benign message and is what you're supposed to use in hooks if you change a message. It does no harm to post the *WM_NULL* message with *PostThreadMessage* even if the thread doesn't have a message queue. And if the thread doesn't have a message queue, such as in a console application, calling *PostThreadMessage* doesn't do any damage. Because console-based applications will always be processing, even if waiting for a keystroke, setting the breakpoint at the current executing instruction will cause the break.

Another issue involves multithreading. If you're going to suspend only a single thread and the application is multithreaded, how do you know which thread to suspend? If you suspend and set the breakpoint in the wrong thread, say one that is blocked waiting on an event that is signaled only when background printing occurs, your breakpoint might never go off unless the user decides to print something. If you want to break on a multithreaded application, the only safe course is to suspend all the threads and set a breakpoint in each one.

Suspending all the threads and setting a breakpoint in each one works just great on an application that has only two threads. If you want to break on an application that has many threads, however, you could leave yourself open to a problem. As you're walking through and suspending each of the debuggee's threads, you're changing the state of the application such that it's possible for you to cause the application to deadlock. To get all the threads suspended, the breakpoints set, and the threads resumed without causing problems, the debugger needs to boost its own thread priority. By boosting the priority to *THREAD_BASE_PRIORITY_LOWRT*, the debugger can have its thread stay scheduled so that the debuggee's threads don't execute as the debugger manipulates them.

So far, my algorithm for breaking in a multithreaded application sounds reasonable. However, the debugger still needs to deal with one last issue to make the Debug Break option work completely. If you have all the breakpoints set in all the threads and you resume the threads, you still face one situation in which the break won't happen. By setting the breakpoints, you're relying on at least one of the threads to execute in order to trigger the breakpoint exception. What do you think happens if the process is in a deadlock situation? Nothing happens—no threads execute and your carefully positioned breakpoints never trigger the exception.

I told you the Debug Break business gets interesting. When you're breaking in a deadlock, you need to set up a timer to mark when you added the break. After your period of time elapses (the Visual C++ debugger uses 3 seconds), you need to take some drastic action. When the Debug Break option times out, you'll need to set one of the thread's instruction pointers to another address, set a breakpoint at that new address, and restart the thread. When that special breakpoint fires, you need to set the thread instruction pointer back to its original location. In WDBG, I didn't implement the anti-deadlock processing, but I left the implementation as an exercise for you in the *CWDBGProjDoc::OnDebugBreak* function in WDBGPROJDOC.CPP on the companion CD. The complete infrastructure is in place to handle the anti-deadlock processing, and it would probably take no more than a couple hours to put in. By the time you had it implemented, you'd have a good idea how WDBG works.

Symbol Tables, Symbol Engines, and Stack Walking

The real black art to writing a debugger involves symbol engines, the code that manipulates symbol tables. Debugging at the straight assembly-language level is interesting for the first couple of minutes you have to do it, but it gets old quickly. Symbol tables, also called debugging symbols, are what turn hexadecimal numbers into source file lines, function names, and variable names. Symbol tables also contain the type information your program uses. This type information allows the debugger to take raw data and display it as the structures and variables you defined in your program. Dealing with modern symbol tables is difficult because the most commonly used format, Program Database (PDB), is undocumented and its owners don't plan to document it anytime soon. Fortunately, you can get at least partial access to the symbol tables.

The Different Symbol Formats

Before diving into a discussion of accessing symbol tables, I need to go over the various symbol formats available. I've found that people are a little confused about what the different formats are and what they offer, so I want to set the record straight.

The first format, SYM, is an older format that used to be common in the MS-DOS and 16-bit Windows days. The only current use of SYM is for the debugging symbols for Windows 98; the SYM format is used here because most of the core kernel is still 16-bit code. WDEB386 is the only debugger actively using them.

Common Object File Format (COFF) was one of the original symbol table formats and was introduced with Windows NT 3.1, the first version of Windows NT. The Windows NT team was experienced with operating system development and wanted to bootstrap Windows NT with some existing tools. The COFF format is part of a larger specification that different UNIX vendors followed to try to make common binary file formats. Although the whole COFF symbol specification is in WINNT.H, the only parts generated by the Microsoft tools are public functions and global variables. Microsoft used to support source and line information but has been gradually moving away from the COFF format in favor of more modern symbol table formats.

The C7, or CodeView, format first appeared as part of Microsoft C/C++ version 7 back in the MS-DOS days. If you're an old timer, you might have heard the name CodeView before—CodeView was the name of the old Microsoft debugger. The C7 format has been updated to support the Win32 operating systems, and you can still generate this format by using the /Z7 command-line switch to CL.EXE or by selecting C7 Compatible from the Debug Info drop-down list on the C/C++ tab of the Project Settings dialog box. On the Link tab of the Project Settings dialog box, uncheck Use Program Database in the Customize category to turn on the /PDB:NONE linker switch. WinDBG and the Visual C++ debugger both support complete source and line debugging with the C7 format. The C7 format is self-contained in the executable module because the linker appends the symbolic information to the binary after it links. Attaching the symbol information to your binary means that your debugging binaries can be quite large; symbol information can easily be larger than your binary file. If you want to see whether a file contains C7 information, open the binary in a hex editor and move to the end of the file. If you see "NB11" followed by 4 bytes, the file has C7 information in it.

If you're interested in symbol tables and would like to write one, the C7 specification is on MSDN. Look for it in the "VC5.0 Symbolic Debug Information" topic. The specification lists only the raw byte structure and type definitions. If you'd like to see the actual type definitions in C, the Dr. Watson source code, included on the MSDN CDs, has some old C7 format header files in its include directory. Although those header files are considerably dated, they can give you an idea what the structures look like.

Although you could use the C7 format for your applications if you wanted to, you probably shouldn't. The main reason for not using C7 is that it automatically turns off incremental linking. With incremental linking turned off, link times increase dramatically. The other reason for avoiding C7 is that it makes binary files incredibly large. Although you could strip out the symbol information with REBASE.EXE, other formats, namely PDB, automatically remove the symbol information for you.

The PDB format is the most common symbol format used today, and both Visual C++ and Visual Basic support it. Unlike the C7 format, PDB symbols are stored in a separate file or files, depending on how the application is linked. By default, Visual C++ 6 links with /PDBTYPE:SEPT, which puts the type information into VC60.PDB and the symbols into <binary name>.PDB. Separating the type information from the debug symbols makes linking faster and requires less disk space. However, the documentation states that if you're building binaries that others could be debugging, you should use /PDBTYPE:CON so that all the type information and debug symbols are consolidated into a single PDB file. Fortunately, Visual Basic automatically uses /PDBTYPE:CON.

To see whether a binary contains PDB symbol information, open it in a hex editor and move to the end of the file. You'll see a marker to the debugging information. If the marker starts with "NB10" and ends with the complete path to the PDB file produced during the link, the binary includes PDB symbols. The debugging format in PDB still resembles the C7 format internally. However, Microsoft optimized the layout for incremental linking and speed. Unfortunately, the low-level interfaces to the PDB file are proprietary and Microsoft hasn't released them.

DBG files are unique because, unlike the other symbol formats, the linker doesn't create them. A DBG file is basically just a file that holds other types of debug symbols, such as COFF or C7. DBG files use some of the same structures defined by the Portable Executable (PE) file format—the format used by Win32 executables. REBASE.EXE produces DBG files by stripping the COFF or C7 debugging information out of a module. There's no need to run REBASE.EXE on a module that was built using PDB files because the symbols are already separate from the module. If you're generating C7 symbols and you need to strip them, read the MSDN documentation on REBASE.EXE to see how to do it. Microsoft distributes the operating system debugging symbols in DBG files, and with Windows 2000, the PDB files are included as well. Before you get your hopes up that the operating system symbols include everything you need to reverse engineer the entire operating system, let me warn you that the files include only the public and global information. Using these files makes it much easier to see where you are when you're dropped into the middle of the Disassembly window.

If you're interested in symbol engines and you start researching how to write one, in your studies you'll run across one other symbol type, OMAP. It appears only in some Microsoft applications, and you can sometimes see it when you use the DUMPBIN.EXE utility with the /SYMBOLS option to dump the symbol information. (DUMPBIN.EXE comes with Visual C++.) OMAP is a completely undocumented symbol format. As far as I can tell, Microsoft has an internal tool that rearranges the compiled binary to put the most frequently called code at the front of the binary. The OMAP symbols have something to do with debugging symbols that take into account this postlink step.

The Working Set Tuner (WST) program that comes with the Platform SDK performs a similar optimization except that Microsoft's tool goes into the functions whereas WST stops at the function level. Microsoft's tool looks like it goes down to what is called the basic block level. The arrows in the following code snippet delineate a basic block.

```
if ( TRUE == bIsError )
{   <- The basic block starts here.

    // Do the error handling here.

}   <- The basic block ends here.
```

The Microsoft tool moves the error handler to the end of the binary so that only the most common code goes into the front. The OMAP symbols seem to be some sort of fixup to the main symbols because the Microsoft tool manipulated the binary after it was built.

Accessing Symbol Information

To access symbol information, you can use Microsoft's DBGHELP.DLL symbol engine. DBGHELP.DLL can read PDB, COFF, and C7 symbol formats. In the past, the symbol engine was in IMAGEHLP.DLL, but Microsoft wisely pulled the symbol engine out of the core system and put it in a DLL that was easier to upgrade. If you have a program that was using the symbol engine when it was part of IMAGEHLP.DLL, IMAGEHLP.DLL still includes the symbol engine exports. The new IMAGEHLP.DLL forwards those functions to DBGHELP.DLL. At the time I was writing this book, the MSDN documentation for the symbol engine was still included as part of IMAGEHLP.DLL.

The DBGHELP.DLL symbol engine allows you to turn an address into the closest public function or global variable. It can also handle the inverse, where you ask it to find the address of a specific function. Finally, you can retrieve the source file and line number for a specific address as well. The DBGHELP.DLL symbol engine doesn't support looking up parameters or local variables, nor does it support type evaluation. As you'll see later in this book, with just this limited functionality, I was able to build some excellent utilities to help you find problems in your applications faster. Microsoft has been slowly improving the symbol table access, and I hope that in the future, DBGHELP.DLL will support our complete symbol table needs.

For WDBG, I used a simple C++ wrapper class, shown in Listing 4-7, that I originally wrote as part of my BUGSLAYERUTIL.DLL library. It is a paper-thin layer of the existing DBGHELP.DLL symbol engine API, but it does provide some workarounds to problems that I've encountered with older IMAGEHLP.DLL symbol engine versions. I left the workarounds in the source code in case you need to use the class with the older IMAGEHLP.DLL symbol engine. I use this class extensively later in the book, so you might want to study it closely.

```
/*----------------------------------------------------------------
"Debugging Applications" (Microsoft Press)
Copyright (c) 1997-2000 John Robbins -- All rights reserved.
----------------------------------------------------------------
This class is a paper-thin layer around the DBGHELP.DLL symbol engine.

This class wraps only those functions that take the unique
HANDLE value. Other DBGHELP.DLL symbol engine functions are global in
scope, so I didn't wrap them with this class.
```

Listing 4-7 *SYMBOLENGINE.H*   *(continued)*

Listing 4-7 *continued*

```
---------------------------------------------------------------------
Compilation Defines:

DO_NOT_WORK_AROUND_SRCLINE_BUG - If defined, the class will NOT work
                                 around the SymGetLineFromAddr bug where
                                 PDB fMile lookups fail after the first
                                 lookup.
USE_BUGSLAYERUTIL - If defined, the class will have another
                    initialization method, BSUSymInitialize, which will
                    use BSUSymInitialize from BUGSLAYERUTIL.DLL to
                    initialize the symbol engine and allow the invade
                    process flag to work for all Win32 operating systems.
                    If you use this define, you must use
                    BUGSLAYERUTIL.H to include this file.
---------------------------------------------------------------------*/


#ifndef _SYMBOLENGINE_H
#define _SYMBOLENGINE_H

// You could include either IMAGEHLP.DLL or DBGHELP.DLL.
#include "imagehlp.h"
#include <tchar.h>

// Include these in case the user forgets to link against them.
#pragma comment (lib,"dbghelp.lib")
#pragma comment (lib,"version.lib")

// The great Bugslayer idea of creating wrapper classes on structures
// that have size fields came from fellow MSJ columnist, Paul DiLascia.
// Thanks, Paul!

// I didn't wrap IMAGEHLP_SYMBOL because that is a variable-size
// structure.

// The IMAGEHLP_MODULE wrapper class
struct CImageHlp_Module : public IMAGEHLP_MODULE
{
    CImageHlp_Module ( )
    {
        memset ( this , NULL , sizeof ( IMAGEHLP_MODULE ) ) ;
        SizeOfStruct = sizeof ( IMAGEHLP_MODULE ) ;
    }
} ;

// The IMAGEHLP_LINE wrapper class
```

```
struct CImageHlp_Line : public IMAGEHLP_LINE
{
    CImageHlp_Line ( )
    {
        memset ( this , NULL , sizeof ( IMAGEHLP_LINE ) ) ;
        SizeOfStruct = sizeof ( IMAGEHLP_LINE ) ;
    }
} ;

// The symbol engine class
class CSymbolEngine
{
/*-------------------------------------------------------------------
                Public Construction and Destruction
---------------------------------------------------------------------*/
public     :
    // To use this class, call the SymInitialize member function to
    // initialize the symbol engine and then use the other member
    // functions in place of their corresponding DBGHELP.DLL functions.
    CSymbolEngine ( void )
    {
    }

    virtual ~CSymbolEngine ( void )
    {
    }

/*-------------------------------------------------------------------
                Public Helper Information Functions
---------------------------------------------------------------------*/
public     :

    // Returns the file version of DBGHELP.DLL being used.
    // To convert the return values into a readable format:
    // wsprintf ( szVer                     ,
    //           _T ( "%d.%02d.%d.%d" ) ,
    //           HIWORD ( dwMS )         ,
    //           LOWORD ( dwMS )         ,
    //           HIWORD ( dwLS )         ,
    //           LOWORD ( dwLS )            ) ;
    //  szVer will contain a string like: 5.00.1878.1
    BOOL GetImageHlpVersion ( DWORD & dwMS , DWORD & dwLS )
    {
        return( GetInMemoryFileVersion ( _T ( "DBGHELP.DLL" ) ,
                                         dwMS                   ,
```

(continued)

129

Listing 4-7 *continued*

```
                                            dwLS                    ) ) ;
}


BOOL GetDbgHelpVersion ( DWORD & dwMS , DWORD & dwLS )
{
    return( GetInMemoryFileVersion ( _T ( "DBGHELP.DLL" ) ,
                                     dwMS                    ,
                                     dwLS                    ) ) ;
}

// Returns the file version of the PDB reading DLLs
BOOL GetPDBReaderVersion ( DWORD & dwMS , DWORD & dwLS )
{
    // First try MSDBI.DLL.
    if ( TRUE == GetInMemoryFileVersion ( _T ( "MSDBI.DLL" ) ,
                                          dwMS                    ,
                                          dwLS                    ) )
    {
        return ( TRUE ) ;
    }
    else if ( TRUE == GetInMemoryFileVersion ( _T ( "MSPDB60.DLL" ),
                                               dwMS                    ,
                                               dwLS                    ) )
    {
        return ( TRUE ) ;
    }
    // Just fall down to MSPDB50.DLL.
    return ( GetInMemoryFileVersion ( _T ( "MSPDB50.DLL" ) ,
                                      dwMS                    ,
                                      dwLS                    ) ) ;
}

// The worker function used by the previous two functions
BOOL GetInMemoryFileVersion ( LPCTSTR szFile ,
                              DWORD & dwMS    ,
                              DWORD & dwLS    )
{
    HMODULE hInstIH = GetModuleHandle ( szFile ) ;

    // Get the full filename of the loaded version.
    TCHAR szImageHlp[ MAX_PATH ] ;
    GetModuleFileName ( hInstIH , szImageHlp , MAX_PATH ) ;

    dwMS = 0 ;
    dwLS = 0 ;
```

```
        // Get the version information size.
        DWORD dwVerInfoHandle ;
        DWORD dwVerSize        ;

        dwVerSize = GetFileVersionInfoSize ( szImageHlp        ,
                                             &dwVerInfoHandle ) ;
        if ( 0 == dwVerSize )
        {
            return ( FALSE ) ;
        }

        // Got the version size, now get the version information.
        LPVOID lpData = (LPVOID)new TCHAR [ dwVerSize ] ;
        if ( FALSE == GetFileVersionInfo ( szImageHlp      ,
                                           dwVerInfoHandle ,
                                           dwVerSize       ,
                                           lpData          ) )
        {
            delete [] lpData ;
            return ( FALSE ) ;
        }

        VS_FIXEDFILEINFO * lpVerInfo ;
        UINT uiLen ;
        BOOL bRet = VerQueryValue ( lpData              ,
                                    _T ( "\\" )         ,
                                    (LPVOID*)&lpVerInfo ,
                                    &uiLen              ) ;
        if ( TRUE == bRet )
        {
            dwMS = lpVerInfo->dwFileVersionMS ;
            dwLS = lpVerInfo->dwFileVersionLS ;
        }

        delete [] lpData ;

        return ( bRet ) ;
    }

/*----------------------------------------------------------------------
                Public Initialization and Cleanup
----------------------------------------------------------------------*/
public    :
    BOOL SymInitialize ( IN HANDLE   hProcess        ,
                         IN LPSTR    UserSearchPath ,
```

(continued)

131

Listing 4-7 *continued*

```
                            IN BOOL      fInvadeProcess  )
   {
       m_hProcess = hProcess ;
       return ( ::SymInitialize ( hProcess       ,
                                  UserSearchPath ,
                                  fInvadeProcess ) ) ;
   }

#ifdef USE_BUGSLAYERUTIL
    BOOL BSUSymInitialize ( DWORD  dwPID          ,
                            HANDLE hProcess       ,
                            PSTR   UserSearchPath ,
                            BOOL   fInvadeProcess  )
    {
        m_hProcess = hProcess ;
        return ( ::BSUSymInitialize ( dwPID          ,
                                      hProcess       ,
                                      UserSearchPath ,
                                      fInvadeProcess ) ) ;
    }
#endif  // USE_BUGSLAYERUTIL
    BOOL SymCleanup ( void )
    {
        return ( ::SymCleanup ( m_hProcess ) ) ;
    }


/*-------------------------------------------------------------------
                    Public Module Manipulation
-------------------------------------------------------------------*/
public     :

    BOOL SymEnumerateModules ( IN PSYM_ENUMMODULES_CALLBACK
                                               EnumModulesCallback,
                    IN PVOID             UserContext )
    {
        return ( ::SymEnumerateModules ( m_hProcess          ,
                                         EnumModulesCallback ,
                                         UserContext         ) ) ;
    }

    BOOL SymLoadModule ( IN   HANDLE hFile      ,
                         IN   PSTR   ImageName  ,
                         IN   PSTR   ModuleName ,
                         IN   DWORD  BaseOfDll  ,
                         IN   DWORD  SizeOfDll   )
```

```
    {
        return ( ::SymLoadModule ( m_hProcess   ,
                                   hFile        ,
                                   ImageName    ,
                                   ModuleName   ,
                                   BaseOfDll    ,
                                   SizeOfDll    ) ) ;
    }

    BOOL EnumerateLoadedModules ( IN PENUMLOADED_MODULES_CALLBACK
                                                EnumLoadedModulesCallback,
                                  IN PVOID          UserContext       )
    {
        return ( ::EnumerateLoadedModules ( m_hProcess                ,
                                            EnumLoadedModulesCallback ,
                                            UserContext               ) );
    }

    BOOL SymUnloadModule ( IN  DWORD BaseOfDll )
    {
        return ( ::SymUnloadModule ( m_hProcess , BaseOfDll ) ) ;
    }

    BOOL SymGetModuleInfo ( IN  DWORD            dwAddr     ,
                            OUT PIMAGEHLP_MODULE ModuleInfo )
    {
        return ( ::SymGetModuleInfo ( m_hProcess   ,
                                      dwAddr       ,
                                      ModuleInfo   ) ) ;
    }

    DWORD SymGetModuleBase ( IN DWORD dwAddr )
    {
        return ( ::SymGetModuleBase ( m_hProcess , dwAddr ) ) ;
    }

/*------------------------------------------------------------------
                     Public Symbol Manipulation
--------------------------------------------------------------------*/
public    :

    BOOL SymEnumerateSymbols ( IN DWORD                       BaseOfDll,
                       IN PSYM_ENUMSYMBOLS_CALLBACK
                                                    EnumSymbolsCallback,
                       IN PVOID                      UserContext )
    {
```

(continued)

Listing 4-7 *continued*

```
        return ( ::SymEnumerateSymbols ( m_hProcess         ,
                                         BaseOfDll          ,
                                         EnumSymbolsCallback ,
                                         UserContext        ) ) ;
    }

    BOOL SymGetSymFromAddr ( IN  DWORD             dwAddr         ,
                             OUT PDWORD            pdwDisplacement ,
                             OUT PIMAGEHLP_SYMBOL  Symbol          )
    {
        return ( ::SymGetSymFromAddr ( m_hProcess      ,
                                       dwAddr          ,
                                       pdwDisplacement ,
                                       Symbol          ) ) ;
    }

    BOOL SymGetSymFromName ( IN  LPSTR             Name   ,
                             OUT PIMAGEHLP_SYMBOL  Symbol )
    {
        return ( ::SymGetSymFromName ( m_hProcess ,
                                       Name       ,
                                       Symbol     ) ) ;
    }

    BOOL SymGetSymNext ( IN OUT PIMAGEHLP_SYMBOL Symbol )
    {
        return ( ::SymGetSymNext ( m_hProcess , Symbol ) ) ;
    }

    BOOL SymGetSymPrev ( IN OUT PIMAGEHLP_SYMBOL Symbol )
    {
        return ( ::SymGetSymPrev ( m_hProcess , Symbol ) ) ;
    }

/*-------------------------------------------------------------------------
                    Public Source Line Manipulation
---------------------------------------------------------------------------*/
public    :

    BOOL SymGetLineFromAddr ( IN  DWORD            dwAddr          ,
                              OUT PDWORD           pdwDisplacement ,
                              OUT PIMAGEHLP_LINE Line              )
    {
#ifdef DO_NOT_WORK_AROUND_SRCLINE_BUG
        // Just pass along the values returned by the main function.
        return ( ::SymGetLineFromAddr ( m_hProcess        ,
```

```
                                                dwAddr              ,
                                                pdwDisplacement ,
                                                Line                ) ) ;

#else
        // The problem is that the symbol engine finds only those source
        // line addresses (after the first lookup) that fall exactly on
        // a zero displacement. I'll walk backward 100 bytes to
        // find the line and return the proper displacement.
        DWORD dwTempDis = 0 ;
        while ( FALSE == ::SymGetLineFromAddr ( m_hProcess       ,
                                                dwAddr - dwTempDis ,
                                                pdwDisplacement  ,
                                                Line                ) )
        {
            dwTempDis += 1 ;
            if ( 100 == dwTempDis )
            {
                return ( FALSE ) ;
            }
        }
        // I found it and the source line information is correct, so I'll
        // change the displacement if I had to search backward to find
        // the source line.
        if ( 0 != dwTempDis )
        {
            *pdwDisplacement = dwTempDis ;
        }
        return ( TRUE ) ;
#endif // DO_NOT_WORK_AROUND_SRCLINE_BUG
    }

    BOOL SymGetLineFromName ( IN     LPSTR          ModuleName      ,
                              IN     LPSTR          FileName        ,
                              IN     DWORD          dwLineNumber    ,
                              OUT    PLONG          plDisplacement  ,
                              IN OUT PIMAGEHLP_LINE Line            )
    {
        return ( ::SymGetLineFromName ( m_hProcess      ,
                                        ModuleName      ,
                                        FileName        ,
                                        dwLineNumber    ,
                                        plDisplacement  ,
                                        Line                ) ) ;
    }
```

(continued)

Listing 4-7 *continued*

```
    BOOL SymGetLineNext ( IN OUT PIMAGEHLP_LINE Line )
    {
        return ( ::SymGetLineNext ( m_hProcess , Line ) ) ;
    }


    BOOL SymGetLinePrev ( IN OUT PIMAGEHLP_LINE Line )
    {
        return ( ::SymGetLinePrev ( m_hProcess , Line ) ) ;
    }


    BOOL SymMatchFileName ( IN  LPSTR    FileName      ,
                            IN  LPSTR    Match         ,
                            OUT LPSTR *  FileNameStop  ,
                            OUT LPSTR *  MatchStop        )
    {
        return ( ::SymMatchFileName ( FileName      ,
                                      Match         ,
                                      FileNameStop  ,
                                      MatchStop        ) ) ;
    }


/*-------------------------------------------------------------------------
                        Public Miscellaneous Members
---------------------------------------------------------------------------*/
public    :

    LPVOID SymFunctionTableAccess ( DWORD AddrBase )
    {
        return ( ::SymFunctionTableAccess ( m_hProcess , AddrBase ) ) ;
    }

    BOOL SymGetSearchPath ( OUT LPSTR SearchPath        ,
                            IN  DWORD SearchPathLength   )
    {
        return ( ::SymGetSearchPath ( m_hProcess        ,
                                      SearchPath        ,
                                      SearchPathLength ) ) ;
    }
    BOOL SymSetSearchPath ( IN LPSTR SearchPath )
    {
        return ( ::SymSetSearchPath ( m_hProcess , SearchPath ) ) ;
    }

    BOOL SymRegisterCallback ( IN PSYMBOL_REGISTERED_CALLBACK
                                                    CallbackFunction,
                               IN PVOID             UserContext    )
```

```
    {
        return ( ::SymRegisterCallback ( m_hProcess        ,
                                         CallbackFunction  ,
                                         UserContext       ) ) ;
    }


/*-------------------------------------------------------------------
                      Protected Data Members
--------------------------------------------------------------------*/
protected   :
    // The unique value that will be used for this instance of the
    // symbol engine. This value doesn't have to be an actual
    // process value, just a unique value.
    HANDLE      m_hProcess      ;

} ;

#endif      // _SYMBOLENGINE_H
```

Before Windows 2000 became available, getting the Microsoft-supplied symbol engine working was no easy task. The main reason for the difficulty was that the symbol engine was in IMAGEHLP.DLL and many programs used it. Because you can't replace a DLL that is currently loaded, getting a newer version of IMAGEHLP.DLL onto your machine was a challenge. Now that DBGHELP.DLL isn't a system DLL, it's much easier to upgrade. The most current version will always be available from the most current Platform SDK, so you should look to install it first. You can download the latest version of the Platform SDK from *www.microsoft.com* or get it as part of your MSDN subscription service. All the code in this book is set up to use DBGHELP.DLL, so you must have DBGHELP.DLL on your computer and in a location specified by the PATH environment variable.

Having DBGHELP.DLL installed is only part of the battle, because you need to ensure that you have your symbol files accessible to the symbol engine in order to load them. For DBG files, the DBGHELP.DLL symbol engine will look for them in the following places:

■ The current working directory of the application using DBGHELP.DLL, not the debuggee

■ The _NT_SYMBOL_PATH environment variable

- The _NT_ALT_SYMBOL_PATH environment variable

- The SYSTEMROOT environment variable

The environment variables must point to directories that are set up a specific way. For example, if your symbols are located in c:\MyFiles, you must create a directory named Symbols under your main directory. Under the Symbols directory, you must create a directory for each extension your binary files use. For example, if you have an EXE and a couple of DLLs, your final directory tree would look like the following. The DBG files for each of your particular extensions go in the appropriate places.

```
c:\MyFiles
   c:\MyFiles\Symbols
   c:\MyFiles\Symbols\Exe
   c:\MyFiles\Symbols\Dll
```

For PDB files, the only difference is that the DBGHELP.DLL symbol engine will look in the binary for the original PDB path and try to load the PDB from that absolute directory. If the DBGHELP.DLL symbol engine can't load the PDB file from that directory, it will attempt to load the PDB file using the same steps I described previously for DBG files.

Walking the Stack

Fortunately for all of us, we don't have to write our own stack-walking code. DBGHELP.DLL provides the *StackWalk* API function. *StackWalk* is straightforward and takes care of all your stack-walking needs. WDBG uses the *StackWalk* API function just as the Visual C++ debugger does. The only snag you might encounter is that the documentation isn't explicit about what needs to be set in the *STACKFRAME* structure. Listing 4-8 shows you the exact fields that need to be filled out in the *STACKFRAME* structure.

StackWalk does such a good job of taking care of the details that you might not be aware that stack walking can be difficult with optimized code. The reason for the difficulty is that the compiler can optimize away the stack frame, the place where the code pushes stack entries, for some functions. The Visual C++ and Visual Basic compilers are aggressive when they do their optimization, and if they can use the stack frame register as a scratch register, they will. To facilitate walking the stack in such situations, the compiler generates what is called Frame Pointer Omission (FPO) data. The FPO data is a table of information that *StackWalk* uses to figure out how to handle those functions missing a normal stack frame. I wanted to mention FPO because occasionally you'll see references to it on MSDN and in various debuggers. If you're curious, WINNT.H contains the FPO data structures.

```
BOOL CPUHELP_DLLINTERFACE __stdcall
    InitializeStackFrameWithContext ( STACKFRAME * pStack ,
                                      CONTEXT *    pCtx    )
{
    ASSERT ( FALSE == IsBadReadPtr ( pCtx , sizeof ( CONTEXT ) ) ) ;
    ASSERT ( FALSE == IsBadWritePtr ( pStack , sizeof ( STACKFRAME ) ) );
    if ( ( TRUE == IsBadReadPtr ( pCtx , sizeof ( CONTEXT ) )        ) ||
         ( TRUE == IsBadWritePtr ( pStack , sizeof ( STACKFRAME ) ) )   )
    {
        return ( FALSE ) ;
    }

    pStack->AddrPC.Offset       = pCtx->Eip ;
    pStack->AddrPC.Mode         = AddrModeFlat  ;
    pStack->AddrStack.Offset    = pCtx->Esp ;
    pStack->AddrStack.Mode      = AddrModeFlat  ;
    pStack->AddrFrame.Offset    = pCtx->Ebp ;
    pStack->AddrFrame.Mode      = AddrModeFlat  ;

    return ( TRUE ) ;
}
```

Listing 4-8 *InitializeStackFrameWithContext from I386CPUHELP.C*

Step Into, Step Over, and Step Out

Now that I've described breakpoints and the symbol engine, I want to explain how debuggers implement the excellent Step Into, Step Over, and Step Out functionality. I didn't implement these features in WDBG because I wanted to concentrate on the core portions of the debugger. Step Into, Step Over, and Step Out require source and disassembly views that allow you to keep track of the current executing line or instruction. After you read the discussion in this section, you'll see that the core architecture of WDBG has the infrastructure you need to wire these features in and that adding these features is mostly an exercise in UI programming.

Step Into, Step Over, and Step Out all work with one-shot breakpoints, which, as you'll recall from earlier in the chapter, are breakpoints that the debugger discards after the breakpoints trigger. In the Debug Break discussion earlier in the chapter, you saw another instance in which the debugger uses one-shot breakpoints to stop the processing.

Step Into works differently depending on whether you're debugging at the source level or the disassembly level. When debugging at the source level, the debugger must rely on one-shot breakpoints because a single high-level language line translates into one or more assembly language lines. If you set the CPU into single-step mode, you would be single stepping individual instructions, not the source lines.

At the source level, the debugger knows the source line you're on. When you execute the debugger's Step Into command, the debugger uses the symbol engine to look up the address of the next line to execute. The debugger will do a partial disassembly at the next line address to see whether the line is a call instruction. If the line is a call instruction, the debugger will set a one-shot breakpoint on the first address of the function the debuggee is about to call. If the next line address isn't a call instruction, the debugger sets a one-shot breakpoint there. After setting the one-shot breakpoint, the debugger will release the debuggee so that it runs to the freshly set one-shot breakpoint. When the one-shot breakpoint triggers, the debugger will replace the opcode at the one-shot location and free any memory associated with the one-shot breakpoint. If the user is working at the disassembly level, Step Into is much easier to implement because the debugger will just force the CPU into single-step execution.

Step Over is similar to Step Into in that the debugger must look up the next line in the symbol engine and does the partial disassembly at the line address. The difference is that in Step Over the debugger will set a one-shot breakpoint after the call instruction if the line is a call.

The Step Out operation is in some ways the simplest of the three. When the user selects the Step Out command, the debugger walks the stack to find the return address for the current function and sets a one-shot breakpoint on that address.

The processing for Step Into, Step Over, and Step Out seems straightforward, but there's one small twist that you need to consider. If you write your debugger to handle Step Into, Step Over, and Step Out, what are you going to do if you've set the one-shot breakpoint for those cases and a regular breakpoint triggers before the one-shot breakpoint? As a debugger writer, you have two choices. The first is to leave your one-shot breakpoints alone so that they trigger. The other option is to remove your one-shot breakpoint when the debugger notifies you that a regular breakpoint triggered. The latter option is what the Visual C++ debugger does.

Either way of handling this case is correct, but by removing the one-shot breakpoint for Step Into, Step Over, and Step Out, you avoid user confusion. If you allow the one-shot breakpoint to trigger after the normal breakpoint, the user can easily be left wondering why the debugger stopped at an odd location.

An Interesting Development Problem with WDBG

In general, I didn't have much trouble developing WDBG. However, one problem that proved to be rather interesting did come up. If you run the Visual C++ debugger, the Output window shows you the complete path to the modules as they load. Because I was trying to make WDBG as complete as I could, I wanted to duplicate that functionality. I didn't think doing so would be that difficult.

If you look at the following definition of the *LOAD_DLL_DEBUG_INFO* structure passed to the debugger on *LOAD_DLL_DEBUG_EVENT* notifications, you'll see a field for *lpImageName*, which you would think would be the name of the module loading. That's exactly what it is, but none of the Win32 operating systems ever fills it out.

```
typedef struct _LOAD_DLL_DEBUG_INFO {
    HANDLE hFile;
    LPVOID lpBaseOfDll;
    DWORD  dwDebugInfoFileOffset;
    DWORD  nDebugInfoSize;
    LPVOID lpImageName;
    WORD   fUnicode;
} LOAD_DLL_DEBUG_INFO;
```

Because I was loading the module into the DBGHELP.DLL symbol engine as I got the *LOAD_DLL_DEBUG_EVENT* notifications, I thought I could just look up the complete module name after loading it. The *SymGetModuleInfo* API function takes an *IMAGEHLP_MODULE* structure, as shown here, and there is space for the complete module name.

```
typedef struct _IMAGEHLP_MODULE {
    DWORD SizeOfStruct;
    DWORD BaseOfImage;
    DWORD ImageSize;
    DWORD TimeDateStamp;
    DWORD CheckSum;
    DWORD NumSyms;
    SYM_TYPE SymType;
    CHAR ModuleName[32];
    CHAR ImageName[256];
    CHAR LoadedImageName[256];
} IMAGEHLP_MODULE, *PIMAGEHLP_MODULE;
```

The puzzling thing I noticed was that *SymGetModuleInfo* would return that the module symbol information was loaded, but the name of the module would be the name of the DBG symbol file or the module name would be missing completely. This behavior surprised me, but when I thought for a minute, I could see how it might be happening. When I got the *LOAD_DLL_DEBUG_INFO* structure, the *hFile* member was valid and I would in turn call *SymLoadModule* with that *hFile*. Because I never gave the DBGHELP.DLL symbol engine a full filename to load, it just looked in the open file designated by *hFile*, found debug information in it, and read in the information. It never needed to know the complete filename.

I just wanted to get the complete name of the module that was loaded. At first, I thought I could use the file handle myself to access the export section of the module and report the module name that I found there. The only problems were that the module could have been renamed so the name in the export section would be wrong, the module could be an EXE or resource-only DLL and not have any exports so it wouldn't have a name, and even if I did retrieve the correct module name, I still wouldn't have the complete path to the module.

After pondering the problem a bit, I figured that there had to be an API function that would take a handle value and tell you the complete name of the open file. When I discovered that there wasn't one, I tried some undocumented means that didn't completely work and that I was hesitant to use in a book like this. I then started poking around with the Tool Help and PSAPI.DLL functions because they will both tell you the modules loaded into a process. The Tool Help functions worked on Windows 98, but on Windows NT 4, PSAPI.DLL failed, and on Windows 2000, the Tool Help functions would hang the debugger hard. The Tool Help functions weren't broken, but they try to start a new thread in the debuggee address space with a call to *CreateRemoteThread*. Because the debuggee was completely stopped in WDBG, the Tool Help functions would hang until the debuggee restarted. After switching to PSAPI.DLL on Windows 2000, instead of hanging, at least it failed as it did on Windows NT 4.

Using the problem-solving approach that I outlined in Chapter 1, I took stock of the situation and set about formulating some hypothesis to explain the problem. As I read up on the PSAPI.DLL *GetModuleFilenameEx* function, I started to realize why it might not work when I was calling it. When I was receiving the *LOAD_DLL_DEBUG_EVENT* notification, it was telling me that a DLL was about to load into the address space, not that the DLL had loaded. Because the memory hadn't been mapped to hold the DLL, the PSAPI.DLL *GetModuleFilenameEx* was failing; when I stepped through it at the assembly-language level, it appeared to be looking through a mapped memory list that the operating system held for each process.

Now that I knew the source of the problem, I just needed a way to find out when the operating system fully mapped the module into memory. Although I probably could have gone to extreme measures to get this information, such as reverse engineer the image loader in NTDLL.DLL and set a breakpoint there, I opted for a solution that was a little easier and that wouldn't break on each service pack release for the operating system. I figured that I just needed to queue up the module load information and check it every once in a while. *PulseModuleNotification* is the function I wrote to handle the details of checking the module load information; you can find its implementation in MODULENOTIFICATION.CPP on the companion CD. If you look at the *DebugThread* function in DEBUGTHREAD.CPP on the companion CD, you'll see that I call *PulseModuleNotification* every time through the debug loop and whenever the *WaitForDebugEvent* function times out. Calling *PulseModuleNotification* continually allows me to report the module load information in a timely manner and with the information that I want.

COMMON DEBUGGING QUESTION

Why can't I step into system functions or set breakpoints in system memory on Windows 98?

If you've ever tried to step into certain system functions on Windows 98, you've seen that the debugger doesn't let you. Windows 2000, on the other hand, allows you to step anywhere you want in your user-mode processes. The reason is that Windows 2000 completely implements copy-on-write, whereas Windows 98 does copy-on-write only for addresses below 2 GB.

As I described in the section "Reading and Writing Memory" earlier in the chapter, copy-on-write allows processes to have their own private copies of mapped memory pages when they, or the debugger, write to a page. Because of the architecture of Windows 98, all processes share the address space above 2 GB. Because Windows 98 doesn't implement copy-on-write for those addresses, if Windows 98 allowed you to set a breakpoint in the shared memory, the first process that executed that address would cause a breakpoint exception. Because that process probably isn't running under a debugger, the process would terminate with a breakpoint exception. Although some system DLLs, such as COMCTL32.DLL, load below 2 GB, the main system DLLs such as KERNEL32.DLL and USER32.DLL load above 2 GB, which means that unless you have a kernel debugger running on Windows 98, you can't step into them with a user-mode debugger.

SO YOU WANT TO WRITE YOUR OWN DEBUGGER

Over the years, I've been amazed at the number of engineers who are interested in writing debuggers. I'm not amazed at why they want to do it since I've lived the debugger writer's life. We got interested in computers and software in the first place because we wanted to know how they worked, and debuggers are the magic looking glass that lets you see anything and everything about them. Consequently, I've received quite a bit of mail asking me what it takes to write a debugger and for advice on how to proceed. Part of my motivation for writing WDBG was to finally get a full example out for engineers to see how debuggers work.

The first step you need to take, after examining WDBG, is to get Jonathan Rosenberg's excellent book *How Debuggers Work* (Wiley, 1996). Although Jonathan's book doesn't present the code for a debugger, it's a wonderful introduction to and discussion about the real-world issues that you'll have to deal with when writing a debugger. Very few engineers have ever written a debugger, so it really helps to get a handle on the issues first.

You'll need to become intimately familiar with the PE file format and the particular CPU you're working on. The companion CD contains PECOFF.DOC, which is the latest PE file specification from Microsoft and is an excellent starting point. You can learn more about the CPU from the Intel CPU manuals available at *www.intel.com*.

Before you tackle a full debugger, you should probably write a disassembler. Writing a disassembler will not only teach you a great deal about the CPU, but it will also result in code you can use in the debugger. The disassembler in WDBG is read-only code. In other words, only the developer who wrote it can read it. Strive to make your disassembler maintainable and extensible. I've done a decent amount of assembly-language programming in the past, but it wasn't until I wrote my own disassembler that I really learned assembly language inside and out.

If you do want to write your own disassembler, the first place to start is with the Intel reference manuals. They have all the information you need about the instructions and their opcodes. Additionally, in the back of Volume 2, is the complete opcode map, which is what you need to know to turn a number into an instruction. The source code to a few disassemblers is floating around the Internet. Before you embark on your writing, you might want to look at some of those disassemblers to get an idea of how others have handled problems.

As I mentioned earlier, the DBGHELP.DLL symbol engine is sufficient for some excellent debugging helper utilities, but it isn't enough for a real debugger. You can always tackle reverse engineering the PDB file format yourself, and we can all hope that Microsoft will someday release the PDB access routines.

WHAT'S NEXT FOR WDBG?

As it stands, WDBG does what it's supposed to do. However, you could improve it in plenty of ways. The following list should give you some ideas about what you can do to enhance WDBG if you're interested. If you do extend WDBG, I'd like to hear about it. In addition, as I mentioned in Chapter 1, examples of your own code are wonderful props to bring to a job interview. If you do add a significant feature to WDBG, you should show it off!

■   The WDBG UI is just enough to get by. The first improvement you could undertake is to implement a better one. All the information is there; you just need to design better ways of displaying it.

■   WDBG supports only simple location breakpoints. BREAKPOINT.H and BREAKPOINT.CPP are ready for you to add additional interesting kinds of breakpoints, such as skip count breakpoints (execute the breakpoint a specific number of times before stopping) or expression breakpoints (break only if an expression is true). Make sure you derive your new breakpoints from *CLocationBP* so that you get the serialization code and you don't have to change anything in WDBG.

■ With a little work, you should be able to extend WDBG to support multiple process debugging. Most of the interfaces are set up to work on a process identification scheme, so you would just need to track which process you're working on during a debug notification.

■ The WDBG interface is set up to allow you to drop in remote debugging and different CPUs and still have the main UI work the same. Write the remote debugging DLLs and extend WDBG to allow the user to choose whether to debug on the local machine or on a remote machine.

■ Finally, you could always write a better disassembler and a C7 symbol engine to make WDBG really useful!

SUMMARY

This chapter was an overview of what debuggers do and how they do it. By learning about your tools, you're better able to maximize their usage. The core Win32 Debugging API was presented, and some of the supporting systems that debuggers use, such as the symbol engine, were covered. You also learned about some of the other debuggers—besides the Visual C++ debugger—that are available. Finally, the WDBG example provided a complete debugger sample that illustrates exactly how debuggers work.

If you had never seen how debuggers operate at this level before, you might have thought that they were magical pieces of code. However, as you look through the code for WDBG, I think you'll agree that debuggers go through the same data grunt work that any software goes through. The biggest deficiency to overcome when writing a Win32 debugger is that the existing symbol engines handle only public functions, global variables, and source and line information. Without local variables, parameters, and types, it's difficult to make a debugger nearly as comprehensive as the Visual C++ debugger or WinDBG.

Chapter 5

Power Debugging with the Visual C++ Debugger

No matter what language you're developing in—C++, Microsoft Visual Basic, or even Java—a crash is a crash. The debugger that works across all these languages is the Microsoft Visual C++ debugger. Over the years, the Visual C++ debugger has continuously improved, and it provides an excellent platform for debugging. This is the first of two chapters about the Visual C++ debugger. In this chapter, I'll cover the advanced features of the Visual C++ debugger (except for the Disassembly window, which I'll save for Chapter 6). These features, including advanced breakpoints and remote debugging, will assist you in solving your coding problems. I'll also provide you with a slew of tips that will help you make the most out of the time you spend in the debugger. In Chapter 6, besides explaining the Disassembly window, I'll tie both these chapters together with some examples that illustrate the power of the Visual C++ debugger.

If you have little or no experience with the Visual C++ debugger, I suggest that you read the Microsoft Visual Studio documentation on MSDN before continuing. I won't be covering the basics of the debugger in this chapter; I'll assume that you'll study the documentation if you need to. Just search for the "Home Page: Debugger" topic on MSDN and you'll find the most pertinent sections.

ADVANCED BREAKPOINTS AND HOW TO USE THEM

Setting a breakpoint on a source line in the Visual C++ debugger with a Win32 Debug or Win32 Unicode Debug project configuration is simple. Just load the source file, put the cursor on the line you want to stop on, roll the mouse to the Insert/Remove Breakpoint button, and click. In debugger terms, this process is called setting a location breakpoint. When the code for that line executes, the debugger will stop at that location. The ease of setting a location breakpoint belies its importance: the location breakpoint on a specific source code line is what separates the modern age of debugging from the debugging dark ages.

In the early days of computing, breakpoints simply didn't exist. Your only "strategy" for finding a bug was to run your program until it crashed and then wade through page after page of hexadecimal core-dump printouts of the state of memory looking for the problem. The only debuggers in the debugging dark ages were trace statements and faith. In the renaissance age of debugging, made possible by the introduction of higher-level languages, developers could set breakpoints but had to debug only at the assembly-language level. The higher-level languages still had no provisions for viewing local variables or seeing a program in source form. As the languages evolved into more sophisticated tools, the debugging modern age began, and developers were able to set a breakpoint on a line of source code and see their variables in a display that interpreted the variables' values into the exact type they specified. This simple location breakpoint is still extremely powerful, and with just it alone, you can solve 99.46 percent of your debugging problems.

However wonderful, though, location breakpoints can get tedious very quickly. What would happen if you set the breakpoint on a line inside a *for* loop that executes from 1 to 10,000 and the bug turned up on the 10,000th iteration? Not only would you give yourself carpal tunnel syndrome from pressing the key assigned to the Go command, but you would also spend hours waiting to get to the iteration that produced the bug. Wouldn't it be nice if there were some way to tell the debugger that you want the breakpoint to execute 9,999 times before stopping?

Fortunately, there is a way: welcome to the realm of advanced breakpoints. In essence, advanced breakpoints allow you to program some smarts into breakpoints, letting the debugger handle the menial chores involved in tracking down bugs and minimizing the time and effort you have to spend in the debugger. Some of the various conditions you can add with advanced breakpoints include having the breakpoint skip for a certain count, break when an expression is true, and break when a variable or memory address changes. The advanced breakpoint capabilities have finally moved debuggers solidly into the modern age, allowing developers to do in minutes what used to take hours with simple location breakpoints.

Advanced Breakpoint Syntax and Location Breakpoints

Before jumping into all the great ways you can use advanced breakpoints, I need to spend a little time going over the advanced breakpoint syntax. This syntax is important because the Breakpoints dialog box displays the breakpoints in this format. Fortunately, the syntax is relatively straightforward. Later in the chapter (Listing 5-1 on page 157), I've included a project, AdvancedBP, that demonstrates each type of advanced breakpoint. This project is also on the companion CD, so you might want to open the project in Visual Studio and refer to it as you're working through this section.

The advanced breakpoint syntax is composed of two parts. The first part is the context portion, and the second part is the location, expression, variable, or Microsoft Windows message condition. You can think of the context portion just as you do the scope of a variable when programming. The context simply provides the debugger with an unambiguous location for your breakpoint.

In debugger terms, the function, the source file, and the binary module specify the context, and the context is delineated in advanced breakpoint syntax as {[function],[source file],[binary module]}. You need to specify only enough context information to get the breakpoint set. In your run-of-the-mill location breakpoint, all the information the debugger needs is the name of the source file. You've probably seen the simple location breakpoint format in the Breakpoints dialog box, perhaps without realizing what it is. If you set a location breakpoint on line 20 of TEST.CPP, for example, the Breakpoints dialog box displays it as {,TEST.CPP,}.20.

The ability to specify the context for a location breakpoint allows you to solve a particularly nasty type of debugging problem. Consider the case in which you have a source file with a diagnostic function, *CheckMyMem*, used by two dynamic-link libraries (DLLs), A.DLL and B.DLL, and the function appears in both DLLs by static linking. Because you're doing lots of proactive programming, you're calling the function a great deal from both DLLs. However, you're experiencing a random crash only in B.DLL. If you set a standard location breakpoint in the *CheckMyMem* source code, "{,CHECKMYMEM.CPP,}.27," the breakpoint will trigger in both DLLs even though you just want to see the calls made in B.DLL. To specify that you want the location breakpoint to trigger only in B.DLL, you would need to use the breakpoint context "{,CHECKMYMEM.CPP,B.DLL}.27."

On the Visual C++ debugger Breakpoints dialog box Location tab, you can type the context syntax directly into the Break At edit box; however, it's easier just to use the Advanced Breakpoint dialog box, shown in Figure 5-1. Click the arrow button to the right of the edit control to bring up the menu. On the menu, select Advanced, and then in the Context group box, type the appropriate information for your breakpoint.

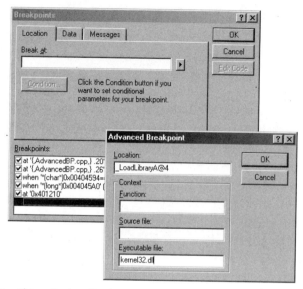

Figure 5-1 *Specifying the breakpoint context in the Advanced Breakpoint dialog box*

The real muscle of advanced breakpoints is found in the second part of the advanced breakpoint syntax, in which you specify the location, expression, variable, or Windows message to break on. I introduced the simple location breakpoint syntax by showing a line location breakpoint. However, you can also break on other types of locations. If you want to break on an absolute address that you know, in the Breakpoints dialog box just type the address in the Break At edit box. For example, as I write this, I'm using the AdvancedBP program, which I compiled for you and which is available on the companion CD. The entry point of the application, *mainCRTStartup*, is 0x401210, so that's the address I'm using for the breakpoint. (Keep in mind that you must include the 0x prefix in the debugger to indicate a hexadecimal number.)

Quickly Breaking on Any Function

Because the Visual C++ debugger is smart enough to evaluate expressions, you have many interesting options for setting breakpoints. Here's one technique I find useful in the midst of my debugging battles: if I know the function I want to break on, instead of hunting all over the source code for the function, I just type the function name in the Break At edit box. If the symbol exists in one of the loaded modules, the debugger will put a breakpoint on the first instruction in the function. If your program is stopped in the debugger and the function you typed is wrong, the debugger will display a message box telling you so. When working with C++ code, type in the class qualifier as well. For example, to break on the base Microsoft Foundation Class (MFC) library *CDialog* class *OnOK* method, you would type *CDialog::OnOK*.

The debugger is also smart enough to know about overloaded class members and will prompt you for a specific version of the function. For example, in an MFC application, if you type *CString::CString* as the function on which to set the breakpoint, the debugger won't know which version of the constructor you're interested in and will prompt you with the Resolve Ambiguity dialog box, shown in Figure 5-2. The Resolve Ambiguity dialog box lists, in advanced breakpoint syntax, the eight *CString* constructors, from which you choose the appropriate version.

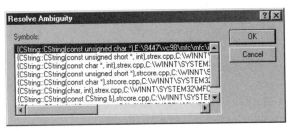

Figure 5-2 *The Resolve Ambiguity dialog box*

The easiest way to set breakpoints on complicated functions, such as class operators, is to type just enough information so that the debugger displays the Resolve Ambiguity dialog box. For example, the MFC *CString* class has overloaded assignment operators, so you would type just *CString::operator=* to see a list of them. You can also specify parameters to the function, if you know them, to set the breakpoint directly. With the *CString::operator=* example, you could type *CString::operator=(const char *)* and bypass the Resolve Ambiguity dialog box altogether.

Breakpoints on System or Exported Functions

This technique of setting a location breakpoint on the first instruction of a function is very powerful. If you try to set a breakpoint on a function that your program imports from a DLL, however, you'll be disappointed. It doesn't work. There's nothing wrong with the debugger; you just need to give it some context information about where it can find the function. Additionally, one other small detail is important: the function name depends on whether symbols for the DLL are loaded. Keep in mind that you can set a breakpoint on a system DLL function only in Microsoft Windows 2000. The lack of copy-on-write protection (discussed in Chapter 4) is the reason you can't set breakpoints on system functions in Windows 98 that load above the 2-GB memory line. To get this technique to work in Windows 2000, you must have Common Object File Format (COFF) and export loading turned on in the debugger. In Visual C++, on the Debug tab of the Options dialog box, make sure Load COFF & Exports is checked.

To illustrate how to set a breakpoint on a system DLL, I'll set a breakpoint on the KERNEL32.DLL *LoadLibrary* function. Because you already know how to set the context for a location breakpoint, you won't be surprised to see that the first part of the breakpoint is {,,KERNEL32.DLL}, to identify the function's module. The Visual C++ debugger follows a hierarchical symbol information approach in which more complete symbols take precedence over the less complete ones. Program Database (PDB) files, which have all the source line, function, variable, and type information possible, always take precedence over COFF/DBG files, which hold only public function symbols, and COFF/DBG files take precedence over exported names, which are a sort of pseudo symbol. If you want to confirm that the debugger loads symbols for a DLL, you need to monitor the Debug tab of the Output window. If the Output window says "Loaded symbols for '*DLL name*'," you have full symbols for your DLL. Conversely, if it says "Loaded '*DLL name*', no matching symbolic information found" or "Loaded exports for '*DLL name*'," no symbols were loaded.

Since we're on the subject of symbols, I'll mention that you should always install the Windows 2000 symbols. They won't help you completely reverse engineer the operating system because they contain symbol names only for public symbols. If the symbols are loaded, however, you'll at least be able to see what function you're in when you're looking at the stack or the Disassembly window. Be aware that you need to update the operating system symbols each time you apply an operating system service pack. For Windows 2000, the symbols are on the Customer Support Diagnostics CD. For Windows NT 4, the Visual Studio setup includes a program, Windows NT Symbols Setup, that installs the symbols for you.

If symbols aren't loaded, the location string you'll use is the name exported from the DLL. You can check the name by running the DUMPBIN utility on the DLL: DUMPBIN /EXPORTS *DLL Name*. If you run DUMPBIN on KERNEL32.DLL, you won't see a *LoadLibrary* function but rather two similarly named functions, *LoadLibraryA* and *LoadLibraryW*. Suffixes indicate the character set used by the function; the *A* suffix stands for ANSI and the *W* stands for Wide, or Unicode. Windows 2000 uses Unicode internally for internationalization. If you compiled your program with *_UNICODE* defined, you'll want to use the *LoadLibraryW* version. If you didn't, you can use *LoadLibraryA*. However, *LoadLibraryA* is just a wrapper that allocates memory to convert the ANSI string to Unicode and calls *LoadLibraryW*, so technically you could use *LoadLibraryW* as well. If you know for sure that your program is going to call only one of these functions, you can just set the breakpoint on that function. If you're not sure, set breakpoints on both functions. If symbols aren't loaded, the breakpoint syntax for breaking on *LoadLibrary* is "{,,KERNEL32.DLL}LoadLibraryA" or "{,,KERNEL32.DLL}LoadLibraryW."

If your application is targeting only Windows 2000, you should use Unicode throughout. You can get a nice performance boost. Matt Pietrek, in his December 1997 "Under the Hood" column in *Microsoft Systems Journal,* reported that the ANSI wrappers had a sizable performance hit associated with them. In addition to having a faster program, you'll be several steps closer to full internationalization by using Unicode.

If symbols are loaded, you need to do some calculations because you'll need to match the decorated symbol name. What you need to know is the calling convention of the exported function and the function prototype. I'll get into much more detail about calling conventions in Chapter 6. For the *LoadLibrary* function, the prototype from WINBASE.H with some macros expanded for clarity, is as follows:

```
__declspec (dllimport)
HMODULE
__stdcall
LoadLibraryA(
    LPCSTR lpLibFileName
    );
```

The *WINBASEAPI* macro expands into the standard call calling convention, *__stdcall*, which, by the way, is the calling convention for all system application programming interface (API) functions. Standard call functions are decorated with an underbar prefix and suffixed with an "@" sign followed by the number of bytes pushed on the stack. Fortunately, calculating the number is easy; it's the sum of the parameter byte count. With the Intel Pentium family of CPUs, you can just count the number of parameters and multiply by 4. In the case of *LoadLibrary*, which takes one parameter, the final name is *_LoadLibraryA@4*. Here are some examples that will give you an idea of what final names look like: *CreateProcess*, which has 10 parameters, is *_CreateProcessA@40*, and *TlsAlloc*, which has no parameters, is *_TlsAlloc@0*. Even if a function doesn't have any parameters, you must keep the "@#" format. As is the case when symbols aren't loaded, the ANSI and Unicode conditions still apply. If symbols are loaded, the breakpoint syntax for breaking on *LoadLibrary* is "{,,KERNEL32.DLL}_LoadLibraryA@4" or "{,,KERNEL32.DLL}_LoadLibraryW@4."

Location Breakpoint Modifiers

After that brief sojourn into how to calculate the correct location of exported functions, you can now set a location breakpoint anywhere in your application with aplomb. Location breakpoints are great, but as I indicated at the opening of this section, you can also add some real smarts to them so that you can use the debugger even more efficiently. The vehicles for these "smarts" are skip counts, conditional expressions, and variable changes.

Skip Counts

The simplest modifier applicable to location breakpoints is a skip count. A skip count tells the debugger that it should put the breakpoint in but not stop on it until the breakpoint executes a specific number of times. With this modifier, breaking inside loops at the appropriate time is trivial.

Adding a skip count to a location breakpoint is easy. First set a regular location breakpoint and bring up the Breakpoints dialog box. Highlight the location breakpoint in the Breakpoints list box, and click the Condition button. Then in the bottom edit control on the Breakpoint Condition dialog box, enter the number of times you want the breakpoint skipped.

What makes skip counts so useful is that when you're stopped in the debugger, the debugger will tell you how many times the breakpoint has executed. If you have a loop that's crashing but you don't know which iteration is crashing, add a location breakpoint to a line in the loop and add a skip count modifier that is larger than the total number of loop iterations. When your program crashes, bring up the Breakpoints dialog box and look at the breakpoint indicated in the Breakpoints list box. After the breakpoint syntax string, you'll see the number of hits remaining. Subtract that number from the skip count to find out how many times the loop executed. The Breakpoints dialog box shown in Figure 5-3 displays the remaining skip count after a crash. Keep in mind that the remaining count works only when your program is running at full speed. Single-stepping over a breakpoint doesn't update the skip count.

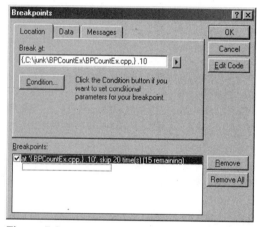

Figure 5-3 *An example of remaining skip count breakpoint executions*

Conditional Expressions

The second modifier for location breakpoints is a conditional expression. A location breakpoint that has a conditional expression triggers only if its expression evaluates to true. A conditional expression is a powerful weapon for gaining control exactly when you need it. The debugger can handle just about any expression you throw at it. To add a conditional expression to your breakpoint, select the breakpoint in the Breakpoints dialog box, click the Condition button, and then enter the expression in the first edit control in the Breakpoint Condition dialog box. The only rules you need to keep in mind are these three:

- You can use only C-style comparison operators.
- The breakpoint conditional expression can't call any functions.
- The breakpoint conditional expression can't contain any macro values.

Because the expression evaluator knows how to evaluate your variables to values, you can use variables directly. Additionally, you can manipulate pointers and do casting if needed.

As you can see, the conditional expression modifier is extremely powerful. Knowing the different pseudoregisters that allow you to access register values and special values and being a little creative are two of the tricks to using conditional expressions. For example, although the Visual C++ debugger doesn't have an explicit method for setting a location breakpoint that fires only in a specific thread under Windows 2000, if you set the expression to "@TIB==*Thread Information Block Linear Address*," you'll break only on the specified thread. The first step is to enter the @TIB pseudoregister into the Watch window and find the thread information block linear address for the thread you want to break on. You might need to use the debugger's Threads dialog box to set the active thread to the one you're interested in checking. If, for example, the thread you want to break on @TIB evaluated to 0x7FFDE000, the expression is "@TIB==0x7FFDE000." For Windows 98, you'll need to look at the Intel CPU FS register, which is unique for each thread, and you can use the expression "@FS==*thread specific value.*"

If you need to break based on a specific last error code, you can use the @ERR pseudoregister. For example, to break after an API call that could have a last error of *ERROR_FILE_NOT_FOUND* according to the Platform SDK documentation, the expression would be "@ERR==2." I looked up *ERROR_FILE_NOT_FOUND* in WINERROR.H to get its value. Table 5-1 lists all the pseudoregisters.

Finally, because you can't call functions in your expressions, breaking on a string with a specific value is difficult. In that case, just set up an expression that checks each character, such as *(szBuff[0]=='P')&&(szBuff[1]=='a')&&(szBuff[2]=='m').*

The other trick you can use with conditional expressions is to combine them with skip counts. That way, you can easily break on the *n*th time the expression is true.

Table 5-1   EXPRESSION AND WATCH WINDOW PSEUDOREGISTERS

Pseudoregister	*Description*
@ERR	Last error value; the same value returned by the *GetLastError* API function
@TIB	Thread information block for the current thread; necessary because the debugger doesn't handle the "FS:0" format
@CLK	Undocumented clock register; usable only in the Watch window
@EAX, @EBX, @ECX, @EDX, @ESI, @EDI, @EIP, @ESP, @EBP, @EFL	Intel CPU registers
@CS, @DS, @ES, @SS, @FS, @GS	Intel CPU segment registers
@ST0, @ST1, @ST2, @ST3, @ST4, @ST5, @ST6, @ST7	Intel CPU floating-point registers

Variable Changes

The final location breakpoint modifier is breaking when a variable changes. The important caveat to remember with this type of location breakpoint modifier is that the variable is checked only when the location breakpoint executes. This modifier comes in handy when you know a memory overwrite is happening in a higher level function but you're trying to narrow down which lower level function is doing the clobbering. When I'm trying to resolve such a situation, I'll set the location breakpoints after each function call and have them check whether the variable value has changed. One benefit of using this variable change is that you can have the debugger look at an entire buffer if needed.

Adding this breakpoint modifier is just like adding the others in that you use the Breakpoint Condition dialog box to set the conditional parameters you want. The only possible confusion is that the edit control you use for entering the variable to watch is the same edit control you use to enter a conditional expression. In the middle edit control of the Breakpoint Condition dialog box, you tell the debugger how many items in an array or memory location you want to watch. If the value you want to break on is a pointer dereference, such as *pMyData*, you enter the number of bytes to watch.

Global Expression and Conditional Breakpoints

Up to this point, I've been talking about a single type of breakpoint—the location breakpoint—and its modifiers. When I originally mentioned the second part of break-point syntax, I referred to three other types in addition to the location breakpoint: expressions, variables, and Windows messages. Expression and variable breakpoints are similar to the location breakpoint modifiers except that they are global in scope. The same rules for their use apply, however. On Intel CPUs, both of these breakpoint types will try to use a hardware breakpoint through one of the CPU's special debug registers.

The debug registers are limited to monitoring an address and 1 byte, 2 bytes, or 4 bytes at that address. If you construct your expression or data change breakpoint so that the debugger can store it in one of the debug registers, your program will be able to run at full speed until it meets your condition or the data changes. If the expression or data can't use the debug registers, however, the debugger will single-step every assembly-language instruction and check the condition after stepping. If your program is forced to single-step at this level of detail, it will run extremely slowly—probably so slowly that it's unusable.

Consequently, no matter whether you're interested in an expression or a data change, the best way for you to ensure that the debugger utilizes the debug registers is to use actual address values for your expressions and data change locations. In the AdvancedBP program in Listing 5-1, I wanted to set a global expression breakpoint to trigger if the first character of the global variable *g_szGlobal* changed to *G*. In the program, I looked up the address for *g_szGlobal*, 0x00404594, and set the expression breakpoint on the Breakpoints dialog box Data tab to "*(char*)0x00404594=='G'." I have to admit that I had to tinker a little to get the expression correct. If you want to see the debugger single-step each instruction, the incorrect expression "WO(0x00404594)=='G' " will show you. I haven't found the global expression breakpoint that useful because it's very hard to find an expression the debugger will accept. The global variable breakpoint is much handier.

```
/*001*/ #include <stdio.h>
/*002*/ #include <string.h>
/*003*/ #include <windows.h>
/*004*/ void LocBPFunc ( void )
/*005*/ {    // {,AdvancedBP.cpp,}.6
/*006*/     printf ( "Hello from LocBPFunc\n" ) ;
/*007*/ }
/*008*/ void SkipLocBPFunc ( void )
/*009*/ {    // {,AdvancedBP.cpp,}.12 skip 99 times(s)
/*010*/     for ( int i = 0 ; i < 100 ; i++ )
/*011*/     {
/*012*/         printf ( "SkipLocBPFunc iteration = %d\n" , i ) ;
/*013*/     }
/*014*/ }
/*015*/ void ExprTrueLocBP ( void )
/*016*/ {    // {,AdvancedBP.cpp,}.20 when 'j==8'
/*017*/     int j = 0 ;
/*018*/     for ( int i = 0 ; i < 10 ; i++ )
/*019*/     {
/*020*/         j = i * 2 ;
/*021*/     }
/*022*/ }
/*023*/ void DataChangeLocBP ( void )
/*024*/ {    // {,AdvancedBP.cpp,}.26 when szBuff[5](length:1) changes
/*025*/     char szBuff[ 10 ] ;
/*026*/     strcpy ( szBuff , "String!" ) ;
/*027*/ }
/*028*/ char g_szGlobal[ 10 ] ;
/*029*/ int g_iInt = 0 ;
/*030*/ void main ( void )
/*031*/ {    // 0x401210 -> BP @ entry point, _mainCRTStartup
/*032*/     LocBPFunc ( ) ;
/*033*/     SkipLocBPFunc ( ) ;
/*034*/     ExprTrueLocBP ( ) ;
/*035*/     DataChangeLocBP ( ) ;
```

Listing 5-1 *ADVANCEDBP.CPP*   *(continued)*

Listing 5-1 *continued*

```
/*036*/
/*037*/        //{,,KERNEL32.DLL}_LoadLibraryA@4   <- w/ symbols
/*038*/        //{,,KERNEL32.DLL}LoadLibrary        <- w/o symbols
/*039*/        LoadLibrary ( "KERNEL32.DLL" ) ;
/*040*/
/*041*/        // (char)0x00404594=='G' <- Global expression BP.
/*042*/        strcpy ( g_szGlobal , "Global!" ) ;
/*043*/
/*044*/        // (long)0x4045A0  <- Global variable BP.
/*045*/        g_iInt = 0x42 ;
/*046*/
/*047*/        printf ( "Done!\n" ) ;
/*048*/ }
```

Like the global expression breakpoint, the global variable breakpoint works best if you use the hexadecimal address of the variable, cast the address to a long pointer, and keep the number of elements to watch set to 1. When the memory at that address changes, the debugger stops. To modify the expression "*(char*)0x00404594=='G' " so that it breaks whenever the memory changes, set the breakpoint at the address "*(long*)(0x00404594)." Generally, it takes a try or two to get the right expression so that you can properly use the debug registers. You should never set the number of elements to watch to anything other than 1 when you're doing the long casts. The 1 indicates that you're monitoring for writes to a double-word memory size, and because the hardware debug registers can't handle more than a double-word reference, you'll force the single-step method of checking memory.

Although there are four debug registers, I've gotten only two global breakpoints working at a time. If you try to set a bunch of global breakpoints, you'll guarantee that the debugger will single-step your program.

Global variable breakpoints are an excellent technique for finding one of the most difficult bugs of all, wild writes. As you'll recall from Chapter 2, a wild write occurs when someone writes to memory using an uninitialized pointer, causing corruption to appear in random places. The only time you notice the problem is either when the program crashes or when some of the data becomes corrupted. Once you get the problem duplicated so that you can get the same variable corrupted even part of the time, set the global variable breakpoint so that you can find out whenever someone writes to that memory. Just be prepared for the breakpoint to go off many times on legitimate writes before you come across the first wild write.

Windows Message Breakpoints

The last type of breakpoint is the Windows message breakpoint. You set this break-point on the Messages tab of the Breakpoints dialog box. With this type of breakpoint, you can have the debugger break when a window procedure receives a specific Windows message. If you have a straight C SDK-style program, setting this breakpoint is a snap because the Break At WndProc drop-down list contains the window procedures in the program when the debuggee is running. Just select the window procedure and set the message you want to break on, and you're done. If the message you want to break on isn't in the list, just type the message's value into the message combo box.

In today's high-speed world, almost everyone uses C++ class libraries, such as MFC, in which it's just barely possible to use a Windows message breakpoint. The issue is that the Windows message breakpoint requires a function, or address, with the four proper window procedure parameters. You can set a Windows message breakpoint on the main MFC window procedure, "{,,MFC42D.DLL}AfxWndProc," and it will work. Unfortunately, because that's the one window procedure for most windows derived from *CWnd*, you might be stopping on the breakpoint all the time. If you need to break on a private Windows message that only one of your classes uses, setting the Windows message breakpoint will work, but you'll still need to step out of *AfxWndProc* to your derived class.

If you need to break on a common message, a better approach is to set a conditional location breakpoint in *CWnd::WindowProc*, the MFC C++ message method for each class. First find the value of the *this* pointer for the class you're interested in, and then look up the value of the Windows message you want to stop on in WINUSER.H. With those two values, you can set a location breakpoint in *CWnd::WindowProc*. I'm running Visual C++ 6.0 Service Pack 3 at the time of this writing, and to break only in my class on a *WM_PAINT* message, the breakpoint syntax is "{,WINCORE.CPP,} .1584 when (this==0x0012FE74)&&(message==0xF)."

When you're using the location breakpoint with the "this...&&...*message*" expression, you'll have to be careful because your *this* pointer will probably change depending on how your class is allocated and on the changes you're making to your code. If you want to get the breakpoint set quickly, you can always add a handler method with the Class Wizard and just set a simple location breakpoint.

I've covered a great deal of ground here with the advanced breakpoints. The AdvancedBP program shows each type of breakpoint except the Windows message, and you might want to experiment a bit with it to see how the various breakpoints work. In the source code, I embedded the breakpoint syntax for each breakpoint so that you can see the syntax without opening the Breakpoints dialog box. I strongly encourage you to take some time to practice using advanced breakpoints in your own code. You'll be amazed at how much you can learn about both the debugger and your project.

COMMON DEBUGGING QUESTION

Why do my breakpoints disappear or jump around?

To keep your source code breakpoints healthy, it helps to edit your source code in the Visual C++ integrated development environment (IDE) editor because it will keep your breakpoints on the appropriate line. If you do happen to edit your source code outside the IDE and your breakpoints don't correspond to an active source code line, the debugger will respond with the following message: "One or more breakpoints are not positioned on valid lines. These breakpoints have been moved to the next valid line." The debugger always moves the breakpoints down, so if you delete code, you might want to double-check the breakpoints to ensure that they appear on the proper lines.

If the debugger can't set a breakpoint at all, you'll get the message, "One or more breakpoints cannot be set and have been disabled. Execution will stop at the beginning of the program." After you click OK to dismiss the message box, you should bring up the Breakpoints dialog box and look for the unchecked breakpoints. Those are the ones that gave the debugger trouble.

The most common reason for the debugger not setting your breakpoints is that you've set a breakpoint in an explicitly loaded DLL—that is, one loaded with an explicit call to the *LoadLibrary* API function. All Component Object Model (COM) DLLs are explicitly loaded DLLs, so this problem occurs with an annoying frequency. The debugger has to resolve all breakpoints at startup, so you'll need to add the explicitly loaded DLLs manually to the additional DLLs list to force the debugger to load symbols for those DLLs when you start debugging. In the Project Settings dialog box, on the Debug tab, select Additional DLLs in the Category combo box. In the Modules list, add all the DLLs that your project might ever load.

Setting compiler optimizations can also move or disable your breakpoints. If you do set compiler optimizations, be aware that the compiler might move code in such a way that the debugger can't resolve the breakpoint location.

REMOTE DEBUGGING

Now that you're well versed in the nuances of advanced breakpoints, I want to turn to one of the hidden gems within the Visual C++ debugger: remote debugging. Remote debugging means that your program and a tiny debug stub run on one machine (the remote machine) and the debugger runs on another (the local machine), communicating with one another through Transmission Control Protocol/Internet Protocol (TCP/IP). Although you can do much of your debugging on a single machine with the Visual C++ debugger, if you encounter any of the following situations, which can be affected by the overhead of a full graphical user interface (GUI) debugger, you'll be glad you've heard of remote debugging:

- When you need to debug critical window activation code

- When you need to debug drawing or painting code

- When you need to free more memory for your application

- When you need to debug on Windows 98

- When you don't want to change the machine configuration drastically by installing the complete Visual C++ IDE

The worst situation you'll face is the first: when you need to debug critical window activation code. It is impossible to single-step through *WM_SETFOCUS* and similar processing on a single machine because the act of stepping causes your program to lose focus to the debugger. GUI debuggers are great, but in this case, the Heisenberg uncertainty principle as it applies to debuggers is alive and well! Moving the debugger to a separate machine allows the debugger and your program each to have its own focus, thus neatly sidestepping the problem.

The second situation in which remote debugging can save the day is when you need to debug drawing or painting code. Although you might be able to scrunch the debugger into one corner of the screen and your application into another for simple cases on a single-monitor system, in the hard cases, the debugger gets in the way. If your application must use a good chunk of screen real estate or your application is a Microsoft DirectX game, you need remote debugging.

The third situation in which you need remote debugging is more subtle but still definitely something to keep in mind. The full-blown GUI debugger uses a fair amount of resources. If you want the power and ease of use of the Visual C++ debugger, your application has to forgo some memory so that the debugger can run. In real-world development with real-world applications, debug builds can be huge. By using remote debugging, you'll free more memory for your application to run. You'll find remote debugging especially useful when you're having trouble testing against minimal requirement machines.

The fourth situation in which I use remote debugging is when I need to debug on Windows 98. Because remote debugging allows you to debug from one operating system to another, I use Windows 2000 for the target machine and Windows 98 for the remote machine because I've found that the Visual C++ debugger runs better on Windows 2000.

The final situation for remote debugging is when you're debugging a machine on which you suspect you might have a system DLL version problem with your application (aka "DLL Hell"). Installing the full Visual C++ IDE on the system in question can cause various system DLLs to be updated, thus destroying the chance to duplicate and fix the bug. By copying just the few files needed to run the remote portion of the debugger to the remote machine, you can still debug the problem.

The Visual Studio documentation does a good job explaining how to set up remote debugging. I don't want to duplicate that explanation here, so I encourage you to search for the "Debugging Remote Applications" topic on MSDN.

What I want to discuss for the rest of this section are the tricks and techniques that will make your remote debugging a pleasurable experience. The documentation does tell you what individual files you need to copy to the remote machine, but it doesn't tell you where you can locate them, so I listed the locations in Table 5-2.

Table 5-2   NECESSARY FILES FOR REMOTE DEBUGGING AND THEIR VISUAL C++ INSTALLED LOCATIONS

Files	Visual C++ Installed Location
MSVCMON.EXE, TLN0T.DLL, DM.DLL, MSDIS110.DLL	\<VS Common>\MSDEV98\BIN
MSVCRT.DLL, MSVCP60.DLL	%SYSTEMROOT%\System32
PSAPI.DLL (Windows 2000 only)	%SYSTEMROOT%\System32

The first key to successful remote debugging is to get the two systems set so that the local machine, on which the debugger runs, can find the same binaries that the remote machine is running. At a minimum, you should have the remote machine share all drives because the local machine will need access to match binaries. The location of your program will depend on its complexity: it can reside on the local machine and run from there on the remote machine; it can reside on both machines; or it can reside only on the remote machine. If your program is just a standard EXE-type program, the remote machine can probably run it off the local machine. In today's brave new COM world, however, deciding where to run your program can get complicated. What has worked for me is to have the program in identical drives and directories on both machines. The second key to remote debugging is to ensure that you have your program completely and correctly installed (wherever you decide to put it) and ready to run on the remote machine before you start remote debugging.

MSVCMON.EXE is the debug stub that runs on the remote machine. MSVCMON.EXE has a Settings button that supposedly lets you specify the local machine network name—but don't bother using it because MSVCMON.EXE ignores the settings. After you start MSVCMON.EXE, make sure that you have your debugging project set up correctly on the local machine. In the Project Settings dialog box, on the Debug tab, put the complete path and file where the binary appears on the *remote* machine in the Remote Executable Path And File Name edit box. When you set the local debugger to debug remotely, the local debugger doesn't actually start the process. MSVCMON.EXE starts the process, so you have to tell it where to find the binary.

After you've set up your project and clicked the Go button, you pretty much debug just as you normally would. The only difference you'll see in remote debugging vs. regular debugging is that the local debugger will occasionally prompt you for the location of a matching DLL. (This is why I mentioned sharing all the remote computer's drives—you'll always need to be able to find the matching binary so that if you experience any sort of problems, you can look at the source.) Although the prompt has a check box for turning off DLL matching, you should never turn off this feature. The problem is that once you've turned off DLL matching there's no way to turn it back on other than by deleting the project OPT file. Additionally, the locations of the remotely matched binaries are stored in the project OPT file, so if later you want to connect to a different machine for remote debugging the same project, the only way to reset the binary file locations is to delete the project OPT as well. Keep in mind that deleting the project OPT will cause you to lose all the project's breakpoints and screen layouts.

You can combine a remote control application, such as Symantec's pcAnywhere, with remote debugging so that you can debug your application on the user's machine. I've done this across a company's intranet, though never on the wild and wooly Internet. Although such a combination could result in some security issues, it still might not be a bad trick to pull out of your debugging bag if needed. This sleight-of-hand might be especially useful if the user's machine is in Singapore, you're in New York, and you have to fix the problem today!

The last two points I want to mention about remote debugging are minor. The first is to remember to set your Visual C++ IDE back to local debugging when you've finished remote debugging. The setting for remote debugging is global to all projects even though, in my opinion, it should be a per-project setting. The last point is that if you're working on a network application or on a system that is sensitive to network traffic, remote debugging uses TCP/IP, so the debugger can get in your way. If you're in either of these situations, use WinDBG, which also supports remote debugging using the serial ports and a null modem cable.

TIPS AND TRICKS

Now it's time to turn to some tricks you can use in the debugger so that you can collect as much information about your problem as possible. As usual, I encourage you to spend some time playing with these tips on your own projects so that you can find innovative ways of applying them.

Setting Breakpoints

You might think I've already covered everything you need to know about breakpoints—but hang on, there's still a little more. Everyone knows that you can set location breakpoints on a source line and in the Disassembly window, but did you know that you can also set them in the Call Stack window? Setting a location breakpoint in a Call Stack window is a great technique when you want to get out of a deeply nested call chain. In the Call Stack window, right-click the function on which you want to break and select Insert/Remove Breakpoint to stop as soon as you return to that function.

Instead of removing breakpoints after a heavy debugging session, I always disable them. You can disable breakpoints either by right-clicking each one in the source window and selecting Disable Breakpoint or by going into the Breakpoints dialog box and turning off the check mark next to the breakpoint. I leave the breakpoints in while I'm fixing a problem so that I can quickly get the application back to the state it was in when the problem occurred. Of course, I update any breakpoints that could have changed before I start debugging. After I've checked the fix, I can safely remove the breakpoints.

To ensure that I get all my breakpoints set easily, I always click the Step Into button to get the debuggee loaded and started before I set any breakpoints other than simple location breakpoints. The debugger can verify your breakpoints and display the Resolve Ambiguity dialog box only when the debuggee is active. The help the debugger gives you means that you get your breakpoints set quicker and that you can be certain they are correct.

The Watch Window

The Watch window is high on the list of important Visual C++ debugger features. In fact, you probably end up looking at the Watch window more than any other window in the debugger. What makes the Watch window so popular is partly its versatility. You can wield it in various ways to gather information about your application. The neatest capability is that you can easily change a variable's value in the Watch window by editing it in the right-hand side of the grid. Recall from earlier in the chapter our discussion of the syntax for the breakpoint expressions. The same expression evaluator is used in the Watch window, so the advanced breakpoint scope syntax and the expression rules and pseudoregisters can be used in the Watch window as well.

Formatting Data and Expression Evaluation

The first "trick" you'll need to master on your way to becoming proficient at manipulating the Watch window is to memorize the formatting symbols in Table 5-3 and

Table 5-3 **FORMATTING SYMBOLS FOR WATCH WINDOW VARIABLES**

Symbol	Format Description	Sample	Displays
d, i	Signed decimal integer	(int)0xF000F065,d	−268373915
u	Unsigned decimal integer	0x0065,u	101
o	Unsigned octal integer	0xF065,o	0170145
x, X	Hexadecimal integer	61541,X	0x0000F065
l, h	Long or short prefix for d, i, u, o, x, X	0x00406042,hx	0x0c22
f	Signed floating-point	3./2.,f	1.500000
e	Signed scientific notation	3./2,e	1.500000e+000
g	Signed floating-point or signed scientific notation, whichever is shorter	3./2,g	1.5
c	Single character	0x0065,c	'e'
s	String	szHiWorld,s	"Hello world"
su	Unicode string	szWHiWorld,su	"Hello world"
st	Unicode string or ANSI string, depending on Unicode Strings setting in AUTOEXP.DAT		
hr	*HRESULT* or Win32 error code	0x00000000,hr	S_OK
wc	Windows class flag	0x00000040,wc	WC_DEFAULTCHAR (Note that although documented, this format doesn't work in Visual C++ 6.)
wm	Windows message numbers	0x0010,wm	WM_CLOSE

Table 5-4, which derive from the Visual C++ documentation on MSDN. The Watch window is wonderfully flexible in how it displays data, and the way you bring out its flexibility is by using the format codes in these tables. As you can see from the tables, the formats are easy to use: follow your variable with a comma and with the format you want to use. The most useful format specifier for COM programming is ",hr." If you keep the expression "@EAX,hr" in your Watch window, as you step over a COM method call, you can see the results of the call in a form you can understand. (@EAX is the Intel CPU register at which return values are stored.) Using the format specifiers will allow you to easily control how you see your data so that you can save huge amounts of time interpreting it.

Table 5-4 FORMATTING SYMBOLS FOR WATCH WINDOW MEMORY DUMPS

Symbol	Format Description	Sample	Displays
ma	64 ASCII characters	0x0012ffac,ma	0x0012ffac .4...0...".0W&.......1W&.0.:W..1 ....."..1.JO&.1.2.."..1...0y....1
m	16 bytes in hexa-decimal followed by 16 ASCII characters	0x0012ffac,m	0x0012ffac b3 34 cb 00 84 30 94 80 ff 22 8a 30 57 26 00 00 .4...0...".0W&..
mb	16 bytes in hexa-decimal followed by 16 ASCII characters	0x0012ffac,mb	0x0012ffac b3 34 cb 00 84 30 94 80 ff 22 8a 30 57 26 00 00 .4...0...".0W&..
mw	8 words	0x0012ffac,mw	0x0012ffac 34b3 00cb 3084 8094 22ff 308a 2657 0000
md	4 double words	0x0012ffac,md	0x0012ffac 00cb34b3 80943084 308a22ff 00002657
mq	4 quadwords	0x0012ffac,mq	0x0012ffac 8094308400cb34b3 00002657308a22ff
mu	2-byte characters (Unicode)	0x0012ffac,mu	0x0012ffac 34b3 00cb 3084 8094 22ff 308a 2657 0000 ?.????.
#	(Undocumented) Expands a pointer to a memory location to the specified number of values	pCharArray,10	Expanded array of 10 characters using +/- expanders

One format specifier not documented is the one that allows you to expand a pointer to a memory location to a specific number of values. If you have a pointer to an array of 10 longs, the Watch window will show only the first value. To see the entire array, follow the variable with the number of values you'd like to see. For example, "pLong,10" would show an expandable array of your 10 items. If you have a large array, you can point into the middle of it and expand just the values you want with "(pBigArray+100),20" to show the 20 elements starting at offset 99. There's a bug in the display: the index values always begin at 0, regardless of the position of the first displayed element. In the *pBigArray* example, the first index, shown as 0, is the 100th array element, 1 is the 101st array element, and so on.

In addition to allowing you to format the data as you'd like it, the Watch window allows you to cast and cajole your data variables so that you can see exactly what you need to see. For example, you can use the *BY*, *WO*, and *DW* expressions mentioned earlier in the chapter to get at pointer offsets. The address-of operator (&) and the pointer operator (*) are also allowed, and both allow you to get the values at memory addresses and to see the results of casts in your code. If you need to be specific, the context specifiers described in the section "Advanced Breakpoint Syntax and Location Breakpoints" earlier in the chapter allow you to explicitly specify the context for a variable in the Watch window. Finally, all the formatting and specifying used in the Watch window also works in the QuickWatch window.

If you haven't guessed by now, the Watch window is much more than a static variable viewer. In fact, it is a whole expression evaluator in which you can check any conditional statements you want. I use the Watch window a lot during my unit testing to verify *if* statements and the like. I put the individual variables for a conditional statement in the Watch window, followed by the conditional statement. With this setup, I can see the values of each variable and the results of the conditional evaluation. If I need to change the evaluation of a conditional statement, I can start changing the values of the individual variables and keep track of the outcome in the Watch window. In addition, because the Watch window handles expressions so well, you no longer need to pull up Microsoft Calculator to do your calculations—just do them in the Watch window.

Timing Code in the Watch Window

Here's another neat trick—using the Watch window to time code. An undocumented pseudoregister, @CLK, can serve as a rudimentary timer. In many cases, you just want a rough idea of the time between two points, and @CLK makes it easy to find out how long it took to execute between two breakpoints. Keep in mind that this time includes the debugger overhead. The trick is to enter two @CLK watches, the first just "@CLK" and the second "@CLK=0". The second watch zeros out the timer after you start running again. Because the time is in microseconds and I prefer the time in milliseconds, I set the first @CLK to "@CLK/1000,d". I include the ",d" to force the display into decimal when I have the Watch window set to Hexadecimal Display. Although not a perfect timer, @CLK is good enough for some ballpark guesses.

Calling Functions in the Watch Window

The last trick with the Watch window is something almost every UNIX developer asks for when converting to Windows programming: a way to execute a function from the debugger. At first, you might wonder what's so desirable about that. If you think like a debugging guru, however, you'll realize that being able to execute a function within the debugger allows you to fully customize your debugging environment. For example, instead of spending 10 minutes looking at 10 different data structures to ensure data coherency, you can write a function that verifies the data and then call it when you need it most—when your application is stopped in the debugger.

The cool part is that your program never has to call the functions you want to use only in the Watch window. In debug builds, your program has all functions linked into it, but in release builds, any function that is never called isn't linked. When you enter a function in the Watch window, you can also pass parameters, so you can write generic functions that can work on different data pointers. You can think of the Watch window as a limited Immediate window like the one in Microsoft Visual Basic.

If your debugging function has no parameters, make sure to use parentheses so that the Visual C++ debugger knows to call your debugging function. For example, if your debugging function is *void MyMemCheck ( )*, you'd call it in the Watch window with "MyMemCheck ( )". If your debugging function takes parameters, just pass them as if you're calling the function normally. If your debugging function returns a value, the right-hand side of the Watch window will display the return value.

You'll face a few limitations when calling debugging functions in the Watch window. These limitations shouldn't cause you any problems, though, as long as you follow a few rules. The first rule is that the function can execute only in a single thread context while it's in the Watch window. If you have a multithreaded program, you should enter the debugging function into the Watch window, check the results, and then immediately delete it from the Watch window. If the debugging function does execute in a thread other than the first one it executed in, the second thread will immediately terminate. The second rule is that the debugging function must execute in less than 20 seconds; if the debugging function has an exception, your entire program will terminate under the debugger. The final rule is common sense: only do memory reads with data verifications. If you have a problem, just call *OutputDebugString* or *printf*. There's no telling what can happen if you start changing memory or calling Windows API functions.

Keep in mind that your debugging function executes whenever the Watch window reevaluates the expressions in it. That happens in the following conditions:

- When the program is running and a breakpoint triggers

- When you single-step a line or an instruction

- When you finish editing the debugging function text in the left-hand side of the Watch window and press Enter

- When an exception occurs in your running program and drops you back to the debugger

I need to stress again that you should get into the habit of entering your special debugging function, letting it evaluate, and immediately deleting it from the Watch window. That way, you avoid any surprises and you control when the debugging function executes. In addition, you don't need to write debugging functions for every little thing in your application. I write them only for the most critical data structures, especially if the structure is one that I need to see in its entirety. I also write them to validate data that must be coordinated. For example, if structure *A* is supposed to have a field that corresponds to a field in structure *B* and both fields need to be updated to keep data coherence, a debugging function that you can call from the Watch window is a good way to coordinate the fields. Finally, don't bother with dump functions for individual structures. The Watch window already expands structures for you, so you needn't waste your time reinventing that particular wheel.

Expanding Your Own Types Automatically

Although the Visual C++ documentation barely mentions this topic, you can have your own types automatically expanded in the Watch window as well as in the QuickWatch window and in DataTips. You've probably seen a few common types, such as *CObject* and *RECT*, expand in the Watch window without realizing that you could easily arrange for your own types to benefit from the Watch window's expansiveness. The magic happens in the AUTOEXP.DAT text file in the <VS Common>\MSDev98\Bin subdirectory. Just add an entry for your own types at the bottom of the file.

As an example, I'll add an auto expand entry for the *PROCESS_INFORMATION* structure that is passed to the *CreateProcess* API function. The first step is to check what the Visual C++ debugger recognizes as the type. In a sample program, I put a *PROCESS_INFORMATION* variable in the Watch window, right-clicked it, and selected Properties from the menu. In the Program Variable Properties dialog box, the type was *_PROCESS_INFORMATION*, which if you look at the structure definition below, matches the structure tag.

```
typedef struct _PROCESS_INFORMATION {
    HANDLE hProcess;
    HANDLE hThread;
    DWORD dwProcessId;
    DWORD dwThreadId;
} PROCESS_INFORMATION
```

The documentation in AUTOEXP.DAT says that the format for an auto expand entry is "type=[text]<member[,format]>...". Table 5-5 shows the meanings for each field. Note that more than one member can be displayed as part of the auto expand.

Table 5-5 **AUTOEXP.DAT AUTO EXPAND ENTRIES**

Field	Description
type	The type name. For template types, this field can be followed by "<*>" to encompass all derived types.
text	Any literal text. This field is generally the member name or a shorthand version of it.
member	The actual data member to display. This field can be an expression, so if you need to add some offsets to various pointers you can include the offsets in the calculation. The casting operators also work.
format	Additional format specifiers for the member variables. These specifiers are the same as the formatting symbols shown in Table 5-3.

With the *PROCESS_INFORMATION* structure, I'm interested in looking at the *hProcess* and *hThread* values, so my auto expand rule would be "_PROCESS-_INFORMATION =hProcess=<hProcess,X> hThread=<hThread,X>." I use the ",X" format specifiers because I always want to see the values as hexadecimal values.

One special formatting code you'll see in the file is "<,t>." This code tells the debugger to put in the type name of the most derived type. For example, if you have a base class *A* with a derived class *B* and only *A* has an auto expand rule, the auto expand for a variable of type *B* will be the class name *B* followed by the auto expand rule for class *A*. The "<,t>" format is very helpful for keeping your classes straight.

The Set Next Statement Command

One of the coolest hidden features in the debugger is the Set Next Statement command. It is accessible in both source windows and the Disassembly window on the right-click menu, but only when you're debugging. What the Set Next Statement command lets you do is change the instruction pointer to a different place in the program. You can also change the instruction pointer in this way by setting the Intel CPU EIP register directly. Changing what the program executes is a fantastic debugging technique when you're trying to track down a bug or when you're unit testing and want to test your error handlers.

I guess I should mention that changing the instruction pointer can easily crash your program if you're not extremely careful. If you're running in a debug build, you can use Set Next Statement without much trouble. In optimized release builds, however, your safest bet is to use Set Next Statement only in the Disassembly window. The compiler will move code around so that source lines might not execute linearly. In addition, you need to be aware if your code is creating temporary variables on the stack when you use Set Next Statement. In the next chapter, I'll cover this last situation in more detail.

If I'm looking for a bug and my hypothesis is that said bug might be in a certain code path, I set a breakpoint in the debugger before the offending function or functions. I check the data and parameters going into the functions, and I single-step over the functions. If the problem isn't duplicated, I use the Set Next Statement command to set the execution point back to the breakpoint and change the data going into the functions. This tactic will allow me to test several hypotheses in one debugging session, thus saving time in the end. As you can imagine, you can't use this technique in all cases because once you execute some code in your program, executing it again can destroy the state. Set Next Statement works best on code that doesn't change the state too much.

As I mentioned earlier, the Set Next Statement command comes in handy during unit testing. For example, Set Next Statement is useful when you want to test error handlers. Say that you have an *if* statement and you want to test what happens if the condition fails. All you need to do is to let the condition execute and use Set Next Statement to move the execution point down to the failure case. In addition to Set Next Statement, the Run To Cursor menu option, also available on the Debug menu, allows you to set a one-shot breakpoint. I also use Run To Cursor quite a bit in testing.

Filling data structures, especially lists and arrays, is another excellent use of Set Next Statement when you're testing or debugging. If you have some code that fills a data structure and adds the data structure to a linked list, you can use Set Next Statement to add some additional items to the linked list so that you can see how your code handles those cases. This use of Set Next Statement is especially handy when you need to set up hard-to-duplicate data conditions when you're debugging.

Debugging Visual Basic Compiled Code

The whole trick to debugging compiled Visual Basic code is to test and debug your application thoroughly as p-code before you ever compile it. Debugging compiled Visual Basic isn't as easy as debugging C code because the debug information that Visual Basic generates doesn't have sufficient type information in it; consequently, the debugger can't decipher the various objects. Before you resort to the Visual C++ debugger, you should use a third-party tool such as Compuware NuMega's SmartCheck because it will make Visual Basic debugging much easier. SmartCheck knows how to convert the obtuse Visual Basic error messages into exactly what conditions lead up to the problem so that you don't need to use the Visual C++ debugger. SmartCheck can also produce a complete flow of your Visual Basic application so that you can see how your program executed. Additionally, for compiled code, you should use conditionally compiled *OutputDebugString* function calls to assist you in tracking the problem. In many ways, I've found it easier to debug compiled Visual Basic code at the assembly-language level. I know that sounds crazy, but with all the gyrations that happen in Visual Basic code, it really is easier. Chapter 6 will help you brush up on your assembly-language skills.

To prepare your Visual Basic files for debugging, you must first generate the PDB files when you compile. You can set this option on the Compile tab of the Project Properties dialog box. It also helps to set the compiler to No Optimizations. Just remember to turn the optimizations back on when you start building for shipping.

In the Visual C++ debugger's Variables window, switch to the Locals tab so that you can see the standard-type local variables. Visual Basic uses many temporary variables, so the tab shows many "unnamed_var1" variables. If you scroll down to the bottom of the window, you'll see the local variables.

When I started playing with Visual Basic, I was confused when I'd get the occasional exception, "Floating-point inexact result." I knew I wasn't doing any floating-point number manipulation, so I had no idea what was causing this message to trigger.

After doing a bit of detective work, I discovered that Visual Basic uses its own version of structured exception handling (SEH). Unfortunately, it uses the *EXCEPTION_FLT_INEXACT_RESULT* value for one of its exception values, and when the exception isn't handled, you and I see the misleading exception message.

One trick I've seen some folks use, especially when they're testing a compiled ActiveX control, is to run the entire Visual Basic environment under the Visual C++ debugger. This trick allows you to debug the ActiveX control and use a p-code program as the test harness. Being able to step between a p-code test program and a compiled component allows you to see both sides of the equation more easily.

SUMMARY

The Visual C++ debugger has many powerful features, and this chapter introduced you to the first set of those features: advanced breakpoints and remote debugging. The most important conclusion you should have drawn is that the debugger can do a considerable amount of work for you if you know how to utilize it effectively. You should strive to make the most of the Visual C++ debugger so that you can minimize the time you spend in it.

Advanced breakpoints help you avoid tedious debugging sessions by allowing you to specify the exact conditions under which a breakpoint triggers. The context part of the advanced breakpoint syntax is what you use to tell the debugger the scope and exact position of the breakpoints. The standard location breakpoint has three modifiers that let you control when the breakpoint will trigger: skip counts, conditional expressions, and variable changes. The other types of breakpoints are the global expression breakpoints and the global data change breakpoints. The global data change breakpoints are the most useful of these two types and let you set a hardware-assisted breakpoint memory location; then when that data location is written to, the breakpoint fires.

Remote debugging is a two-machine debugging solution that's a great addition to your debugging toolkit. It's one of the few ways that you can debug difficult situations such as working with window activation code, handling painting problems, freeing up memory for your application, debugging in Windows 98, and avoiding state changes in the machine.

Another useful addition to your debugging repertoire is the many tips and tricks that help you stretch the uses of the Visual C++ debugger. The Watch window, with its wonderful flexibility, is where you can do amazing things to speed up your debugging. In addition to letting you change your variable values, the Watch window offers all sorts of formatting options so that you can view your data in exactly the way you want to. The Watch window also lets you call functions in your program from the debugger. This feature allows you to create and use special debugging functions to automate your most tedious debugging tasks. Finally, you can also define auto expansion rules for your own types so that with a quick glance you can see the important members of your structures and classes.

Chapter 6

Power Debugging with x86 Assembly Language and the Visual C++ Debugger Disassembly Window

In many cases when your application crashes, the real difference between solving the bug and screaming in frustration comes down to how well you can read a little assembly language. Although we'd all prefer our crashes to occur in a module with source code and a complete call stack, many crashes just don't happen that way. When you do crash, you're generally left looking at the Disassembly window in the Microsoft Visual C++ debugger and wondering how you're going to figure out where you are in the program, let alone why you crashed.

By no means am I saying that you need to know assembly language well enough to write all your programs using Microsoft Macro Assembler (MASM). The key is to learn enough assembly language to be comfortable reading it. My goal for this chapter is to present the information you need to have a working knowledge of assembly language. By the time you finish reading this chapter and practice for a couple of hours, you'll know more than enough assembly language to get by. That small investment of time can be the difference between flailing around in the debugger practicing your primal scream therapy and fixing your bugs.

Developers are sometimes wary of learning assembly language because they think some sort of black magic is involved. There's really nothing mysterious about assembly language, though; a single assembly language instruction does one thing and one thing only. Once you see the pattern and understand how the CPU carries out instructions, you'll realize that assembly language is actually quite elegant. If you want to look at black magic, take a single line in Microsoft Visual Basic, such as *db.Connect ("Foo")*. That single line can call 30 to 40 different functions and make an incredible number of assumptions. To me, Visual Basic is sometimes far more mystifying than assembly language.

After introducing you to assembly language, I'll turn back to the Visual C++ debugger and show you how to survive in the Disassembly window. For example, I'll show you how to look up parameters on the stack and navigate within the Disassembly window. I'll also explain the relationship between the Memory window and the Disassembly window as well as supply you with tips and tricks that will help you debug at the assembly-language level.

THE BASICS OF THE CPU

The Intel instruction set has been around for quite a while and has its roots in the 8086 CPU that Intel first released in 1978. In the days of MS-DOS and 16-bit Microsoft Windows, assembly language used to be a little quirky and hard to use because of the way the CPU handled memory, which was through 64-KB blocks of memory called *segments*. Fortunately, today on Microsoft Windows 98 and Microsoft Windows 2000, the CPU has direct access to the entire address space, which means that assembly language is much easier to deal with.

The assembly language that I'll be introducing in this chapter will be the basic 32-bit instruction set that is compatible across all x86 architecture CPUs from both Intel and Advanced Micro Devices (AMD). The advanced features on the Intel Pentiums, such as MMX, aren't generally an issue because Windows uses relatively few such features. I won't get into the real grungy parts of assembly-language instruction formats such as the ModR/M and SIB bytes, which both indicate ways to access memory. For the purposes of this chapter, memory access is memory access. I also won't be covering floating-point instructions. Operations on the Intel CPU floating-point unit (FPU) are similar to normal instructions. The main differences are that the FPU has its own set of registers and the floating-point instructions use a register stack–based architecture. If this chapter inspires you to learn more about the Intel family of CPUs—and I hope it does—you should download the three-volume "Intel Architecture Software Developer's Manual" Adobe PDF files from *www.intel.com*. Intel even offers the manuals in book form for free if you want to be cool and have them on your bookshelf.

One key point to remember is that the x86 CPUs are very flexible and provide you with many ways to carry out similar operations. Fortunately for us, the Microsoft compilers do a good job of picking the fastest way to do an operation and reusing that construct wherever applicable, so recognizing what a section of code is doing is easier. In this chapter, I'll cover the most commonly used instructions you'll see in assembly language. If you're interested in all the assembly-language instructions, you can consult the Intel manuals.

Registers

The first topic I want to cover is the registers. Because every bit of data that your application handles passes through the registers at one time or another, knowing the purpose of each register can help you recognize code gone awry. x86 CPUs have eight general-purpose registers (EAX, EBX, ECX, EDX, ESI, EDI, ESP, and EBP), six segment registers (CS, DS, ES, SS, FS, and GS), an instruction pointer (EIP), and a flags register (EFLAGS). The CPU has other registers as well, such as the debug and machine control registers, but they are special-purpose registers and you won't encounter them in normal user-mode debugging. The general-purpose registers, which are listed in Table 6-1, are all 32-bit registers. Notice that some of the registers allow mnemonics

TABLE 6-1   GENERAL-PURPOSE REGISTERS

32-Bit Register	*16-Bit Access*	*Low-Byte Access (bits 0–7)*	*High-Byte Access (bits 8–15)*	*Special Uses*
EAX	AX	AL	AH	Integer function return values are stored here.
EBX	BX	BL	BH	
ECX	CX	CL	CH	Loop instruction counters use this register for counting.
EDX	DX	DL	DH	The high 32 bits of 64-bit values are stored here.
ESI	SI			In memory move or compare instructions, the source address is stored here.
EDI	DI			In memory move or compare instructions, the destination address is stored here.
ESP	SP			The stack pointer. This register is changed implicitly when calling functions, returning from functions, making room on the stack for local variables, and cleaning up the stack.
EBP	BP			Base/frame pointer. This register holds the stack frame for a procedure.

to access different portions of the complete 32-bit register. The only segment register of interest for this chapter is the FS register, which holds the thread information block (TIB) that describes the currently executing thread. The other segment registers are used, but the operating system configures them in such a way that they are transparent to normal operation. The instruction pointer holds the address of the currently executing instruction.

The flags register, EFLAGS, contains the status flags and the control flags. Various instructions set bits in EFLAGS to indicate the result of those instructions. For example, the ZF (Zero Flag) bit is set to 1 if the result of an instruction is 0. In Chapter 4, I described setting the CPU into single-step mode, which involved setting the TF (Trap Flag) in the EFLAGS register. Figure 6-1 shows the Registers window from the Visual C++ debugger. The Registers window displays the EFLAGS register as EFL. Notice that I'm not showing floating-point registers in the Registers window. You can hide the floating-point registers by right-clicking in the Registers window and unchecking Floating-Point Registers on the menu.

Figure 6-1 *Visual C++ Registers window*

Table 6-2 lists the flag values shown in the Registers window. The Visual C++ documentation doesn't mention what the flag values in the Registers window mean, so you might never have seen these values before. Unfortunately, the mnemonics Visual C++ uses for these flags doesn't correspond to the Intel mnemonics, so you'll have to translate when referring to the Intel documentation.

One minor problem with the Registers window is that the flags update, but unlike the regular registers, which turn a different color when they change, the flags stay the same color even when they change. You need to keep an eye on the particular flag you're interested in to see it change. Fortunately, you rarely need to look at the individual flag values. What I do to make spotting flag changes easier is to click the New File button and open a new scratch file. I then copy the existing flags from the Registers window and paste them into the scratch text window to compare the values before and after.

Table 6-2   REGISTERS WINDOW FLAG VALUES

Registers Window Flag	Meaning	Intel Manual Mnemonic	Notes
OV	Overflow Flag	OF	Set to 1 if the operation resulted in an integer overflow or underflow.
UP	Direction Flag	DF	Set to 1 if string instructions are processed from highest address to lowest address (autodecrement). 0 means that string instructions are processed from lowest address to highest address (autoincrement).
EI	Interrupt Enable Flag	IF	Set to 1 if interrupts are enabled. This flag will always be 1 in a user-mode debugger.
PL	Sign Flag	SF	Reflects the most significant bit of an instruction result. Set to 0 for positive values, 1 for negative values.
ZR	Zero Flag	ZF	Set to 1 if the instruction result is 0. This flag is important for compare instructions.
AC	Auxiliary Carry Flag	AF	Set to 1 if a binary-coded decimal (BCD) operation generated a carry or a borrow.
PE	Parity Flag	PF	Set to 1 if the least significant byte of the result contains an even number of bits set to 1.
CY	Carry Flag	CF	Set to 1 if an arithmetic operation generates a carry or a borrow out of the most significant bit of the result. Also set to 1 on an overflow condition for unsigned integer arithmetic.

One important feature of the Registers window is that you can edit the values in it. Although the Registers window looks like a standard text window, such as the Output window, you can change the values in it if you put the cursor on the first number to the right of the equal sign for the register you want to change and type in your revision.

Instruction Format and Memory Addressing

The basic instruction format for the Intel CPUs is below. All instructions follow the same pattern.

```
[prefix] instruction [operands]
```

For the most part, you see prefixes only on some string functions. (I'll cover the common situations in which string functions use prefixes in the "String Manipulation" section later in the chapter.) The operands format, shown below, indicates the direction of the operation. The source goes into the destination, so read the operands from right to left.

```
Single-instruction operands : XXX source
Two-instruction operands: XXX destination, source
```

The source operand can be a register, a memory reference, or an immediate value—that is, a hard-coded value. The destination operand can be a register or a memory reference. The Intel CPUs don't allow both a source and a destination to be memory references.

Memory references are those operands that appear within brackets. For example, the memory reference [0040129Ah] means "get the value at memory location 0x0040129A." The *h* is the assembly language way of specifying a hexadecimal number. Using [0040129Ah] is the same as accessing a pointer to an integer in C with *pIVal*. Memory references can be through registers, as in [EAX], which means "get the memory at the address in EAX." Another common memory reference specifies an address by adding an offset to a register value. [EAX+0Ch] means "add 0xC to the value in EAX and get that memory." Some memory references, such as [EAX+EBX*2], which indicates that the memory reference is from a calculation involving several registers, become fairly complicated.

To differentiate the sizes of memory references, you'll often see a memory reference preceded by a pointer size. The pointer sizes are shown as BYTE PTR, WORD PTR, and DWORD PTR for byte, word, and double-word references, respectively. You can think of these just as you think of a C++ cast. If the disassembly doesn't specify a pointer size, the size is a double word.

Sometimes an instruction's memory reference is straightforward and you can easily see the address for that memory. For example, a reference to [EBX] is just a reference to the memory held in the EBX register, so you can simply pull up the Memory window and type in *EBX* to look at it. Other times, however, it isn't possible to figure out the memory reference without performing some complicated hexadecimal multiplication. Fortunately, the Registers window will show you what memory the instruction is about to reference.

Notice the line "0012F988 = 0012F9D4" at the bottom of Figure 6-1. That line is the *effective address* display. The current instruction, in this case at 0x5F42D8B8, is referencing the address 0x0012F988, the left-hand side of the line. The right-hand side of the line is the value at the 0x0012F988 memory location, 0x0012F9D4. Only those instructions that access memory will show the effective address in the Registers window. Because x86 CPUs allow only one of the operands to be a memory reference, just keeping an eye on the effective address display can show you what memory you're about to access and what the value is at that memory location.

If the memory access isn't valid, the CPU generates either a General Protection Fault (GPF) or a page fault. A GPF indicates that you're trying to access memory that you don't have access to. A page fault indicates that you're trying to access a memory location that doesn't exist. If you're looking at a line of assembly language that crashes, the part to look at is the memory reference. That will tell you which values were invalid. For example, if the memory reference is [EAX], you need to look at the value in EAX. If EAX holds an invalid address, you need to start scanning backward in the assembly-language listing to see what instruction set EAX to the invalid value. Keep in mind that you might need to go back several calls to find the instruction. I'll show you how to walk the stack manually in the section "The Memory Window and the Disassembly Window" later in the chapter.

A WORD ABOUT THE VISUAL C++ INLINE ASSEMBLER

Before I jump into the assembly-language instructions, I want to talk for a bit about the inline assembler in Visual C++. Like most professional C++ compilers, the Visual C++ compiler allows you to embed assembly-language instructions directly in line with your C and C++ code. Although using inline assembly language generally isn't recommended because it restricts your code's portability, it's sometimes the only way to accomplish a task. In Chapters 12 and 14, I'll show you how to hook imported functions by using inline assembly language.

At the beginning of the chapter, I said that you don't need to know how to write your programs in assembly language, and I'm not contradicting myself. Learning to use the inline assembler isn't the same as learning to write an entire program in MASM—your C/C++ program still provides the application infrastructure. You can think of the inline assembler as the programming equivalent of a Zoom feature. When you create a bitmap, for example, you start out by painting with broad strokes; when it comes time to put on the finishing touches, you zoom in so that you can control the individual pixels. In the same way, the inline assembler lets you "paint" your program in broad C/C++ strokes but allows you to zoom in when you need to control the individual assembly-language instructions. I want to show you how to use the inline assembler because inline assembly language will make the examples easier to understand. Additionally, you can use the inline assembler to play around with the instructions I show you in this chapter so that you can see how they behave.

To show you the format for inline assembly language, I'll need to introduce your first instruction:

NOP No operation

NOP is the instruction that does nothing. The compiler sometimes uses NOP for padding inside functions to keep those functions aligned on proper memory reference boundaries.

The inline assembler keyword is *__asm*. After *__asm*, you enter the assembly-language instruction you want to execute. If you want to enter multiple instructions, use *__asm* and enclose within braces as many assembly-language instructions as you'd like. The following two routines show you the format of inline assembly-language instructions. These routines are functionally equivalent.

```
void NOPFuncOne ( void )
{
    __asm NOP
    __asm NOP
}

void NOPFuncTwo ( void )
{
    __asm
    {
        NOP
        NOP
    }
}
```

Throughout the chapter, I'll use the inline assembler to illustrate assembly-language operations, such as parameter and variable access. If you want to see how each instruction operates, open the ASMer sample program on the companion CD. This sample program contains all the assembly-language examples that follow.

INSTRUCTIONS YOU NEED TO KNOW

There are many different instructions on Intel CPUs; the Intel Instruction Set Reference chapter for the Pentium Pro is 467 pages. That doesn't mean there are 467 instructions; it means that it takes 467 pages to describe what the instructions do. Fortunately, many of the instructions aren't used in user-mode programs, so you don't need to be concerned with them. I'll cover only the instructions that are frequently used and the situations in which you'll commonly need them. The format I'll use is to describe a couple of instructions and then demonstrate scenarios in which they apply.

Stack Manipulation

PUSH Push a word or a double word onto the stack

POP Pop a value from the stack

Intel CPUs use the stack extensively. Other CPUs, which have many more registers, might pass parameters to functions in the registers, but the Intel CPUs pass most parameters on the stack. The stack starts in high memory and grows downward. Both these instructions implicitly change the ESP register, which reflects the current top of the stack. After a PUSH, the value in the ESP register decreases. After a POP, ESP increases.

You can push registers, memory locations, or hard-coded numbers. Popping an item from the stack usually moves the item into a register. The key characteristic of the CPU stack is that it's a last in, first out (LIFO) data structure; if you push three registers to save their values, you must pop them off in reverse order, as shown here:

```
void PushPop ( void )
{
    __asm
    {
        // Save the values in EAX, ECX, and EDX.
        PUSH EAX
        PUSH ECX
        PUSH EDX

        // Do some operation here that might destroy the values in each
        // of those registers.

        // Restore the previously saved registers. Notice that they are
        // removed from the stack in LIFO order.
        POP EDX
        POP ECX
        POP EAX
    }
}
```

Even though there are far more efficient ways of exchanging values, the PUSH and POP instructions allow you to swap register values. The swap happens when you reverse the order of the POP instructions.

```
void SwapRegistersWithPushAndPop ( void )
{
    __asm
    {
        // Swap the EAX and EBX values using the stack. The sequence gives
        // you an idea of how to make this swap.
        PUSH EAX
        PUSH EBX

        POP EAX
        POP EBX
    }
}
```

PUSHAD Push all general-purpose registers

POPAD Pop all general-purpose registers

Occasionally when you're debugging through system code, you'll run into these two instructions. Instead of having long chains of PUSH instructions to save all general registers followed later by an equally long set of POP instructions to retrieve all general registers, the Intel CPU offers these two instructions to save and retrieve the registers for you.

Very Common Simple Instructions

MOV Move

The MOV instruction is the most common instruction used on the CPU because it's the way to move values from one place to another. I just showed you how to swap two registers by using only PUSH and POP; now I'll show you how to make the same swap with the MOV command.

```
void SwapRegisters ( void )
{
    __asm
    {
        // The EAX register is a temporary holder. Swap the ECX and
        // EBX values.
        MOV EAX , ECX
        MOV ECX , EBX
        MOV EBX , EAX
    }
}
```

SUB Subtract

The SUB instruction is the subtract operation. It subtracts the source operand from the destination operand and stores the result in the destination operand.

ADD Add

The ADD instruction adds the source operand to the destination operand and stores the result in the destination operand.

INT 3 Breakpoint

INT 3 is the breakpoint instruction for Intel CPUs. Microsoft compilers use this instruction as padding between functions in a file. The padding keeps Portable Executable (PE) sections aligned based on the linker's /ALIGN switch, which defaults to 4 KB.

LEAVE High-level procedure exit

The LEAVE instruction restores the CPU state when leaving a function. I'll go into more detail about LEAVE in the following section.

Common Sequence: Function Entry and Exit

The majority of the functions in Windows and in your program set up and leave functions in the same manner. The setup is called the *prolog,* and the leaving is called the *epilog;* the compiler generates both automatically. When setting up the prolog, the code is setting up to access the function's local variables and parameters. The access is called a *stack frame*. Although the x86 CPU doesn't explicitly specify any stack frame scheme, the design of the CPU and some instructions make it easiest for operating systems to use the EBP register to hold the pointer to the stack frame.

```
__asm
{
    // Standard prolog setup
    PUSH EBP            // Save the stack frame register.
    MOV  EBP , ESP      // Set the local function stack frame to ESP.
    SUB  ESP , 20h      // Make room on the stack for 0x20 bytes of
                        // local variables. The SUB instruction appears
                        // only if the function has local variables.
}
```

This sequence is common in both debug and release builds. In some release build functions, however, you might see some instructions interspersed between PUSH and MOV. CPUs with multiple pipelines, such as those in the Pentium family, can decode multiple instructions at a time, so the optimizer will try to set up the instruction stream to take advantage of this capability.

Depending on the optimizations you chose when compiling your code, you can also have functions that don't use EBP as the frame pointer. Those procedures have what is called Frame Pointer Omission (FPO) data. When you look at the disassembly for functions with FPO data, the code in the function looks as if it just starts manipulating data. You'll find out how to identify one of these functions in the following section.

The following common epilog undoes the operations of the prolog and is the one you'll see the most in debug builds. This epilog matches the prolog above.

```
__asm
{
    // Standard epilog teardown
    MOV ESP , EBP      // Restore the stack value.
    POP EBP            // Restore the saved stack frame register.
}
```

In release builds, using the LEAVE instruction introduced earlier is faster than using the MOV/POP sequence, so you might see that the epilog will be just a LEAVE instruction. The LEAVE instruction is identical to the MOV/POP sequence. In debug builds, the compilers default to MOV/POP. Interestingly, the x86 CPU has a corresponding ENTER instruction to set up the prolog, but it's slower than the PUSH/MOV/ADD sequence, so the compilers don't use it.

How compilers choose to generate code depends a great deal on whether your program is optimized for speed or for size. If you optimize for size, as I strongly recommend in Chapter 2, many of your functions will use more standard stack frames. Optimizing for speed leads to the more convoluted FPO generation.

Variable Access: Global Variables, Parameters, and Local Variables

Now let's turn to accessing variables. Global variables are the easiest to access because they're just a memory reference with a fixed address. If you have symbols for the particular module at the address, you might get to see the name of the global variable. The following example shows how to access a global variable through the inline assembler. With the inline assembler, you can use your variables as either the source or the destination, depending on the instruction, just as you would in straight C programming. In comments below the code, I note what the Disassembly window can show for the operation depending on whether symbols are loaded.

```
int g_iVal = 0 ;

void AccessGlobalMemory ( void )
{
    __asm
    {
        // Set the global variable to 48,059.
        MOV g_iVal , 0BBBBh

        // If symbols are loaded, the Disassembly window will show
        // MOV DWORD PTR [g_iVal (00403060)],0BBBBh.

        // If symbols are not loaded, the Disassembly window will show
        // MOV DWORD PTR [00403060],0BBBBh.
    }
}
```

If a function has standard stack frames, parameters are positive offsets from the EBP register. If you don't change EBP for the life of the function, parameters appear at the same positive offsets because you push the parameters on the stack before you call the procedure. The following code shows parameter access.

```
void AccessParameter ( int iParam )
{
    __asm
    {
        // Move the iParam value into EAX.
        MOV EAX , iParam

        // If symbols are loaded, the Disassembly window will show
        // MOV EAX,DWORD PTR [iParam].

        // If symbols are not loaded, the Disassembly window will show
        // MOV EAX,DWORD PTR [EBP+8].
    }
}
```

If you're debugging through optimized code and you see references that are positive offsets from the ESP stack register, you're looking at a function that has FPO data. Because ESP can change throughout the life of the function, you have to work a little harder to keep the parameters straight. When dealing with optimized code, you'll need to keep track of the items pushed onto the stack because a reference to [ESP+20h] can be the same reference as [ESP+8h] earlier in the function. In the process of debugging optimized code, I always take notes about where parameters are located when I'm single-stepping through the assembly language.

If the standard frames are used, local variables are negative offsets from EBP. The SUB instruction reserves the space, as shown in the preceding section "Common Sequence: Function Entry and Exit." The following code shows how to set a local variable to a new value:

```
void AccessLocalVariable ( void )
{
    int iLocal ;

    __asm
    {
        // Set the local variable to 23.
        MOV iLocal , 017h

        // If symbols are loaded, the Disassembly window will show
        // MOV DWORD PTR [iLocal],017h.

        // If symbols are not loaded, the Disassembly window will show
        // MOV [EBP-4],017h.
    }
}
```

If standard frames aren't used, finding local variables can be difficult—if you can find them at all. The problem is that local variables appear as positive offsets from ESP, just as parameters do. The trick in that case is to try to find the SUB instruction so that you can see how many bytes are devoted to local variables. If the ESP offset is larger than the number of bytes set aside for local variables, that offset reference is probably a parameter.

Stack frames are a bit confusing the first time you encounter them, so I think a final example and a couple of illustrations might help clarify the subject. The following code, a very simple C function, will show you why parameters are at positive offsets from EBP and why local variables are at negative offsets with standard stack frames. The disassembly for the function as it was compiled in the ASMer sample program appears after the C function.

```
void AccessLocalsAndParamsExample ( int * pParam1 , int * pParam2 )
{
    int iLocal1 = 3 ;
```

(continued)

```
        int iLocal2 = 0x42 ;

        iLocal1 = *pParam1 ;
        iLocal2 = *pParam2 ;
}


// The AccessLocalsAndParamsExample disassembly with addresses
// Standard function prolog
00401097  PUSH EBP
00401098  MOV  EBP , ESP
0040109A  SUB  ESP , 8

// int iLocal1 = 3 ;
0040109D  MOV  DWORD PTR [EBP-8h] , 3

// int iLocal2 = 0x42 ;
004010A4  MOV  DWORD PTR [EBP-4h] , 42h

// iLocal1 = *pParam1 ;
004010AB  MOV  EAX , DWORD PTR [EBP+8h]
004010AE  MOV  ECX , DWORD PTR [EAX]
004010B0  MOV  DWORD PTR [EBP-08h] , ECX

// iLocal2 = *pParam2 ;
004010B3  MOV  EDX , DWORD PTR [EBP+0Ch]
004010B6  MOV  EAX , DWORD PTR [EDX]
004010B8  MOV  DWORD PTR [EBP-4h] , EAX

// Standard function epilog
004010BB  MOV  ESP , EBP
004010BD  POP  EBP
004010BE  RET
}
```

If you set a breakpoint at the start of the *AccessLocalsAndParamsExample* function, address 0x00401097, you'll see the stack and register values depicted in Figure 6-2.

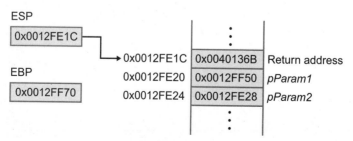

Figure 6-2 *Stack before the* AccessLocalsAndParamsExample *function prolog*

The first three assembly-language instructions in *AccessLocalsAndParams-Example* comprise the function prolog. After the prolog executes, the stack and the base pointer have been set up, the parameters are accessed through positive offsets from EBP, and the local variables are accessible through negative offsets from EBP. Figure 6-3 shows the stack and the base pointer values after each of the prolog instructions executes.

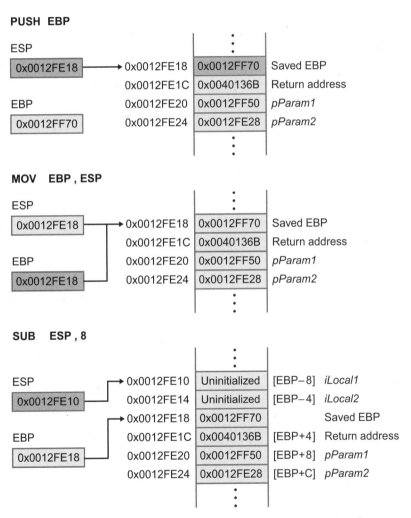

Figure 6-3 *Stack during and after execution of the* AccessLocalsAndParamsExample *function prolog*

Calling Procedures and Returning

CALL Call a procedure

RET Return from a procedure

Now that you've seen what procedures look like, I want to show you how to call them and return from them. The CALL instruction is straightforward. When a CALL executes, the CALL implicitly pushes the return address on the stack, so if you stop at the first instruction of the called procedure and look at ESP, the address at the top of the stack is the return address.

The operand to the CALL instruction can be almost anything, and if you browse through the Disassembly window, you'll see calls that go through registers, memory references, parameters, and global offsets. You can use the effective address field of the Registers window to see exactly the procedure you're about to call if the CALL is going through a pointer memory reference.

If you're calling a local function, your call will be a direct call to an address. However, many times you'll see calls that are through pointers, which are generally calls through your import address table (IAT) to imported functions. If the symbols are loaded for the binary you're stepping through, you'll see something like the first CALL instruction shown in the *CallSomeFunctions* example below. This code indicates that you're calling through the IAT. The "__imp__" is a dead giveaway. The *CallSomeFunctions* example also shows how to call a local function.

```
void CallSomeFunctions ( void )
{
    __asm
    {
        // Call the imported function, GetLastError, which takes no
        // parameters. EAX will hold the return value. This is a
        // call through the IAT, so it is a call through a pointer.
        CALL DWORD PTR [GetLastError]

        // If symbols are loaded, the Disassembly window will show
        // CALL DWORD PTR [__imp__GetLastError@0 (00402000)].

        // If symbols are not loaded, the Disassembly window will show
        // CALL DWORD PTR [00402000].

        ////////////////////////////////////////////////////////////
        // Call a function inside this file.
        CALL NOPFuncOne

        // If symbols are loaded, the Disassembly window will show
        // CALL NOPFuncOne (00401000).

        // If symbols are not loaded, the Disassembly window will show
        // CALL 00401000.
    }
}
```

The RET instruction returns to the caller by using the address that's at the top of the stack, with no checking whatsoever when the instruction is executed. As you can imagine, a corrupt stack can cause you to return anywhere in your application. The RET instruction is sometimes followed by a fixed number. This number specifies how many bytes to pop off the stack to account for parameters pushed on the stack and passed to the function.

CALLING CONVENTIONS

Before I move into other instructions, let's take a brief detour into calling conventions. The few instructions presented in the last section will help you do some excellent debugging. However, I need to tie procedure calling and calling conventions together so that I can start showing you how to decipher the Disassembly window.

A calling convention specifies how parameters are passed to a function and how stack cleanup occurs when the function returns. The programmer who codes a function dictates the calling convention that everyone must follow when calling that function. The CPU doesn't dictate any specific calling conventions. If you understand the calling conventions, you'll find it much easier to look up parameters in the Memory window and to determine the flow of the assembly language in the Disassembly window.

There are five calling conventions in all, but only three are common: the standard call (__*stdcall*), the C declaration (__*cdecl*), and the *this* call. Although you can specify the standard call and the C declaration yourself, the *this* call is automatically applied when you're using C++ code and dictates how the *this* pointer is passed. The other two calling conventions are the fast call (__*fastcall*) and the provocatively named *naked* calling conventions. By default, Win32 operating systems don't use the fast-call calling convention in user-mode code because it isn't portable to other CPUs. The naked calling convention is used in virtual device driver (VxD) programming and when you want to control the prolog and epilog generation yourself, as you'll see in Chapters 12 and 14.

Table 6-3 lists all the calling conventions. Recall from Chapter 5 the description of the name decoration scheme for setting breakpoints on system functions. In Table 6-3, you'll see that the calling convention dictates the name decoration scheme.

If you've never been exposed to the different calling conventions, you might wonder why the different types exist. The differences between the C declaration and the standard call are subtle. In a standard call function, the callee cleans up the stack, so it has to know exactly how many parameters to expect. Therefore, a standard call function can't be a variable argument function such as *printf*. Because C declaration functions have the caller cleaning up the stack, variable argument functions are just fine. Standard call is the default for Win32 system functions as well as for Visual Basic functions.

Table 6-3   CALLING CONVENTIONS

Calling Convention	Argument Passing	Stack Maintenance	Name Decoration	Notes
__cdecl	Right to left.	Caller removes arguments from the stack. This calling convention is the only one that allows variable argument lists.	Underscore prefixed to function names, as in _Foo	The default for C and C++ functions.
__stdcall	Right to left.	Callee removes its own arguments from the stack.	Underscore prefixed to function name, and @ appended followed by the number of decimal bytes in the argument list, as in _Foo@12.	Used by almost all system functions; the default for Visual Basic internal functions.
__fastcall	First two DWORD parameters are passed in ECX and EDX; the rest are passed right to left.	Caller removes arguments from the stack.	An @ is prefixed to the name, and @ is appended followed by the number of decimal bytes in the argument list, as in @Foo@12.	Applies only to Intel CPUs. This calling convention is the default calling convention for Borland Delphi compilers.
this	Right to left. The this parameter is passed in the ECX register.	Caller removes arguments from the stack.	None	Used automatically by C++ class methods unless you specify standard call. COM methods are declared as standard call.
naked	Right to left	Caller removes arguments from the stack.	None	Used by VxDs and when you need custom prolog and epilog.

Calling Conventions Example

To tie together the instructions I've shown so far and the calling conventions, Listing 6-1 shows an example of all the calling conventions from the Visual C++ debugger's Disassembly window. The sample source code, CALLING.CPP, is on the companion CD if you want to take a look at it.

The code in Listing 6-1 is a debug build to make it easier to follow; also, the code doesn't actually do anything. I call each calling convention function in turn. Pay special attention to how the parameters are pushed to each function and to how the stack is cleaned up. I inserted NOP instructions between each of the functions to make the listing easier to read.

```
 6:    // The strings passed to each function
 7:    static char * g_szStdCall  = "__stdcall"  ;
 8:    static char * g_szCdeclCall = "__cdecl"    ;
 9:    static char * g_szFastCall  = "__fastcall" ;
10:    static char * g_szNakedCall = "__naked"    ;
11:
12:    // The extern "C" turns off all C++ name decoration.
13:    extern "C"
14:    {
15:
16:    // The __cdecl function
17:    void CDeclFunction ( char *         szString ,
18:                         unsigned long ulLong   ,
19:                         char          chChar    ) ;
20:
21:    // The __stdcall function
22:    void __stdcall StdCallFunction ( char *         szString ,
23:                                     unsigned long ulLong    ,
24:                                     char          chChar     ) ;
25:    // The __fastcall function
26:    void __fastcall FastCallFunction ( char *         szString ,
27:                                       unsigned long ulLong    ,
28:                                       char          chChar     ) ;
29:
30:    // The naked function. The declspec goes on the definition, not on
31:    // the declaration.
32:    int NakedCallFunction ( char *         szString ,
33:                            unsigned long ulLong   ,
34:                            char          chChar    ) ;
35:    }
```

Listing 6-1 *Calling conventions example*

Listing 6-1 *continued*

```
36:
37:    void main ( void )
38:    {
00401000 55                      push        ebp
00401001 8B EC                   mov         ebp,esp
00401003 53                      push        ebx
00401004 56                      push        esi
00401005 57                      push        edi
39:        // Call each function to generate the code. I separate each
40:        // function with a couple of NOP bytes to make it easier to read
41:        // the disassembly.
42:        __asm NOP __asm NOP
00401006 90                      nop
00401007 90                      nop
43:        CDeclFunction ( g_szCdeclCall , 1 , 'a' ) ;
00401008 6A 61                   push        61h
0040100A 6A 01                   push        1
0040100C A1 14 30 40 00          mov         eax,[g_szCdeclCall (00403014)]
00401011 50                      push        eax
00401012 E8 45 00 00 00          call        CDeclFunction (0040105c)
00401017 83 C4 0C                add         esp,0Ch
44:        __asm NOP __asm NOP
0040101A 90                      nop
0040101B 90                      nop
45:        StdCallFunction ( g_szStdCall , 2 , 'b' ) ;
0040101C 6A 62                   push        62h
0040101E 6A 02                   push        2
00401020 8B 0D 10 30 40 00       mov         ecx,dword ptr
                                                 [g_szStdCall (00403010)]
00401026 51                      push        ecx
00401027 E8 3D 00 00 00          call        StdCallFunction (00401069)
46:        __asm NOP __asm NOP
0040102C 90                      nop
0040102D 90                      nop
47:        FastCallFunction ( g_szFastCall , 3 , 'c' ) ;
0040102E 6A 63                   push        63h
00401030 BA 03 00 00 00          mov         edx,3
00401035 8B 0D 18 30 40 00       mov         ecx,dword ptr
                                                 [g_szFastCall (00403018)]
0040103B E8 38 00 00 00          call        FastCallFunction (00401078)
48:        __asm NOP __asm NOP
00401040 90                      nop
00401041 90                      nop
49:        NakedCallFunction ( g_szNakedCall , 4 , 'd' ) ;
00401042 6A 64                   push        64h
```

```
00401044 6A 04                    push        4
00401046 8B 15 1C 30 40 00        mov         edx,dword ptr
                                              [g_szNakedCall (0040301c)]
0040104C 52                       push        edx
0040104D E8 40 00 00 00           call        NakedCallFunction (00401092)
00401052 83 C4 0C                 add         esp,0Ch
50:        __asm NOP __asm NOP
00401055 90                       nop
00401056 90                       nop
51:
52:    }
00401057 5F                       pop         edi
00401058 5E                       pop         esi
00401059 5B                       pop         ebx
0040105A 5D                       pop         ebp
0040105B C3                       ret
53:
54:    void CDeclFunction ( char *          szString ,
55:                         unsigned long ulLong     ,
56:                         char            chChar    )
57:    {
0040105C 55                       push        ebp
0040105D 8B EC                    mov         ebp,esp
0040105F 53                       push        ebx
00401060 56                       push        esi
00401061 57                       push        edi
58:        __asm NOP __asm NOP
00401062 90                       nop
00401063 90                       nop
59:    }
00401064 5F                       pop         edi
00401065 5E                       pop         esi
00401066 5B                       pop         ebx
00401067 5D                       pop         ebp
00401068 C3                       ret
60:
61:    void __stdcall StdCallFunction ( char *          szString ,
62:                                     unsigned long ulLong     ,
63:                                     char            chChar    )
64:    {
00401069 55                       push        ebp
0040106A 8B EC                    mov         ebp,esp
0040106C 53                       push        ebx
0040106D 56                       push        esi
0040106E 57                       push        edi
```

(continued)

Listing 6-1 *continued*

```
65:        __asm NOP __asm NOP
0040106F 90                     nop
00401070 90                     nop
66:    }
00401071 5F                     pop        edi
00401072 5E                     pop        esi
00401073 5B                     pop        ebx
00401074 5D                     pop        ebp
00401075 C2 0C 00               ret        0Ch
67:
68:    void __fastcall FastCallFunction ( char *        szString ,
69:                                        unsigned long ulLong    ,
70:                                        char          chChar    )
71:    {
00401078 55                     push       ebp
00401079 8B EC                  mov        ebp,esp
0040107B 83 EC 08               sub        esp,8
0040107E 53                     push       ebx
0040107F 56                     push       esi
00401080 57                     push       edi
00401081 89 55 F8               mov        dword ptr [ebp-8],edx
00401084 89 4D FC               mov        dword ptr [ebp-4],ecx
72:        __asm NOP __asm NOP
00401087 90                     nop
00401088 90                     nop
73:    }
00401089 5F                     pop        edi
0040108A 5E                     pop        esi
0040108B 5B                     pop        ebx
0040108C 8B E5                  mov        esp,ebp
0040108E 5D                     pop        ebp
0040108F C2 04 00               ret        4
74:
75:    __declspec(naked) int NakedCallFunction ( char *        szString ,
76:                                               unsigned long ulLong    ,
77:                                               char          chChar    )
78:    {
00401092 90                     nop
00401093 90                     nop
79:        __asm NOP __asm NOP
80:        // Naked functions must explicitly do a return.
81:        __asm RET
00401094 C3                     ret
```

MORE INSTRUCTIONS YOU NEED TO KNOW

The instructions covered in this section apply to data and pointer manipulation, comparing and testing, jumping and branching, looping, and string manipulation.

Data Manipulation

AND Logical-AND

OR Logical-OR (inclusive)

The AND and OR instructions perform the bitwise operations that should be familiar to everyone because they are the basis of bit manipulation.

NOT One's complement negation

NEG Two's complement negation

The NOT and NEG instructions sometimes cause some confusion because they look similar but they certainly don't indicate the same operation. The NOT instruction is a bitwise operation that turns each binary 1 into a 0 and each 0 into a 1. The NEG instruction is the equivalent of subtracting the operand from 0. The following code snippet shows the differences between these two instructions:

```
void NOTExample ( void )
{
    __asm
    {
        MOV EAX , 0FFh
        MOV EBX , 1
        NOT EAX      // EAX now holds 0FFFFFF00h.
        NOT EBX      // EBX now holds 0FFFFFFFEh.
    }
}

void NEGExample ( void )
{
    __asm
    {
        MOV EAX , 0FFh
        MOV EBX , 1
        NEG EAX      // EAX now holds 0FFFFFF01h ( 0 - 0FFh ).
        NEG EBX      // EBX now holds 0FFFFFFFFh ( 0 - 1 ).
    }
}
```

XOR Logical-OR (exclusive)

You'll see the XOR instruction used quite a bit, not because people are keenly interested in exclusive OR operations but because it's the fastest way to zero out a value.

Using XOR on two operands will set each bit to 1 if the same bit in each operand is different. If each bit is the same, the result is 0. Because "XOR EAX, EAX" is faster than "MOV EAX, 0" (because the former takes fewer clock cycles), the Microsoft compilers use it to zero out registers.

INC Increment by 1

DEC Decrement by 1

These instructions are straightforward, and you can figure out what they do just from their names. The compiler often uses these instructions when optimizing certain code sequences because each of them executes in a single clock cycle. Additionally, these instructions map directly to the C integer ++ and the -- arithmetic operators.

SHL Shift left, multiply by 2

SHR Shift right, divide by 2

Binary manipulation bit shifts are faster than the corresponding multiplication and division instructions in x86 CPUs. These instructions are akin to the C << and >> bitwise operators, respectively.

DIV Unsigned division

MUL Unsigned multiplication

These seemingly straightforward instructions are in fact a little odd. Both instructions perform their unsigned operations on the EAX register. But the output implicitly uses the EDX register. The high bytes of double-word and higher size multiplications are placed in the EDX register. The DIV instruction stores the remainder in EDX and the quotient in EAX. Both instructions operate on the value in EAX only with register or memory values.

IDIV Signed division

IMUL Signed multiplication

These instructions are similar to the DIV and MUL instructions except that they treat operands as signed values. The same result gyrations happen with the IDIV and IMUL instructions as with the DIV and MUL instructions. An IMUL instruction sometimes has three operands. The first operand is the destination, and the last two are source operands. IMUL is the only three-operand instruction in the x86 instruction set.

LOCK Assert LOCK# signal prefix

LOCK isn't an actual instruction but rather a prefix to other instructions. The LOCK prefix tells the CPU that the memory accessed by the following instruction needs to be an atomic operation, so the CPU executing the instruction locks the memory bus and prevents any other CPUs on the system from accessing that memory.

MOVSX Move with sign-extend

MOVZX Move with zero-extend

These two instructions copy smaller size values to larger size values and dictate how the larger values fill the upper bits. MOVSX indicates that the sign value on the source operand will extend through the upper bits of the destination register. MOVZX fills the upper bits of the destination register with 0. These are two instructions to watch for when you're tracking down sign errors.

Pointer Manipulation

LEA Load effective address

LEA loads the destination register with the address of the source operand. The following code snippet shows two examples of the LEA instruction. The first example shows how to assign an address to an integer pointer. The second shows how to retrieve the address of a local character array with the LEA instruction and pass the address as a parameter to the *GetWindowsDirectory* API function.

```
void LEAExamples ( void )
{
    int * pInt ;
    int iVal ;

    // The following instruction sequence is identical to the C code
    // pInt = &iVal ;.
    __asm
    {
        LEA EAX , iVal
        MOV [pInt] , EAX
    }


    ////////////////////////////////////////////////////////////////

    char szBuff [ MAX_PATH ] ;

    // Another example of accessing a pointer through LEA. This
    // instruction sequence is identical to the C code
    // GetWindowsDirectory ( szBuff , MAX_PATH ) ;.
    __asm
    {
        PUSH 104h            // Push MAX_PATH as the second parameter.
        LEA  ECX , szBuff    // Get the address of szBuff.
        PUSH ECX             // Push the address of szBuff as the first
                             // parameter.
        CALL DWORD PTR [GetWindowsDirectory]
    }
}
```

Comparing and Testing

CMP Compare two operands

The CMP instruction compares the first and second operands by subtracting the second operand from the first operand, discarding the results, and setting the appropriate flags in the EFLAGS register. You can think of the CMP instruction as the conditional part of the C *if* statement. Table 6-4 shows the different flags and the values they correspond to when the CMP instruction executes.

Table 6-4   RESULT VALUES AND THEIR FLAG SETTINGS

Result (First Operand Compared to Second Operand)	Register Window Flag Settings	Intel Manual Flag Settings
Equal	ZR = 1	ZF = 1
Less than	PL != OV	SF != OF
Greater than	ZR = 0 and PL = OV	ZF = 0 and SF = OF
Not equal	ZR = 0	ZF = 0
Greater than or equal	PL = OV	SF = OF
Less than or equal	ZR = 1 or PL != OV	ZF = 1 or SF != OF

TEST Logical compare

The TEST instruction does a bitwise logical AND of the operands and sets the PL, ZR, and PE (SF, ZF, and PF for the Intel manuals) flags accordingly. The TEST instruction checks whether a bit value was set.

Jump and Branch Instructions

JMP Absolute jump

Just as the name implies, the JMP moves execution to the absolute address.

JE Jump if equal

JL Jump if less than

JG Jump if greater than

JNE Jump if not equal

JGE Jump if greater than or equal

JLE Jump if less than or equal

The CMP and TEST instructions aren't much good if you don't have a way to act on their results. The conditional jumps allow you to branch accordingly. The instructions above are the most common ones you'll see in the Disassembly window, though there are 31 different conditional jumps, many of which perform the same action except that the mnemonic is expressed with "not." For example, JLE (jump if less than or equal) has the same opcode as JNG (jump if not greater than). If you're using a disassembler other than the Visual C++ debugger, you might see some of the other instructions. You should get the Intel manuals and look up the "Jcc" codes so that you can decode all the jump instructions.

I listed the conditional jump instructions in the same order as they're shown in Table 6-4 so that you can match them up. One of the conditional jumps closely follows any CMP or TEST instructions. Optimized code might have a few instructions interspersed between the check and the jump, but those instructions are guaranteed not to change the flags.

When you're looking at a disassembly, you'll notice that the conditional check is generally the opposite of what you typed in. The first section in the following code shows an example.

```
void JumpExamples ( int i )
{
    // Here is the C code statement. Notice that the conditional is
    // "i > 0," but the compiler generates the opposite. The assembly
    // language that I show is similar to what the compiler generates.
    // Different optimization methods generate different code.
    // if ( i > 0 )
    // {
    //     printf ( "i > 0\n" ) ;
    // }
    char szGreaterThan[] = "i > 0\n" ;
    __asm
    {
        CMP  i , 0          // Compare i to 0 by subtracting (i - 0).
        JLE  JE_LessThanOne // If i is less than or equal to 0, jump to
                            // the label.
        PUSH i              // Push the parameter on the stack.
        LEA  EAX , szGreaterThan // Push the format string.
        PUSH EAX
        CALL DWORD PTR [printf]  // Call printf. Notice that you can
                            // tell printf probably comes from a DLL
                            // because I'm calling through a pointer.
        ADD  ESP , 8        // printf is __cdecl, so I need to clean up
                            // the stack in the caller.

JE_LessThanOne:             // With the inline assembler, you can jump
                            // to any C label.
    }
```

(continued)

```
//////////////////////////////////////////////////////////////
// Take the absolute value of the parameter and check again.
// The C code:
// int y = abs ( i ) ;
// if ( y >=5 )
// {
//      printf ( "abs(i) >= 5\n" ) ;
// }
// else
// {
//      printf ( "abs(i) < 5\n" ) ;
// }

char szAbsGTEFive[] = "abs(i) >= 5\n" ;
char szAbsLTFive[] = "abs(i) < 5\n" ;
__asm
{
    MOV   EBX , i         // Move i's value into EBX.
    CMP   EBX , 0         // Compare EBX to 0 (EBX - 0).
    JG    JE_PosNum       // If the result is greater than 0, EBX
                         // is positive.
    NEG   EBX            // Turn negative into positive.

JE_PosNum:

    CMP   EBX , 5         // Compare EBX to 5 (EBX - 5).
    JL    JE_LessThan5    // Jump if less than 5.
    LEA   EAX , szAbsGTEFive // Get the pointer to the correct format
                         // string into EAX.
    JMP   JE_DoPrintf    // Go to the printf call.

JE_LessThan5:

    LEA   EAX , szAbsLTFive  // Get the pointer to the correct format
                         // string into EAX.

JE_DoPrintf:

    PUSH EAX             // Push the string.
    CALL DWORD PTR [printf] // Print it.
    ADD   ESP , 4        // Restore the stack.
}
}
```

As you can see, the result in the first example is correct. The idea to remember is that it's more efficient to check the opposite condition and jump around than to jump someplace to execute what's inside the *if* statement and then jump back.

JA Jump if above

JBE Jump if below or equal

JC Jump if carry

JNC Jump if not carry

JNZ Jump if not 0

JZ   Jump if 0

These conditional branch instructions aren't as common as the ones listed earlier, but you might see them in the Disassembly window. You should be able to intuit the condition from the jump names.

Looping

LOOP Loop according to ECX counter

You might not run into too many LOOP instructions because the Microsoft compilers don't generate them that much. In some parts of the operating system core, however (parts that look as if Microsoft wrote them in assembly language), you'll occasionally see them. Using the LOOP instruction is easy. Set ECX equal to the number of times to loop, and then execute a block of code. Immediately following the code is the LOOP instruction, which decrements ECX and then jumps to the top of the block if ECX isn't equal to 0. When ECX reaches 0, the LOOP instruction falls through.

Most of the loops you'll see are a combination of conditional jumps and absolute jumps. In many ways, these loops look like the *if* statement code presented a moment ago except that the bottom of the *if* block is a JMP instruction back to the top. The following example is representative of your average code-generation loop.

```
void LoopingExample ( int q )
{
    // Here's the C code:
    // for ( ; q < 10 ; q++ )
    // {
    //     printf ( "q = %d\n" , q ) ;
    // }

    char szFmt[] = "q = %d\n" ;
    __asm
    {
        JMP   LE_CompareStep       // First time through, check against
                                   // 10 immediately.

LE_IncrementStep:
        INC   q                    // Increment q.
```

(continued)

```
LE_CompareStep:
        CMP   q , 0Ah             // Compare q to 10.
        JGE   LE_End              // If q is >= 10, this function is done.

        MOV   ECX , DWORD PTR [q] // Get the value of q into ECX.
        PUSH  ECX                 // Get the value onto the stack.
        LEA   ECX , szFmt         // Get the format string.
        PUSH  ECX                 // Push the format string onto the stack.
        CALL  DWORD PTR [printf]  // Print the current iteration.
        ADD   ESP , 8             // Clean up the stack.

        JMP   LE_IncrementStep    // Increment q, and start again.

LE_End:                           // The loop is done.

    }
}
```

String Manipulation

The Intel CPUs are adept at manipulating strings. In the vernacular of CPUs, being good at string manipulation means that the CPU can manipulate large chunks of memory in a single instruction. All the string instructions I'll show you have several mnemonics, which you'll see if you look them up in the Intel reference manuals, but the Visual C++ Disassembly window always disassembles string instructions into the forms I show. All these instructions can work on byte, word, and double-word size memory.

MOVS Move data from string to string

The MOVS instruction moves the memory address at ESI to the memory address at EDI. The MOVS instruction operates only on values that ESI and EDI point to. You can think of the MOVS instruction as the implementation of the C *memcpy* function. The Visual C++ Disassembly window always shows the size of the operation with the size specifier, so you can tell at a glance how much memory is being moved. After the move is completed, the ESI and EDI registers are incremented or decremented depending on the Direction Flag in the EFLAGS register (shown as the UP field in the Visual C++ Registers window). If the UP field is 0, the registers are incremented. If the UP field is 1, the registers are decremented. The increment and decrement amounts depend on the size of the operation: 1 for bytes, 2 for words, and 4 for double words.

SCAS Scan string

The SCAS instruction compares the value at the memory address specified by the EDI register with the value in AL, AX, or EAX, depending on the requested size. The various flag values in EFLAGS are set to indicate the comparison values. The flag settings are the same as those shown in Table 6-4 on page 200. If you scan the string for a *NULL* terminator, the SCAS instruction can be used to duplicate the functionality of the C *strlen* function. Like the MOVS instruction, the SCAS instruction autoincrements or autodecrements the EDI register.

STOS Store string

The STOS instruction stores the value in AL, AX, or EAX, depending on the requested size, into the address specified by the EDI register. The STOS instruction is similar to the C *memset* function. Like both the MOVS and SCAS instructions, the STOS instruction autoincrements or autodecrements the EDI register.

CMPS Compare strings

The CMPS instruction compares two string values and sets the flags in EFLAGS accordingly. Whereas the SCAS instruction compares a string with a single value, the CMPS instruction walks the characters in two strings. The CMPS instruction is similar to the C *memcmp* function. Like the rest of the string manipulators, the CMPS instruction compares different size values and autoincrements and autodecrements the pointers to both strings.

REP Repeat for ECX count

REPE Repeat while equal or ECX count isn't 0

REPNE Repeat while not equal or ECX count isn't 0

The string instructions, though convenient, aren't worth a great deal if they can manipulate only a single unit at a time. The repeat prefixes allow the string instructions to iterate for a set number of times (in ECX) or until the specified condition is met. If you use the Step Into key when a repeat instruction is executing in the Disassembly window, you'll stay on the same line because you're executing the same instruction. If you use the Step Over key, you'll step over the entire iteration. If you're looking for a problem, you might want to use the Step Into key to check the strings in ESI or EDI as appropriate. Another trick when looking at a crash in a repeat prefixed string instruction is to look at the ECX register to see which iteration crashed.

In talking about the string instructions, I mentioned which C run-time library function each was similar to. The following code shows, without obvious error checking, what the assembly-language equivalents could look like:

```
void MemCPY ( char * szSrc , char * szDest , int iLen )
{
    __asm
    {

        MOV ESI , szSrc        // Set the source string.
        MOV EDI , szDest       // Set the destination string.
```

(continued)

```
            MOV ECX , iLen          // Set the length to copy.

                                    // Copy away!
            REP MOVS BYTE PTR [EDI] , BYTE PTR [ESI]
        }
    }

int StrLEN ( char * szSrc )
{
    int iReturn ;
    __asm
    {
        XOR EAX , EAX           // Zero out EAX.
        MOV EDI , szSrc         // Move the string to check into EDI.
        MOV ECX , 0FFFFFFFFh    // The maximum number of characters to
                                // check.

        REPNE SCAS BYTE PTR [EDI] // Compare until ECX=0 or found.

        CMP ECX , 0             // If ECX is 0, a
        JE  StrLEN_NoNull       // NULL wasn't found in the string.

        NOT ECX                 // ECX was counted down, so convert it
                                // to a positive number.
        DEC ECX                 // Account for hitting the NULL.
        MOV EAX , ECX           // Return the count.
        JMP StrLen_Done         // Return.

StrLEN_NoNull:
        MOV EAX , 0FFFFFFFFh    // Because NULL wasn't found, return -1.

StrLEN_Done:

    }
    __asm MOV iReturn , EAX ;
    return ( iReturn ) ;
}

void MemSET ( char * szDest , int iVal , int iLen )
{
    __asm
    {
        MOV EAX , iVal          // EAX holds the fill value.
        MOV EDI , szDest        // Move the string into EDI.
        MOV ECX , iLen          // Move the count into ECX.

        REP STOS BYTE PTR [EDI] // Fill the memory.
    }
}
```

```
int MemCMP ( char * szMem1 ,  char * szMem2 , int iLen )
{
    int iReturn ;
    __asm
    {
        MOV ESI , szMem1       // ESI holds the first memory block.
        MOV EDI , szMem2       // EDI holds the second memory block.
        MOV ECX , iLen         // The maximum bytes to compare

                               // Compare the memory blocks.
        REPE CMPS BYTE PTR [ESI], BYTE PTR [EDI]

        JL  MemCMP_LessThan    // If szSrc < szDest
        JG  MemCMP_GreaterThan // If szSrc > szDest

                               // The memory blocks are equal.
        XOR EAX , EAX          // Return 0.
        JMP MemCMP_Done

MemCMP_LessThan:
        MOV EAX , 0FFFFFFFFh   // Return -1.
        JMP MemCMP_Done

MemCMP_GreaterThan:
        MOV EAX , 1            // Return 1.
        JMP MemCMP_Done

MemCMP_Done:
    }
    __asm MOV iReturn , EAX
    return ( iReturn ) ;
}
```

COMMON ASSEMBLY-LANGUAGE CONSTRUCTS

Up to this point, I've just been covering basic assembly-language instructions. Now I want to start looking at various assembly-language constructs that you'll encounter and explain how you identify them and translate them into higher level operations.

FS Register Access

In Win32 operating systems, the FS register is special because the pointer to the thread information block (TIB) is stored in it. The TIB is also called the thread environment block (TEB). The TIB holds all the thread-specific data so that the operating system can keep your thread access straight. This thread-specific data includes all the structured exception handling (SEH) chains, thread local storage, and other information needed internally. For more information about SEH, see Chapter 9. For an example of thread local storage, see the MemStress discussion in Chapter 15.

The TIB is stored in a special memory segment, and when the operating system needs to access the TIB, it converts the FS register plus an offset into a normal linear address. When you see an instruction accessing the FS register, one of the following operations is underway: an SEH frame is being created or destroyed, the TIB is being accessed, or thread local storage is being accessed.

Creating or Destroying an SEH Frame

The first instructions after setting up the stack frame are often something like the following code, which is standard code to start a __try block. The first node in the chain of SEH handlers is at offset 0 in the TIB. In the disassembly below, the compiler is pushing a data value and a pointer to a function on the stack. That function is __except_handler3. The first MOV instruction is accessing the TIB; the offset of 0 indicates that a node is being added to the top of the exception chain. The last two instructions indicate where the code moves the actual node to the chain.

```
PUSH 004060d0
PUSH 004014a0
MOV  EAX , FS:[00000000]
PUSH EAX
MOV  DWORD PTR FS:[0] , ESP
```

Although this example is nice and clean, the compiler doesn't always produce such tidy code. Sometimes it spreads the SEH frame creation throughout the code. Depending on the code generation and optimization flags, the compiler moves instructions around to take better advantage of the CPU's pipelining. The following disassembly example, in which KERNEL32.DLL symbols are loaded, shows the start of the Microsoft Windows NT 4 *IsBadReadPtr* function.

```
MOV   EAX , FS:[00000000h]
PUSH  EBP
MOV   EBP , ESP
PUSH  0FFh
PUSH  77F3D1E8h
PUSH  _except_handler3
PUSH  EAX
MOV   EAX , [BaseStaticServerData]
MOV   DWORD PTR FS:[00000000h] , ESP
```

Destroying an SEH frame is much more mundane than creating one, as the following code shows. The key item to remember is that any access of FS:[0] means SEH.

```
MOV ECX , DWORD PTR [EBP-10h]
MOV DWORD PTR FS:[0] , ECX
```

Accessing the TIB

The value at FS:[18] is the linear address of the TIB structure. In the following code, the Windows 2000 implementation of *GetCurrentThreadId* gets the linear address of the TIB, and at offset 0x24, it gets the actual thread ID.

```
GetCurrentThreadId:
MOV EAX , FS:[00000018h]
MOV EAX , DWORD PTR [EAX+024h]
RET
```

Accessing Thread Local Storage

Thread local storage is a Win32 mechanism that allows you to have variables that are global, but each thread has its own instance of the global variables. Offset 0x2C in the TIB structure is the pointer to the thread local storage array. The following disassembly shows how to access the thread local storage pointer.

```
MOV ECX , DWORD PTR FS:[2Ch]
MOV EDX , DWORD PTR [ECX+EAX*4]
```

Structure and Class References

Because so much of Windows development is structures and classes, I want to spend some time going over how you access that memory. Although structures and classes are convenient to deal with in high-level languages, at the assembly-language level they really don't exist. In high-level languages, a structure and a class are just shorthand ways to specify offsets into a blob of memory. If you're dealing with Visual Basic code, a Visual Basic form is identical to a class at the assembly-language level.

For the most part, the compilers lay out memory for your structures and classes just as you specify. Occasionally, the compiler will pad fields to keep them on natural memory boundaries, which for x86 CPUs is 4 or 8 bytes.

Structure and class references are denoted by a register and a memory offset. In *MyStruct* below, the comments to the right of each member show the offset from the beginning of the structure for each member. After the *MyStruct* definition, I show various ways of accessing the structure fields.

```
typedef struct tag_MyStruct
{
    DWORD dwFirst ;              // 0-byte offset
    char  szBuff[ 256 ] ;       // 4-byte offset
    int   iVal ;                // 260-byte offset
} MyStruct , * PMyStruct ;
```

(continued)

```
void FillStruct ( PMyStruct pSt )
{
    char szName[] = "Pam\n" ;

    __asm
    {
        MOV  EAX , pSt   // Place pSt into EAX. Below, I'm using the
                         // direct offsets in the assembly language to show
                         // what they look like in a disassembly. The
                         // inline assembler allows you to use the normal
                         // <struct>.<field> references.

        // C code : pSt->dwFirst = 23 ;
        MOV  DWORD PTR [EAX] , 17h

        // C code: pSt->iVal = 0x33 ;
        MOV  DWORD PTR [EAX + 0104h] , 0x33

        // C code: strcpy ( pSt->szBuff , szName ) ;
        LEA  ECX , szName       // Push szName on the stack.
        PUSH ECX

        LEA  ECX , [EAX + 4]    // Get to the szBuff field.
        PUSH ECX

        CALL strcpy
        ADD  ESP , 8            // strcpy is a __cdecl function.

        // C code: pSt->szBuff[ 1 ] = 'A' ;
        MOV  BYTE PTR [EAX + 5] , 41h

        // C code: printf ( pSt->szBuff ) ;
        MOV  EAX , pSt          // Get pSt back. EAX was destroyed
                                // on the call to strcpy.
        LEA  ECX , [EAX + 4]
        PUSH ECX
        CALL DWORD PTR [printf]
        ADD ESP , 4             // printf is a __cdecl function.
    }
}
```

A COMPLETE EXAMPLE

Now that I've covered all the important parts of Intel assembly language, I want to show a complete example of a Win32 API function before turning to the Disassembly window. Listing 6-2 shows the completely commented disassembly of the *lstrcpyA* function from the Windows NT 4 Service Pack 4 KERNEL32.DLL. The *lstrcpyA* function copies one string into another string. I chose this function because it shows a little bit of everything that I've discussed so far in this chapter and because the purpose of the function is easily understood. I made the comments, delineated by semicolons, as detailed as possible.

```
; Function prototype:
; LPTSTR lstrcpy ( LPTSTR lpString1 , LPCTSTR lpString2 )

lstrcpyA:

; Start preparing to set up an SEH frame.
77F127E6: MOV        EAX , FS:[00000000h]

; Do the regular stack frame setup.
77F127EC: PUSH       EBP
77F127ED: MOV        EBP , ESP

; Continue with the SEH frame setup.
77F127EF: PUSH       0FFh
77F127F1: PUSH       77F3CD48h
77F127F6: PUSH       _except_handler3
77F127FB: PUSH       EAX
77F127FC: MOV        DWORD PTR FS:[00000000h] , ESP

; Save 12 bytes for local variables.
77F12803: SUB        ESP , 00Ch

; Save register values that will be destroyed as part of this function.
77F12806: PUSH       EBX
77F12807: PUSH       ESI
77F12808: PUSH       EDI

; Save the current top of the stack into a local variable. This
; line is part of the SEH setup as well.
77F12809: MOV        DWORD PTR [EBP-018h] , ESP

; Initialize this local variable to 0. This line indicates that the
; function is entering the __try block.
77F1280C: MOV        DWORD PTR [EBP-004h] , 00000000h

; The first step after setting up is to get the length of the string to
; copy. The string to copy is the second parameter.

; Move the second parameter, the string to be copied, into EDI.
77F12813: MOV        EDI , DWORD PTR [EBP+00Ch]
```

Listing 6-2 lstrcpyA—*A complete assembly-language example*   *(continued)*

Listing 6-2 *continued*

```
; lstrcpy will look through 4,294,967,295 bytes for the NULL terminator.
; EDX is used later with a value of -1, so it's initialized here.
; Remember that ECX is what REPNE SCAS uses to count the loop.
77F12816: MOV        EDX , FFFFFFFFh
77F1281B: MOV        ECX , EDX


; Zero out EAX so that SCAS will look for the NULL character.
77F1281D: SUB        EAX , EAX


; Look for the NULL character.
77F1281F: REPNE      SCAS BYTE PTR [EDI]


; Because ECX is counted down, switch all the bits so that the length of
; the string is in ECX. The length here includes the NULL character.
77F12821: NOT        ECX


; Because the REPNE SCAS also incremented EDI, subtract the length of the
; string from EDI so that EDI points back to the start of the string.
77F12823: SUB        EDI , ECX


; Hold the string length in EAX.
77F12825: MOV        EAX , ECX


; Move the second parameter into ESI since ESI is the source operand for
; the string instructions.
77F12827: MOV        ESI , EDI


; Move the first parameter, the destination string, into EDI.
77F12829: MOV        EDI , DWORD PTR [EBP+008h]


; The string length was counted in bytes. Divide the string length by
; 4 to get the number of DWORDs. If the number of characters is odd,
; the REPE MOVS won't copy them all. Any remaining bytes are copied
; right after the REPE MOVS.
77F1282C: shr        ECX , 002h


; Copy the second parameter string into the first parameter string.
77F1282F: REPE       MOVS DWORD PTR [EDI] , DWORD PTR [ESI]


; Move the saved string length into ECX.
77F12831: MOV        ECX , EAX


; AND the count with 3 to get the remaining bytes to copy.
77F12833: AND        ECX , 003h
```

```
; Copy the remaining bytes from string to string.
77F12836: REPE     MOVS BYTE PTR [EDI] , BYTE PTR [ESI]


; lstrcpy returns the first parameter, so move the return value
; into EAX.
77F12838: MOV      EAX , DWORD PTR [EBP+008h]


; Set the local variable to -1, which indicates that the function is
; leaving this try/except block.
77F1283B: MOV      DWORD PTR [EBP-004h] , EDX


; The function has completed; jump out and move home.
77F1283E: JMP      77F12852h


; If you look through this function, you'll notice that no instruction
; actually jumps or branches to 0x77F12840. This address is the
; exception filter part of the SEH. The exception filter is a piece of
; code that tells the SEH unwinding what to do. The exception filter here
; is equivalent to __except ( EXCEPTION_EXECUTE_HANDLER ). The unwinding
; code should execute the handler, which is the code right after the RET
; instruction. To learn more about exception filters, see MSDN or
; Jeffrey Richter's "Programming Applications for Microsoft Windows"
; (Microsoft Press, 1999).


77F12840: MOV      EAX , 00000001h
77F12845: RET


; The next three instructions are the exception block for the function.


; Restore the stack saved earlier.
77F12846: MOV   ·  ESP , DWORD PTR [EBP-018h]


; Set the local variable to -1, which indicates that the function is
; leaving this try/except block.
77F12849: MOV      DWORD PTR [EBP-004h] , FFFFFFFFh


; Set up to return 0, the bad return value.
77F12850: XOR      EAX , EAX


; Get the previous SEH frame.
77F12852: MOV      ECX , DWORD PTR [EBP-010h]


; Restore the previously pushed EDI.
77F12855: POP      EDI
```

(continued)

Listing 6-2 *continued*

```
; Undo the SEH frame.
77F12856: MOV        DWORD PTR FS:[00000000h] , ECX

; Restore the previously pushed ESI.
77F1285D: POP        ESI

; Restore the previously pushed EBI.
77F1285E: POP        EBX

; Undo the normal stack frame setup.
77F1285F: MOV        ESP , EBP
77F12861: POP        EBP

; Return to the caller and clean off 8 bytes from the stack.
; lstrcpy is a __sdtcall function.
77F12862: RET        00008h
```

THE DISASSEMBLY WINDOW

Now that you've learned some assembly language, the Visual C++ debugger Disassembly window shouldn't be so daunting. The Disassembly window offers many features that will help you with your debugging work. In this section, I'll talk about some of those features and how to minimize the time you spend in the Disassembly window.

Navigating

If you've ever worked with a debugger that didn't have navigation features that let you steer a course through disassembled code, you know that the lack of good navigation tools can lead to a very frustrating debugging experience. Fortunately, the Disassembly window offers several efficient ways to get where you need to go in the debuggee.

The first avenue for getting to a specific location in the debuggee is via the Go To dialog box, which you can reach through Go To on the Edit menu or through an accelerator, Ctrl+G. If you know the address you want to go to, you can just type it in and jump right to it. The Go To dialog box can also interpret symbols and context information, so you can jump to areas even if you don't know the exact address.

The only small problem is that you're stuck with the symbol formatting issues I brought up in Chapter 5. You'll have to do the same translations to account for name decoration that you have to do when setting a breakpoint on a system or an exported function. For example, if you have symbols loaded for KERNEL32.DLL and you want to jump to *LoadLibrary* in the Disassembly window, you'll need to enter *{,,kernel-32}_LoadLibraryA@4* in the Go To dialog box to jump to the correct place.

One cool capability that the Disassembly window supports is drag and drop. If you're working through a section of assembly language and you need to quickly check where in memory an operation is going, you can select the address and drag it a couple of pixels. When you release the mouse button, the Disassembly window automatically jumps to that address.

As you're frolicking around the Disassembly window with abandon, don't be surprised if you realize that you've forgotten where you started—it's easy to get lost in the Disassembly window. To get back to where the instruction pointer is sitting, just right-click in the Disassembly window and select Show Next Statement. The Show Next Statement command is also available in source code windows.

You should always use the Go To dialog box to move around in the Disassembly window, especially when you're moving to lower memory. If you try to page or cursor up, you can get into situations in which the Disassembly window needs to disassemble from the beginning of memory to figure out what to display. This complete disassembly can hang the debugger.

Viewing Parameters on the Stack

In Chapter 5, you saw how to set breakpoints on system and exported functions. One of the main reasons for setting breakpoints on these functions is so that you can view the parameters that go into a given function. To demonstrate how to look up items on the stack, I want to use a real-world example instead of a contrived, simple example.

Ever since Visual Basic 5 first came out with the native-code feature, I've wanted to see how the native compilation worked. I saw that the Visual Basic directory included LINK.EXE and C2.EXE. These two programs are also part of Visual C++, and I was curious to see how Visual Basic used them so that I'd have a good idea of how the compilation worked. As you can tell from the name, LINK.EXE links the object files together and produces the executable binary. C2.EXE is a little obtuse. In Visual C++, C2.EXE is the code generator that produces the machine code. I wanted to see whether Visual Basic uses C2.EXE in the same way that Visual C++ does.

From the Visual C++ integrated development environment (IDE), I opened VB6.EXE as the program to debug. Because I had symbols loaded, I needed to set a breakpoint on *{,,kernel32}_CreateProcessA@40*. When Visual Basic started, I created a simple project, set the project properties to create native code, and selected File–Make from the Visual Basic IDE. The breakpoint on *_CreateProcessA@40* gives the debugger control when starting either C2.EXE or LINK.EXE.

On Windows 2000 RC2, the breakpoint on _CreateProcessA@40 stops the debugger at address 0x77E8D7E6 when the instruction about to be executed is PUSH EBP to set up the standard stack frame. Because the breakpoint is on the first instruction of CreateProcess, the top of the stack contains the parameters and the return address. I opened the Memory window by selecting the View–Debug Windows–Memory command. I then entered ESP in the Address field, which is the stack pointer register, to see what was on the stack.

The default format for the Memory window displays all its contents in byte format, and searching through this output can be mind-numbing when you're looking for values that are multiple bytes because you have to do all the Endian conversions in your head. (If you're unfamiliar with the term "Endian," refer to the section "Endians" on page 222.) One day I right-clicked in the Memory window and, lo and behold, the memory window showed different formats: byte, short hex (2 byte or WORD), and long hex (4 byte or DWORD)

Figure 6-4 shows the stack in the debugger Memory window at the start of the CreateProcess breakpoint. The first value is the return address for the instruction 0xFB6B3F6; the next 10 are the parameters to CreateProcess. (See Table 6-5.) CreateProcess has 40 bytes of parameters; each parameter is 4 bytes long. The stack grows from high memory to low memory, and the parameters are pushed in right-to-left order, so the parameters appear in the Memory window in the same order as in the function definition.

Figure 6-4 *The stack displayed in the Visual C++ debugger Memory window*

You can view the individual parameter values for the first two parameters in two ways. The first way is to use the Memory window by switching its format to byte format and viewing the particular address. The second and easier way is to drag the address you want to view to the Watch window. In the Watch window, use a cast operator to view the address. For example, to view the *lpApplicationName* parameter in the example, you'd put "(char*)0x0012EAC4" in the Watch window. Either way of viewing works; both should show the following values:

```
0x0012EAC4 "c:\vb\C2.EXE"
0x0012EBC4 "C@ -il "e:\temp\VB815574
              -f "c:\junk\vb\Form1.frm -W 3 -Gy -G5
              -Gs4096 -dos -Z1
              -Fo"c:\junk\vb\Form1.OBJ" -Zi -QIfdiv
              -ML -basic"
```

Table 6-5   PARAMETERS THAT VB6.EXE PASSES TO *CREATEPROCESS*

Value	Type	Parameter
0x0012EAC4	*LPCTSTR*	*lpApplicationName*
0x0012EBC4	*LPTSTR*	*lpCommandLine*
0x00000000	*LPSECURITY_ATTRIBUTES*	*lpProcessAttributes*
0x00000000	*LPSECURITY_ATTRIBUTES*	*lpThreadAttributes*
0x00000001	*BOOL*	*bInheritHandles*
0x08000000	*DWORD*	*dwCreationFlags*
0x00000000	*LPVOID*	*lpEnvironment*
0x00000000	*LPCTSTR*	*lpCurrentDirectory*
0x0012EA3C	*LPSTARTUPINFO*	*lpStartupInfo*
0x0012EC60	*LPPROCESS_INFORMATION*	*lpProcessInformation*

It was easy to get the preceding parameters because I stopped the function on the first instruction before it had a chance to push additional items. If you need to check the parameters when you're in the middle of a function, you have to do a little more work. If you can find the positive offsets from EBP, that helps. Sometimes the best technique is just to open the Memory window and start looking.

The Set Next Statement Command

Like source windows, the Disassembly window has a Set Next Statement command available from the right-click menu, so you can change EIP to another location to execute. You can get away with being a little sloppy with the Set Next Statement line in a source view, but you must be very careful with the Set Next Statement command in the Disassembly window.

The key to getting EIP set right—so that you don't crash—is to pay attention to the stack. Stack pops should balance out stack pushes; if they don't, you'll eventually crash your program. I don't mean to scare you off from changing execution on the fly; in fact, I encourage you to experiment with it. Changing execution with Set Next Statement is a powerful technique and can greatly speed up your debugging. If you take care of the stack, the stack will take care of you.

For example, if you want to reexecute a function without crashing immediately, make sure to change the execution so that the stack stays balanced. Here I want to execute the call to the function at 0x00401005 twice.

```
00401032 PUSH EBP
00401033 MOV  EBP , ESP
00401035 PUSH 404410h
0040103A CALL 00401005h
```

(continued)

```
0040103F ADD   ESP , 4
00401042 POP   EBP
00401043 RET
```

As I step through the disassembly twice, I need to make sure that I let the ADD instruction at address 0x0040103F execute to keep the stack balanced. As the discussion of the different calling conventions earlier in the chapter indicated, the assembly-language snippet shows a call to a __cdecl function because of the ADD instruction right after the call. To reexecute the function, I'd set the instruction pointer to 0x00401035 to ensure that the PUSH occurs properly.

The Memory Window and the Disassembly Window

The Memory window and the Disassembly window have a symbiotic relationship. As you're trying to determine what a sequence of assembly-language operations is doing in the Disassembly window, you need to have the Memory window open so that you can look at the addresses and values being manipulated. Assembly-language instructions work on memory, and memory affects the execution of assembly language; the Disassembly window and the Memory window together allow you to observe the dynamics of this relationship.

On its own, the Memory window is just a sea of numbers, especially when you crash. By combining the two windows, however, you can start figuring out some nasty crash problems. Using these windows together is especially important when you're trying to debug optimized code and the debugger can't walk the stack as easily. To solve the crash, you have to walk the stack manually.

The first step in figuring out how to walk the stack is to know where your binaries are loaded into memory. In version 6, the Visual C++ debugger added a dialog box, Module List, that shows you all the binaries loaded in your program. This dialog box shows you the module name, the path to the module, the load order, and most important, the address range where the module was loaded. Because this dialog box is modal to the debugger, you might want to write down the module names and their load addresses because you'll be referring to this information often. By comparing items on the stack with the list of address ranges, you can get an idea of which items are addresses in your modules.

After you look at the load address ranges, you need to open both the Memory and Disassembly windows. In the Memory window, enter ESP, the stack register, into the Address field and show the values in double-word format by right-clicking within the window and selecting Long Hex Format. Using either your written list of load addresses or the Module List dialog box, start looking at the Memory window numbers across and down. When you see a number that looks as if it belongs to one of your loaded modules, select the entire number and drag it to the Disassembly window. The Disassembly window will show the assembly language at that address, and if you built your application with full debugging information, you should be able to see what the caller function was.

If the ESP register dump doesn't show anything that looks like a module address, you can also dump the EBP register in the Memory window and do the same sorts of lookups. As you get more comfortable with assembly language, you'll start looking at the disassembly around the address that crashed. Studying the crash crime scene should give you some hints about where the return address might be located, either in ESP or in EBP.

The downside to looking up items on the stack manually is that you might have to hunt a considerable way down the stack before you start finding addresses that make sense. If you have an idea of where the modules loaded, however, you should be able to pick out the appropriate addresses quickly.

Let me backtrack a minute before I go any further. Before you use the Memory window, you should know about some of its strengths and weaknesses. On the plus side, the Memory window is the only place where you can view character strings over 255 characters—all other views in the debugger stop at 255. You can also select and drag any variable or memory into the Memory window to view it.

On the downside, the Memory window has two problems. The first problem is that you can view only one piece of memory at a time with the Visual C++ debugger, and there's no way around this limitation. If enough of us ask, however, perhaps future versions of the Visual C++ debugger will allow us to view more than one memory block at a time.

The other problem with the Memory window is that the memory address that you're interested in viewing can bounce around in the display. This bouncing around happens mostly when you right-click to change the memory format. For example, if you position the memory at 0x0012FDBC at the top of the Memory window and then change the memory format, the display can shift down so that the address appears in the middle of the window. As you're concentrating on the problem at hand, you can easily miss the fact that the address you need to see has moved and you start looking at the top line, which is something completely different. I don't know how many times this "jumping memory address" problem has messed up a debugging session.

To work around the memory-address-as-moving-target problem, I've found it best to right-click only on the address I need to see—and nowhere else in the Memory window. Apparently, the Memory window keeps track of where it displays the current address line. For example, if the current address line is the tenth line from the top of the window and you type a new address in the Address field, the new address gets displayed as the tenth line. When you right-click in the window and change the memory format, the Memory window moves the current address line to the right-click location—the result can be extremely confusing.

DEBUGGING WAR STORY

What can go wrong in *GlobalUnlock*? It's just a pointer dereference.

The Battle

A team called me in to help them debug an extremely nasty crash—one severe enough to prevent them from releasing the product. The team had spent nearly a month trying to duplicate the crash and still had no idea what was causing it. The only clue they had was that the crash happened only after they brought up the Print dialog box and changed some settings. After they closed the Print dialog box, the crash occurred a little later in a third-party control. The crash call stack indicated that the crash happened in the middle of *GlobalUnlock*.

The Outcome

At first I wasn't sure that anyone was still using the handle-based memory functions (*GlobalAlloc*, *GlobalLock*, *GlobalFree*, and *GlobalUnlock*) in Win32 programming. After looking at a disassembly of the third-party control, however, I saw that the control writer obviously ported the control from a 16-bit code base. My first hypothesis was that the control wasn't properly dealing with the handle-based memory API functions.

To test my hypothesis, I set some breakpoints on *GlobalAlloc*, *GlobalLock*, and *GlobalUnlock* so that I could find the places in the third-party control where memory was being allocated or manipulated. Once I got the breakpoints set in the third-party control, I started watching how the control used the handle-based memory. Everything seemed normal until I started working through the steps to duplicate the crash.

At some point after closing the Print dialog box, I noticed that *GlobalAlloc* was starting to return handle values that ended in odd values, such as 5. Because the handle-based memory in Win32 just needs a pointer dereference to turn the handle into a memory value, I immediately saw that I was on to a critical problem. Every memory allocation in Win32 must end in 0, 4, 8, or a C hex digit, because all pointers must be double-word aligned. The handle values coming out of *GlobalAlloc* were evidence that something serious was corrupted.

Armed with this information, the product manager was ready to jump on the phone and demand the source code for the third-party control because he was sure that the control was causing the crash and holding up his release. After calming him down, I told him that what we had found didn't prove anything and that I needed to be absolutely sure the control was the culprit before we made life miserable for the vendor. I continued to look at the control's memory usage and spent the next several hours chasing down all the handle-based memory manipulations in the control. The control was properly using the handle-based memory, and my new hypothesis became that the team's application contained the real problem. The crash in the third-party control was just a coincidence.

After looking through the team's code, I was more confused than ever because the application was a complete Win32 application and did nothing with handle-based memory. I then turned to their printing code and started looking at it. The code looked fine.

I went back and started to narrow down the minimum case that would duplicate the crash. After a few runs, I found that all I needed to do to crash was to bring up the Print dialog box and change the paper orientation. After closing the Print dialog box, I just needed to reopen it, and the crash would happen shortly after I closed it the second time. I was happy to get the problem duplicated to this minute level because the page orientation was probably just changing a byte somewhere in memory and causing the problem.

Although the code looked fine on the initial read, I went back through each line and double-checked it against the MSDN documentation. After 10 minutes, I found the bug. The team was saving the *PRINTDLG* data structure used to initialize the Print dialog box with the *PrintDlg* API function. The third field in the *PRINTDLG* structure, *hDevMode*, is a handle-based memory value that the Print dialog box allocates for you. The bug was that the team was using that memory value as a regular pointer and not properly dereferencing the handle or calling *GlobalLock* on the handle. When they would go to change values in the *DEVMODE* structure, they were actually writing to the global handle table for the process. The global handle table is a chunk of memory in which all handle-based heap allocations are stored. By having the wild writes to the global handle table, a call to *GlobalAlloc* would use invalid offsets and values calculated from the global handle table so that *GlobalAlloc* was returning pointers that were incorrect.

The Lesson
The first lesson is to read the documentation carefully. If the documentation says that the data structure is a "movable global memory object," the memory is handle-based memory and you need to dereference that memory handle properly or use *GlobalLock* on it. Even though 16-bit Windows 3.1 seems like ancient history, some 16-bit-isms are still in the Win32 API, and you must pay attention to them.

(continued)

Another lesson that I learned was that the global handle table is stored in writable memory. I would have thought that such an important operating system structure would have been in read-only memory. After pondering the reasons Microsoft wouldn't protect that memory, I can only hazard a guess about why they didn't choose to make the global handle table read-only. Technically, the handle-based memory is just for backward compatibility, and Win32 applications should be using the Win32-specific memory types. Protecting the global handle table would require two context switches, from user mode to kernel mode, on each handle-based memory function call. Because those context switches are very expensive in processing time, I can see why Microsoft didn't protect the global handle table.

The final lesson I learned was that I spent too much time concentrating on the third-party control. In all, it took me around seven hours to find the bug. However, the fact that the bug could be duplicated only by bringing up the Print dialog box, which went through the team's code, should have tipped me off that the problem was closer to home.

TIPS AND TRICKS

In Chapter 5, I presented some tips and tricks that can make your life in the debugger easier. In this chapter, I'll continue to provide you with suggestions, but here I'll concentrate on tips that will help you with debugging at the assembly-language level.

Endians

The "Endianness" of a CPU refers to which end of a byte is stored first. Intel CPUs are "Little Endian," which means that the little end of a multibyte value is stored first. For example, the value 0x1234 is stored in memory as 0x34 0x12. It's important that you keep the Little Endian storage in mind when you're looking at memory in the debugger. You'll need to convert it in your head so that you're interpreting the correct values. If you use the Memory window to look at one of your link list nodes and the next pointer value is 0x12345678, the value will be displayed in byte format as 0x78 0x56 0x34 0x12.

If you're curious, the term "Endian" comes from Jonathan Swift's *Gulliver's Travels*, and the computer meaning came from a 1980 Request for Comments (RFC) concerning byte ordering by Danny Cohen. Danny's paper is at *http://www.op.net/docs/RFCs/ien-137* for those who want to know the entire story.

Garbage Code

As a crash dumps you into the Disassembly window, you have to determine whether or not you're looking at real code, which is sometimes a difficult task. Here are some tips that will help you figure out whether you're looking at something other than executable code.

- I've found that turning on the Code Bytes from the Disassembly window right-click menu to see the opcodes for the instructions is useful. As you'll see in the following tips, knowing what opcode patterns to look for can help you decide whether you're looking at legitimate code.

- If you're looking at a series of identical ADD BYTE PTR [EAX] , AL instructions, you're not looking at valid assembly-language code. You're looking at a series of zeros.

- If you see symbols but the offsets added to the symbols are very large numbers, generally over 0x1000, you're probably outside a code section. However, very large numbers can also mean that you're debugging a module that doesn't have private symbols available.

- If you're looking at a bunch of instructions that I didn't cover in this chapter, you're probably looking at data.

- If the Visual C++ disassembler can't disassemble an instruction, it displays "???" as the opcode.

Registers and the Watch Window

The Visual C++ debugger Watch window knows how to decode all the registers to values. Therefore, you can put a register in the Watch window and cast it to the type you want to observe. For example, if you're looking at a string manipulation instruction, you can enter *(char*)@EDI* in the Watch window to view the data in a format that's easier to read.

Learn from ASM Files

If you'd like to see more mixed assembly language and source code, you can have Visual C++ generate the assembly listings for your source files. If you type the /FAs option into the Project Settings dialog box, C++ tab, Project Options edit control, the compiler will generate an ASM file for each of your source code files. You might not want to generate the ASM files for every build, but they can be instructive, letting you see what the compiler is generating. The ASM files don't require you to fire up your application every time you're curious about assembly language.

The files generated are nearly ready to compile with the Microsoft Macro Assembler (MASM), so they can be a challenge to read. Much of the files consist of MASM directives, but the main parts of the files show your C code with the assembly-language code below each construct. After reading this chapter, you shouldn't have any trouble following the flow of ASM files.

SUMMARY

This chapter presented the Intel CPU assembly language that you need to know to survive in the Disassembly window. It started by covering the basics of Intel CPUs, such as setting registers and interpreting status flags, and then moved on to the instructions required to manipulate stacks, data, pointers, and strings; compare and test operands; and jump, branch, and loop, among other actions. After the assembly-language code were tips and tricks that will help you get the most out of debugging at the assembly-language level.

Being able to read assembly language makes all the difference in the world when you're in the debugger trying to figure out why your program crashed. Despite the fact that some people try to avoid it like the plague, assembly language isn't that hard, and there's certainly nothing mysterious about it. The information in this chapter will give you the power to solve many nasty bugs that once stumped you.

Chapter 7

Power Debugging with the Visual Basic Debugger

The Microsoft Visual Basic debugger is an interesting beast—developers either love it or hate it. On the positive side, the Visual Basic debugger makes debugging some applications, such as Microsoft ActiveX controls written in Visual Basic, trivial. The Visual Basic debugger is also easy to use. Finally, the Immediate window is a model for what all debuggers should include to make power debugging a snap.

On the negative side, the Visual Basic debugger has some serious problems. The first problem, which happens to be extremely annoying when you're trying to track down difficult bugs over multiple debugging sessions, is that the Visual Basic integrated development environment (IDE) doesn't save your breakpoints or your Watch window watches between sessions. Unfortunately, there's nothing you can do to work around this problem. The second problem, which I'll cover in detail later in this chapter, is that the debugger and the debuggee share the same address space, so when one crashes, the other follows. The final problem is that you're debugging interpreted p-code, which isn't exactly what your users will be running.

In this chapter, I'll explain how the Visual Basic debugger works and offer some recommendations for getting around its limitations with your sanity intact. I'll start by defining what it means to debug in Visual Basic. Then I'll go over the error trapping options and show you how to get the most out of the Locals, Immediate, and Watch windows. Finally, as I did in the chapters on the Microsoft Visual C++ debugger, I'll provide some tips and tricks to maximize your debugging pleasure.

VISUAL BASIC P-CODE

Experienced developers know all about Visual Basic's p-code, but I want to make sure that everyone understands exactly what happens when a Visual Basic application executes. I also want to be sure that you know the ramifications of debugging Visual Basic applications. As with other aspects of debugging, understanding how the debugger operates can help you out tremendously when you're experiencing problems. To help set up your frame of reference, I need to start with a little history lesson.

A P-Code History Lesson

Visual Basic 1, introduced in 1991, was an intriguing advance in programming tools. In the early 1990s, if you did any Microsoft Windows development at all, you had to write your code in C at the SDK level, which was generally a painful experience. Visual Basic promised, and mostly delivered, the ability to draw your user interface (UI) with a What-You-See-Is-What-You-Get (WYSIWYG) tool and an easy way to connect code to user events such as clicking a button. The unusual twist in Visual Basic 1 was that it didn't compile the final applications to native executables but to a form called *p-code*.

P-code, short for "packed code," was a method of reducing the memory footprint for binary files—p-code is much smaller than regular Intel x86 assembly language. When you "compiled" your applications in Visual Basic 1, you produced a regular executable, but that was just a shell around the p-code. When the "compiled" binary started, the run time started, hunted down the p-code at a specific offset in memory, and started executing the p-code. As everyone knows, the large run-time dynamic-link library (DLL) VBRUN100.DLL, which contained the p-code interpreter, also had to be shipped with your application.

The p-code interpreter is a stack-based engine that translates the special opcodes into operations on the CPU. Microsoft used to offer the ability to generate a different form of p-code as part of C/C++ version 7 back in the days of MS-DOS and 16-bit Windows. In fact, the original 16-bit versions of Microsoft's Word, Excel, and PowerPoint products used the p-code in C/C++ version 7 extensively in their UI code to achieve the size-to-performance trade-offs necessary to make those applications run on the limited memory systems available when Windows 3 and 3.1 were released. You can search MSDN for the "Microsoft P-Code Technology" topic to get an idea of the implementation of p-code in C/C++ version 7, which is probably close to the implementation of p-code in Visual Basic.

All versions of Visual Basic from 1 through 4 generated only p-code. The biggest problem with using p-code was that it was slower than native code. The old joke was that you could tell a Visual Basic application from a mile away because the application was slow and it used three-dimensional text controls for all the buttons. Although Microsoft couldn't do anything about the developers' choice of controls, it did heed the number-one plea of Visual Basic developers: "We want native code generation!"

Starting with Visual Basic 5 in 1997, Microsoft added an option that allowed you to produce native code as part of the compilation process. Microsoft developers also rewrote the Visual Basic run time to make it faster. The result of both changes was a fantastic performance boost for Visual Basic applications. The only hitch was that Microsoft just grafted on the native compilation feature to fulfill a bullet point on the feature chart rather than completely integrating the compilation and debugging with the Visual Basic IDE. After you compiled your application to native code, you were completely on your own to debug it. As I discussed in the section "Debugging Visual Basic Compiled Code" in Chapter 5, Visual Basic binaries don't have sufficient debugging symbols, so you're almost forced to debug raw assembly language.

The biggest hole in the native compilation feature is that the Visual Basic IDE understands only interpreted p-code. Thus, what you're debugging with the Visual Basic debugger, p-code, isn't what you're building, native compiled code. From a debugging and testing perspective, the situation is troublesome—even if you choose to compile to a p-code binary, you're still not debugging the exact bits you're sending to the customers. Unfortunately, other than suffering through debugging your compiled Visual Basic binaries under the Visual C++ debugger, there's nothing you can do about the situation. We can only hope that a future version of Visual Basic or Microsoft Visual Studio will rectify this problem so that we can debug exactly what we're shipping to our customers.

Ramifications of Using P-Code

Recall that in the section "MinDBG: A Simple Win32 Debugger" in Chapter 4, I talked about how much more stable debugging is under Win32 systems than it was in 16-bit versions of Windows because in Win32 systems the debuggee is outside the debugger's address space. Because the Visual Basic debugger understands only interpreted p-code, the upshot is that your Visual Basic debuggee runs in the same address space as the debugger. As most developers who have used Visual Basic have found out, although Visual Basic doesn't have the pointer problems you can encounter in C, an errant component your application loads can crash the Visual Basic IDE, causing you to lose parts of your project.

The following three concrete rules have helped me maintain my sanity when using the Visual Basic debugger:

■ Be very, very careful when subclassing or using *AddressOf.*

■ In general, treat source code as read-only when debugging.

■ Don't use the rest of the IDE when debugging.

Be Very, Very Careful When Subclassing or Using *AddressOf*

Most Visual Basic applications run fine under the debugger. However, if your application is subclassing Windows controls or you're otherwise using the *AddressOf* operator to pass one of your routines as a hook callback or timer procedure, you must be extremely cautious because your application runs in the same address space as the Visual Basic debugger. You can still debug your application, but you must be aware that callbacks and timers can still execute after you've stopped your application, causing the IDE to crash.

If you're subclassing a window procedure and you're in break mode inside the Visual Basic debugger, when the window you've subclassed receives a message, the IDE will crash. Fortunately, because subclassing windows is such a common operation, Microsoft provides a solution with a utility DLL named DBGWPROC.DLL. This DLL allows you to subclass windows at will and still debug your application using the Visual Basic debugger. You can download DBGWPROC.DLL from *http://msdn.microsoft.com/vbasic/downloads/controls.asp*.

If you're using the *AddressOf* operator to pass one of your application's routines to any hook, callback, or timer functions in the operating system, there's nothing like DBGWPROC.DLL to help you out. If you do want to debug your application with the Visual Basic debugger, you can. However, you should always run your application to completion so that any hooks and callbacks can be undone. If you use the End command on the Run menu or Ctrl+Break to stop your application, you can encounter situations in which your procedure is no longer in memory, so the IDE crashes.

Another technique I've used to circumvent the *AddressOf* problem is to have a debug function that cleans up any hooks, callbacks, or timers that I can call either from a special button in my application or through the Immediate window. With such a function, I stand a better chance of avoiding errant calls into my application that could crash the IDE.

In General, Treat Source Code as Read-Only When Debugging

The Visual Basic IDE is set up to make it easy to edit your source code and continue execution during your debugging sessions, and many Visual Basic developers feel that this capability is one of the debugger's best features. As great a perk as being able to edit code during a debugging session might be, however, you still must proceed with utmost care when you do it.

You should set the IDE option to save all your source files automatically when you start your applications in the debugger by checking Save Changes on the Environment tab of the Options dialog box. If you're revising your source code on the fly, you should frequently save your changes in case the Visual Basic debugger crashes. Personally, I don't make any changes while my application is running in the debugger, and I advise you not to either. I believe that when you're in the debugger you should be debugging, not editing. With this feature, it's just as easy to add a bug as it is to remove one, so you should avoid the temptation to debug and edit simultaneously so you don't work at cross purposes.

Don't Use the Rest of the IDE When Debugging

Because the IDE is doing all the work to run your application when you're debugging, you can cause some problems for your application if you try to access nondebugging features in the IDE. For example, if your application uses a timer notification for background processing, you can stop the timer messages from getting through to your timer procedure if you bring up a modal window such as the Open Project dialog box or the Options dialog box.

When debugging in the Visual Basic debugger, just use the debugging windows supplied. If you have specialized code such as timers or modeless dialog boxes, any additional interaction that you have with the IDE can result in predicaments in which your application is receiving messages that aren't a normal part of the application process. Additionally, because your application's windows are part of the same thread message queue as the IDE, in certain cases you can't easily debug with the debugger because of the tight interaction between debugger and debuggee. The worst of those cases is if you need to debug a key down or a mouse down message. In those situations, you can use only *Debug.Print* statements to debug your code.

ERROR TRAPPING: BREAK IN OR BREAK ON OPTIONS

Now I want to turn to the different error trapping options you can use. The Visual Basic IDE can run in three modes: design mode, for when you're coding; run mode, for when your application is running under the debugger; and break mode, for when your application is stopped under the debugger.

When your application hits a location breakpoint, the IDE automatically drops into break mode. When your application generates an error, however, the IDE might or might not drop into break mode, depending on which of the following three options is set:

■ Break On All Errors

■ Break On Unhandled Errors

■ Break In Class Module

When I first started programming in Visual Basic, I couldn't get a class that had a run-time error I was handling to drop into break mode. After much gnashing of teeth, I finally found the secret menu that allowed me to set these error trapping options.

You can set the default error trapping option on the General tab of the Options dialog box. The Visual Basic default is Break In Class Module. You can also change the error trapping option on the fly by right-clicking in a source window, selecting the Toggle pop-up menu, and choosing a different error trapping option.

Break On All Errors

Just as the name Break On All Errors implies, whenever the Visual Basic debugger encounters an error, the debugger will stop with the run-time error dialog box shown in Figure 7-1. Any error will cause a break, even if you have an error handler for the error in your code. Generally, this error trapping option isn't that useful. I use this option only if I need to see where a particular error is raised when it occurs in a function without any error handlers.

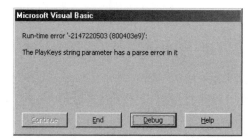

Figure 7-1 *The Visual Basic run-time error dialog box*

Essentially, when you set the Break On All Errors error trapping, you're turning off all error handlers built into your code. When your application breaks on the error, you can continue running by dragging the currently executing line arrow down to the next executable line after the location that raised the error or by using the Set Next Statement option on the right-click menu. The only problem with changing the executing line is that Visual Basic won't raise the actual error for you to handle.

Break On Unhandled Errors

As its name suggests, Break On Unhandled Errors will force the debugger into break mode if an error is raised and you don't have an error handler for the raised error. Break On Unhandled Errors works great for almost all situations, and I've set this as my default error trapping option.

Unfortunately, if you're debugging Component Object Model (COM) server systems, both in-process and out-of-process, you won't break on errors from your class modules. COM does the right thing and packages your raised errors and transmits them back to the client as normal COM errors. If you want to break in COM servers, you need to set the error trapping option to Break In Class Modules.

Break In Class Modules

Break In Class Modules is for debugging COM servers. When you select this error trapping option, you're telling the debugger that you want to treat all errors in class modules as if there are no error handlers. Although Break In Class Modules allows you to get to errors in COM servers, you're still stuck with the fact that your error handlers are ignored.

A Final Plea for Decent Error Trapping

As you can tell from this discussion, error trapping in the Visual Basic debugger leaves quite a bit to be desired. If you want to break on errors, you can do so, but at the expense of being able to step through your error handlers. The only real workaround is to set breakpoints on all the error handlers you're interested in stepping through and to set the error trapping option to Break On Unhandled Errors. What we really need is a way to break on errors but still process them through our normal error handling after breaking.

I hope that the Visual Basic development team will take pity on those of us who want to debug our applications completely and allow us to trap errors yet still let us test the error handlers from the point at which an error is raised. The artificial limits imposed on error trapping in the Visual Basic debugger make it difficult to debug applications.

Because the error trapping problems are related directly to the On Error GoTo constructs in Visual Basic, you need to pay special attention to how you use error handlers in your code. I was going to write a section in this chapter about proper error handling, but Peet Morris wrote what I consider the definitive text in Chapter 1, "On Error GoTo Hell," in the book *Advanced Microsoft Visual Basic 6.0* by The Mandelbrot Set (2nd ed., Microsoft Press, 1998). If you're even thinking about doing Visual Basic development, Peet's chapter is a mandatory read.

VISUAL BASIC DEBUGGER WINDOWS

So far, I've concentrated mostly on the Visual Basic debugger's limitations, not its strengths. But as I mentioned at the beginning of this chapter, the Visual Basic debugger has several features that developers love. For starters, the Visual Basic debugger is much simpler to operate than the Visual C++ debugger. It also includes some excellent supporting windows that make debugging simple. In this section, I'll go over the three Visual Basic debugger windows: Locals, Immediate, and Watch.

The Locals Window

Although the Locals window is straightforward, I want to make sure everyone knows about three key points that affect its use. The first is that, unlike the Watch window in the Visual C++ debugger, the Visual Basic Locals window doesn't require you to mess around with any sort of casting and cajoling to see the value in the appropriate format. The second is that the most important variable shown in the Locals window is the *Me* object. Like the C++ *this* pointer, the *Me* object is a generic construct that fully describes the current object and its properties.

The last point about the Locals window is that you can sometimes change local variables through it by selecting the variable you want to change and clicking on the Value field. If Visual Basic will allow you to change the variable, the Value field will let you edit the text. Visual Basic doesn't allow you to change objects and certain *Variant* variables. For example, you can't change any of the properties of controls in a form's *Controls* collection. However, if you have variables in your form with the actual control types, such as *CommandButton*, you can change the controls' properties through the variables. In cases in which you can't change a variable's value in the Locals window, you can use the Immediate window to effect the change.

The Immediate Window

In my opinion, the Visual Basic Immediate window is amazing. I wish all debuggers had such great debugging capabilities built in. While debugging, you can do anything you want to the debuggee through the Immediate window. The Immediate window is basically (excuse the pun) a mini-Basic interpreter that allows you to execute snippets of code.

The Immediate window shows the output from your *Debug.Print* trace statements. Keep in mind, however, that the Immediate window does limit the number of items you can display to 200 lines, so trace strings might scroll off before you read them. Unfortunately, there's no programmatic way to clear the Immediate window to ensure that you can see your important trace statements. I hope a future version of Visual Basic will offer a *Debug.Clear* method.

The Immediate window's main claim to fame is that you can change variable values and call routines directly in your application. To see the value of a specific variable, say *frmFoo.x*, in your program, you use the *?* or *Print* statement to print out the value *?frmFoo.x*. The beauty of the Immediate window is that all the wonderful Microsoft IntelliSense is built in. If you type a valid object name, IntelliSense does the work of displaying the object's methods and properties so that you can choose the one you want.

To change the value of a variable, simply type a line of Visual Basic code in the Immediate window, just as you would if you were assigning a variable in a source window. The Immediate window knows all about read-only properties and the appropriate syntax, and it will tell you through a message box if your assignment fails.

One great trick you can do in the Immediate window is to create quick test harnesses. For example, if you're developing a class, you can test that class in the Immediate window as soon as you type the code into the source editor. If the class is *clsMyClass* and has a method named *DoSomethingMagical*, you can enter the following code, line by line, into the Watch window and test the method. Make sure you always set object variables back to *Nothing* so that you don't run the risk of leaving initialized variables active in the Immediate window. If you have breakpoints set in *DoSomethingMagical*, you can single-step through your method.

```
Set x = New clsMyClass
x.DoSomethingMagical
Set x = Nothing
```

Another debugging trick you can perform in the Immediate window is to call your debug-only functions all you want. If you remember the byzantine rules for and limitations on calling a debugging function from the Visual C++ Watch window (see the section "Calling Functions in the Watch Window" in Chapter 5), you'll greatly appreciate the ease of using the Immediate window. The only restriction on calling functions in the Visual Basic Immediate window is that the function must exist in your program. I don't know how you could make a powerful debugging feature any easier to use.

Although the Immediate window lets you leap tall buildings in a single bound, you can't write your entire application in it. A couple of built-in constraints will prevent you from using the Immediate window the same way you use a source window. The first constraint is that you can't write functions in the Immediate window. The second is that the Immediate window executes only a single line of code at a time. Some control structures, such as *For...Next* loops, require multiple statements; you can use the special ":" operator to allow those control structures on a single line. The following code shows how to execute a *For...Next* loop in the Immediate window:

```
For i = 1 to UBound(a) : ? a(i) : Next i
```

The Watch Window

As you can guess, the Watch window is where you can watch the values of variables inside your program. You can set the scope of the variable you want to watch in the Watch window, so you can easily avoid any confusion over same-name variables in different parts of your application. The Watch window is also the place where you set your conditional breakpoints.

The Watch window lets you set only two types of conditional breakpoints: Break When Value Changes and Break When Value Is True. Setting conditional breakpoints is trivial in that you just right-click in a source window and select Add Watch from the pop-up menu. To break when the value of an expression changes, type the expression you want to watch in the Expression field and select Break When Value Changes in the Watch Type group box. To break when an expression evaluates to true, type the expression in the Expression field and select Break When Value Is True. When your application does break into the debugger, make sure you look at the Watch window because the highlighted line indicates which condition caused the breakpoint to trigger.

If you want to use skip count breakpoints such as those offered in the Visual C++ debugger, you'll need to use a counter variable that holds the number of times the function is called and use that variable in a conditional breakpoint to stop after a specific count. For the counter variable, I like to use a static local variable.

You can drag and drop variables right out of your source windows into the Watch window. What makes the drag and drop even cooler is that Visual Basic is smart enough to figure out the context for that variable, so you don't have to set it manually. Although you can also drag and drop to the Immediate window, the IDE treats such a move as a cut operation, so you'll change your source files. If you want to edit the result of a drag-and-drop watch, just right-click in the Watch window and select Edit Watch from the pop-up menu.

Before moving on to the tips and tricks section, I want to mention two final aspects of the Watch window. The first is that you can edit the values by clicking on the Value field. Just as in the Locals window, if Visual Basic will allow you to edit, you can change the value. You can also edit your expressions in place as well.

The other is that I always like to put special values, such as *Err.Description*, in the Watch window. That way, I can keep an eye on any error values that I might have encountered and handled as I step over entire functions. If my application also takes command-line parameters, I put *Command* in the Watch window so that I can quickly test the various command-line options my application might use without having to set them each time on the Make tab of the Project Properties dialog box. Unfortunately, as I mentioned at the beginning of the chapter, an incredibly annoying feature of Visual Basic is that it forgets your carefully constructed watches and breakpoints once you leave the IDE, so you must reenter them every time you start a new debugging session.

TIPS AND TRICKS

As I did in the two chapters on the Visual C++ debugger, I'll end the Visual Basic debugger chapter with some tips and tricks that can make your life easier.

Add the Run To Cursor Button to the Debug Toolbar

Like the Visual C++ debugger, the Visual Basic debugger allows you to run to the cursor position. By default, Run To Cursor is assigned to the Ctrl+F8 key combination, but I like to use the mouse when debugging, and this wonderful command isn't on the Debug toolbar. In the Customize dialog box, on the Command tab, select the Debug category and drag the Run To Cursor button to your Debug toolbar.

You might notice in Visual Basic 6 that if you do create the Run To Cursor button on the toolbar, the ToolTip for the Run To Cursor menu item says, "Step To Cursor." Just ignore the ToolTip—the button is still the Run To Cursor command. You're only seeing a small bug.

Avoid Compile On Demand

Visual Basic wants to help you debug faster by compiling only enough of your application to get it turning over in the debugger. Although the idea is sound, the problem is that you can be merrily debugging away on your application and if you hit a section that hasn't been compiled, you can have your debugging session abruptly stopped with a syntax error. If you finally got that one bug that was driving you crazy almost duplicated, stopping with a syntax error can be enough to make you throw your computer out your office door.

I always start my debugging sessions with Start With Full Compile so that I can avoid any syntax surprises. I even added a button for this command to my Debug toolbar so that I always remember to start the correct way. I also turned off Compile On Demand by unchecking it on the General tab of the Options dialog box. If you're working on a large application, you'll increase your initial debugging startup time, but at least a syntax error won't get the drop on you in the middle of a debugging session.

Group Projects Are the Way to Go for Debugging

Visual Basic 5 introduced the concept of a Group project. A Group project allows you to house all your ActiveX components along with a test harness, or your main EXE (provided it's written in Visual Basic), into one project. With all your components in the same project, you can single-step from your EXE right through your controls and DLLs. For an example, see TESTER.VBG, part of the code from Chapter 13, on the companion CD.

Visual Basic Debugging and Reality Might Conflict

As I stated earlier in this chapter, in the "Visual Basic P-Code" section, Visual Basic can debug objects only at the interpreted p-code level. In the brave new world of COM+ and Component Services, you can debug your objects with the Visual Basic debugger, but most of the documentation strongly suggests that you debug Visual Basic objects at the compiled level with the Visual C++ debugger.

For Component Services applications, I've followed the steps listed in the Visual Basic 6 README VB.HTM file installed as part of Visual Studio. The section "Building and Debugging MTS Components in Visual Basic 6" tells you exactly what to do to debug your applications. For COM+ applications, search MSDN for the Platform SDK topics "Debugging Components Written in Visual Basic" and "COM+ Visual Basic Debugging Support Contrasted with MTS."

To fully debug any Component Services and COM+ objects, I just compile the objects and use either SoftICE or the Visual C++ debugger. Although debugging compiled Visual Basic code isn't easy, I lighten the burden by using a slew of trace statements to view all variables and other state information I need. In the end, I feel it's better to debug Component Services and COM+ applications as compiled applications instead of working around the limitations of the Visual Basic debugger.

SUMMARY

This chapter presented an overview of various features of and issues relevant to the Visual Basic debugger. If you understand the limitations of the Visual Basic debugging environment, primarily the fact that the debugger understands only interpreted p-code and runs the debuggee inside the same address space as the debugger, you can better adjust your programming to accommodate these requirements. For you to debug raised errors appropriately, you need to have the error trapping set to the specific option that will work best based on what you're debugging. The most useful parts of the debugger are the Immediate and Watch windows. If your application can be debugged cleanly with the Visual Basic debugger, you should become familiar with these windows because they can speed up your debugging considerably.

As you've seen in this chapter, the Visual Basic debugger is a study in opposites; some parts of the debugger help you tremendously, whereas others cause you some serious problems. Visual Basic has made it possible to develop Windows applications faster than ever before. Unfortunately, the weaknesses of the Visual Basic debugger have meant that when you do run into any problem the IDE isn't equipped to handle, you have to figure out a solution pretty much on your own.

Part III

Power Tools and Techniques

Chapter 8

Finding Source and Line Information with Just a Crash Address

Your program has crashed. You have the crash address because the operating system is nice enough to give it to you when your application dies. Now what do you do? My friend Chris Sells calls this scenario the "my program went on vacation and all I got was this lousy address" problem. Although having the address is better than nothing, having the source file and the line number of the crash would be much more convenient. I suppose you could always give the source code to your users and have them debug it for you, but I just don't see that happening any time soon.

That crash address is generally all you're going to get. Even if you have access to a full Dr. Watson log, you still have only the address of the problem. (Refer to Appendix A for detailed information about Dr. Watson logs and how to interpret them.) Obviously, you need a way to convert that address to the source file and line number in your application. In this chapter, I'll explain how to accomplish that. I'll concentrate on the two main ways of converting the address: using MAP files and using CrashFinder, a utility included on the book's companion CD.

To maximize the techniques in this chapter, you need to have your program compilation set up as I described in Chapter 2. You need to be building your release builds with full debugging symbols and generating MAP files for them. Additionally, you must fix any dynamic-link library (DLL) load address conflicts. If you don't take these steps, the techniques I present in this chapter won't completely work and the only way you'll be able to figure out the source file and line number for a crash address is through pure guessing.

CREATING AND READING A MAP FILE

Many people have asked me why I keep recommending that everyone create MAP files with their release builds. Simply put, MAP files are the only textual representation of your program's global symbols and source file and line number information. Although using CrashFinder is far easier than deciphering a MAP file, your MAP files can be read anywhere and anytime, without requiring a supporting program and without requiring all your program's binaries to get the same information. Trust me, at some point in the future, you're going to need to figure out where a crash happened on an older version of your software, and the only way you'll be able to find the information is with your MAP file.

You can create MAP files for modules compiled in both Microsoft Visual C++ and Microsoft Visual Basic. In Visual C++, on the Link tab of the Project Settings dialog box, type the switches /MAPINFO:EXPORTS and /MAPINFO:LINES in the Project Options edit box. Select Debug in the Category list box, and check Generate Mapfile.

If you're working on a real-world project, you probably have your binary files going to their own output directory. By default, the linker writes the MAP file to the same directory as the intermediate files, so you need to specify that the MAP file goes to the binary file output directory. In the Mapfile Name edit box, you can type *$(OUTDIR)\<project>.MAP* where *<project>* is the name of your particular project. The $(OUTDIR) is an NMAKE.EXE macro that the build system will substitute with the real output directory. Figure 8-1 shows the completed MAP file settings for the MapDLL project, which is included on the companion CD.

Creating a MAP file for a Visual Basic module involves setting the same flags but in a different, interesting way. Visual Basic uses the same LINK.EXE as Visual C++, and you can set some of the command-line switches through the LINK environment variable. If you set the LINK environment variable to "/MAP:<project>.MAP /MAPINFO:EXPORTS /MAPINFO:LINES," Visual Basic will generate the MAP file in the link step of the compilation. After you set the environment variable in a Command Prompt window, you must start Visual Basic from that same window so that the LINK environment variable is visible to VB6.EXE.

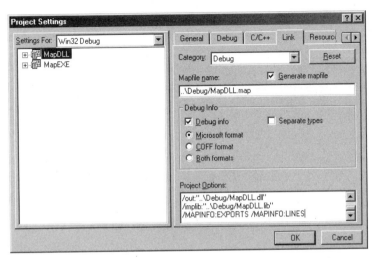

Figure 8-1 *The MAP file settings in the Project Settings dialog box*

Although you might not need the MAP files in your day-to-day operation, chances are that you'll need them in the future. CrashFinder and your debugger rely on symbol tables and a symbol engine to read them. If the format of the symbol table changes or if you forget to save the Program Database (PDB) files, you're completely out of luck. Forgetting to save the PDB files is your fault, but you have no control over symbol table formats. They change frequently. For example, many people who upgraded from Microsoft Visual Studio 5 to Visual Studio 6 noticed that tools such as CrashFinder quit working with programs compiled with Visual Studio 6. Microsoft changed the symbol table format and does so on a regular basis. MAP files are your only savior at that time.

Even though you, as a developer, might be up to Windows 2005 with Visual Studio 11 Service Pack 6 in five years, I can assure you that you'll still have customers who will be running the software you released back in 1999. When they call you in alarm and give you a crash address, you could spend the next two days trying to find the Visual Studio 6 CDs so that you can read your saved PDB files. Or if you have the MAP files, you can find the problem in five minutes.

MAP File Contents

Listing 8-1 shows an example MAP file. The top part of the MAP file contains the module name, the timestamp indicating when LINK.EXE linked the module, and the preferred load address. After the header comes the section information that shows which sections the linker brought in from the various OBJ and LIB files.

After the section information, you get to the good stuff, the public function information. Notice the "public" part. If you have static-declared C functions, they won't show up in the MAP file. Fortunately, the line numbers will still reflect the static functions.

The important parts of the public function information are the function names and the information in the Rva+Base column, which is the starting address of the function. The line information follows the public function section. The lines are shown as follows:

```
10 0001:00000030
```

The first number is the line number, and the second is the offset from the beginning of the code section in which this line occurred. Yes, that sounds confusing, but later I'll show you the calculation you need to convert an address into a source file and line number.

If the module contains exported functions, the final section of a MAP file lists the exports. You can get this same information by running "DUMPBIN /EXPORTS <modulename>."

```
MapDLL

Timestamp is 37f41936 (Thu Sep 30 22:15:18 1999)

Preferred load address is 03900000

Start            Length    Name              Class
0001:00000000 00001421H .text              CODE
0002:00000000 0000012cH .rdata             DATA
0002:00000130 00000193H .edata             DATA
0003:00000000 00000104H .CRT$XCA           DATA
0003:00000104 00000104H .CRT$XCZ           DATA
0003:00000208 00000104H .CRT$XIA           DATA
0003:0000030c 00000104H .CRT$XIZ           DATA
0003:00000410 00000176H .data              DATA
0003:00000588 00000030H .bss               DATA
0004:00000000 00000014H .idata$2           DATA
0004:00000014 00000014H .idata$3           DATA
0004:00000028 00000050H .idata$4           DATA
0004:00000078 00000050H .idata$5           DATA
0004:000000c8 00000179H .idata$6           DATA

Address          Publics by Value          Rva+Base    Lib:Object

0001:00000030    _DllMain@12               03901030 f  MapDLL.obj
```

Listing 8-1 *Example MAP file*

```
0001:0000004c    ?MapDLLFunction@@YAHXZ       0390104c f  MapDLL.obj
0001:00000076    ?MapDLLHappyFunc@@YAPADPAD@Z 03901076 f  MapDLL.obj
0001:000000f6    _printf                      039010f6 f  MSVCRTD:MSVCRTD.dll
0001:000000fc    __chkesp                     039010fc f  MSVCRTD:MSVCRTD.dll
0001:00000110    __CRT_INIT@12                03901110 f  MSVCRTD:crtdll.obj
0001:00000220    __DllMainCRTStartup@12       03901220 f  MSVCRTD:crtdll.obj
0001:00000314    __free_dbg                   03901314 f  MSVCRTD:MSVCRTD.dll
0001:0000031a    __initterm                   0390131a f  MSVCRTD:MSVCRTD.dll
0001:00000320    __onexit                     03901320 f  MSVCRTD:atonexit.obj
0001:00000360    _atexit                      03901360 f  MSVCRTD:atonexit.obj
0001:00000378    __malloc_dbg                 03901378 f  MSVCRTD:MSVCRTD.dll
0001:0000037e    ___dllonexit                 0390137e f  MSVCRTD:MSVCRTD.dll
0002:0000001c    ??_C@_08JKC@crtdll?4c?$AA@   0390301c   MSVCRTD:crtdll.obj
0003:00000000    ___xc_a                      03904000   MSVCRTD:cinitexe.obj
0003:00000104    ___xc_z                      03904104   MSVCRTD:cinitexe.obj
0003:00000208    ___xi_a                      03904208   MSVCRTD:cinitexe.obj
0003:0000030c    ___xi_z                      0390430c   MSVCRTD:cinitexe.obj
0003:0000058c    __adjust_fdiv                0390458c   <common>
0003:00000598    ___onexitend                 03904598   <common>
0003:000005a8    ___onexitbegin               039045a8   <common>
0003:000005ac    __pRawDllMain                039045ac   <common>
0004:00000000    __IMPORT_DESCRIPTOR_MSVCRTD  03905000   MSVCRTD:MSVCRTD.dll
0004:00000014    __NULL_IMPORT_DESCRIPTOR     03905014   MSVCRTD:MSVCRTD.dll
0004:00000078    __imp___malloc_dbg           03905078   MSVCRTD:MSVCRTD.dll
0004:0000007c    __imp___chkesp               0390507c   MSVCRTD:MSVCRTD.dll
0004:00000080    __imp___free_dbg             03905080   MSVCRTD:MSVCRTD.dll
0004:00000084    __imp___initterm             03905084   MSVCRTD:MSVCRTD.dll
0004:00000088    __imp__printf                03905088   MSVCRTD:MSVCRTD.dll
0004:0000008c    __imp___adjust_fdiv          0390508c   MSVCRTD:MSVCRTD.dll
0004:00000090    __imp___dllonexit            03905090   MSVCRTD:MSVCRTD.dll
0004:00000094    __imp___onexit               03905094   MSVCRTD:MSVCRTD.dll
0004:00000098    \177MSVCRTD_NULL_THUNK_DATA  03905098   MSVCRTD:MSVCRTD.dll


entry point at        0001:00000220


Line numbers for .\Debug\MapDLL.obj(D:\MapFile\MapDLL\MapDLL.cpp)
   segment .text


   10 0001:00000030    12 0001:0000003b   19 0001:00000041   20 0001:00000046
   24 0001:0000004c    25 0001:00000050   26 0001:00000067   27 0001:0000006c
   35 0001:00000076    36 0001:0000007a   37 0001:0000007f   38 0001:00000096
   39 0001:0000009c    40 0001:0000009f   30 0001:000000a9   31 0001:000000ad
   32 0001:000000c4
```

(continued)

Listing 8-1 *continued*

```
Line numbers for g:\vc\LIB\MSVCRTD.lib(atonexit.c) segment .text

  84 0001:00000320    89 0001:00000324    98 0001:0000035b   103 0001:00000360
 104 0001:00000363   105 0001:00000376

Line numbers for g:\vc\LIB\MSVCRTD.lib(crtdll.c) segment .text

 135 0001:00000110   140 0001:00000114   141 0001:0000011a   142 0001:00000123
 143 0001:00000130   147 0001:00000132   156 0001:00000139   164 0001:00000147
 170 0001:0000014d   175 0001:00000175   177 0001:0000017c   179 0001:00000187
 184 0001:00000193   189 0001:000001a5   192 0001:000001b4   219 0001:000001bc
 220 0001:000001c5   222 0001:000001cd   227 0001:000001e1   228 0001:000001e9
 236 0001:000001ee   238 0001:00000202   242 0001:0000020c   243 0001:00000211
 251 0001:00000220   252 0001:00000224   258 0001:0000022b   259 0001:0000023a
 261 0001:00000241   263 0001:0000024d   264 0001:00000256   266 0001:0000026b
 267 0001:00000271   269 0001:00000285   270 0001:0000028b   273 0001:0000028f
 276 0001:000002a3   284 0001:000002af   287 0001:000002be   289 0001:000002ca
 290 0001:000002df   292 0001:000002e6   293 0001:000002f5   296 0001:0000030a
 297 0001:0000030d

Exports

 ordinal   name

       1   ?MapDLLFunction@@YAHXZ (int __cdecl MapDLLFunction(void))
       2   ?MapDLLHappyFunc@@YAPADPAD@Z (char * __cdecl MapDLLHappyFunc(char *))
```

Finding the Function, Source File, and Line Number

The algorithm for extracting the function, source file, and line number from a MAP file is straightforward, but you need to do a few hexadecimal calculations when using it. As an example, let's say that a crash in MAPDLL.DLL, the module shown in Listing 8-1, occurs at address 0x03901099.

The first step is to look in your project's MAP files for the file that contains the crash address. First look at the preferred load address and the last address in the public function section. If the crash address is between those values, you're looking at the correct MAP file.

To find the function—or the closest public function if the crash occurred in a C static function—scan down the Rva+Base column until you find the first function address that's greater than the crash address. The preceding entry in the MAP file is the function that had the crash. For example, in Listing 8-1, the first function address greater than the 0x3901099 crash address is 0x39010F6, so the function that crashed is "?MapDLLHappyFunc@@YAPADPAD@Z." Any function name that starts with a question mark is a C++ decorated name. To translate the name, pass it as a command-line parameter to the Platform SDK program UNDNAME.EXE. In the example, "?MapDLLHappyFunc@@YAPADPAD@Z" translates into *MapDLLHappyFunc*, which you probably could figure out just by looking at the decorated name. Other C++ decorated names are harder to decipher, especially when overloaded functions are used.

To find the line number, you get to do a little hexadecimal subtraction using the following formula:

```
(crash address) - (preferred load address) - 0x1000
```

Remember that the addresses are offsets from the beginning of the first code section, so the formula does that conversion. You can probably guess why you subtract the preferred load address, but you earn extra credit if you know why you still have to subtract 0x1000. The crash address is an offset from the beginning of the code section, but the code section isn't the first part of the binary. The first part of the binary is the PE (Portable Executable) header, which is 0x1000 bytes long.

I'm not sure why the linker still generates MAP files that require this odd calculation. The linker team put in the Rva+Base column a while ago, so I don't see why they didn't just fix up the line number at the same time.

Once you've calculated the offset, look through the MAP file line information until you find the closest number that isn't over the calculated value. Keep in mind that during the generation phase the compiler can jiggle the code around so that the source lines aren't in ascending order. With my crash example, I used the following formula:

```
0x03901099 - 0x03900000 - 0x1000 = 0x99
```

If you look through the MAP file in Listing 8-1, you'll see that the closest line that isn't over is 38 0001:00000096 (Line 38) in MAPDLL.CPP.

If you're reading a MAP file for a module written in Visual Basic, you need to be aware that the line numbers reported in the MAP file (and in CrashFinder as well) don't correspond to the lines that you see in the Visual Basic editor. The compiled binaries take into account the complete header at the top of the source file, which Visual Basic hides from view. To find the line that the compiler reports, you need to open the Visual Basic file in a text editor, such as the Visual C++ editor, and go to the line listed in the MAP file.

USING CRASHFINDER

As you just saw, reading a MAP file isn't too terribly difficult. It is rather tedious, however, and certainly not a scalable solution to others on your team, such as quality engineers, technical support staff, and even managers. To address the issue of scalability in CrashFinder, I decided to make CrashFinder usable for all members of the development team, from individual developers, through test engineers, and on to the support engineers so that all crash reports include as much information as possible about the crash. If you follow the steps outlined in Chapter 2 for creating the appropriate debug symbols, everyone on your team will be able to use CrashFinder without a problem.

When using CrashFinder in a team setting, you need to be especially vigilant about keeping the binary images and their associated PDB files accessible because CrashFinder doesn't store any information about your application other than the paths to the binary images. CrashFinder stores only the filenames to your binary files, so you can use the same CrashFinder project throughout the production cycle. If CrashFinder stored more detailed information about your application, such as symbol tables, you'd probably need to produce a CrashFinder project for each build. If you take this advice and allow easy access to your binaries and PDB files, when your application crashes, all your test or support engineers will have to do is fire up CrashFinder and add a vital piece of information to the bug report. As we all know, the more information an engineer has about the particular problem, the easier correcting the problem will be.

You'll probably need to have multiple CrashFinder projects for your application. If you opt to include system DLLs as part of your CrashFinder project, you'll need to create separate CrashFinder projects for each operating system you support. You'll also need to have a CrashFinder project for each version of your application that you send to testers outside your immediate development team, so you'll have to store separate binary images and PDBs for each version you send out.

Figure 8-2 shows the CrashFinder user interface with one of my personal projects loaded as a project. The left portion of the child window is a tree control that shows the executable and its associated DLLs. The check marks indicate that the symbols for each of the binary images have been loaded properly. If CrashFinder couldn't load the symbols, an X would indicate that there was a problem. The right side of the child window is an edit control that lists the symbol information about the currently selected binary image in the tree.

You add a binary image to a CrashFinder project through the Add Image command on the Edit menu. When you're adding binary images, keep in mind that CrashFinder will accept only a single EXE for the project. For your applications comprising multiple EXEs, create a separate CrashFinder project for each EXE. Because CrashFinder is a multiple-document interface (MDI) application, you can easily open all the projects for each of your EXEs to locate the crash location. When you add DLLs, CrashFinder checks that there are no load address conflicts with any other DLLs already in the project. If CrashFinder detects a conflict, it will allow you to change the load address for the conflicting DLL just for the current instance of the CrashFinder project. This option is handy when you have a CrashFinder project for a debug build and you accidentally forget to rebase your DLLs. As I pointed out in Chapter 2, you should always set the base addresses of all your DLLs.

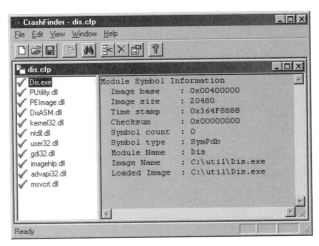

Figure 8-2 *The CrashFinder user interface*

As your application changes over time, you can remove binary images by selecting the Remove Image command from the Edit menu. At any time, you can also change a binary image's load address through the Image Properties command on the Edit menu. In addition, it's a good idea to add any system DLLs that your project uses so that you can locate the problem when you crash in them. As I mentioned in Chapter 5, having the Windows 2000 debugging symbols installed can sometimes help you immensely when you have to step through the disassembly of a system module. Now you have an even better reason for installing the Windows 2000 debugging symbols—CrashFinder can use them, so you can look up crashes even in system modules.

CrashFinder's raison d'être is to turn a crash address into a function name, source file, and line number. Selecting the Find Crash command from the Edit menu brings up the Find Crash dialog box, shown in Figure 8-3. For each crash address you want to look up, all you need to do is type the hexadecimal address in the edit control and click the Find button.

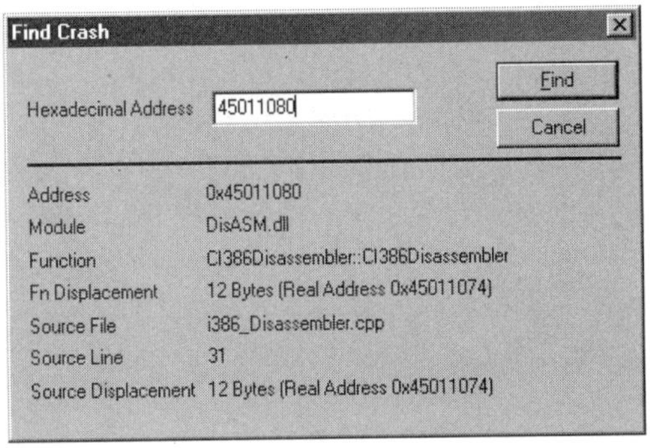

Figure 8-3 *Finding the location of a crash by using CrashFinder*

The lower part of the Find Crash dialog box lists all the information about the last address looked up. Most of the fields in the lower part of the dialog box should be self-explanatory. The Fn Displacement field shows how many code bytes from the start of the function the address is. The Source Displacement field tells you how many code bytes from the start of the closest source line the address is. Remember that many assembly-language instructions can make up a single source line, especially if you use function calls as part of the parameter list. When using CrashFinder, keep in mind that you can't look up an address that isn't a valid instruction address. If you're programming in C++ and you blow out the *this* pointer, you can cause a crash in an address such as 0x00000001. Fortunately, those types of crashes aren't as prevalent as the usual memory access violation crashes, which you can easily find with CrashFinder.

Implementation Highlights

CrashFinder itself is a straightforward Microsoft Foundation Class (MFC) library application, so most of it should be familiar. I want to point out three key areas and explain their implementation highlights so that you can extend CrashFinder more easily with some of the suggestions I offer in the section "What's Next for CrashFinder?" later in the chapter. The first area is the symbol engine, the second is where the work gets done in CrashFinder, and the last is the data architecture.

CrashFinder uses the DBGHELP.DLL symbol engine introduced in Chapter 4. The only detail of interest is that I need to force the symbol engine to load all source file and line number information by passing the *SYMOPT_LOAD_LINES* flag to *SymSetOptions*. The DBGHELP.DLL symbol engine doesn't load source file and line number information by default, so you must explicitly tell the symbol engine to load it.

The second point about CrashFinder's implementation is that all the work is essentially done in the document class, *CCrashFinderDoc*. It holds the *CSymbolEngine* class, does all the symbol lookup, and controls the view. The key function, *CCrashFinderDoc::LoadAndShowImage*, is shown in Listing 8-2. This function is where the binary image is validated and checked against the existing items in the project for load address conflicts, the symbols are loaded, and the image is inserted at the end of the tree. This function is called both when a binary image is added to the project and when the project is opened. By letting *CCrashFinderDoc::LoadAndShowImage* handle all these chores, I ensure that the core logic for CrashFinder is always in one place and that the project needs to store only the binary image names instead of copies of the symbol table.

```
BOOL CCrashFinderDoc :: LoadAndShowImage ( CBinaryImage * pImage          ,
                                           BOOL            bModifiesDoc )
{
    // Check the assumptions from outside the function.
```

Listing 8-2 *The* CCrashFinderDoc::LoadAndShowImage *function*

```
ASSERT ( this ) ;
ASSERT ( NULL != m_pcTreeControl ) ;

// A string that can be used for any user messages
CString    sMsg                      ;
// The state for the tree graphic
int        iState = STATE_NOTVALID ;
// A Boolean return value holder
BOOL       bRet                      ;

// Make sure the parameter is good.
ASSERT ( NULL != pImage ) ;
if ( NULL == pImage )
{
    // Nothing much can happen with a bad pointer.
    return ( FALSE ) ;
}

// Check to see whether this image is valid. If it is, make sure
// that it isn't already in the list and that it doesn't have
// a conflicting load address. If it isn't a valid image, I add
// it anyway because it isn't good form just to throw out user
// data. If the image is bad, I just show it with the invalid
// bitmap and don't load it into the symbol engine.
if ( TRUE == pImage->IsValidImage ( ) )
{

    // Here I walk through the items in the data array so that I can
    // look for three problem conditions:
    // 1. The binary image is already in the list. If so, I can
    //    only abort.
    // 2. The binary is going to load at an address that's already
    //    in the list. If that's the case, I'll display the
    //    Properties dialog box for the binary image so that its
    //    load address can be changed before adding it to the list.
    // 3. The project already includes an EXE image, and pImage is
    //    also an executable.

    // I always start out assuming that the data in pImage is valid.
    // Call me an optimist!
    BOOL bValid = TRUE ;
    int iCount = m_cDataArray.GetSize ( ) ;
    for ( int i = 0 ; i < iCount ; i++ )
    {
        CBinaryImage * pTemp = (CBinaryImage *)m_cDataArray[ i ] ;

        ASSERT ( NULL != pTemp ) ;
```

(continued)

Listing 8-2 *continued*

```
            if ( NULL == pTemp )
            {
                // Not much can happen with a bad pointer!
                return ( FALSE ) ;
            }

            // Do these two CString values match?
            if ( pImage->GetFullName ( ) == pTemp->GetFullName ( ) )
            {
                // Tell the user!!
                sMsg.FormatMessage ( IDS_DUPLICATEFILE       ,
                                    pTemp->GetFullName ( )   ) ;
                AfxMessageBox ( sMsg ) ;

                return ( FALSE ) ;
            }

            // If the current image from the data structure isn't
            // valid, I'm up a creek. Although I can check
            // duplicate names above, it's hard to check load
            // addresses and EXE characteristics. If pTemp isn't valid,
            // I have to skip these checks. Skipping them can lead
            // to problems, but since pTemp is marked in the list as
            // invalid, it's up to the user to reset the properties.
            if ( TRUE == pTemp->IsValidImage ( FALSE ) )
            {

                // Check that I don't add two EXEs to the project.
                if ( 0 == ( IMAGE_FILE_DLL &
                        pTemp->GetCharacteristics ( ) ) )
                {
                    if ( 0 == ( IMAGE_FILE_DLL &
                            pImage->GetCharacteristics ( ) ) )

                    {
                        // Tell the user!!
                        sMsg.FormatMessage ( IDS_EXEALREADYINPROJECT ,
                                        pImage->GetFullName ( ) ,
                                        pTemp->GetFullName ( )   ) ;
                        AfxMessageBox ( sMsg ) ;
                        // Trying to load two images marked as EXEs will
                        // automatically have the data thrown out for
                        // pImage.
                        return ( FALSE ) ;
                    }
                }
```

```
            // Check for load address conflicts.
            if ( pImage->GetLoadAddress ( ) ==
                 pTemp->GetLoadAddress( )          )
            {
                sMsg.FormatMessage ( IDS_DUPLICATELOADADDR       ,
                                     pImage->GetFullName ( )      ,
                                     pTemp->GetFullName ( )          ) ;

                if ( IDYES == AfxMessageBox ( sMsg , MB_YESNO ) )
                {
                    // The user wants to change the properties by
                    // hand.
                    pImage->SetProperties ( ) ;

                    // Check that the load address really did
                    // change and that it doesn't now conflict with
                    // another binary.
                    int iIndex ;
                    if ( TRUE ==
                            IsConflictingLoadAddress (
                                    pImage->GetLoadAddress(),
                                    iIndex                   ))
                    {
                        sMsg.FormatMessage
                                    ( IDS_DUPLICATELOADADDRFINAL ,
                                      pImage->GetFullName ( )     ,
((CBinaryImage*)m_cDataArray[iIndex])->GetFullName());
                        AfxMessageBox ( sMsg ) ;

                        // The data in pImage isn't valid, so go
                        // ahead and exit the loop.
                        bValid = FALSE ;
                        break ;
                    }
                }
                else
                {
                    // The data in pImage isn't valid, so go
                    // ahead and exit the loop.
                    bValid = FALSE ;
                    break ;
                }
            }
        }
    }
```

(continued)

Listing 8-2 *continued*

```
        if ( TRUE == bValid )
        {
            // This image is good (at least up to the symbol load).
            iState = STATE_VALIDATED ;
        }
        else
        {
            iState = STATE_NOTVALID ;
        }
    }
    else
    {
        // This image isn't valid.
        iState = STATE_NOTVALID ;
    }

    if ( STATE_VALIDATED == iState )
    {
        // Try to load this image into the symbol engine.
        bRet =
            m_cSymEng.SymLoadModule(NULL                             ,
                                    (PSTR)(LPCSTR)pImage->GetFullName() ,
                                    NULL                             ,
                                    pImage->GetLoadAddress ( )       ,
                                    0                                );
        // Watch out. SymLoadModule returns the load address of the
        // image, not TRUE.
        ASSERT ( FALSE != bRet ) ;
        if ( FALSE == bRet )
        {
            TRACE ( "m_cSymEng.SymLoadModule failed!!\n" ) ;
            iState = STATE_NOTVALID ;
        }
        else
        {
            iState = STATE_VALIDATED ;
        }
    }

    // Set the extra data value for pImage to the state of the symbol
    // load.
    if ( STATE_VALIDATED == iState )
    {
        pImage->SetExtraData ( TRUE ) ;
    }
    else
    {
```

```
        pImage->SetExtraData ( FALSE ) ;
}


// Put this item into the array.
m_cDataArray.Add ( pImage ) ;

// Does adding the item modify the document?
if ( TRUE == bModifiesDoc )
{
    SetModifiedFlag ( ) ;
}

CCrashFinderApp * pApp = (CCrashFinderApp*)AfxGetApp ( ) ;
ASSERT ( NULL != pApp ) ;

// Put the string into the tree.
HTREEITEM hItem =
    m_pcTreeControl->InsertItem ( pApp->ShowFullPaths ( )
                                ? pImage->GetFullName ( )
                                : pImage->GetName ( )        ,
                              iState                       ,
                              iState                         ) ;
ASSERT ( NULL != hItem ) ;

// Put a pointer to the image in the item data. The pointer
// makes it easy to update the module symbol information whenever
// the view changes.
bRet = m_pcTreeControl->SetItemData ( hItem , (DWORD)pImage ) ;
ASSERT ( bRet ) ;

// Force the item to be selected.
bRet = m_pcTreeControl->SelectItem ( hItem ) ;

// All OK, Jumpmaster!
return ( bRet ) ;
}
```

The last point I want to mention is about CrashFinder's data architecture. The main data structure is a simple array of *CBinaryImage* classes. The *CBinaryImage* class represents a single binary image added to the project and serves up any core information about a single binary—details such as load address, binary properties, and name. When a binary image is added, the document adds the *CBinaryImage* to the main data array and puts the pointer value for it into the tree node's item data slot. When selecting an item in the tree view, the tree view passes the node back to the document so that the document can get the *CBinaryImage* and look up its symbol information.

WHAT'S NEXT FOR CRASHFINDER?

Now that you've seen a little bit about how CrashFinder works, let's talk about how you can add some functionality to it. Although CrashFinder is a fairly complete application as it stands, I know of some tweaks that would make it much easier to use and also more powerful. If you want to learn more about binary images, I encourage you to add some of the following features to CrashFinder.

- Automatically add dependent DLLs. CrashFinder now makes you add each binary image for the project by hand. It would be much nicer if Crash-Finder prompted for the EXE and then automatically added all dependent DLLs when creating a new project. Of course, this feature wouldn't find dynamically loaded DLLs (DLLs loaded by a call to *LoadLibrary*), but it would still save you some time adding individual binaries.

- Show more information in the informational edit control. The *CBinaryImage* class has the functionality to show more information after the symbol information through the *GetAdditionalInfo* method. You could add the ability to show information from the binary image, such as header information, imported functions, and exported functions.

- Allow pasting in of DLL lists to automatically add them to the project. The debugger Output window lists all the DLLs that an application loads. You could extend CrashFinder to allow the user to paste in the Output window text and have CrashFinder scan through the text looking for DLL names.

SUMMARY

This chapter helped demystify the process of what you do to pinpoint the location of a crash when the only information you have is the crash address. The first technique for finding out the source file and line number of a particular crash is to refer to a MAP file. MAP files are the only textual representation of your symbols, and you should create them routinely for every release build of your application. The second technique for converting a crash address to a function, source file, and line number is to use CrashFinder. The CrashFinder utility takes all the work out of making this conversion and allows others on your team to report as much information as possible when the application crashes on them. Although CrashFinder is easier to use than MAP files, you still need to get into the habit of creating MAP files because symbol file formats change—and when they do, only your MAP files will save your soul when the ghost of applications past comes knocking at your door.

Chapter 9

Crash Handlers

This news flash shouldn't come as a shock, but I'm going to let you in on a little secret: your users really hate seeing that Application Error dialog box pop up when your application crashes. The fact that you're reading this book means that you're trying hard to avoid crashes in the first place. As we all know, however, crashes happen even in the best applications, and you need to be prepared for them.

Instead of just letting the Application Error dialog box make an appearance and irritate your users, wouldn't it be nice if a user-friendly dialog box popped up and reported the problem, and asked the users exactly what they were doing at the time of the crash? Wouldn't it be even better if, in addition to recording the usual crash address and call stack that utilities such as Dr. Watson give you, this kinder and gentler dialog box recorded the internal state of your program so that you could get the processing and data states at the time of the crash? And wouldn't it just be icing on the cake if the dialog box would automatically e-mail the crash information to you and log a bug report directly in to your bug tracking system?

Crash handlers can turn such wishful thinking into reality, providing you with all the cool information I fantasized about in the preceding paragraph. *Crash handlers* is the term I've come up with to describe both exception handlers and unhandled exception filters. If you've done any C++ programming, you should be familiar with exception handlers. You might know less about unhandled exception filters, which are interesting routines that allow you to gain control right before that Application Error dialog box that drives your users crazy pops up. Whereas exception handlers are C++ specific, unhandled exception filters work for both Microsoft Visual C++ and Microsoft Visual Basic.

In this chapter, I'll present code that you can drop into your applications to get crash information such as registers and call stacks. In addition, the code will hide much of the dirty work of gathering this information for you so that you can concentrate on reporting the information that is unique to your application and on presenting a better face to the user. Before I can jump into the code, however, I need to spend some time describing the various types of exception handling in Microsoft Win32 systems.

STRUCTURED EXCEPTION HANDLING VS. C++ EXCEPTION HANDLING

Getting up to speed on exception handling can be tough partly because C++ can use two main types of exception handling: structured exception handling (SEH), which the operating system provides, and C++ exception handling, which the C++ language provides. Just figuring out which type of exception handling to use when can be a challenge, and it doesn't help that many people talk about both types as if they were interchangeable. I assure you that each type of exception handling has a distinctly different approach. I think what confuses some people is that you can combine both types. In the following sections, I'll touch on the differences and similarities between these two types of exception handling. I'll also describe how to combine them in a way that will let you avoid some of the problems that can crop up when you use them together.

Structured Exception Handling

The operating system provides SEH, and it deals directly with crashes such as access violations. SEH is language-independent but is usually implemented in C and C++ programs with the *__try/__except* and *__try/__finally* keyword pairs. The way you use the *__try/__except* pair is to set your code inside a *__try* block and then determine how to handle the exception in the *__except* block (also called an exception handler). In a *__try/__finally* pair, the *__finally* block (also called a termination handler) ensures that a section of code will always be executed upon leaving a function, even if the code in the *__try* block terminates prematurely.

Listing 9-1 shows a typical function with SEH. The *__except* block looks almost like a function call, but the parentheses specify the value of a special expression called an *exception filter*. The exception filter value in Listing 9-1 is *EXCEPTION_EXECUTE_HANDLER*, which indicates that the code in the *__except* block must be executed every time any exception occurs inside the *__try* block. The two other possible exception filter values are *EXCEPTION_CONTINUE_EXECUTION*, which allows an exception to be ignored, and *EXCEPTION_CONTINUE_SEARCH*, which passes the exception up the call chain to the next *__except* block. You can make the exception filter expression as simple or as complicated as you like so that you target only those exceptions you're interested in handling.

```
void Foo ( void )
{
    __try
    {
        __try
        {
            // Execute code to accomplish something.
        }
        __except ( EXCEPTION_EXECUTE_HANDLER )
        {
            // This block will be executed if the code in the __try
            // block causes an access violation or some other hard crash.
            // The code in here is also called the exception handler.
        }
    }
    __finally
    {
        // This block will be executed regardless of whether the function
        // causes a crash. Mandatory cleanup code goes here.
    }
}
```

Listing 9-1 *Example SEH handler*

The process of finding and executing an exception handler is sometimes called *unwinding the exception*. Exception handlers are kept on an internal stack; as the function call chain grows, the exception handler (if one exists) for each new function is pushed onto this internal stack. When an exception occurs, the operating system finds the thread's exception handler stack and starts calling the exception handlers until one exception handler indicates that it will handle the exception. As the exception works its way down the exception handler stack, the operating system cleans up the call stack and executes any termination handlers it finds along the way. If the unwinding continues to the end of the exception handler stack, the Application Error dialog box pops up.

Your exception handler can determine the exception value by calling the special *GetExceptionCode* function, which can be called only in exception filters. If you were writing a math package, for example, you might have an exception handler that handles divide-by-zero attempts and returns NaN (not a number). The code in Listing 9-2 shows an example of such an exception handler. The exception filter calls *GetExceptionCode*, and if the exception is divide-by-zero, the exception handler executes. If any other exception occurs, *EXCEPTION_CONTINUE_SEARCH* tells the operating system to execute the next *__except* block up the call chain.

```
long IntegerDivide ( long x , long y )
{
    long lRet ;

    __try

    {
        lRet = x / y ;
    }
    __except ( EXCEPTION_INT_DIVIDE_BY_ZERO ==
            GetExceptionCode ( )
                ? EXCEPTION_EXECUTE_HANDLER
                : EXCEPTION_CONTINUE_SEARCH
            )
    {
        lRet = NaN ;
    }
    return ( lRet ) ;
}
```

Listing 9-2 *Example SEH handler with exception filter processing*

If your exception filter requires more complexity, you can even call one of your own functions as the exception filter as long as it specifies how to handle the exception by returning one of the valid exception filter values. In addition to calling the special *GetExceptionCode* function, you can also call the *GetExceptionInformation* function in the exception filter expression. *GetExceptionInformation* returns a pointer to an *EXCEPTION_POINTERS* structure that completely describes the reason for a crash and the state of the CPU at that time. You might have guessed that the *EXCEPTION_POINTERS* structure will come in handy later in this chapter.

SEH isn't limited just to handling crashes. You can also create your own exceptions with the *RaiseException* API function. Most developers don't use *RaiseException*, but it does offer a way to quickly leave deeply nested conditional statements in code. The *RaiseException* exit technique is cleaner than using the old *setjmp* and *longjmp* run-time functions.

Before you dive in and start using SEH, you need to be aware of two of its limitations. The first is minor: your custom error codes are limited to a single unsigned integer. The second limitation is a little more serious: SEH doesn't mix well with C++ programming because C++ exceptions are implemented with SEH and the compiler complains when you try to combine them indiscriminately. The reason for the conflict is that when straight SEH unwinds out of a function, it doesn't call any of the C++ object destructors for objects created on the stack. Because C++ objects can do all sorts of initialization in their constructors, such as allocating memory for internal data structures, skipping the destructors can lead to memory leaks and other problems.

If you'd like to learn more about SEH, I recommend two references in addition to perusing the Microsoft Developer Network (MSDN). The best overview of SEH is in Jeffrey Richter's *Programming Applications for Microsoft Windows* (Microsoft Press, 1999). If you're curious about the actual SEH implementation, check out Matt Pietrek's article "A Crash Course on the Depths of Win32 Structured Exception Handling" in the January 1997 *Microsoft Systems Journal.*

C++ Exception Handling

Because C++ exception handling is part of the C++ language specification, it's probably more familiar to most programmers than SEH. The keywords for C++ exception handling are *try* and *catch*. The *throw* keyword allows you to initiate an exception unwind. Whereas SEH error codes are limited to just a single unsigned integer, a C++ *catch* statement can handle any variable type, including classes. If you derive your error handling classes from a common base class, you can handle just about any error you need to in your code. This class hierarchy approach to error handling is exactly what the Microsoft Foundation Class (MFC) library does with its *CException* base class. Listing 9-3 shows C++ exception handling in action with an MFC *CFile* class read.

```
BOOL ReadFileHeader ( CFile * pFile , LPHEADERINFO pHeader )
{
    ASSERT ( FALSE == IsBadReadPtr ( pFile , sizeof ( CFile * ) ) ) ;
    ASSERT ( FALSE == IsBadReadPtr ( pHeader ,
                                     sizeof ( LPHEADERINFO ) ) ) ;
    if ( ( TRUE == IsBadReadPtr ( pFile , sizeof ( CFile * ) ) ) ||
         ( TRUE == IsBadReadPtr ( pHeader ,
                                  sizeof ( LPHEADERINFO )   ) )   )
    {
        return ( FALSE ) ;
    }

    BOOL bRet ;
    try
    {
        pFile->Read ( pHeader , sizeof ( HEADERINFO ) ) ;
        bRet = TRUE ;
    }
    catch ( CFileException * e )
    {
        // If the header couldn't be read because the file was
        // truncated, handle it; otherwise, continue the unwind.
        if ( CFileException::endOfFile == e->m_cause )
```

Listing 9-3 *C++ exception handler example*   *(continued)*

Listing 9-3 *continued*

```
        {
            e->Delete();
            bRet = false;
        }
        else
        {
            // The throw keyword just by itself throws the same exception
            // as passed to this catch block.
            throw ;
        }
    }
    return ( bRet ) ;
}
```

You need to keep in mind the following drawbacks when you're using C++ exception handling: First, it doesn't handle your program crashes automatically. (Later in the chapter, I'll show you how you can work around this limitation.) Second, C++ exception processing isn't free. The compiler might do a great deal of work setting up and removing the *try* and *catch* blocks even if you never throw any exceptions, so if you're working on performance-sensitive code you might not be able to afford that much overhead. Although these performance-sensitive cases are rare, they do occur. If you're new to C++ exception handling, MSDN is a great place to start learning about it.

Combining SEH and C++ Exception Handling

As mentioned earlier, there is a way to combine both SEH and C++ exceptions; the result is that you have to use only C++ exception handling in your code. The C runtime library function *_set_se_translator* lets you set a translator function that will be called when a structured exception happens so that you can throw a C++ exception. This powerful function is a hidden gem. The following code snippet shows all that a translator function must do:

```
void SEHToCPPException ( UINT uiEx ,
                        EXCEPTION_POINTERS * pExp )
{
    // CSEHException is a class derived from the MFC CException
    // class.
    throw CSEHException ( uiEx , pExp ) ;
}
```

The first parameter is the SEH code returned through a call to *GetExceptionCode*. The second parameter is the exception state from a call to *GetExceptionInformation*.

When using the *_set_se_translator* function in your code, you should catch exception classes thrown out of your translator function only if you're expecting a crash. For example, if you allow users to extend your application with DLLs, you can wrap the calls to the DLLs with *try...catch* blocks to handle potential crashes. In the course of normal processing, however, you should end the application when you get a hard SEH crash. In one of my own programs, I accidentally handled an access violation instead of just crashing. As a result, instead of leaving the user's data alone, I proceeded to wipe out her data files.

The reason you should be careful about handling hard SEH exceptions as C++ exceptions is that the process is in an unstable state. You can show dialog boxes and write out crash information to a file as part of your handling. However, you need to be aware that the stack might be blown and so you don't have the room to call many functions. Because the exception code is passed to your translator function, you need to check it for *EXCEPTION_STACK_OVERFLOW* and degrade your error handling gracefully if there is insufficient stack space.

As you can see in the preceding code snippet that translates the SEH exception into the C++ exception, you can throw any class you'd like. Implementing the exception class is trivial; the interesting part is in translating the *EXCEPTION_POINTERS* information into human-readable form. Before delving into that code, though, I want to explain asynchronous and synchronous C++ exception handling.

Asynchronous vs. Synchronous C++ Exception Handling

When using C++ exception handling, you must understand the difference between asynchronous and synchronous exception handling. Unfortunately, the words *asynchronous* and *synchronous* don't adequately describe the difference between these two types of C++ exception handling. The real difference between asynchronous and synchronous C++ exception handling comes down to this distinction: how the compiler assumes that exceptions will be thrown dictates how the compiler generates the exception handling code for the program.

In asynchronous C++ exception handling, the compiler assumes that each instruction could generate an exception and that the code must be prepared to handle the exceptions anywhere. The default exception model for Visual C++ 5 was asynchronous exception handling. The problem with asynchronous exception handling is that the compiler has to track the lifetime of objects and be prepared to unwind the exceptions at any point in the code. All the additional code generated can be substantial, and the resulting code bloat is a waste because the extra code often isn't needed.

With synchronous exception handling, the default for Visual C++ 6, the compiler expects you to throw exceptions only with an explicit *throw* statement. Thus the compiler doesn't have to track the lifetime of an object and doesn't have to generate the code needed to handle the unwinding if the object's lifetime doesn't over-lap a function call or a *throw* statement. You can think of asynchronous as "all func-tions track lifetimes of objects" and synchronous as "some functions track lifetimes of objects."

The impact of the switch to synchronous exception handling as the default is that in your release builds you can end up in situations in which your carefully con-structed *_set_se_translator* function never gets called, your code doesn't catch the translated exception, and your application crashes as a normal application would. The default /GX switch maps to /EHsc (synchronous exceptions), so to turn on asyn-chronous exceptions, you need to explicitly use /EHa (asynchronous exceptions). Fortunately, you don't have to enable asynchronous exceptions projectwide—you can compile different source files with different exception handling and link them together without problems.

If you want to compile with asynchronous exception handling, /EHa, but with-out the overhead of the object lifetime tracking on functions that don't throw excep-tions, you can use *__declspec(nothrow)* to declare or define those functions. Although you have to do more work by manually declaring *__declspec(nothrow)*, you reap the benefits of *_set_se_translator* and tighter code.

The code in Listing 9-4 shows a program using *_set_se_translator* that doesn't work if compiled as a release build with the default synchronous exceptions. The code must be compiled with /EHa. In your programs, if you want to ensure that you can use *_set_se_translator* anywhere, including in functions outside classes, you must compile with /EHa and take the hit of the extra code overhead. If you have a C++ program, especially one written using MFC, you might get by with using synchro-nous exceptions if the only places you'll be using the class thrown by your *_set_se_translator* function are in member functions.

```
// Compile as a Win32 Release configuration using /GX to see that the
// translator function won't be called. /GX maps to /EHsc. To make
// this program work in a release build, compile with /EHa.
#include "stdafx.h"

class CSEHError
{
public :
    CSEHError ( void )
    {
        m_uiErrCode = 0 ;
    }
```

Listing 9-4 *An example in which synchronous exceptions don't work*

```
    CSEHError ( unsigned int u )
    {
        m_uiErrCode = u ;
    }

    ~CSEHError ( void )
    {
    }

    unsigned int m_uiErrCode ;
} ;
void TransFunc ( unsigned int u , EXCEPTION_POINTERS * pEP )
{
    printf ( "In TransFunc\n" ) ;

    throw CSEHError ( u ) ;
}

void GrungyFunc ( char * p )
{
    *p = 'p' ;
    printf ( "This output should never be seen!\n" ) ;
}

void DoBadThings ( void )
{
    try
    {
        GrungyFunc ( (char*)0x1 ) ;
    }
    catch ( CSEHError e )
    {
        printf ( "Got an exception! -> 0x%08X\n" , e.m_uiErrCode ) ;
    }
}

int main ( int argc, char* argv[] )
{
    _set_se_translator ( TransFunc ) ;
    DoBadThings ( ) ;
    return 0;
}
```

THE *SETUNHANDLEDEXCEPTIONFILTER* API FUNCTION

In C++ code, you have the opportunity to handle crashes by guarding the sections of code in which you think a hard crash might occur. As we all know, however, crashes have a habit of never happening where you expect them. Unfortunately, when your users experience crashes in your program, they just see the Application Error dialog box, and then maybe Dr. Watson gives them a little information to send to you to figure out the problem. As I mentioned early in this chapter, you can devise your own dialog boxes to get the information you really need to solve the crash. The way you do this is through the magic of the *SetUnhandledExceptionFilter* API function. I've always referred to these handlers as crash handlers. Amazingly, this functionality has been in Microsoft Win32 since Microsoft Windows NT 3.5, but it's almost undocumented. In the July 1999 MSDN, this function was mentioned in only nine topics.

In my experience, crash handlers have excellent debugging capabilities. In one project I worked on, when a crash occurred, in addition to putting up a dialog box with our technical support number on it, I logged all the information I could about the crash, including the state of the user's system, into a file. I also iterated through the program's main objects so that I could report down to the class level which objects were active and what they contained. I was logging almost too much information about the program's state. With a crash report, I had a 90 percent chance of duplicating the user's problem. If that isn't proactive debugging, I don't know what is!

Needless to say, I find *SetUnhandledExceptionFilter* powerful. Just by looking at the function name—*SetUnhandledExceptionFilter*—you can probably guess what the function does. The one parameter to *SetUnhandledExceptionFilter* is a pointer to a function that is called in the final __*except* block for the application. This function returns the same value that any exception filter would return: *EXCEPTION_EXECUTE-_HANDLER, EXCEPTION_CONTINUE_EXECUTION,* or *EXCEPTION_CONTINUE_SEARCH.* You can do any exception handling you want in the filter function, but as I warned earlier in the C++ *_set_se_translator* discussion, you need to be careful about blown stacks in your filter function. To be on the safe side, you might want to avoid any C run-time library calls as well as MFC. If you write your exception filter function in Visual Basic, you should be extra careful about what you access from the Visual Basic run-time library. Although I'm obligated to warn you about these possibilities, I can assure you that the vast majority of your crashes will be access violations—you shouldn't have any problems if you write a complete crash handling system in your function provided you check the exception reason first and avoid function calls if the stack is blown.

Your exception filter also gets a pointer to an *EXCEPTION_POINTERS* structure. In Listing 9-5, I'll present several routines that translate this structure for you. Because each company has different crash handler needs, I'll let you write your own.

You need to keep in mind a couple of issues when you're using *SetUnhandled-ExceptionFilter*. The first is that you can't use standard user-mode debuggers to debug any unhandled exception filter you set. This is a known bug. Knowledge Base article Q173652 says that under a debugger the unhandled exception filter isn't called. This bug can be a bit of a pain, but in a C++ program, one workaround you can use to debug your unhandled exception filter is to call it from a regular SEH exception filter. You can find an example of this workaround in the *Baz* function in CH_TESTS.CPP, which is part of this book's source code.

Another issue is that the crash handler you specify by calling *SetUnhandled-ExceptionFilter* is global to your process. If you build the coolest crash handler in the world for your ActiveX control and the container crashes—even if it's not your fault—your crash handler will be executed. Don't let this possibility keep you from using *SetUnhandledExceptionFilter*, though; I have some code that might help you out.

USING THE CRASHHANDLER API

In the reusable module BUGSLAYERUTIL.DLL, I wrote the CrashHandler API, which you can use to limit your crash handler to a specific module or modules. The way that I limit your crash handler is that all exceptions pass through an unhandled exception filter that I set. When my unhandled exception filter is called, I check the module that the exception came from. If the exception is from one of the modules requested, I call your crash handler, but if it's from a module outside those requested, I call the unhandled exception filter I replaced. Calling the replaced exception filter means that multiple modules can use my CrashHandler API without stepping on one another. You can see all the CrashHandler API functions in Listing 9-5.

```
/*--------------------------------------------------------------------
"Debugging Applications" (Microsoft Press)
Copyright (c) 1997-2000 John Robbins -- All rights reserved.

CONDITIONAL COMPILATION :
    WORK_AROUND_SRCLINE_BUG - Define this symbol to work around the
                              SymGetLineFromAddr bug; this bug causes PDB
                              file lookups to fail after the first lookup.
                              This bug is fixed in DBGHELP.DLL, but I
```

Listing 9-5 *CRASHHANDLER.CPP*   *(continued)*

Listing 9-5 *continued*

```
                                still keep the workaround for users
                                who might need to use the old IMAGEHLP.DLL
                                versions.
-------------------------------------------------------------------------*/

#include "pch.h"
#include "BugslayerUtil.h"
#include "CrashHandler.h"

// The project internal header file
#include "Internal.h"


/*///////////////////////////////////////////////////////////////////////
                        File Scope Defines
///////////////////////////////////////////////////////////////////////*/
// The maximum symbol size handled in the module
#define MAX_SYM_SIZE   256
#define BUFF_SIZE 1024
#define SYM_BUFF_SIZE 512


/*///////////////////////////////////////////////////////////////////////
                    File Scope Global Variables
///////////////////////////////////////////////////////////////////////*/
// The custom unhandled exception filter (crash handler)
static PFNCHFILTFN g_pfnCallBack = NULL ;

// The original unhandled exception filter
static LPTOP_LEVEL_EXCEPTION_FILTER g_pfnOrigFilt = NULL ;

// The array of modules to limit crash handler to
static HMODULE * g_ahMod = NULL ;
// The size, in items, of g_ahMod
static UINT g_uiModCount = 0 ;

// The static buffer returned by various functions. This buffer
// allows data to be transferred without using the stack.
static TCHAR g_szBuff [ BUFF_SIZE ] ;

// The static symbol lookup buffer
static BYTE g_stSymbol [ SYM_BUFF_SIZE ] ;

// The static source file and line number structure
static IMAGEHLP_LINE g_stLine ;

// The stack frame used in walking the stack
```

```
static STACKFRAME g_stFrame ;

// The flag indicating that the symbol engine has been initialized
static BOOL g_bSymEngInit = FALSE ;

/*///////////////////////////////////////////////////////////////////////
                    File Scope Function Declarations
///////////////////////////////////////////////////////////////////////*/
// The exception handler
LONG __stdcall CrashHandlerExceptionFilter ( EXCEPTION_POINTERS *
                                             pExPtrs              ) ;

// Converts a simple exception to a string value
LPCTSTR ConvertSimpleException ( DWORD dwExcept ) ;

// The internal function that does all the stack walking
LPCTSTR __stdcall
          InternalGetStackTraceString ( DWORD              dwOpts  ,
                                         EXCEPTION_POINTERS * pExPtrs );

// The internal SymGetLineFromAddr function
BOOL InternalSymGetLineFromAddr ( IN  HANDLE          hProcess        ,
                                  IN  DWORD           dwAddr          ,
                                  OUT PDWORD          pdwDisplacement ,
                                  OUT PIMAGEHLP_LINE  Line            );

// Initializes the symbol engine if needed
void InitSymEng ( void ) ;

// Cleans up the symbol engine if needed
void CleanupSymEng ( void ) ;

/*///////////////////////////////////////////////////////////////////////
                          Destructor Class
///////////////////////////////////////////////////////////////////////*/
// See the note in MEMDUMPVALIDATOR.CPP about automatic classes.
// Turn off warning: initializers put in library initialization area
#pragma warning (disable : 4073)
#pragma init_seg(lib)
class CleanUpCrashHandler
{
public :
    CleanUpCrashHandler ( void )
    {
    }
```

(continued)

Listing 9-5 *continued*

```
    ~CleanUpCrashHandler ( void )
    {
        // Are there any outstanding memory allocations?
        if ( NULL != g_ahMod )
        {
            VERIFY ( HeapFree ( GetProcessHeap ( ) ,
                                0                     ,
                                g_ahMod               ) ) ;
            g_ahMod = NULL ;
        }
        if ( NULL != g_pfnOrigFilt )
        {
            // Restore the original unhandled exception filter.
            SetUnhandledExceptionFilter ( g_pfnOrigFilt ) ;
        }
    }
} ;

// The static class
static CleanUpCrashHandler g_cBeforeAndAfter ;

/*/////////////////////////////////////////////////////////////////////
                Crash Handler Function Implementation
//////////////////////////////////////////////////////////////////////*/

BOOL __stdcall SetCrashHandlerFilter ( PFNCHFILTFN pFn )
{
    // A NULL parameter unhooks the callback.
    if ( NULL == pFn )
    {
        if ( NULL != g_pfnOrigFilt )
        {
            // Restore the original unhandled exception filter.
            SetUnhandledExceptionFilter ( g_pfnOrigFilt ) ;
            g_pfnOrigFilt = NULL ;
            if ( NULL != g_ahMod )
            {
                free ( g_ahMod ) ;
                g_ahMod = NULL ;
            }
            g_pfnCallBack = NULL ;
        }
    }
    else
```

```
    {
        ASSERT ( FALSE == IsBadCodePtr ( (FARPROC)pFn ) ) ;
        if ( TRUE == IsBadCodePtr ( (FARPROC)pFn ) )
        {
            return ( FALSE ) ;
        }
        g_pfnCallBack = pFn ;

        // If a custom crash handler isn't already in use, enable
        // CrashHandlerExceptionFilter and save the original unhandled
        // exception filter.
        if ( NULL == g_pfnOrigFilt )
        {
            g_pfnOrigFilt =
                SetUnhandledExceptionFilter( CrashHandlerExceptionFilter );
        }
    }
    return ( TRUE ) ;
}

BOOL __stdcall AddCrashHandlerLimitModule ( HMODULE hMod )
{
    // Check the obvious cases.
    ASSERT ( NULL != hMod ) ;
    if ( NULL == hMod )
    {
        return ( FALSE ) ;
    }__

    // Allocate a temporary array. This array must be allocated from
    // memory that's guaranteed to be around even if the process is
    // toasting. If the process is toasting, the RTL heap probably isn't
    // safe, so I allocate the temporary array from the process heap.
    HMODULE * phTemp = (HMODULE*)
                HeapAlloc ( GetProcessHeap ( )              ,
                            HEAP_ZERO_MEMORY |
                                HEAP_GENERATE_EXCEPTIONS    ,
                        ( sizeof ( HMODULE ) * ( g_uiModCount+1 ) ) ) ;
    ASSERT ( NULL != phTemp ) ;
    if ( NULL == phTemp )
    {
        TRACE0 ( "Serious trouble in the house! - "
                "HeapAlloc failed!!!\n"          );
        return ( FALSE ) ;
    }
```

(continued)

269

Listing 9-5 *continued*

```
    if ( NULL == g_ahMod )
    {
        g_ahMod = phTemp ;
        g_ahMod[ 0 ] = hMod ;
        g_uiModCount++ ;
    }
    else
    {
        // Copy the old values.
        CopyMemory ( phTemp        ,
                     g_ahMod       ,
                     sizeof ( HMODULE ) * g_uiModCount ) ;
        // Free the old memory.
        VERIFY ( HeapFree ( GetProcessHeap ( ) , 0 , g_ahMod ) ) ;
        g_ahMod = phTemp ;
        g_ahMod[ g_uiModCount ] = hMod ;
        g_uiModCount++ ;
    }
    return ( TRUE ) ;
}

UINT __stdcall GetLimitModuleCount ( void )
{
    return ( g_uiModCount ) ;
}

int __stdcall GetLimitModulesArray ( HMODULE * pahMod , UINT uiSize )
{
    int iRet ;

    __try
    {
        ASSERT ( FALSE == IsBadWritePtr ( pahMod ,
                                          uiSize * sizeof ( HMODULE ) ) ) ;
        if ( TRUE == IsBadWritePtr ( pahMod ,
                                     uiSize * sizeof ( HMODULE ) ) )
        {
            iRet = GLMA_BADPARAM ;
            __leave ;
        }

        if ( uiSize < g_uiModCount )
```

```
        {
            iRet = GLMA_BUFFTOOSMALL ;
            __leave ;
        }

        CopyMemory ( pahMod      ,
                     g_ahMod      ,
                     sizeof ( HMODULE ) * g_uiModCount ) ;

        iRet = GLMA_SUCCESS ;
    }
    __except ( EXCEPTION_EXECUTE_HANDLER )
    {
        iRet = GLMA_FAILURE ;
    }
    return ( iRet ) ;
}

LONG __stdcall CrashHandlerExceptionFilter ( EXCEPTION_POINTERS* pExPtrs )
{
    LONG lRet = EXCEPTION_CONTINUE_SEARCH ;

    // If the exception is an EXCEPTION_STACK_OVERFLOW, there isn't much
    // you can do because the stack is blown. If you try to do anything,
    // the odds are great that you'll just double-fault and bomb right
    // out of your exception filter. Although I don't recommend doing so,
    // you could play some games with the stack register and
    // manipulate it so that you could regain enough space to run these
    // functions. Of course, if you did change the stack register, you'd
    // have problems walking the stack.
    // I take the safe route and make some calls to OutputDebugString here.
    // I still might double-fault, but because OutputDebugString does very
    // little on the stack (something like 8-16 bytes), it's worth a
    // shot. You can have your users download Mark Russinovich's
    // DebugView/Enterprise Edition (www.sysinternals.com) so that they can
    // at least tell you what they see.
    // The only problem is that I can't even be sure there's enough
    // room on the stack to convert the instruction pointer.
    // Fortunately, EXCEPTION_STACK_OVERFLOW doesn't happen very often.

    // Note that I still call your crash handler. I'm doing the logging
    // work here in case the blown stack kills your crash handler.
    if ( EXCEPTION_STACK_OVERFLOW ==
                        pExPtrs->ExceptionRecord->ExceptionCode )
```

(continued)

Listing 9-5 *continued*

```
{
    OutputDebugString ( "!!!!!!!!!!!!!!!!!!!!!!!!!!!!!!!!!!!!!\n" ) ;
    OutputDebugString ( "EXCEPTION_STACK_OVERFLOW occurred\n" ) ;
    OutputDebugString ( "!!!!!!!!!!!!!!!!!!!!!!!!!!!!!!!!!!!!!\n" ) ;
}


__try
{

    if ( NULL != g_pfnCallBack )
    {

        // The symbol engine has to be initialized here so that
        // I can look up the base module information for the
        // crash address as well as get the symbol engine
        // ready.
        InitSymEng ( ) ;

        // Check the g_ahMod list.
        BOOL bCallIt = FALSE ;
        if ( 0 == g_uiModCount )
        {
            bCallIt = TRUE ;
        }
        else
        {
            HINSTANCE hBaseAddr = (HINSTANCE)
                SymGetModuleBase ((HANDLE)GetCurrentProcessId ( ) ,
                                  (DWORD)pExPtrs->
                                        ExceptionRecord->
                                             ExceptionAddress ) ;
            if ( NULL != hBaseAddr )
            {
                for ( UINT i = 0 ; i < g_uiModCount ; i ++ )
                {
                    if ( hBaseAddr == g_ahMod[ i ] )
                    {
                        bCallIt = TRUE ;
                        break ;
                    }
                }
            }
        }
        if ( TRUE == bCallIt )
```

```
                {
                    // Check that the crash handler still exists in memory
                    // before I call it. The user might have forgotten to
                    // unregister, and the crash handler is invalid because
                    // it got unloaded. If some other function loaded
                    // back into the same address, however, there isn't much
                    // I can do.
                    ASSERT ( FALSE == IsBadCodePtr( (FARPROC)g_pfnCallBack ) );
                    if ( FALSE == IsBadCodePtr ( (FARPROC)g_pfnCallBack ) )
                    {
                        lRet = g_pfnCallBack ( pExPtrs ) ;
                    }
                }
                else
                {
                    // Call the previous filter but only after it checks
                    // out. I'm just being a little paranoid.
                    ASSERT ( FALSE == IsBadCodePtr( (FARPROC)g_pfnOrigFilt ) );
                    if ( FALSE == IsBadCodePtr ( (FARPROC)g_pfnOrigFilt ) )
                    {
                        lRet = g_pfnOrigFilt ( pExPtrs ) ;
                    }
                }
                CleanupSymEng ( ) ;
        }
    }
    __except ( EXCEPTION_EXECUTE_HANDLER )
    {
        lRet = EXCEPTION_CONTINUE_SEARCH ;
    }
    return ( lRet ) ;
}

/*/////////////////////////////////////////////////////////////////////////
        EXCEPTION_POINTER Translation Functions Implementation
/////////////////////////////////////////////////////////////////////////*/

LPCTSTR __stdcall GetFaultReason ( EXCEPTION_POINTERS * pExPtrs )
{
    ASSERT ( FALSE == IsBadReadPtr ( pExPtrs ,
                                     sizeof ( EXCEPTION_POINTERS ) ) ) ;

    if ( TRUE == IsBadReadPtr ( pExPtrs ,
                                sizeof ( EXCEPTION_POINTERS ) ) )
```

(continued)

Listing 9-5 *continued*

```
{
    TRACE0 ( "Bad parameter to GetFaultReasonA\n" ) ;
    return ( NULL ) ;
}


// The variable that holds the return value
LPCTSTR szRet ;


__try
{

    // Initialize the symbol engine in case it isn't initialized.
    InitSymEng ( ) ;

    // The current position in the buffer
    int iCurr = 0 ;
    // A temporary value holder. This holder keeps the stack usage to a
    // minimum.
    DWORD dwTemp ;

    iCurr += BSUGetModuleBaseName ( GetCurrentProcess ( ) ,
                                    NULL                   ,
                                    g_szBuff               ,
                                    BUFF_SIZE              ) ;

    iCurr += wsprintf ( g_szBuff + iCurr , _T ( " caused an " ) ) ;

    dwTemp = (DWORD)
        ConvertSimpleException ( pExPtrs->ExceptionRecord->
                                                    ExceptionCode );

    if ( NULL != dwTemp )
    {
        iCurr += wsprintf ( g_szBuff + iCurr ,
                        _T ( "%s" )          ,
                        dwTemp              ) ;
    }
    else
    {
        iCurr += ( FormatMessage ( FORMAT_MESSAGE_IGNORE_INSERTS |
                                FORMAT_MESSAGE_FROM_HMODULE,
                            GetModuleHandle (_T("NTDLL.DLL") ) ,
                            pExPtrs->ExceptionRecord->
                                                    ExceptionCode,
```

```
                                        0                         ,
                                        g_szBuff + iCurr          ,
                                        BUFF_SIZE ,
                                        0                         )
                    * sizeof ( TCHAR ) ) ;
    }

    ASSERT ( iCurr < ( BUFF_SIZE - MAX_PATH ) ) ;

    iCurr += wsprintf ( g_szBuff + iCurr , _T ( " in module " ) ) ;

    dwTemp =
        SymGetModuleBase ( (HANDLE)GetCurrentProcessId ( ) ,
                           (DWORD)pExPtrs->ExceptionRecord->
                                                 ExceptionAddress ) ;
    ASSERT ( NULL != dwTemp ) ;

    if ( NULL == dwTemp )
    {
        iCurr += wsprintf ( g_szBuff + iCurr , _T ( "<UNKNOWN>" ) );
    }
    else
    {
        iCurr += BSUGetModuleBaseName ( GetCurrentProcess ( )   ,
                                        (HINSTANCE)dwTemp        ,
                                        g_szBuff + iCurr         ,
                                        BUFF_SIZE - iCurr         ) ;

    }

#ifdef _WIN64
    iCurr += wsprintf ( g_szBuff + iCurr    ,
                        _T ( " at %016X" )  ,
                        pExPtrs->ExceptionRecord->ExceptionAddress );
#else
    iCurr += wsprintf ( g_szBuff + iCurr                       ,
                        _T ( " at %04X:%08X" )                 ,
                        pExPtrs->ContextRecord->SegCs          ,
                        pExPtrs->ExceptionRecord->ExceptionAddress );
#endif

    ASSERT ( iCurr < ( BUFF_SIZE - 200 ) ) ;

    // Start looking up the exception address.
    PIMAGEHLP_SYMBOL pSym = (PIMAGEHLP_SYMBOL)&g_stSymbol ;
    FillMemory ( pSym , NULL , SYM_BUFF_SIZE ) ;
```

(continued)

Listing 9-5 *continued*

```
pSym->SizeOfStruct = sizeof ( IMAGEHLP_SYMBOL ) ;
pSym->MaxNameLength = SYM_BUFF_SIZE - sizeof ( IMAGEHLP_SYMBOL );

DWORD dwDisp ;
if ( TRUE ==
     SymGetSymFromAddr ( (HANDLE)GetCurrentProcessId ( )       ,
                         (DWORD)pExPtrs->ExceptionRecord->
                                            ExceptionAddress   ,
                         &dwDisp                               ,
                         pSym                                  ) )
{
    iCurr += wsprintf ( g_szBuff + iCurr , _T ( ", " ) ) ;

    // Copy no more of the symbol information than there's
    // room for.
    dwTemp = lstrlen ( pSym->Name ) ;
    // Make sure there's enough room for the longest symbol
    // and the displacement.
    if ( (int)dwTemp > ( ( BUFF_SIZE - iCurr ) -
                         ( MAX_SYM_SIZE + 50 ) ) )
    {
        lstrcpyn ( g_szBuff + iCurr       ,
                   pSym->Name             ,
                   BUFF_SIZE - iCurr - 1  ) ;
        // Gotta leave now
        szRet = g_szBuff ;
        __leave ;
    }
    else
    {
        if ( dwDisp > 0 )
        {
            iCurr += wsprintf ( g_szBuff + iCurr       ,
                                _T ( "%s()+%04d byte(s)" ),
                                pSym->Name             ,
                                dwDisp                 ) ;
        }
        else
        {
            iCurr += wsprintf ( g_szBuff + iCurr ,
                                _T ( "%s " )     ,
                                pSym->Name       ) ;
        }
    }
}
```

```
        else
        {
            // If the symbol wasn't found, the source and line won't
            // be found either, so leave now.
            szRet = g_szBuff ;
            __leave ;
        }

        ASSERT ( iCurr < ( BUFF_SIZE - 200 ) ) ;

        // Look up the source file and line number.
        ZeroMemory ( &g_stLine , sizeof ( IMAGEHLP_LINE ) ) ;
        g_stLine.SizeOfStruct = sizeof ( IMAGEHLP_LINE ) ;

        if ( TRUE ==
             InternalSymGetLineFromAddr ( (HANDLE)
                                                GetCurrentProcessId ( )    ,
                                          (DWORD)pExPtrs->
                                                      ExceptionRecord->
                                                          ExceptionAddress ,
                                          &dwDisp                          ,
                                          &g_stLine                     ) )
        {
            iCurr += wsprintf ( g_szBuff + iCurr , _T ( ", " ) ) ;

            // Copy no more of the source file and line number
            // information than there's room for.
            dwTemp = lstrlen ( g_stLine.FileName ) ;
            if ( (int)dwTemp > ( BUFF_SIZE - iCurr -
                          MAX_PATH - 50        ) )
            {
                lstrcpyn ( g_szBuff + iCurr        ,
                           g_stLine.FileName       ,
                           BUFF_SIZE - iCurr - 1 ) ;
                // Gotta leave now
                szRet = g_szBuff ;
                __leave ;
            }
            else
            {
                if ( dwDisp > 0 )
                {
                    iCurr += wsprintf ( g_szBuff + iCurr         ,
                                  _T("%s, line %04d+%04d byte(s)"),
```

(continued)

Listing 9-5 *continued*

```
                                        g_stLine.FileName       ,
                                        g_stLine.LineNumber     ,
                                        dwDisp                  ) ;
            }
            else
            {
                iCurr += wsprintf ( g_szBuff + iCurr    ,
                                    _T ( "%s, line %04d" ),
                                    g_stLine.FileName     ,
                                    g_stLine.LineNumber ) ;
            }
        }
    }
    szRet = g_szBuff ;
    }
    __except ( EXCEPTION_EXECUTE_HANDLER )
    {
        ASSERT ( !"Crashed in GetFaultReason" ) ;
        szRet = NULL ;
    }
    return ( szRet ) ;
}

BOOL __stdcall GetFaultReasonVB ( EXCEPTION_POINTERS * pExPtrs ,
                                  LPTSTR                szBuff  ,
                                  UINT                  uiSize  )
{
    ASSERT ( FALSE == IsBadWritePtr ( szBuff , uiSize ) ) ;
    if ( TRUE == IsBadWritePtr ( szBuff , uiSize ) )
    {
        return ( FALSE ) ;
    }

    LPCTSTR szRet ;

    __try
    {

        szRet = GetFaultReason ( pExPtrs ) ;

        ASSERT ( NULL != szRet ) ;
        if ( NULL == szRet )
        {
            __leave ;
        }
```

```
        lstrcpyn ( szBuff  ,
                   szRet   ,
                   min ( (UINT)lstrlen ( szRet ) + 1, uiSize ) ) ;
    }
    __except ( EXCEPTION_EXECUTE_HANDLER )
    {
        szRet = NULL ;
    }
    return ( NULL != szRet ) ;
}



LPCTSTR BUGSUTIL_DLLINTERFACE __stdcall
          GetFirstStackTraceString ( DWORD                 dwOpts  ,
                                     EXCEPTION_POINTERS * pExPtrs )
{
    // All the error checking is in the InternalGetStackTraceString
    // function.

    // Initialize the STACKFRAME structure.
    ZeroMemory ( &g_stFrame , sizeof ( STACKFRAME ) ) ;

#ifdef _X86_
    g_stFrame.AddrPC.Offset       = pExPtrs->ContextRecord->Eip ;
    g_stFrame.AddrPC.Mode         = AddrModeFlat              ;
    g_stFrame.AddrStack.Offset    = pExPtrs->ContextRecord->Esp ;
    g_stFrame.AddrStack.Mode      = AddrModeFlat              ;
    g_stFrame.AddrFrame.Offset    = pExPtrs->ContextRecord->Ebp ;
    g_stFrame.AddrFrame.Mode      = AddrModeFlat              ;
#else
    g_stFrame.AddrPC.Offset       = (DWORD)pExPtrs->ContextRecord->Fir ;
    g_stFrame.AddrPC.Mode         = AddrModeFlat ;
    g_stFrame.AddrReturn.Offset   =
                          (DWORD)pExPtrs->ContextRecord->IntRa ;
    g_stFrame.AddrReturn.Mode     = AddrModeFlat ;
    g_stFrame.AddrStack.Offset    =
                          (DWORD)pExPtrs->ContextRecord->IntSp ;
    g_stFrame.AddrStack.Mode      = AddrModeFlat ;
    g_stFrame.AddrFrame.Offset    =
                          (DWORD)pExPtrs->ContextRecord->IntFp ;
    g_stFrame.AddrFrame.Mode      = AddrModeFlat ;
#endif

    return ( InternalGetStackTraceString ( dwOpts , pExPtrs ) ) ;
}
```

(continued)

Listing 9-5 *continued*

```
LPCTSTR BUGSUTIL_DLLINTERFACE __stdcall
            GetNextStackTraceString ( DWORD                    dwOpts  ,
                                       EXCEPTION_POINTERS * pExPtrs )
{
    // All error checking is in InternalGetStackTraceString.
    // Assume that GetFirstStackTraceString has already initialized the
    // stack frame information.
    return ( InternalGetStackTraceString ( dwOpts , pExPtrs ) ) ;
}


BOOL __stdcall CH_ReadProcessMemory ( HANDLE                    ,
                                      LPCVOID  lpBaseAddress     ,
                                      LPVOID   lpBuffer          ,
                                      DWORD    nSize             ,
                                      LPDWORD  lpNumberOfBytesRead   )
{
    return ( ReadProcessMemory ( GetCurrentProcess ( ) ,
                                 lpBaseAddress      ,
                                 lpBuffer           ,
                                 nSize              ,
                                 lpNumberOfBytesRead     ) ) ;
}


// The internal function that does all the stack walking
LPCTSTR __stdcall
        InternalGetStackTraceString ( DWORD                    dwOpts  ,
                                      EXCEPTION_POINTERS * pExPtrs  )
{

    ASSERT ( FALSE == IsBadReadPtr ( pExPtrs                      ,
                                     sizeof ( EXCEPTION_POINTERS ) ) ) ;
    if ( TRUE == IsBadReadPtr ( pExPtrs                      ,
                                sizeof ( EXCEPTION_POINTERS ) ) )
    {
        TRACE0 ( "GetStackTraceString - invalid pExPtrs!\n" ) ;
        return ( NULL ) ;
    }

    // The value that is returned
    LPCTSTR szRet ;
    // A temporary variable for all to use. This variable saves
    // stack space.
    DWORD dwTemp ;
    // The module base address. I look this up right after the stack
```

```
        // walk to ensure that the module is valid.
        DWORD dwModBase ;

        __try
        {
            // Initialize the symbol engine in case it isn't initialized.
            InitSymEng ( ) ;

#ifdef _WIN64
#define CH_MACHINE IMAGE_FILE_MACHINE_IA64
#else
#define CH_MACHINE IMAGE_FILE_MACHINE_I386
#endif
            // Note:  If the source file and line number functions are used,
            //         StackWalk can cause an access violation.
            BOOL bSWRet = StackWalk ( CH_MACHINE                         ,
                                      (HANDLE)GetCurrentProcessId ( )    ,
                                      GetCurrentThread ( )               ,
                                      &g_stFrame                         ,
                                      pExPtrs->ContextRecord             ,
                                      (PREAD_PROCESS_MEMORY_ROUTINE)
                                               CH_ReadProcessMemory      ,
                                      SymFunctionTableAccess             ,
                                      SymGetModuleBase                   ,
                                      NULL                               ) ;
            if ( ( FALSE == bSWRet ) || ( 0 == g_stFrame.AddrFrame.Offset ) )
            {
                szRet = NULL ;
                __leave ;
            }

            // Before I get too carried away and start calculating
            // everything, I need to double-check that the address returned
            // by StackWalk really exists. I've seen cases in which
            // StackWalk returns TRUE but the address doesn't belong to
            // a module in the process.
            dwModBase = SymGetModuleBase ( (HANDLE)GetCurrentProcessId ( ) ,
                                           g_stFrame.AddrPC.Offset          ) ;

            if ( 0 == dwModBase )
            {
                szRet = NULL ;
                __leave ;
            }

            int iCurr = 0 ;
```

(continued)

Listing 9-5 *continued*

```
        // At a minimum, put in the address.
#ifdef _WIN64
        iCurr += wsprintf ( g_szBuff + iCurr          ,
                            _T ( "0x%016X" )           ,
                            g_stFrame.AddrPC.Offset ) ;
#else
        iCurr += wsprintf ( g_szBuff + iCurr                  ,
                            _T ( "%04X:%08X" )                ,
                            pExPtrs->ContextRecord->SegCs     ,
                            g_stFrame.AddrPC.Offset         ) ;
#endif

        // Output the parameters?
        if ( GSTSO_PARAMS == ( dwOpts & GSTSO_PARAMS ) )
        {
            iCurr += wsprintf ( g_szBuff + iCurr             ,
                                _T ( " ( 0x%08X 0x%08X "\
                                     "0x%08X 0x%08X )" ) ,
                                g_stFrame.Params[ 0 ]        ,
                                g_stFrame.Params[ 1 ]        ,
                                g_stFrame.Params[ 2 ]        ,
                                g_stFrame.Params[ 3 ]      ) ;
        }
        // Output the module name.
        if ( GSTSO_MODULE == ( dwOpts & GSTSO_MODULE ) )
        {
            iCurr += wsprintf ( g_szBuff + iCurr , _T ( " " ) ) ;

            ASSERT ( iCurr < ( BUFF_SIZE - MAX_PATH ) ) ;
            iCurr += BSUGetModuleBaseName ( GetCurrentProcess ( ) ,
                                            (HINSTANCE)dwModBase   ,
                                            g_szBuff + iCurr       ,
                                            BUFF_SIZE - iCurr    ) ;
        }

        ASSERT ( iCurr < ( BUFF_SIZE - MAX_PATH ) ) ;
        DWORD dwDisp ;

        // Output the symbol name?
        if ( GSTSO_SYMBOL == ( dwOpts & GSTSO_SYMBOL ) )
        {

            // Start looking up the exception address.
            PIMAGEHLP_SYMBOL pSym = (PIMAGEHLP_SYMBOL)&g_stSymbol ;
```

```
ZeroMemory ( pSym , SYM_BUFF_SIZE ) ;
pSym->SizeOfStruct = sizeof ( IMAGEHLP_SYMBOL ) ;
pSym->MaxNameLength = SYM_BUFF_SIZE -
                     sizeof ( IMAGEHLP_SYMBOL ) ;

if ( TRUE ==
     SymGetSymFromAddr ( (HANDLE)GetCurrentProcessId ( )  ,
                          g_stFrame.AddrPC.Offset         ,
                          &dwDisp                          ,
                          pSym                            ) )
{
    iCurr += wsprintf ( g_szBuff + iCurr , _T ( ", " ) ) ;

    // Copy no more symbol information than there's room for.
    dwTemp = lstrlen ( pSym->Name ) ;
    if ( dwTemp > (DWORD)( BUFF_SIZE - iCurr -
                         ( MAX_SYM_SIZE + 50 ) ) )
    {
        lstrcpyn ( g_szBuff + iCurr       ,
                   pSym->Name             ,
                   BUFF_SIZE - iCurr - 1 ) ;
        // Gotta leave now
        szRet = g_szBuff ;
        __leave ;
    }
    else
    {
        if ( dwDisp > 0 )
        {
            iCurr += wsprintf ( g_szBuff + iCurr         ,
                                _T( "%s()+%04d byte(s)") ,
                                pSym->Name               ,
                                dwDisp                   ) ;
        }
        else
        {
            iCurr += wsprintf ( g_szBuff + iCurr ,
                                _T ( "%s" )      ,
                                pSym->Name       ) ;
        }
    }
}
else
{
    // If the symbol wasn't found, the source file and line
```

(continued)

Listing 9-5 *continued*

```
                    // number won't be found either, so leave now.
                    szRet = g_szBuff ;
                    __leave ;
            }


    }


    ASSERT ( iCurr < ( BUFF_SIZE - MAX_PATH ) ) ;

    // Output the source file and line number information?
    if ( GSTSO_SRCLINE == ( dwOpts & GSTSO_SRCLINE ) )
    {
        ZeroMemory ( &g_stLine , sizeof ( IMAGEHLP_LINE ) ) ;
        g_stLine.SizeOfStruct = sizeof ( IMAGEHLP_LINE ) ;

        if ( TRUE ==
                InternalSymGetLineFromAddr ( (HANDLE)
                                                GetCurrentProcessId ( ),
                                              g_stFrame.AddrPC.Offset   ,
                                              &dwDisp                   ,
                                              &g_stLine                 ) )
        {
            iCurr += wsprintf ( g_szBuff + iCurr , _T ( ", " ) ) ;

            // Copy no more of the source file and line number
            // information than there's room for.
            dwTemp = lstrlen ( g_stLine.FileName ) ;
            if ( dwTemp > (DWORD)( BUFF_SIZE - iCurr -
                            ( MAX_PATH + 50      ) ) )
            {
                lstrcpyn ( g_szBuff + iCurr      ,
                           g_stLine.FileName     ,
                           BUFF_SIZE - iCurr - 1 ) ;
                // Gotta leave now
                szRet = g_szBuff ;
                __leave ;
            }
            else
            {
                if ( dwDisp > 0 )
                {
                    iCurr += wsprintf(g_szBuff + iCurr          ,
                                _T("%s, line %04d+%04d byte(s)"),
                                    g_stLine.FileName            ,
                                    g_stLine.LineNumber          ,
```

```
                                        dwDisp                    ) ;
                }
                else
                {
                    iCurr += wsprintf ( g_szBuff + iCurr     ,
                                        _T ( "%s, line %04d" ) ,
                                        g_stLine.FileName      ,
                                        g_stLine.LineNumber    ) ;
                }
            }
        }
    }

    szRet = g_szBuff ;
    }
    __except ( EXCEPTION_EXECUTE_HANDLER )
    {
        ASSERT ( !"Crashed in InternalGetStackTraceString" ) ;
        szRet = NULL ;
    }
    return ( szRet ) ;
}

BOOL __stdcall
        GetFirstStackTraceStringVB ( DWORD                 dwOpts  ,
                                     EXCEPTION_POINTERS * pExPtrs ,
                                     LPTSTR                szBuff  ,
                                     UINT                  uiSize  )
{
    ASSERT ( FALSE == IsBadWritePtr ( szBuff , uiSize ) ) ;
    if ( TRUE == IsBadWritePtr ( szBuff , uiSize ) )
    {
        return ( FALSE ) ;
    }

    LPCTSTR szRet ;

    __try
    {
        szRet = GetFirstStackTraceString ( dwOpts , pExPtrs ) ;
        if ( NULL == szRet )
        {
            __leave ;
        }
        lstrcpyn ( szBuff   ,
```

(continued)

Listing 9-5 *continued*

```
                    szRet    ,
                    min ( (UINT)lstrlen ( szRet ) + 1 , uiSize ) ) ;
    }
    __except ( EXCEPTION_EXECUTE_HANDLER )
    {
        szRet = NULL ;
    }
    return ( NULL != szRet ) ;
}

BOOL __stdcall
         GetNextStackTraceStringVB ( DWORD                dwOpts  ,
                                     EXCEPTION_POINTERS * pExPtrs ,
                                     LPTSTR               szBuff  ,
                                     UINT                 uiSize  )
{
    ASSERT ( FALSE == IsBadWritePtr ( szBuff , uiSize ) ) ;
    if ( TRUE == IsBadWritePtr ( szBuff , uiSize ) )
    {
        return ( FALSE ) ;
    }

    LPCTSTR szRet ;

    __try
    {
        szRet = GetNextStackTraceString ( dwOpts , pExPtrs ) ;
        if ( NULL == szRet )
        {
            __leave ;
        }
        lstrcpyn ( szBuff   ,
                   szRet    ,
                   min ( (UINT)lstrlen ( szRet ) + 1 , uiSize ) ) ;
    }
    __except ( EXCEPTION_EXECUTE_HANDLER )
    {
        szRet = NULL ;
    }
    return ( NULL != szRet ) ;
}

LPCTSTR __stdcall GetRegisterString ( EXCEPTION_POINTERS * pExPtrs )
{
    // Check the parameter.
```

```
    ASSERT ( FALSE == IsBadReadPtr ( pExPtrs                      ,
                                    sizeof ( EXCEPTION_POINTERS ) ) ) ;
    if ( TRUE == IsBadReadPtr ( pExPtrs                     ,
                                sizeof ( EXCEPTION_POINTERS ) ) )
    {
        TRACE0 ( "GetRegisterString - invalid pExPtrs!\n" ) ;
        return ( NULL ) ;
    }

#ifdef _WIN64
    ASSERT ( !"IA64 is not supported (YET!) " ) ;
#else
    // This call puts 48 bytes on the stack, which could be a problem when
    // the stack is blown.
    wsprintf ( g_szBuff ,
               _T ( "EAX=%08X   EBX=%08X   ECX=%08X   EDX=%08X   ESI=%08X\n"\
                    "EDI=%08X   EBP=%08X   ESP=%08X   EIP=%08X   FLG=%08X\n"\
                    "CS=%04X    DS=%04X   SS=%04X   ES=%04X    "\
                    "FS=%04X   GS=%04X" ) ,
                    pExPtrs->ContextRecord->Eax       ,
                    pExPtrs->ContextRecord->Ebx       ,
                    pExPtrs->ContextRecord->Ecx       ,
                    pExPtrs->ContextRecord->Edx       ,
                    pExPtrs->ContextRecord->Esi       ,
                    pExPtrs->ContextRecord->Edi       ,
                    pExPtrs->ContextRecord->Ebp       ,
                    pExPtrs->ContextRecord->Esp       ,
                    pExPtrs->ContextRecord->Eip       ,
                    pExPtrs->ContextRecord->EFlags    ,
                    pExPtrs->ContextRecord->SegCs     ,
                    pExPtrs->ContextRecord->SegDs     ,
                    pExPtrs->ContextRecord->SegSs     ,
                    pExPtrs->ContextRecord->SegEs     ,
                    pExPtrs->ContextRecord->SegFs     ,
                    pExPtrs->ContextRecord->SegGs     ) ;

#endif
    return ( g_szBuff ) ;

}

BOOL __stdcall GetRegisterStringVB ( EXCEPTION_POINTERS * pExPtrs ,
                                     LPTSTR               szBuff  ,
                                     UINT                 uiSize  )
```

(continued)

Listing 9-5 *continued*

```
{
    ASSERT ( FALSE == IsBadWritePtr ( szBuff , uiSize ) ) ;
    if ( TRUE == IsBadWritePtr ( szBuff , uiSize ) )
    {
        return ( FALSE ) ;
    }

    LPCTSTR szRet ;

    __try
    {
        szRet = GetRegisterString ( pExPtrs ) ;
        if ( NULL == szRet )
        {
            __leave ;
        }
        lstrcpyn ( szBuff   ,
                   szRet    ,
                   min ( (UINT)lstrlen ( szRet ) + 1 , uiSize ) ) ;
    }
    __except ( EXCEPTION_EXECUTE_HANDLER )
    {
        szRet = NULL ;
    }
    return ( NULL != szRet ) ;

}

LPCTSTR ConvertSimpleException ( DWORD dwExcept )
{
    switch ( dwExcept )
    {
        case EXCEPTION_ACCESS_VIOLATION         :
            return ( _T ( "EXCEPTION_ACCESS_VIOLATION" ) ) ;
        break ;

        case EXCEPTION_DATATYPE_MISALIGNMENT    :
            return ( _T ( "EXCEPTION_DATATYPE_MISALIGNMENT" ) ) ;
        break ;

        case EXCEPTION_BREAKPOINT               :
            return ( _T ( "EXCEPTION_BREAKPOINT" ) ) ;
        break ;
```

```
case EXCEPTION_SINGLE_STEP               :
    return ( _T ( "EXCEPTION_SINGLE_STEP" ) ) ;
break ;

case EXCEPTION_ARRAY_BOUNDS_EXCEEDED     :
    return ( _T ( "EXCEPTION_ARRAY_BOUNDS_EXCEEDED" ) ) ;
break ;

case EXCEPTION_FLT_DENORMAL_OPERAND      :
    return ( _T ( "EXCEPTION_FLT_DENORMAL_OPERAND" ) ) ;
break ;

case EXCEPTION_FLT_DIVIDE_BY_ZERO        :
    return ( _T ( "EXCEPTION_FLT_DIVIDE_BY_ZERO" ) ) ;
break ;

case EXCEPTION_FLT_INEXACT_RESULT        :
    return ( _T ( "EXCEPTION_FLT_INEXACT_RESULT" ) ) ;
break ;

case EXCEPTION_FLT_INVALID_OPERATION     :
    return ( _T ( "EXCEPTION_FLT_INVALID_OPERATION" ) ) ;
break ;

case EXCEPTION_FLT_OVERFLOW              :
    return ( _T ( "EXCEPTION_FLT_OVERFLOW" ) ) ;
break ;

case EXCEPTION_FLT_STACK_CHECK           :
    return ( _T ( "EXCEPTION_FLT_STACK_CHECK" ) ) ;
break ;

case EXCEPTION_FLT_UNDERFLOW             :
    return ( _T ( "EXCEPTION_FLT_UNDERFLOW" ) ) ;
break ;

case EXCEPTION_INT_DIVIDE_BY_ZERO        :
    return ( _T ( "EXCEPTION_INT_DIVIDE_BY_ZERO" ) ) ;
break ;

case EXCEPTION_INT_OVERFLOW              :
    return ( _T ( "EXCEPTION_INT_OVERFLOW" ) ) ;
break ;
```

(continued)

Listing 9-5 *continued*

```
        case EXCEPTION_PRIV_INSTRUCTION          :
            return ( _T ( "EXCEPTION_PRIV_INSTRUCTION" ) ) ;
        break ;

        case EXCEPTION_IN_PAGE_ERROR             :
            return ( _T ( "EXCEPTION_IN_PAGE_ERROR" ) ) ;
        break ;

        case EXCEPTION_ILLEGAL_INSTRUCTION       :
            return ( _T ( "EXCEPTION_ILLEGAL_INSTRUCTION" ) ) ;
        break ;

        case EXCEPTION_NONCONTINUABLE_EXCEPTION :
            return ( _T ( "EXCEPTION_NONCONTINUABLE_EXCEPTION" ) ) ;
        break ;

        case EXCEPTION_STACK_OVERFLOW            :
            return ( _T ( "EXCEPTION_STACK_OVERFLOW" ) ) ;
        break ;

        case EXCEPTION_INVALID_DISPOSITION       :
            return ( _T ( "EXCEPTION_INVALID_DISPOSITION" ) ) ;
        break ;

        case EXCEPTION_GUARD_PAGE                :
            return ( _T ( "EXCEPTION_GUARD_PAGE" ) ) ;
        break ;

        case EXCEPTION_INVALID_HANDLE            :
            return ( _T ( "EXCEPTION_INVALID_HANDLE" ) ) ;
        break ;

        default :
            return ( NULL ) ;
        break ;
    }
}


BOOL InternalSymGetLineFromAddr ( IN  HANDLE          hProcess        ,
                                  IN  DWORD           dwAddr          ,
                                  OUT PDWORD          pdwDisplacement ,
                                  OUT PIMAGEHLP_LINE  Line            )
{
#ifdef WORK_AROUND_SRCLINE_BUG
```

```
    // The problem is that the symbol engine finds only those source
    // line addresses (after the first lookup) that fall exactly on
    // a zero displacement. I'll walk backward 100 bytes to
    // find the line and return the proper displacement.
    DWORD dwTempDis = 0 ;
    while ( FALSE == SymGetLineFromAddr ( hProcess           ,
                                          dwAddr -
                                           dwTempDis          ,
                                          pdwDisplacement    ,
                                          Line               ) )
    {
        dwTempDis += 1 ;
        if ( 100 == dwTempDis )
        {
            return ( FALSE ) ;
        }
    }

    // I found the line, and the source line information is correct, so
    // change the displacement if I had to search backward to find
    // the source line.
    if ( 0 != dwTempDis )
    {
        *pdwDisplacement = dwTempDis ;
    }
    return ( TRUE ) ;

#else  // WORK_AROUND_SRCLINE_BUG
    return ( SymGetLineFromAddr ( hProcess           ,
                                  dwAddr             ,
                                  pdwDisplacement    ,
                                  Line               ) ) ;
#endif
}

// Initializes the symbol engine if needed
void InitSymEng ( void )
{
    if ( FALSE == g_bSymEngInit )
    {
        // Set up the symbol engine.
        DWORD dwOpts = SymGetOptions ( ) ;

        // Turn on line loading and deferred loading.
        SymSetOptions ( dwOpts                     |
```

(continued)

Listing 9-5 *continued*

```
                           SYMOPT_DEFERRED_LOADS |
                           SYMOPT_LOAD_LINES        ) ;

        // Force the invade process flag no matter what operating system
        // I'm on.
        HANDLE hPID = (HANDLE)GetCurrentProcessId ( ) ;
        VERIFY ( BSUSymInitialize ( (DWORD)hPID ,
                                    hPID        ,
                                    NULL        ,
                                    TRUE         ) ) ;
        g_bSymEngInit = TRUE ;
    }
}

// Cleans up the symbol engine if needed
void CleanupSymEng ( void )
{
    if ( TRUE == g_bSymEngInit )
    {
        VERIFY ( SymCleanup ( (HANDLE)GetCurrentProcessId ( ) ) ) ;
        g_bSymEngInit = FALSE ;
    }
}
```

To set your filter function, simply call *SetCrashHandlerFilter*. Internally, *SetCrashHandlerFilter* saves your filter function to a static variable and calls *SetUnhandledExceptionFilter* to set the real exception filter, *CrashHandler-ExceptionFilter*. If you don't add any modules that limit the exception filtering, *CrashHandlerExceptionFilter* will always call your exception filter no matter which module had the hard crash. Calling your exception filter if no modules were added was by design—so that you'd have to use only one API call to set your final exception handling. It's best if you call *SetCrashHandlerFilter* as soon as you can and make sure that you call it again with *NULL* right before you unload so that you allow my crash handler code to remove your filter function.

AddCrashHandlerLimitModule is where you add a module to limit the crash handling. All you need to pass to this function is the *HMODULE* for the module in question. If you have multiple modules that you want to limit crash handling to, just call *AddCrashHandlerLimitModule* for each one. The array of module handles is allocated from the main process heap.

As you look at the various functions in Listing 9-5, you'll notice that I don't make any C run-time library calls. Because the crash handler routines are called only in extraordinary situations, I can't rely on the run time being in a stable state. To clean up any memory that I allocated, I use an automatic static class whose destructor is called when BUGSLAYERUTIL.DLL is unloaded. I also provide a couple of functions that allow you to get the limit module size and a copy of the array—*GetLimitModuleCount* and *GetLimitModulesArray*. I'll leave it up to you to write a *RemoveCrashHandlerLimitModule* function.

One interesting aspect of the implementation in CRASHHANDLER.CPP is how I handle initializing the DBGHELP.DLL symbol engine. Because the crash handler code can be called at any time, I needed a way to get all the process's modules loaded at the time of the crash. *SymInitialize* will take care of this automatically for you by setting its third parameter, *fInvadeProcess*, to *TRUE*. Unfortunately, invading the process and loading all the modules will work only on Windows 2000, not on Windows 98. However, the *BSUSymInitialize* function from BUGSLAYERUTIL.DLL will hunt down all the loaded modules and load them one at a time so that you can have the same behavior on Windows 98.

TRANSLATING *EXCEPTION_POINTERS* STRUCTURES

Now that you've written your exception handlers and crash handlers, it's time to talk about those *EXCEPTION_POINTERS* structures each is passed. Because these structures are where all the interesting information about the crash is stored, I wanted to develop a set of functions that you can call to translate the information into human-readable form. With these functions, all you need to concentrate on is the display of information to the user in a manner that's appropriate for your particular application. You can find all these functions in Listing 9-5.

I tried to keep the functions as simple as possible. All you need to do is to pass in the *EXCEPTION_POINTERS* structures. Each function returns a pointer to a constant string that holds the text. If you looked at the code, you might have noticed that each function has a corresponding function whose name ends in "VB". I tried to come up with a way for Visual Basic to use the same static buffers that the C functions use. I used the static buffers because the *EXCEPTION_POINTERS*-handling functions will be called in crash situations, and I can't rely on allocated memory or use too much stack space when my crash handler functions are called. Unfortunately, I couldn't come up with a clean way other than having Visual Basic use its own string buffer that you must pass in. With the C versions, because I could return the static string buffers directly, I wanted to make the functions easier to use. When calling the crash handler functions from Visual Basic, declare a global string variable early in the program so that the memory is available.

The *GetRegisterString* function simply returns the formatted register string. The *GetFaultReason* function is a little more interesting in that it returns a complete description of the problem. The returned string shows the process, the reason for the exception, the module that caused the exception, the address of the exception, and—if symbol information is available—the function, source file, and line number where the crash occurred.

```
CH_TESTS.EXE caused an EXCEPTION_ACCESS_VIOLATION in module CH_TESTS.EXE at
001B:004010FB, Baz()+0064 bytes, CH_Tests.cpp, line 0060+0003 bytes
```

The most interesting functions are *GetFirstStackTraceString* and *GetNextStackTraceString*. As their names indicate, these functions let you walk the stack. As with the *FindFirstFile* and *FindNextFile* API functions, you can call *GetFirstStackTraceString* and then continue to call *GetNextStackTraceString* until it returns *FALSE* to walk the entire stack. In addition to an *EXCEPTION_POINTERS* structure, these functions take a flag option parameter that lets you control the amount of information that you want to see in the resultant string. The following string shows all the options turned on:

```
001B:004018AA (0x00000001 0x008C0F90 0x008C0200 0x77F8FE94)
CH_TESTS.EXE, main()+1857 bytes, CH_Tests.cpp,
line 0341+0007 bytes
```

The values in parentheses are the first four possible parameters to the function. Table 9-1 shows the options flags and what each will include in the output string.

**Table 9-1   *GetFirstStackTraceString* AND
GetNextStackTraceString OPTIONS**

Option	Output
0	Just the stack address
GSTSO_PARAMS	The first four possible parameters
GSTSO_MODULE	The module name
GSTSO_SYMBOL	The symbol name of the stack address
GSTSO_SRCLINE	The source file and line number information of the stack address

To see these functions in action, I included two sample test programs on the companion CD. The first, CH_TEST, is a C/C++ example. The second program, CrashTest, is a Visual Basic–based example. Between these two programs, you should get a pretty good idea of how to use all the functions I've presented. Figure 9-1 shows CrashTest displaying its crash dialog box.

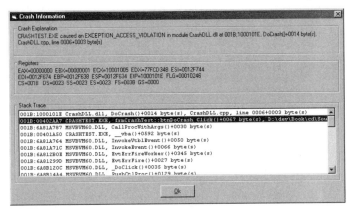

Figure 9-1 *CrashTest dialog box*

SUMMARY

This chapter covered crash handlers, which are exception handlers and unhandled exception filters. Both allow you to get more information about a crash and provide a better face to the user when your application does have problems. Whereas unhandled exception filters work in both Visual C++ and Visual Basic code, exception handling works only with Visual C++.

C++ exceptions and SEH exceptions are sometimes confused. The C++ language specification provides C++ exceptions, whereas the operating system provides SEH; the two kinds of exception handling are completely different. Fortunately, you can combine C++ exceptions and SEH with the run-time library function *_set_se_translator*.

One key point you need to make sure that you understand is the differences between asynchronous and synchronous C++ exception handling. The easiest way to keep the differences between these two types of C++ exception handling straight is to think of asynchronous as "all functions track lifetimes of objects" and synchronous as "some functions track lifetimes of objects."

The magic function that does the work to make crash handlers possible is *SetUnhandledExceptionFilter*, which allows you to set the final SEH exception filter. The final exception filter allows you to gain control right before the Application Error dialog box pops up so that you can record all sorts of great information about why you crashed. The CrashHandler code presented will make it easier to set unhandled exception filters and will do the hard work of translating the crash information for you so that you can concentrate on the display and the unique parts of your application.

Chapter 10

Debugging Windows 2000 Services and DLLs That Load into Services

Next to device drivers, the hardest code to debug involves Microsoft Windows 2000 services and dynamic-link libraries (DLLs) that load into services. You might think that because services are really just user-mode processes without a user interface, debugging them would be as easy as debugging a console application. Unfortunately, the story isn't that simple. In fact, so many issues come into play with Windows 2000 services and with DLLs that load into services, especially issues related to Windows 2000 security, that you might find yourself wanting to pull out your hair in frustration trying to work with them. In the early days of Microsoft Windows NT, very few developers wrote services or even knew what they were. In today's world of COM+, Microsoft Internet Information Services (IIS), Microsoft Exchange Server extensions, and Microsoft Cluster Servers (MSCSs), however, many developers must start dealing with services—and debugging them.

In this chapter, I'll provide an overview of the basic characteristics of services. To understand how to debug services themselves and DLLs that load into services, such as Internet Server API (ISAPI) filters and extensions, you need to know how services operate. I'll then explain issues directly related to debugging services. As I walk you through the different stages of debugging a service, I'll point out issues that apply to specific Microsoft service technologies.

SERVICE BASICS

A service has three basic characteristics:

- A service runs all the time, even when the computer doesn't have anyone logged on or when the computer first starts.
- A service doesn't have a user interface.
- A service can be managed and controlled by both local and remote clients.

When deciding whether you need to write your application as a service or as a normal user-mode application, you need to ask yourself whether the development problem you're trying to solve has these three requirements. If it does, you should consider writing your application as a service. And if you do decide to write a service—and want to be able to debug it—you need to make sure you have a solid understanding of how a service operates. The information I'll present in this section will be just enough to give you an idea of what you're getting yourself into. If you'd like to learn more about services, I suggest you take a look at Jeffrey Richter's article, "Design a Windows NT Service to Exploit Special Operating System Facilities," in the October 1997 *Microsoft Systems Journal* available on MSDN.

A perfect example of when to write a service is when you're writing an application that needs to monitor an uninterruptible power supply (UPS). All the UPS software needs to do is to monitor when the UPS hardware reports a power failure; and when the power does go out, the UPS software needs to initiate a controlled shutdown. Obviously, if the UPS software isn't running all the time (the first criterion for deciding whether your application should be a service), the shutdown won't happen and the computer will just stop when the UPS hardware runs out of battery power. The UPS software doesn't really need a user interface (the second criterion) because it just needs to run in the background and monitor the UPS hardware. Finally, if you're working on UPS hardware for use in data centers, system administrators will definitely want to check on the health of remote UPS hardware (the third criterion).

Sounds simple enough—so far. Now we'll turn to the way services operate. The first aspect of services I'll cover is the specific API functions that you call to turn a normal user-mode process into a service.

The API Dance

Services have some unique qualities that will require some maneuvering on your part to accommodate. First, the entry point you use in services—*main* or *WinMain*—doesn't matter. Because your service doesn't have any user interface, you can use console or graphical user interface (GUI) entry points interchangeably.

Inside your *main* or *WinMain* processing, the first call you have to make is to the *StartServiceCtrlDispatcher* API function. You pass a *SERVICE_TABLE_ENTRY* structure to *StartServiceCtrlDispatcher* in which you indicate your service name and the main entry point of your service. The Service Control Manager (SCM), which starts all services and is what *StartServiceCtrlDispatcher* eventually talks to in order to set up your service, is an operating system feature that, as its name implies, controls all services. If your service doesn't call *StartServiceCtrlDispatcher* within 2 minutes of starting for Windows NT 4 or within 30 seconds of starting for Windows 2000, the SCM will terminate your service. As you'll see later in the chapter, this time limit can make debugging startup a little more interesting.

As soon as you call into the SCM, the SCM spawns a thread to call your service's entry point. Your service's entry point has one hard requirement: it must call *RegisterServiceCtrlHandler* within 1 second of starting. If your service doesn't make the call within a second, the SCM thinks your service has failed, though it doesn't terminate the service. If your service eventually does call *RegisterServiceCtrlHandler*, your service will run normally. Although you'd expect that the SCM would terminate your service if it thought your service had failed, it doesn't. Odd as this behavior is, it does make debugging as your service continues to run much easier.

RegisterServiceCtrlHandler takes yet another pointer to a function, called the handler function. The SCM calls into the handler function to control your service's performance on operations such as stopping, pausing, or continuing.

When your service is transitioning from the states of starting, stopping, and pausing, it communicates with the SCM through the *SetServiceStatus* API function. Most services just need to call *SetServiceStatus* and indicate the basic state to which they're changing—there's nothing fancy about this API function.

I've glossed over a few of the details involved with the API functions, but basically the calls to *StartServiceCtrlDispatcher*, *RegisterServiceCtrlHandler*, and *SetServiceStatus* are all that the operating system requires of your service to get it up and running. Notice that I didn't mention anything about requirements concerning communications protocols your service uses to communicate between a controller user interface you write and your service. Fortunately, services have access to all the regular Windows API functions, so you can use memory mapped files, mail slots, and named pipes. With services, you really have all the same options as you do in normal cross-process communications. The most challenging issue with services, as I pointed out at the beginning of the chapter, is security.

The Security Dance

Unless you specify otherwise, services run in a special account called the System Account. Because Windows 2000 has user-based security for all objects, the System Account is validated for the machine, not for the network as a whole. Consequently, a System Account process can't access network resources. For many services, such as the UPS example mentioned earlier in this chapter, the security issues might never arise during development. But if you're trying to share mapped memory from your service to the UI client application, for example, and your security isn't set correctly, you'll run into access-denied errors from your client applications as they attempt to map the shared memory.

Unfortunately, no amount of debugging will solve security problems; you have to make sure that you program both your services and your client applications with the security aligned correctly. Complete Windows 2000 security programming is a book unto itself, so be prepared to spend some time planning your security programming from the beginning of development. For a quick introduction to the range of security issues with services, I strongly suggest that you read Frank Kim's article "Why Do Certain Win32 Technologies Misbehave in Windows NT Services?" in the March 1998 *Microsoft Systems Journal.* Another excellent resource is Keith Brown's "Security Briefs" column in *Microsoft Systems Journal,* in which Keith covers nothing except security.

Some of you who have been around the block a few times might be thinking that instead of doing all this weird service development you'll just whip out the Windows 2000 Resource Kit SRVANY.EXE program that allows you to turn any application into a service and be done with it. That solution might work in some cases, but in Frank's article you'll find some of the reasons that using SRVANY.EXE isn't the panacea you might think it is.

Now that you've had a whirlwind tour of services, let's turn to the real heart of this chapter: how to debug services.

DEBUGGING SERVICES

As you've seen, the unique nature of services alone means that you need to deal with many issues that don't come up when you're programming regular user-mode applications. Keep in mind that the discussion so far has been about the bare minimum functionality necessary for getting a service up and running. I haven't even touched on the fundamental requirement of ensuring that your general algorithms and implementation work for the one-of-a-kind pieces of your service. The easiest and best way to debug services without becoming completely overwhelmed is to approach the debugging in stages.

Three main stages are involved when you're debugging services:

- Debugging the core code
- Debugging the basic service
- Debugging for real

In the following sections, I'll describe what you need to do in each stage to make sure that you stand the best chance of debugging your service with a minimal amount of hassle.

Debugging the Core Code

Before you even consider running your application as a service, you need to run and test your application as a standard user-mode executable until you've debugged all your core code. Once you've done that, you can start working on the issues specific to services.

When debugging your core code, you should debug everything on the same machine, running under your developer account; that is, your service core code as well as any client code should be on the same machine. With this approach, you won't have to worry about any security or network issues. Once you debug your logic, you can move on to the joy of other problems you'll encounter with services, such as security and service initialization orders.

COM+ Services

If you're building a COM+ service with the Active Template Library (ATL), such as the TraceSrv utility in Chapter 11, you don't have to do anything with security. By default, ATL runs as a user-mode executable until you register your application with the *-Service* command-line option.

ISAPI Filters and Extensions

The exported functions you must provide for your filters and extensions are fairly simple, and you can easily write a test harness that acts as a fake IIS system. You can test all your core algorithms in a controlled environment so that you have them completely debugged before you run your service under IIS proper.

Exchange Server

You can build Exchange service applications that run as console applications if you use the helper functions in WINWRAP.LIB. Starting your service with the *notserv* startup parameter will force running as a normal process. The *notserv* parameter must be the first parameter specified.

Debugging the Basic Service

After you test and debug your general logic, you can start debugging your code while running as a service. All your initial debugging should take place on a system on which you can control everything. Ideally, you should have a second machine sitting right next to your main development machine that you can use for your initial debugging. The second machine should have the version and flavor of Windows you're recommending to your customers for the environment your service will run under. Whereas the reason for debugging the core code was to verify your basic logic, the reason for preliminary service debugging is to shake out your basic service-specific code. You need to complete four tasks as part of debugging your first-cut service code:

- Turn on Allow Service To Interact With Desktop.
- Set your service identity.
- Attach to your service.
- Debug your startup code.

As I discuss each task, I'll mention particular issues relevant to the different technologies as appropriate.

Turn On Allow Service To Interact With Desktop

No matter what type of service you're debugging, you'll want to turn on Allow Service To Interact With Desktop on the Log On tab of your service's Properties dialog box. Although you shouldn't have any user interface elements with your service, having assertion message boxes that allow you to gain control with the debugger is very helpful. Assertion message boxes combined with excellent logging code, such as the code that ATL gives you for writing to the Event Log, can make it much easier to debug services.

In the initial stages of development, I turn on *SUPERASSERT* message box assertions just so I can quickly gauge the general health of my code. (For more information on *SUPERASSERT*, see Chapter 3.) As I get more and more of the service running, however, I set the assertion options so that all assertions just go through trace statements.

Until I'm confident of the service code, I generally leave the Allow Service To Interact With Desktop setting checked. One nasty bug that cropped up in a service I once wrote took me a while to track down because I turned off this option and I still had a message box assertion that popped up. Because the operating system security won't allow normal services to show a message box, my service just appeared to hang. Before I do turn off Allow Service To Interact With Desktop, I double-check that my service—and any DLLs that it uses—don't call message boxes by using DUMPBIN /IMPORTS to verify that neither *MessageBoxA* nor *MessageBoxW* are imported when I don't expect them to be.

Set Your Service Identity

To avoid security problems when you're trying to get your service running, you can set the identity of your service. By default, all services run under the System Account, which is sometimes referred to as the LocalSystem account. However, you can set your service to start under a user account with higher security access, such as someone who is a member of the machine's Administrator group—like you, for example!

In your service's Properties dialog box, click on the Log On tab. Select the This Account radio button, click the Browse button, and choose the appropriate account from the Select User dialog box. After selecting the user, you'll need to type in and confirm the password for that account. For COM+ services, DCOMCNFG.EXE can also set the logon identity of your service if you're more comfortable using it.

Attach to Your Service

Once your service has started, debugging isn't usually that difficult. All you need to do is to attach to your service process from the Microsoft Visual C++ debugger. Depending on your service and the complexity of your code, attaching to the service with a debugger might be all you need to do to debug. Follow these simple steps to attach to an active process from the Visual C++ debugger:

1. Start MSDEV.EXE.

2. From the Build menu, select Start Debug to bring up the pop-up menu, and then click Attach To Process.

3. Check the Show System Processes check box so that you can see all the service processes.

4. Select the process you want to debug from the list, and click OK.

An alternative method of attaching the debugger is just to call the *DebugBreak* API function. When the Application Error dialog box pops up, simply click the Cancel button and debug as you normally would. Keep in mind that if you're building a COM+ service, you should make the *DebugBreak* call outside any COM method or property invocations. If you don't, COM will eat the breakpoint exception generated by *DebugBreak* and you'll never get a debugger attached. In addition, you shouldn't call *DebugBreak* as part of your service's initial startup code; see the section "Debug Your Startup Code" on page 305 for reasons why.

Yet another means to attach the debugger to your service is to use Task Manager. Bring up Task Manager, select the Processes tab, right-click on the process you want to debug, and select Debug from the pop-up menu. The operating system makes it easy to attach your debugger if you know what process you want to debug.

If the Debug option on the right-click menu is disabled in Task Manager, don't be alarmed—you're just seeing Windows 2000 security having some fun. Only users who are authenticated as Administrators on the local machine are allowed to attach a debugger to services. If the software engineers in your company typically log on with a domain account, you should add that domain account to the Administrators group on each of their machines.

IIS ISAPI filters and extensions

Internet Information Services 5 changed the rules about where ISAPI filters and extensions execute. In previous versions of IIS, all filters and extensions ran inside

INETINFO.EXE, the main IIS service. In IIS 5, extensions run in DLLHOST.EXE because of the new pooled out-of-process model. ISAPI filters still run inside the IIS process, INETINFO.EXE. The new model makes IIS much more stable, and according to Microsoft, much more scalable. The only problem for debugging is that you might not know which DLLHOST.EXE process your extension is running under.

The new pooled out-of-process model for extensions applies only to Web sites created after you upgrade to IIS 5. If you upgrade your existing server to IIS 5, your existing Web shares will run extensions as they were with IIS 4. If your extension is handling its own thread pooling or using any form of *RevertToSelf*, you'll need to set up your extension to run inside IIS's address space. Search MSDN for the topic "Pooled Out-of-Process Model for ISAPI" to learn more about setting up your extension.

The IIS documentation also mentions that you should set up your extensions to run inside IIS so that you can debug them. The only problem with changing where your extensions run is that you should deploy your extensions so that you use the pooled out-of-process model. Because I'm a believer in debugging what you ultimately run, I want to show you the trick to debugging extensions even when they're running under DLLHOST.EXE, which is how your extensions will run.

Before I talk about using the debugger, though, I need to talk about how to figure out which process is running your filter or extension because multiple instances of DLLHOST.EXE will be running. First, you need to download a fantastic free utility, HandleEx for Windows NT, from Mark Russinovich and Bruce Cogswell's Web site, *www.sysinternals.com*. HandleEx will show you the handles that a process has open and, most important, which DLLs are loaded into which processes. To find your DLL using HandleEx, press F3 and type the filename of your DLL in the HandleEx Search dialog box. Click the Search button, and HandleEx will list the names and process IDs (PIDs) of the processes that have your DLL loaded. Figure 10-1 shows HandleEx reporting which process the Simple extension is running under.

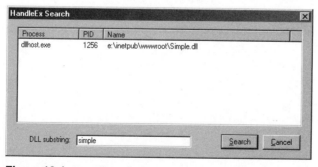

Figure 10-1 *HandleEx finding an IIS 5 extension running in the out-of-process pool manager*

After you have the PID, you can attach the Visual C++ debugger to the process using the Attach To Process command. Keep in mind that once you attach to the process with the debugger, you must keep the debugger running even when you finish debugging your particular DLL. If you shut down the debugger, the process you're debugging will stop.

Because you're looking for a loaded DLL, you obviously have to make sure that it loads before you can debug it. Filters run inside INETINFO.EXE, so you can't attach the debugger before the IIS service starts. Therefore, you're out of luck if you want to debug the initialization. If you're debugging extensions, you can debug your initialization if you're ingenious. The idea is to create a dummy extension that you force IIS to load by connecting to your Web site with Microsoft Internet Explorer, which will make IIS start the DLLHOST.EXE pooled out-of-process executable. After you hunt down the PID for the new DLLHOST.EXE, you can attach the debugger. You can then set a breakpoint on *LdrpRunInitializeRoutines* so that you can step directly into your extension's *DllMain*. Matt Pietrek clarifies exactly what you need to do to set the *LdrpRunInitializeRoutines* breakpoint in his "Under the Hood" column from the September 1999 *Microsoft Systems Journal*. After you've set the breakpoint, you can load your real extension with Internet Explorer and debug your initialization.

Debug Your Startup Code

The hardest part of debugging services is debugging the startup code. The SCM will wait only 2 minutes under Windows NT 4 or 30 seconds under Windows 2000 for a service to get started and call *StartServiceCtrlDispatcher* to indicate that the service is running fine. Although both times are almost a lifetime on the CPU, you can easily spend that amount of time single-stepping through your code looking at variables.

The only clean way to debug your service startup code is to use trace statements if all you have is the Visual C++ debugger. Using Mark Russinovich's DebugView/ Enterprise Edition, which I refer to in Chapter 3, you can see the statements as your service rolls along. Fortunately, your service startup code is generally more lightweight than the main service code, so debugging with trace statements isn't too painful.

The SCM timeout limits can cause problems for services that can't start quickly. A slow piece of hardware or the nature of your service can sometimes dictate a long startup time. The *SERVICE_STATUS* structure you pass to *SetServiceStatus* has two fields, *dwCheckPoint* and *dwWaitHint*, which might help you if your service is likely to time out on startup.

When your service does start, you can tell the SCM that you're entering the *SERVICE_START_PENDING* state, place a large hint in the *dwWaitHint* field (the time is in milliseconds), and set the *dwCheckPoint* field to 0 so that the SCM won't use the default times. If you need more time in your service startup, you can repeat the call to *SetServiceStatus* as many times as necessary as long as you increment the *dwCheckPoint* field before each successive call.

The final point I want to address about debugging startup code is that the SCM will add entries to the Event Log explaining why it can't start a particular service. In the Event Viewer, look in the Source column for "Service Control Manager." If you also use the Event Log for your lightweight tracing, between the SCM entries and your tracing, you should be able to solve many of your startup problems. If you use the Event Log, make sure your service dependencies are set so that your service will be started after the Event Log service.

Debugging for Real

The limitations of GUI debuggers make debugging services an interesting challenge. Even so, though you might find it a little painful, you can debug your services with the debuggers that come with Microsoft Visual Studio or the Platform SDK.

If you're developing services that have complicated processing requirements with heavy Win32 synchronization or memory sharing, or DLLs that load into services such as IIS, you might want to consider using Compuware NuMega's SoftICE debugger. SoftICE runs between the CPU and the operating system and can debug user-mode code with ease. Because GUI debuggers sometimes don't allow you to debug what you need to debug, such as the service startup or cross-process communications, SoftICE can make your debugging chores much easier. With SoftICE, you simply load your module's source code and set a breakpoint, and no matter how or where your module loads into memory, you can concentrate on debugging without worrying about the issues associated with GUI debuggers. Granted, SoftICE has a much steeper learning curve than the Visual C++ debugger, but if you're developing services and DLLs that load into services, you'll save yourself considerable amounts of time in the end if you take the time to learn how to use it.

SUMMARY

This chapter covered some of the trials and tribulations that are a part of debugging Windows 2000 services and DLLs that load into services. Services have a special status in the operating system, and because of the security issues involved, you need to have an excellent understanding of what services are and how they behave. Service debugging takes more planning up front than most debugging.

The first step in debugging services and any DLLs that load into services is to debug as much of the core code as possible while running as a normal application. The second step is to ensure that you take advantage of the environment for services, such as by turning on interaction with the desktop and by using tools such as HandleEx to find the information you need to debug faster. Finally, if you're writing large, complicated services, as I described in the "Debugging for Real" section, you might want to consider using Compuware NuMega's SoftICE to assist in your debugging.

Chapter 11

Multimachine, Multiprocess Tracing

These days it's common for an application to have a front end written in one language, three or four components written in other languages, and yet another part that is running in a different process or on a completely different machine. Trying to track down a bug that occurs between the Microsoft Visual Basic, Scripting Edition (VBScript), code in an Active Server Pages Web page and an object that the code calls on another machine can be a hair-raising experience. Unfortunately, no debuggers currently exist that will allow you to single-step across machines or even do something you'd think would be simple, such as step from VBScript into a C++ control. Debugging modern applications is definitely not easy.

In this chapter, I'll present a tool, TraceSrv, that allows you to easily add trace statements to all the parts of your applications, no matter what machine they reside on, and lets you view all the output in the same place. Although not as useful as the ultimate debugger—in which you'd be able to single-step everything, everywhere—TraceSrv at least gives you a fighting chance of tracking down problems in your multilanguage, multiprocess, and multimachine development. As all good developers know, trace statements are right up there with *ASSERT* macros in the Good Things list. You can never have enough of either.

In presenting TraceSrv, I'll start by laying out the set of requirements I had and the underlying technology decisions I made, and then I'll highlight what went on as I was designing and developing this tool. Most of the code for TraceSrv isn't rocket science. I originally thought that TraceSrv would be fairly easy to develop, but as it turned out I spent a great deal of time filling many holes in my knowledge. I hope I can save you from some of the frustrations that I had to deal with.

TraceSrv Requirements

First let's go over my design objectives for TraceSrv because the best way for you to understand TraceSrv is to see what I set out to accomplish. Here are the requirements that I started with:

1. TraceSrv must be compatible with most common programming languages, including, at a minimum, C++, Visual Basic, Borland Delphi, Visual Basic for Applications, Java, JScript, and VBScript.

2. TraceSrv must be very simple to use inside a programming language.

3. TraceSrv must always be running so that any application can connect to it at any time.

4. The trace statements of a program that runs on multiple machines should go to the same place.

5. The trace statements should be viewable on multiple machines at the same time by trace viewer applications.

6. The following trace statement options processing should be available:

    ❑   Prefix the trace statement with the time the trace statement was received.

    ❑   Prefix the trace statement with the number of the trace statement.

    ❑   Prefix the process ID of the process that sent the trace statement.

    ❑   Append a carriage return and line feed if needed.

    ❑   Send the trace statement through to a kernel debugger where the TraceSrv process is running.

7. If one of the TraceSrv options in requirement 6 is changed, all the currently active viewers should be notified so that all viewers, even on other machines, are coordinated with the current options.

At first glance, the TraceSrv requirements might look daunting because of the need for multilanguage programming and network development. I thought I could address multilanguage issues with a simple dynamic-link library (DLL) that anyone could load. Because I'm primarily a systems programmer, not a Web developer, my ignorance of VBScript and Java began to get in my way. Particularly when I looked at VBScript, I realized that no matter how much hacking I did, I wasn't going to get VBScript to call a DLL directly. The light finally started to dawn when I saw that VBScript supported *CreateObject*; I just needed a Component Object Model (COM) object, and VBScript would be able to use it just fine. Because COM works in almost all languages, I decided to make TraceSrv a simple COM object.

COM made the network programming problem go away fairly easily. You basically get COM+ for free. COM+ solves the "running all the time" problem because you can have your COM+ servers running as Microsoft Win32 services. The object is always ready if you use an automatic start service.

My first brush with COM+ services (then known as DCOM services) way back in the Microsoft Windows NT 4 alpha days was rather scary. Not only did you have to write the services—not the easiest thing in the world—but you also had to do all sorts of weird stuff with COM to get them hooked up. Fortunately, the Active Template Library (ATL) that comes with Microsoft Visual C++ 6 handles all the grunge work of writing COM+ services and even provides a wizard to help generate the code.

Once I figured out the basic development direction, I needed to define the interface for TraceSrv. TRACESRV.IDL, shown in Listing 11-1, is the main interface for TraceSrv. Basically, I use the *Trace* method of the *ITrace* interface to have a trace statement sent to TraceSrv. To accommodate the broadest number of languages, I decided to set the string type passed as a *BSTR*.

```
/*-----------------------------------------------------------------
"Debugging Applications" (Microsoft Press)
Copyright (c) 1997-2000 John Robbins -- All rights reserved.
-----------------------------------------------------------------*/
import "oaidl.idl";
import "ocidl.idl";
    [
        object ,
        uuid ( 4D42A00C-7774-11D3-9F57-00C04FA34F2C ) ,
        dual ,
        helpstring ( "ITrace Interface" ) ,
        pointer_default ( unique )
    ]
    interface ITrace : IDispatch
    {
        [ id ( 1 ) ,
          helpstring ( "method Trace" ) ]
          HRESULT Trace ( [ in ] BSTR bstrText ) ;
```

Listing 11-1 *TRACESRV.IDL*   *(continued)*

Listing 11-1 *continued*

```
    [ id ( 2 ) ,
      helpstring ( "method FullTrace" ) ]
      HRESULT FullTrace ( [ in ] BSTR bstrText , [ in ] long dwPID ) ;

    [ propget, id ( 3 ) ,
      helpstring ( "property ShowTimeStamps" ) ]
      HRESULT ShowTimeStamps ( [ out, retval ] VARIANT_BOOL *pVal ) ;
    [ propput, id ( 3 ) ,
      helpstring ( "property ShowTimeStamps" ) ]
      HRESULT ShowTimeStamps ( [ in ] VARIANT_BOOL newVal ) ;

    [ propget,
      id ( 4 ) ,
      helpstring ( "property ShowTraceAsODS" ) ]
      HRESULT ShowTraceAsODS ( [ out, retval ] VARIANT_BOOL *pVal ) ;
    [ propput,
      id ( 4 ) ,
      helpstring ( "property ShowTraceAsODS" ) ]
      HRESULT ShowTraceAsODS ( [ in ] VARIANT_BOOL newVal ) ;

    [ propget,
      id ( 5 ) ,
      helpstring ( "property ShowItemNumber" ) ]
      HRESULT ShowItemNumber ( [ out, retval ] VARIANT_BOOL *pVal ) ;
    [ propput,
      id ( 5 ) ,
      helpstring ( "property ShowItemNumber" ) ]
      HRESULT ShowItemNumber ( [ in ] VARIANT_BOOL newVal ) ;

    [ propget,
      id ( 6 ) ,
      helpstring ( "property ShowPID" ) ]
      HRESULT ShowPID ( [ out, retval ] VARIANT_BOOL *pVal ) ;
    [ propput,
      id ( 6 ) ,
      helpstring ( "property ShowPID" ) ]
      HRESULT ShowPID ( [ in ] VARIANT_BOOL newVal ) ;

    [ propget,
      id ( 7 ) ,
      helpstring ( "property AddCRLF" ) ]
      HRESULT AddCRLF ( [ out, retval ] VARIANT_BOOL *pVal ) ;
    [ propput,
      id ( 7 ) ,
      helpstring ( "property AddCRLF" ) ]
```

```
        HRESULT AddCRLF ( [ in ] VARIANT_BOOL newVal ) ;
    } ;


[
    uuid ( 4D42A000-7774-11D3-9F57-00C04FA34F2C ) ,
    version ( 1.0 ) ,
    helpstring ( "TraceSrv 1.0 Type Library" )
]
library TRACESRVLib
{
    importlib ( "stdole32.tlb" ) ;
    importlib ( "stdole2.tlb" ) ;

    [
        uuid ( 4D42A00E-7774-11D3-9F57-00C04FA34F2C ) ,
        helpstring ( "_ITraceEvents Interface" )
    ]
    dispinterface _ITraceEvents
    {
        properties:
        methods:
        [ id ( 1 ) ,
          helpstring ( "method TraceEvent" ) ]
          HRESULT TraceEvent ( BSTR bstrText ) ;

        [ id ( 2 ) ,
          helpstring ( "method ChangeShowTimeStamps" ) ]
          HRESULT ChangeShowTimeStamps ( VARIANT_BOOL bNewVal ) ;

        [ id ( 3 ) ,
          helpstring ( "method ChangeShowTraceAsODS" ) ]
          HRESULT ChangeShowTraceAsODS ( VARIANT_BOOL bNewVal ) ;

        [ id ( 4 ) ,
          helpstring ( "method ChangeShowItemNumber" ) ]
          HRESULT ChangeShowItemNumber ( VARIANT_BOOL bNewVal ) ;

        [ id ( 5 ) ,
          helpstring ( "method ChangeShowPID" ) ]
          HRESULT ChangeShowPID ( VARIANT_BOOL bNewVal ) ;

        [ id ( 6 ) ,
          helpstring ( "method ChangeAddCRLF" ) ]
          HRESULT ChangeAddCRLF ( VARIANT_BOOL bNewVal ) ;
    } ;
```

(continued)

Listing 11-1 *continued*

```
[
    uuid ( 4D42A00D-7774-11D3-9F57-00C04FA34F2C ) ,
    helpstring ( "Trace Class" )
]
coclass Trace
{
    [ default ] interface ITrace ;
    [ default, source ] dispinterface _ITraceEvents ;
} ;
} ;
```

To write a trace statement viewer, all you need to do is handle the events from the *_ITraceEvents* interface. The TraceSrv properties, which implement the trace statement options requirement listed earlier in this section, are on the *ITrace* interface in case an application using TraceSrv might want to change them. When a TraceSrv property is changed, TraceSrv generates an event that a trace viewer should handle. The TraceView program I'll go over later shows how to handle each event that TraceSrv generates.

The ATL COM AppWizard cranked out a COM+ service that seemed to be almost 90 percent complete. The only parts that I had to code were the TraceSrv interface and the handlers. Most of the code that I wrote is in TRACE.H and TRACE.CPP, which are on the book's companion CD. Most of the work is setting and getting properties and firing events. The only out-of-the-ordinary function, *CTrace::ProcessTrace*, is shown in Listing 11-2. I do the processing on the trace strings in *CTrace::ProcessTrace*.

```
HRESULT CTrace :: ProcessTrace ( BSTR bstrText , long dwPID)
{
    // Always double-check everything. Trust nothing.
    ASSERT ( this ) ;
    ASSERT ( NULL != bstrText ) ;

    // The length of the input string. The length is found after the
    // pointer is validated.
    int iInputLen = 0 ;

    if ( NULL == bstrText )
    {
        return ( Error ( IDS_NULLSTRINGPASSED ,
                         GUID_NULL            ,
                         E_INVALIDARG             ) ) ;
    }
```

Listing 11-2 *The* CTrace::ProcessTrace *function*

```
// I have some form of pointer in bstrText. Make sure that what the
// pointer holds is valid.
ASSERT ( FALSE == IsBadReadPtr ( bstrText , sizeof ( BSTR ) ) ) ;
ASSERT ( L'\0' != *bstrText ) ;

if ( ( TRUE == IsBadReadPtr ( bstrText , sizeof ( BSTR ) ) ) ||
     ( L'\0' == *bstrText                                   )   )
{
    return ( Error ( IDS_INVALIDSTRING ,
                     GUID_NULL          ,
                     E_INVALIDARG       ) ) ;
}

// Get the input length in characters now that the pointer is
// validated.
iInputLen = lstrlenW ( bstrText ) ;

// Calculate the maximum number of bytes needed for the input
// string.
UINT uiSize = ( iInputLen * sizeof ( OLECHAR ) ) +
                  k_SIZE_FULLFORMATBYTES  ;

// Grab the lock to protect the m_cOutput class.
ObjectLock lock ( this ) ;

// If this is the first call to ProcessTrace, m_lBuffSize is 0, so
// this if block serves as the initial allocation point.
if ( uiSize >= m_cOutput.BufferSize ( ) )
{
    // Delete the existing buffer, and allocate a bigger one.
    m_cOutput.Free ( ) ;

    // Allocate a buffer twice as large as the input string. The
    // input string is the largest seen so far, so bump up the
    // memory so that I do allocations only rarely.
    // I'll take the trade-off of extra space not being used
    // over the time to allocate over and over.
    // Also, multiplying by 2 ensures that I keep the memory
    // size an even number. I'm working with Unicode characters
    // in this program, so I don't want odd memory allocations.
    UINT uiAllocSize = uiSize * 2 ;

    // Make sure I get a minimum buffer size. The minimum buffer
    // size is 2 KB, so in most cases, I'll execute the code
    // in this if block only once.
```

(continued)

Listing 11-2 *continued*

```
        if ( k_MIN_TRACE_BUFF_SIZE > uiAllocSize )
        {
            uiAllocSize = k_MIN_TRACE_BUFF_SIZE ;
        }
        OLECHAR * pTemp = m_cOutput.Allocate ( uiAllocSize ) ;
        ASSERT ( NULL != pTemp ) ;
        if ( NULL == pTemp )
        {
            return ( Error ( IDS_OUTOFMEMORY ,
                             GUID_NULL        ,
                             E_OUTOFMEMORY    ) ) ;
        }
    }

    // Everything checked out; now start the real work.

    // Increment the total.
    m_dwCurrCount++ ;

    // Is it time to wrap?
    if ( 100000 == m_dwCurrCount )
    {
        m_dwCurrCount = 0 ;
    }

    // Have the marker pointer start at the beginning of the output
    // buffer.
    OLECHAR * pCurr = m_cOutput.GetDataBuffer ( ) ;

    if ( -1 == m_vbShowItemNumber )
    {
        pCurr += wsprintfW ( pCurr , L"%05d " , m_dwCurrCount ) ;
    }
    if ( -1 == m_vbShowTimeStamps )
    {
        // Show the timestamp based on the user's locale (here at the
        // server, not at the client!). I force the timestamp to use
        // the 24-hour military time format.
        int iLen = GetTimeFormatW ( LOCALE_USER_DEFAULT         ,
                                    LOCALE_NOUSEROVERRIDE     |
                                        TIME_FORCE24HOURFORMAT |
                                        TIME_NOTIMEMARKER      ,
                                    NULL                      ,
                                    NULL                      ,
                                    pCurr                     ,
                                    k_SIZE_TIME               ) ;
```

```
        ASSERT ( 0 != iLen ) ;

        // Move the pointer along, but remember to account for the
        // NULL character.
        pCurr += ( iLen - 1 ) ;

        // GetTimeFormat doesn't tack on the extra space, so add the
        // space now.
        *pCurr = L' ' ;
        pCurr++ ;
    }

    if ( -1 == m_vbShowPID )
    {
        pCurr += wsprintfW ( pCurr , L"[%04X] " , dwPID ) ;
    }

    // Now put the actual message in and copy the NULL terminator as
    // well.
    lstrcpynW ( pCurr , bstrText , iInputLen + 1 ) ;

    // Move pCurr to point at the NULL terminator.
    pCurr += iInputLen ;

    // Check to see whether the string needs CRLFs.
    if ( -1 == m_vbAddCRLF )
    {
        if ( ( L'\x0D' != *( pCurr - 2 ) ) ||
             ( L'\x0A' != *( pCurr - 1 ) )   )
        {
            *( pCurr ) = L'\x0D' ;
            *( pCurr + 1 ) = L'\x0A' ;
            pCurr += 2 ;
            *pCurr = L'\0' ;
        }
    }

    // Is the input supposed to get shot to a kernel debugger?
    if ( -1 == m_vbShowTraceAsODS )
    {
        OutputDebugStringW ( (OLECHAR*) m_cOutput ) ;
    }


    // Calculate the string's length.
    m_cOutput.GetStringByteLength ( ) ;


    // Finally, let viewers know about the trace.
```

(continued)

Listing 11-2 *continued*

```
#ifdef _DEBUG
    HRESULT hr =
#endif
    Fire_TraceEvent ( m_cOutput ) ;

#ifdef _DEBUG
    if ( ! SUCCEEDED ( hr ) )
    {
        ASSERT ( SUCCEEDED ( hr ) ) ;
        TRACE ( _T ( "!!!!!!!!!!!!!!!!!!!!!!!!!!!!!!!!!!!!!\n" ) ) ;
        TRACE ( _T ( "TraceSrv Fire_TraceEvent failed!!\n" ) ) ;
        TRACE ( _T ( "!!!!!!!!!!!!!!!!!!!!!!!!!!!!!!!!!!!!!\n" ) ) ;
    }
#endif

    return ( S_OK ) ;
}
```

Overall, the implementation of TraceSvr is straightforward. The Implement Connection Point command in ClassView makes handling the *IConnectionPoint* code a piece of cake. Compared with the Microsoft Visual C++ 5 ATL Proxy Generator, the Implement Connection Point command is a huge improvement.

I paid careful attention to the *BSTR* string processing. Because I could think of scenarios in which the trace statements would be coming in fast and furiously, I wanted to make sure the strings were handled as rapidly as possible. The *CTrace:: ProcessTrace* function in TRACE.CPP does a lot of string manipulation, especially considering the different items that I can place on the front and the end of the final string output by TraceSrv. I had originally used the *CComBSTR* class for the string manipulation. But when I started stepping through the code and looking at what *CComBSTR* did, I noticed that for almost every method and operator in the class, it allocated or deallocated memory each time with the *SysXXXString* functions. Although using *CComBSTR* is perfectly legitimate in some applications, using it in programs that do a good deal of string manipulation, such as TraceSrv, can result in some real performance problems.

To speed up the string processing, I wrote a simple class named *CFastBSTR* that handles the *BSTR* manipulation directly. The class is in FASTBSTR.H. Its sole job is to allocate a single buffer for the data and to play games with the leading size *DWORD* in the *GetStringByteLength* function. Some developers might argue that I should have stuck religiously with the semantics of Automation *BSTRs*, but I felt that in this case enhanced performance was more important than conservative programming. You can easily change the code in *CFastBSTR* to use the *SysXXXString* functions if the liberties I took with *BSTR* make you uncomfortable.

The only other detail I need to point out is that the project workspace has four different build configurations: debug and release for multibyte character builds and debug and release for Unicode builds. The multibyte builds allow you to register TraceSrv on Windows 98 machines. As I pointed out in Chapter 5, if you're targeting Windows 2000 exclusively, you should compile your programs to use full Unicode. Because I designed TraceSrv as a Windows 2000 service, which definitely won't run on Windows 98, you should compile the version you install on the server machine with one of the Unicode builds.

Now that you've seen a little of the TraceSrv code, I want to cover what happens after you build TraceSrv and want to use it. The Visual C++ 6–based project that's on the companion CD is basically the one that the ATL COM AppWizard generated, so the last step of the build is to register TraceSrv. The registration portions are all part of the ATL code that you get for free, but TraceSrv is registered only as a local server EXE. TraceSrv won't run as a Win32 service unless you specify the *-Service* command-line switch. Although I could've made the service registration part of the build, I chose not to because debugging a Win32 service without a kernel debugger such as SoftICE isn't simple. Also, if you're in the middle of a fix-compile-debug cycle, it's a real pain to have to shell out to a command prompt and run *net stop tracesrv* just to get the build to work. After you've done sufficient debugging and testing with TraceSrv running as a local server, you can register it and run it as a service.

TRACESRV AND DCOMCNFG

You don't have to run TraceSrv as a service to allow access to it across a network—TraceSrv works just as well running as a COM+ remote server. This flexibility is convenient for debugging because all you need to do is start TraceSrv in the debugger and you can watch clients connect to it and debug when appropriate. What worked best for me was to run both the client and TraceSrv under debuggers on their respective machines; when either application hit a breakpoint, I would break on the other to avoid any possible timeout problems. I always compiled the Visual Basic client down to native code and ran it under the Visual C++ debugger. This tactic ensured that when the client hit a breakpoint, it was stopped dead in the debugger. The reason you can't stop the client under the Visual Basic debugger is that the client that connects to TraceSvr is actually the Visual Basic debugger, not the application being debugged.

When you want to use TraceSrv across a network, you need to run the DCOM-CNFG.EXE program to get the proper information set in the registry. The first thing you need to do is to get the default COM+ properties set up for your machine. Because you could leave your machine exposed to some serious security problems, you might want to check with your network administrators before changing the default COM+

properties in a company environment. If you have a small network and are King of the Domain, as I am, you can use the settings listed in Table 11-1. These are the settings that worked best for me on all the machines I tested TraceSrc on.

Table 11-1   DCOMCNFG DEFAULT SETTINGS

On the Default Properties Tab in DCOMCNFG	
Enable Distributed COM On This Computer	Checked
Default Authentication Level	Connect
Default Impersonation Level	Identify

On the Default Security Tab in DCOMCNFG.EXE		
Default Access Permissions	Everyone	Allow Access
	INTERACTIVE	Allow Access
	NETWORK	Allow Access
	SYSTEM	Allow Access
Default Launch Permissions	Administrators	Allow Launch
	Everyone	Allow Launch
	INTERACTIVE	Allow Launch
	NETWORK	Allow Launch
	SYSTEM	Allow Launch
Default Configuration Permissions	Administrators	Full Control
	CREATOR OWNER	Full Control
	Everyone	Read
	INTERACTIVE	Special Access (Check all except Create Link, Write DAC, and Write Owner)
	SYSTEM	Full Control

After you've registered TraceSrv (either as part of the build or with the *-RegServer* command-line switch), start DCOMCNFG, select TraceSrv (or Trace Class on Windows 98), and click the Properties button. I changed settings only on the Location tab. If you want to run TraceSrv only on the local machine, check Run Application On This Computer and leave the other options unchecked. If you want to run TraceSrv only on another machine, check Run Application On The Following Computer, and specify the server. (Note that DCOMCNFG will let you put the current computer name in the box, but then it won't create the server.) To avoid lots of headaches, double-check that all the options on the Security tab are set to use the defaults.

For the most part, you shouldn't have to change the settings in DCOMCNFG. For fun, try setting different security and identity options to see what effect they have on starting and connecting to TraceSrv. If you get into a situation in which you can no longer start TraceSrv, simply run TraceSrv with the *-UnRegServer* command-line switch—the registry will be cleaned out so that you can start fresh again. Automatic registration and unregistration are handy features of ATL.

Now that you know how I designed, built, and set up TraceSrv, you probably think you've reached the end of this chapter. Originally, I thought so too, but then some really nasty bugs showed up when I started using TraceSrv.

INITIAL PROBLEMS WITH TRACESRV

The first problem occurred after I got TraceSrv up and running and had connected to it from multiple client processes. My design requirements state that all clients will use the same instance of TraceSrv. When I was testing, each process that was connecting was getting its own copy of the *ITrace* interface, so there was no way that a trace viewer would ever see the output from multiple processes.

This problem had me stumped because I didn't think it would be that hard to make a single-instance interface. After fumbling around for a day, I was ready to override *IClassFactory::CreateInstance* and force it always to return a single *ITrace* interface. Although this modification would've changed the expected behavior of *CreateInstance*, at least it would've allowed only one instance. Fortunately, while poking through the ATL code, I ran across the *CComClassFactorySingleton* class, which the documentation says is used to create a single instance—exactly what I needed. This class is handled by the *DECLARE_CLASSFACTORY_SINGLETON (CTrace)* macro in TRACE.H. This bug was caused by my ignorance of ATL.

Once I started using TraceSrv, I noticed that *CComBSTR* was doing all those allocations and deallocations on almost every method call. After developing the *CFastBSTR* class, I thought I was ready for smooth testing. As I started testing various scenarios, I was getting an assertion at the end of *CTrace::ProcessTrace*, which you can see in Listing 11-2. In TraceSrv, I'm using the assertion macros that I introduced in Chapter 3, and because TraceSrv is designed to be a service, I called *SetDiagAssertOptions* and turned off the message box display.

I was getting the assertion when I was running TraceSrv with no viewers attached. I walked through *Fire_TraceEvent* code, which was generated by the Implement Connection Point command in the integrated development environment (IDE), and noticed something very interesting. The code for the original *Fire_TraceEvent* is shown in Listing 11-3. Take a careful look at the code and see whether you can spot the bug.

```
HRESULT Fire_TraceEvent( BSTR bstrText )
{
    CComVariant varResult;
    T* pT = static_cast<T*>( this );
    int nConnectionIndex;
    CComVariant* pvars = new CComVariant[1];
    int nConnections = m_vec.GetSize( );

    for ( nConnectionIndex = 0;
          nConnectionIndex < nConnections;
          nConnectionIndex++ )
    {
        pT->Lock();
        CComPtr<IUnknown> sp = m_vec.GetAt( nConnectionIndex );
        pT->Unlock( );
        IDispatch* pDispatch = reinterpret_cast<IDispatch*>( sp.p );
        if (pDispatch != NULL)
        {
            VariantClear( &varResult );
            pvars[0] = bstrText;
            DISPPARAMS disp = { pvars, NULL, 1, 0 };
            pDispatch->Invoke( 0x1,
                               IID_NULL,
                               LOCALE_USER_DEFAULT,
                               DISPATCH_METHOD,
                               &disp,
                               &varResult,
                               NULL,
                               NULL );
        }
    }
    delete[] pvars;
    return varResult.scode;
}
```

Listing 11-3 Fire_TraceEvent *with a bug*

Keep in mind that my assertion triggered only when I didn't have any viewers attached to TraceSrv. As you look carefully at *Fire_TraceEvent*, you'll see that the *for* loop never executes when a viewer isn't attached. However, the generated code returns *varResult.scode*, which is initialized only inside the *for* loop. Consequently, the function returns an uninitialized value when no viewers are attached. In debug builds, *Fire_TraceEvent* was returning 0xCCCCCCCC, the fill pattern the /GZ compiler switch puts into local variables.

The workaround to the uninitialized variable problem was rather simple. I renamed the file that Implement Connection Point generated, TRACESRVCP.H, to CORRECTEDTRACESRVCP.H, and after the declaration of *varResult*, I set *varResult.scode* equal to *S_OK*. Although using uninitialized variables isn't a recommended programming practice, at least the Visual C++ developers are now returning the results of *IDispatch::Invoke* calls. In previous versions of Visual C++, they didn't. Once I fixed this small problem, TraceSrv was up and running fairly well.

Before I can wrap up this chapter, I need to cover TraceView, Win32 security, and calling TraceSrv from your code.

TRACEVIEW AND SECURITY

TraceSrv by itself is useful, but a viewer that shows the trace statements really enhances it. I wrote TraceView in Visual Basic because it was fairly simple to do. When you look at the source code for TraceView, you shouldn't see much that hasn't been done before.

I tried to make TraceView a little more useful than a plain edit control by giving it a toolbar and a status bar as well as adding support for saving and restoring the window position, saving files, searching forward and backward, and allowing the window to stay on top. For internalization ease, I kept all the strings in a resource file instead of hard-coding them. I won't get into the resource string loading, but I will mention that I modified the generated *LoadResStrings* function (which I renamed *LoadFormResStrings*) so that it notifies you about which resource items failed to load.

When I first started using TraceView, it worked great. Nevertheless, when I started testing all the different ways to connect TraceView to TraceSrv, I encountered some problems. If TraceView and TraceSrv were on the same machine, TraceView could connect to TraceSrv if it ran as a service or as a local server. TraceView could also connect properly if TraceSrv ran as a local server on another machine using COM+. When I tried to have TraceView connect to TraceSrv running as a COM+ service on another machine, however, it would always fail, giving me the Visual Basic error message "Run-time error -2147023071 (80070721) Automation Error." I looked up the error value in WINERROR.H; the ID is *RPC_S_SEC_PKG_ERROR*, "A security package specific error occurred."

I had never seen this error ID before. When I searched MSDN for it, all I got back was that it was in WINERROR.H and that it was listed in the system error appendixes. After fiddling with this problem for several days, I found that I could get a Visual Basic–based program to connect to the remote TraceSrv service only if I didn't use the *WithEvents* keyword in the declaration of the *Trace* object. If I used the *WithEvents* keyword, I'd always get the *RPC_S_SEC_PKG_ ERROR* error. I was perplexed by this bug until a friend pointed out that I didn't have the security for the service set correctly.

When I stepped back and walked through what happened, the bug started to make sense. The *WithEvents* keyword sets up an *IConnectionPoint* interface that the server uses to call in to the client—in essence a callback. To call back in to the client, the server must have the correct security permissions. When TraceSrv runs on the same machine as TraceView, TraceSrv—whether started as a local server or as a service— runs under the same user identification as TraceView or is trusted. Running TraceSrv on one machine as a COM+ remote server and TraceView on another machine worked because I was lucky. On both Windows NT Workstation machines without a domain controller, I was logged in as "John" with the same password. According to Knowledge Base article Q158508, "COM Security Frequently Asked Questions," Windows NT Workstation "falls back to a 'matching account names and passwords' mode. If you use the same ASCII names on the two machines running Windows NT Workstation and the accounts have the same passwords, then DCOM and other [Windows] NT security (such as filesystem) should work as though you were really logged on to the two machines with the same account." When I logged on to the remote machine as "Bob," started TraceSrv as a remote server, and tried to connect TraceView on the client machine logged on as "John," I got the *RPC_S_SEC_PKG_ERROR* error. My test case, running TraceSrv as a remote server on a separate machine, didn't take into account all the permutations for connections.

Getting a remote server started with proper security is fairly easy—just log on as a user who has network permission—but getting a Win32 service working with proper security takes a little more effort. By default, Win32 services have no security credentials, so TraceSrv caused a security error whenever it tried to do anything with the *IConnectionPoint* interface it was passed. What I needed was a way to have the client tell COM+ the security level it will allow for its own interfaces. You specify the security level for your client's interfaces through the *CoInitializeSecurity* function call, which should be called immediately after your application calls *CoInitialize*. In TraceView, which is written in Visual Basic, calling *CoInitializeSecurity* won't work. If you try calling *CoInitializeSecurity* as the first statement in your *Sub Main*, you'll get the error code 0x80010119 (*RPC_E_ TOO_LATE*), which means "Security must be initialized before any interfaces are marshaled or unmarshaled. It cannot be changed once initialized." As you can see, Visual Basic is happily marshaling away long before your code ever gets called.

You can get around this Visual Basic roadblock in two ways. The first way is to fire up DCOMCNFG and set the Default Authentication Level (on the Default Properties tab) to None. Although this solution might be fine for my little sealed network at home, it isn't the best fix in a real development shop. The second approach is more secure and appropriate: on the machine that will be running TraceSrv, register TraceSrv as a service, start up Control Panel, and click the Services icon. Select the TraceSrv entry, and click the Start Service button. Click the Properties button to display the TraceSrv Properties dialog box. On the Log On tab, under Log On As, select the This Account radio button and type the user name and password for the account TraceSrv is supposed to use in order to run. Now the service will be able to get the security it needs from a known account on the network. As the "COM Security Frequently Asked Questions" article points out, "Localsystem is a very privileged account locally.... However, it has no network privileges and cannot leave the machine via any [Windows] NT-secured mechanism, including file system, named pipes, DCOM, or secure RPC." Once I got the service started under the proper account, TraceView worked fine. If you're working with a domain server, you might want to consider creating a specific account that you can use just for starting tools such as TraceSrv. For example, if you have a Build account that your build machines use to send mail, you might want to use that.

USING TRACESRV

As you can imagine, using TraceSrv is fairly easy. In fact, after all the fun of getting the service running, explaining the details would be anticlimactic. The code on the companion CD calls TraceSrv from three different languages. I wanted to show you the VBScript example, which is in Listing 11-4, to give you an idea of how easy TraceSrv is to use. The C++ example is more interesting in that you need to convert your trace strings to *BSTR*s before you can call in to TraceSrv. Listing 11-5 show the DCOMTEST.CPP program in action.

```
<SCRIPT LANGUAGE="VBScript"><!--
Dim g_TraceObj
set g_TraceObj = CreateObject ( "TraceSrv.Trace.1" )
g_TraceObj.Trace( "This is a test of the...?" + vbCRLF )

Sub ButtonOne_OnClick
    g_TraceObj.Trace ( "Hey! I'm Button One!" + vbCRLF )
End Sub
Sub ButtonTwo_OnClick
    g_TraceObj.Trace ( "VBScript is dangerous!" + vbCRLF )
End Sub
--></SCRIPT>
```

Listing 11-4 *Calling TraceSrv from VBScript*

```
void main ( void )
{
    HRESULT       hr ;
    ITrace *      lpTrace ;
    IUnknown *    lpUnknown ;


    // Initialize the COM+ libraries.
    hr = CoInitializeEx ( NULL , COINIT_APARTMENTTHREADED ) ;
    if ( FAILED ( hr ) )
    {
        printf ( "Unable to initialize COM+\n" ) ;
        return ;
    }


    hr = CoCreateInstance ( CLSID_Trace      ,
                            NULL             ,
                            CLSCTX_SERVER    ,
                            IID_IUnknown     ,
                            (LPVOID*)&lpUnknown ) ;
    if ( FAILED ( hr ) )
    {
        LPVOID lpMsgBuf;

        FormatMessage( FORMAT_MESSAGE_ALLOCATE_BUFFER |
                       FORMAT_MESSAGE_FROM_SYSTEM |
                       FORMAT_MESSAGE_IGNORE_INSERTS,
                       NULL,
                       hr,
                       MAKELANGID ( LANG_NEUTRAL, SUBLANG_DEFAULT ),
                       (LPTSTR) &lpMsgBuf,
                       0,
                       NULL );
        printf ( "CoCreateInstanceEx failed: 0x%08X\n" , hr ) ;
        printf ( "FormatMessage returned: %s\n" , lpMsgBuf ) ;
        return ;
    }


    hr = lpUnknown->QueryInterface ( IID_ITrace       ,
                                     (LPVOID*)&lpTrace ) ;
    lpUnknown->Release ( ) ;
    if ( FAILED ( hr ) )
    {
        LPVOID lpMsgBuf;
```

Listing 11-5 *Calling TraceSrv from a C++ program* (DCOMTEST.CPP)

```
                FormatMessage( FORMAT_MESSAGE_ALLOCATE_BUFFER |
                               FORMAT_MESSAGE_FROM_SYSTEM |
                               FORMAT_MESSAGE_IGNORE_INSERTS,
                               NULL,
                               hr,
                               MAKELANGID ( LANG_NEUTRAL, SUBLANG_DEFAULT ),
                               (LPTSTR) &lpMsgBuf,
                               0,
                               NULL );
        printf ( "QueryInterface failed: 0x%08X\n" , hr ) ;
        printf ( "FormatMessage returned: %s\n" , lpMsgBuf ) ;
        return ;
    }


    OLECHAR * pszTemp ;

    pszTemp = SysAllocString ( OLESTR ( "Hello from a C++ program!!!" ) );
    lpTrace->Trace ( pszTemp ) ;
    SysFreeString ( pszTemp ) ;


    lpTrace->Release ( ) ;


    CoUninitialize ( ) ;
}
```

SUMMARY

Armed with TraceSrv, you now have a way to start debugging your cross-language, cross-process, cross-machine applications. The requirements for TraceSrv and most of its implementation are fairly simple, but TraceSrv is one of those applications that let you get into the morass of Windows 2000 security issues. Because more and more of our development is COM-based, security is becoming a much greater part of our daily programming lives. With security adding another layer in which programs can fail in strange and subtle new ways, you need to devote some time to mastering security. As I pointed out in Chapter 1, the more you know about the operating system, the faster you'll be able to solve problems. That advice is true for security problems as well as for other, more traditional, bugs.

I encourage you to experiment with TraceSrv in your applications. Never underestimate the power of tracing—it can be one of the best debugging tools in your arsenal.

Chapter 12

Multithreaded Deadlocks

Without a doubt, the hardest problems to solve in modern software development are multithreaded deadlocks. Even if you think you planned for every situation, your multithreaded application can stop dead when you least expect it. The biggest obstacle to debugging multithreaded deadlocks is that by the time your application is deadlocked, it's almost too late to start debugging.

In this chapter, I'll go over some tricks and techniques that have worked for me when I've done multithreaded programming. I'll also present a utility I wrote, Deadlock-Detection, that lets you see the flow of events that led up to your deadlock, which is about the only evidence you'll have to help you track down what went wrong and figure out how to avoid the same deadlock in the future. The information in this chapter and the DeadlockDetection utility will help you avoid the minefield of multithreaded deadlocks.

MULTITHREADING TIPS AND TRICKS

As I've been emphasizing throughout this book, one of the keys to debugging is up-front planning. With multithreaded programming, up-front planning is the only way you can avoid the dreaded deadlocks. I break down the necessary planning for multithreaded applications into the following categories:

- Don't do it
- Multithread only small, discrete pieces
- Synchronize at the lowest level
- Review the code—and review the code again
- Test on multiprocessor machines

Don't Do It

This first tip might seem a little facetious, but I'm absolutely serious. Make sure there's no other way you can structure your program before you decide to incorporate multithreading into your application. When you include multithreading in your application, you're easily adding a minimum of an extra month of development and testing to your schedule.

If you need your program to do some lightweight background processing, check to see whether the work can be handled either through the Microsoft Foundation Class (MFC) library *OnIdle* processing or through a background periodic timer event. With a little creative thinking, you can probably find a way to avoid multithreading and the headaches that go with it.

Multithread Only Small, Discrete Pieces

If you must multithread, try to keep it to small, discrete pieces. The rule of thumb I use is to not multithread the user interface (UI). Stick to small pieces of work that are generally devoid of any UI elements. For example, printing in the background is a smart use of multithreading because your application's UI will be able to accept input while data is printing.

Synchronize at the Lowest Level

Put your synchronization methods at the lowest level possible in your code. If you need a critical section for protecting a piece of data, put *EnterCriticalSection* and *LeaveCriticalSection* around just the actual data access. This placement ensures that you're indeed protecting only the item you're supposed to protect and nothing more. Restricting the scope of your synchronization objects is your best defense against inadvertent deadlocks. One of the nastiest deadlock problems I ever caused was the result of grabbing the synchronization object two functions above where I should have.

Review the Code—And Review the Code Again

If you really do need to multithread your application, you must allow plenty of time to walk through your multithreaded code in full code reviews. The trick is to assign one person to each thread in your code and one person to each synchronization object. In many ways, the code review in multithreaded programming is really a "multithreaded" review.

When you review the code, pretend that each thread is running at real-time priority on its own dedicated CPU. Each "thread person" walks through the code paying attention only to the particular code that his thread is supposed to be executing. When the "thread person" is ready to acquire a synchronization object, the "object person" literally moves behind the "thread person." When the "thread person" releases a synchronization object, the "object person" goes to a neutral corner of the room. In addition to the thread and object representatives, you should have some developers who are monitoring the overall thread activity so that they can assess the program's flow and help determine the points at which different threads deadlock.

As you're working through the code review, keep in mind that the operating system has its own synchronization objects that it applies to your process and that those objects can cause deadlocks as well. The process critical section, explained in the Debugging War Story sidebar "The Deadlock Makes No Sense" on the following page, and the infamous Microsoft Windows 98 Win16 mutex are both synchronization objects that the operating system uses in your process. Message handling can also cause deadlocks if you're not careful. If thread A is a UI thread and is waiting for a critical section currently owned by thread B, and if thread B sends a message to an *HWND* in thread A via *SendMessage*, you'll deadlock. Again, be sure to monitor these activities during your code review.

Test on Multiprocessor Machines

As I mentioned, a multithreaded application requires a much higher level of testing than a single-threaded one. The most important tip I have for testing your multithreaded application is to test it thoroughly on multiprocessor machines. And I don't mean simply running your application through a few paces; I mean continually testing your program in all possible scenarios. Even if your application runs perfectly on single-processor machines, a multiprocessor machine will turn up deadlocks you never thought possible.

The best approach to this kind of testing is to have the team's developers running the application on multiprocessor machines every day. If you're a manager and you don't have any multiprocessor machines in your shop, stop reading right now and immediately equip half your developers and QA testers with multiprocessor machines! If you're a developer without a multiprocessor machine, show this chapter to your manager and demand the proper equipment to do your job!

DEADLOCKDETECTION REQUIREMENTS

As you might have noticed in the preceding tips and tricks section, I didn't provide any suggestions about what to do when an unexpected deadlock paralyzes your code. The recommendations there were more preventive measures you can take to try to avoid deadlocks in the first place rather than prescriptions for fixing them whey they do occur. In this section, you'll see that solving deadlocks isn't easy with just the debugger and that you almost always need some additional help. A utility that can come to your rescue when you need that extra assistance is DeadlockDetection.

Here's the list of basic requirements I worked with when I developed DeadlockDetection:

1. Show exactly where the deadlock happens in the user's code. A tool that tells only that *EnterCriticalSection* is blocked doesn't help much. To be really effective, the tool needs to let you get back to the address, and consequently the source file and line number, where the deadlock occurred so that you can fix it quickly.

DEBUGGING WAR STORY

The Deadlock Makes No Sense

The Battle

A team (that I wasn't a member of) was developing an application and ran into a nasty deadlock that made no sense. After struggling with the deadlock for a couple of days—an ordeal that brought development to a standstill—the team asked me to come help them figure out the bug.

The product they were working on had an interesting architecture and was heavily multithreaded. The deadlock they were running into occurred only at a certain time, and it always happened in the middle of a series of dynamic-link library (DLL) loads. The program deadlocked when *WaitForSingleObject* was called to check whether a thread was able to create some shared objects.

The team was good and had already double-checked and triple-checked their code for potential deadlocks—but they remained completely stumped. I asked if they had walked through the code to check for deadlocks, and they assured me that they had.

The Outcome

I remember this situation fondly because it was one of the few times that I've gotten to look like a hero within 5 minutes of starting the debugger. Once the team duplicated the deadlock, I took a quick look at the Call Stack window and noticed that the program was waiting on a thread handle inside *DllMain*. As part of their architecture, when a certain DLL loads, that DLL's *DllMain* starts another thread and then immediately calls *WaitForSingleObject* on an acknowledge event object to ensure that the spawned thread was able to properly initialize some important shared objects before continuing with the rest of the *DllMain* processing.

What the team didn't know is that each process has something called a "process critical section" that the operating system uses to synchronize various

---

2. Show what synchronization object caused the deadlock.

3. Show what Windows function is blocked and the parameters passed to the function. It helps to see timeout values and the values passed to the function.

4. Determine which thread caused the deadlock.

5. The utility must be lightweight so that it interferes with the user's program as little as possible.

---

actions that happen behind the scenes in a process. One situation in which the process critical section is used is to serialize the execution of *DllMain* for the four cases in which *DllMain* is called: *DLL_PROCESS_ATTACH*, *DLL_THREAD_ATTACH*, *DLL_THREAD_DETACH*, and *DLL_PROCESS_DETACH*. The second parameter to *DllMain* indicates the reason the call to *DllMain* occurred.

In the team's application, the call to *LoadLibrary* caused the operating system to grab the process critical section so that the operating system could call the DLL's *DllMain* for the *DLL_PROCESS_ATTACH* case. The DLL's *DllMain* function then spawned a second thread. Whenever a process spawns a new thread, the operating system grabs the process critical section so that it can call the *DllMain* function of each loaded DLL for the *DLL_THREAD_ATTACH* case. In this particular program, the second thread blocked because the first thread was holding the process critical section. Unfortunately, the first thread then called *WaitForSingleObject* to ensure that the second thread was able to properly initialize some shared objects. Because the second thread was blocked on the process critical section, held by the first thread, and the first thread blocked while waiting on the second thread, the result was the usual deadlock.

The Lesson

The obvious lesson is to avoid doing any *Wait** calls inside *DllMain*. However, the issues with the process critical section extend beyond the *Wait** functions. The operating system acquires the process critical section behind your back in *CreateProcess*, *GetModuleFileName*, *GetProcAddress*, *LoadLibrary*, and *FreeLibrary*, so you shouldn't call any of these functions in *DllMain*. Because *DllMain* acquires the process critical section, only one thread at a time is ever executing a *DllMain*.

As you can see, even experienced developers can get bitten by multithreaded bugs—and as I mentioned earlier, this kind of bug is often in the place you least expect it.

6. The information output processing must be extensible. The information collected in a deadlock detection system can be processed in many ways, and the utility needs to allow others, not just you, to extend the information as they see fit.

7. The tool must integrate easily with the user's programs.

One of the key points to keep in mind with a utility such as DeadlockDetection is that it definitely affects the behavior of the application it's observing. Once again, it's the Heisenberg uncertainty principle in action. DeadlockDetection can produce deadlocks in your programs you might not otherwise see because the work it does to gather information slows down your threads. I almost defined this behavior as a feature because any time you can cause a deadlock in your code, you've identified a bug, which is the first step toward correcting it—and as always, it's better for you to find the bugs than for your customers to find them.

HIGH-LEVEL DESIGN ISSUES WITH DEADLOCKDETECTION

I had to figure out how to implement DeadlockDetection given the preceding requirements. I first needed to determine what functions I needed to monitor so that I could report the complete deadlock trace. Table 12-1 lists all the functions, grouped by type, I decided I needed to monitor to implement DeadlockDetection.

After pondering the problem of how to collect the information I needed to satisfy the first four requirements, I realized that I was going to have to intercept (or hook) the functions in Table 12-1 to record the acquisition and release of synchronization objects. Hooking functions isn't a trivial task, and I'll explain how I implemented the code in the section "Hooking Imported Functions" later in this chapter. The one constraint that hooking imported functions imposed on DeadlockDetection is that the code for DeadlockDetection must reside in a DLL because the hooks apply only to the address space in which they're created. This constraint means that the user must load the DeadlockDetection DLL into her address space, a requirement that isn't too harsh given the benefits. As a DLL, the utility would integrate easily with a user program, a condition specified in requirement 7 in the list in the preceding section.

Gathering the information to satisfy requirements 1 through 4 follows as a direct consequence of choosing the in-process function hooking approach. This approach means that each of the multithreading and synchronization functions will be calling directly into the DeadlockDetection code with all the information I need.

Making DeadlockDetection as lightweight as possible (requirement 5) was a tough condition to satisfy. I tried to code efficiently, but efficient code went only so far toward fulfilling the goal I set out to achieve. Figuring that you would know best

Table 12-1 **FUNCTIONS THAT DEADLOCKDETECTION MONITORS**

Type	*Function*
Thread-related functions	*CreateThread*
	ExitThread
	SuspendThread
	ResumeThread
	TerminateThread
Critical-section functions	*InitializeCriticalSection*
	InitializeCriticalSectionAndSpinCount
	DeleteCriticalSection
	EnterCriticalSection
	LeaveCriticalSection
	SetCriticalSectionSpinCount
	TryEnterCriticalSection
Mutex functions	*CreateMutexA*
	CreateMutexW
	OpenMutexA
	OpenMutexW
	ReleaseMutex
Semaphore functions	*CreateSemaphoreA*
	CreateSemaphoreW
	OpenSemaphoreA
	OpenSemaphoreW
	ReleaseSemaphore
Event functions	*CreateEventA*
	CreateEventW
	OpenEventA
	OpenEventW
	PulseEvent
	ResetEvent
	SetEvent
Blocking functions	*WaitForSingleObject*
	WaitForSingleObjectEx
	WaitForMultipleObjects
	WaitForMultipleObjectsEx
	MsgWaitForMultipleObjects
	MsgWaitForMultipleObjectsEx
	SignalObjectAndWait
Special functions	*CloseHandle*
	ExitProcess
	GetProcAddress

what types of synchronization objects you're using in your program, I grouped the object types so that you can specify just those functions you want to hook. For example, if you're concerned only about deadlock problems on mutexes, you can process only mutex functions.

To make DeadlockDetection even more useful, you can specify, on the fly, which sets of synchronization object functions you want to watch. You can also turn DeadlockDetection on and off as many times as needed. You might even want to give your application an accelerator key or a special menu option that toggles the entire DeadlockDetection system. Allowing this narrow scope meets requirement 5 and helps with requirement 7.

The only requirement left is 6: making the output processing as extensible as possible. I wanted to give you the ability to slice and dice the output, rather than force you to make do with some arbitrary, hard-coded format. By keeping the main hooking and processing separate from the output code, I can achieve greater code reuse because the only part being changed, the output side, is much easier to develop than the core side. I named the output portions DeadlockDetection extensions, or DeadDetExt for short. A DeadDetExt is simply a DLL that has several exported functions that DeadlockDetection looks for and calls when appropriate.

Now it's time to explain how to use DeadlockDetection. If you understand the requirements I set out and understand how to use this utility, you'll find it easier to see how I implemented it.

Using DeadlockDetection

The first step in using DeadlockDetection is to put DEADLOCKDETECTION.DLL, its initialization file, and the appropriate DeadDetExt DLL in the same place. The initialization file is a simple INI file that, at a minimum, must specify the name of the DeadDetExt file to load. The following sample is a DEADLOCKDETECTION.INI file that loads the supplied TEXTFILEDDEXT.DLL:

```
[Initialization]
; The only mandatory value, the name of the DeadDetExt
; file that will handle the output
ExtDll = "TextFileDDExt.dll"
; If StartInDllMain is 1, DeadlockDetection will
; initialize in its DllMain so that logging can start
; at the earliest possible time.
StartInDllMain = 0
; If StartInDllMain is 1, InitialOpts specifies the
; initial options for DeadlockDetection. This value is a
; combination of the DDOPT_* flags.
; InitialOpts = 0
```

As you can see from some of the INI settings, DeadlockDetection can initialize just by having *LoadLibrary* called on it. A good proactive debugging idea would be to create a backdoor in your application initialization that calls *LoadLibrary* on the specified DLL name if your application sees a special registry key or an environment variable. This alternate approach to initializing your application would mean that you wouldn't need conditional compilation and you'd have a means of getting DLLs into your address space cleanly. Of course, all this assumes that the DLLs you're loading in this way are smart enough to initialize themselves completely in their *DllMain*s and don't require you to call any other exported functions in the DLL.

Having your code set the DeadlockDetection initialization options, rather than using an INI file, means that you'll need to include DEADLOCKDETECTION.H in your application and have your application link against DEADLOCKDETECTION.LIB. If you want to initialize DeadlockDetection yourself, all you need to do is call *OpenDeadlockDetection* when appropriate. *OpenDeadlockDetection* takes a single parameter, the initial reporting options. Table 12-2 lists all the *DDOPT_** flags. You'll want to call *OpenDeadlockDetection* before your application starts creating threads so that you can record all the key information about your synchronization objects.

At any point, you can change the reporting options by calling *SetDeadlockDetection-Options*. This function takes the same OR'd set of flags as the *OpenDeadlockDetection* function. To see what the current options are, call *GetDeadlockDetectionOptions*. You can change the current options as many times as you like during your program's execution. If you want to suspend and resume logging, call the *SuspendDeadlock-Detection* and *ResumeDeadlockDetection* functions.

Along with the DeadlockDetection source code on the companion CD, I've included a DeadDetExt DLL that I wrote, TEXTFILEDDEXT.DLL. This relatively simple extension writes all the information to a text file. When you run DeadlockDetection with TEXTFILEDDEXT.DLL, the extension creates a text file in the same directory as the executable program. The text file will use the name of the executable with a DD extension. For example, if you run SIMPTEST.EXE, the resulting file will be SIMPTEST.DD. Listing 12-1 shows some sample output from TEXTFILEDDEXT.DLL.

Table 12-2 DEADLOCKDETECTION REPORTING OPTIONS

Flag	*Limits Logging to*
DDOPT_THREADS	Thread-related functions
DDOPT_CRITSEC	Critical-section functions
DDOPT_MUTEX	Mutex functions
DDOPT_SEMAPHORE	Semaphore functions
DDOPT_EVENT	Event functions
DDOPT_ALL	All hooked functions

```
TID         Ret Addr    C/R Ret Value  Function & Params
0x000000F7 [0x004011AC] (R) 0x00000000 InitializeCriticalSection 0x00403110
0x000000F7 [0x004011C6] (R) 0x00000290 CreateEventA 0x00000000, 1, 0,
                                          0x004030F0 [The event name]
0x000000F7 [0x004011E9] (R) 0x00000294 CreateThread 0x00000000, 0x00000000,
                                          0x00401000, 0x00000000,
                                          0x00000000, 0x0012FF68
0x000000F7 [0x0040120C] (R) 0x00000298 CreateThread 0x00000000, 0x00000000,
                                          0x004010BC, 0x00000000,
                                          0x00000000, 0x0012FF68
0x000000F7 [0x00401223] (C)            EnterCriticalSection 0x00403110
0x000000F7 [0x00401223] (R) 0x00000000 EnterCriticalSection 0x00403110
0x000000F7 [0x00401238] (C)            WaitForSingleObject 0x00000290,
                                          INFINITE
0x000000FF [0x1020B973] (C)            EnterCriticalSection 0x1025CE90
0x000000FF [0x1020B973] (R) 0x00000000 EnterCriticalSection 0x1025CE90
0x0000010C [0x004010F3] (R) 0x000002A4 OpenEventA 0x001F0003, 0, 0x004030BC
                                          [The event name]
```

Listing 12-1 *DeadlockDetection output using TESTFILEDDEXT.DLL*

Notice that the function and parameter information is wrapped in Listing 12-1 to display on the page. The output shows the information in the following order:

1. The ID of the executing thread.

2. The return address to indicate which of your functions called the synchronization function. Using the CrashFinder utility from Chapter 8, you can look up the return addresses and discover how you got into the deadlock situations.

3. The call or return indicator to help identify actions that occur before and after specific functions.

4. The return value of the function if your program is reporting function returns.

5. The synchronization function name.

6. The parameter list for the synchronization function. Items in brackets are the human-readable data. I concentrated on showing string values, but it would be trivial to add more data, such as individual flags.

When you run your application and it deadlocks, kill the process and view the output file to see the last synchronization item called. TEXTFILEDDEXT.DLL keeps the file up to date by flushing the file buffers each time you call a *WaitFor** function, *EnterCriticalSection*, or *TryEnterCriticalSection*.

A word of caution: if you turn on full logging of all functions, you can generate some extremely large files in no time. Using the MTGDI Visual C++ sample application, I generated an 11-MB text file in a minute or two by creating a couple of threads.

IMPLEMENTING DEADLOCKDETECTION

As you can see, using DeadlockDetection is fairly simple. Beneath the simplicity of use, however, is a fairly sophisticated implementation. The first part of Deadlock-Detection's implementation I'll go over is how to hook functions.

Hooking Imported Functions

There are many ways to hook the function calls a program makes. The hard way is to hunt down all the CALL instructions and replace the address with one of your own. This approach is difficult and extremely error prone. Fortunately, with Deadlock-Detection, the functions I need to hook are imported functions and are much easier to handle than CALL instructions.

An imported function is a function that comes out of a DLL. For example, when your program calls *OutputDebugString*, it's calling a function that resides in KERNEL32.DLL. When I first started doing Microsoft Win32–based programming, I thought that calling an imported function would be just like calling any other function—a CALL or branch instruction would jump to an address and start executing the imported function. The only difference might be that with an imported function the operating system program loader would have to run through the executable and fix up the addresses to reflect where the DLL being called would be loaded into memory. When I looked at how a call to an imported function really is implemented, I was amazed at the simplicity and beauty of the design.

The problem with the way I was thinking becomes apparent when you consider how many API functions there are and that you can easily call the same ones many times throughout your program. If the loader had to find and replace each occurrence of a call to *OutputDebugString*, for example, loading a program could take forever. Even if the linker generated a complete table that specified where each call to *OutputDebugString* took place in the code, the huge amount of looping and memory writing would make load times excruciatingly slow.

So how does the loader tell your application where to find an imported function? The solution is fiendishly clever. If you think about where the calls to *Output-DebugString* go, you'll soon realize that each call must go to the same address: the address where *OutputDebugString* is loaded into memory. Of course, your application can't know this address ahead of time, so instead, all your *OutputDebugString* calls get routed through a single, indirect address. When the program loader loads your executable and its dependent DLLs, the loader fixes up this one indirect address so that it corresponds to the final load address of *OutputDebugString*. The compiler makes this indirect addressing work by generating a jump to the indirect address any time your code calls the imported function. This indirect address is stored in the *.idata* (or import) section of the executable. If you import through *__declspec(dllimport)*, instead of being an indirect jump, the code is an indirect call, thus saving a couple of instructions per function call.

Hooking an imported function is a matter of finding the imports section of the executable, looking for the address of the particular function you want to hook, and then writing the hook function address in its place. Although hunting down and replacing function addresses might sound like a lot of work, it's not that bad because the Win32 Portable Executable (PE) file format is so nicely organized.

In Chapter 10 of his excellent book *Windows 95 System Programming Secrets* (IDG Books, 1995), Matt Pietrek describes a method for hooking imported functions. Matt's code simply finds a module's imports section and, using the value returned from a call to *GetProcAddress*, loops through the imported functions. When Matt's code finds the function it's looking for, it overwrites the original imported function address with the hook function.

Not surprisingly, given that 1995 is a past lifetime in software development circles, two small issues have changed since Matt's book came out. The first is that when Matt wrote his book, most developers didn't merge their imports section with other PE sections. Therefore, if the imports section is in read-only memory, you cause an access violation by writing the hook address. I fixed the read-only memory issue by setting the virtual memory protection to read-write before the hook function address is written to memory. The second issue, which is a little tougher to work around, is that under certain conditions you can't hook imported functions under Windows 98.

When you use DeadlockDetection, you want to be able to have the threading functions redirected any time you run your application, even when the application is running under the debugger. Although you wouldn't think that hooking functions while running under a debugger would be a problem, it is. In Microsoft Windows 2000, or when running a program in Windows 98 outside a debugger, when you call *GetProcAddress* to find a function and then look through the imports section for that address, you'll always find it. But under Windows 98, calling *GetProcAddress* in your program while it's running under a debugger returns a different address than when it runs outside a debugger. What *GetProcAddress* actually returns when running under the debugger is a *debug thunk*—a special wrapper around the real call.

Windows 98 doesn't implement copy-on-write in the operating system, as I explained in Chapter 4. The debug thunk returned when running under a debugger is a means by which Windows 98 keeps debuggers from attempting to step into system functions above the 2-GB line. Overall, the lack of copy-on-write isn't much of an issue for most developers—only those who write debuggers or who want to hook functions correctly whether or not they're running under a debugger.

Fortunately, getting the real address for an imported function isn't too difficult—it just takes a little more work, and you have to avoid *GetProcAddress*. The PE file *IMAGE_IMPORT_DESCRIPTOR* structure, which holds all the information about functions imported from a specific DLL, has pointers to two arrays in the executable. These arrays are called import address tables (IATs), or sometimes thunk data arrays. The first pointer references the real IAT, which the program loader fixes up when the executable is loaded. The second pointer references the original IAT, which is untouched by the loader and lists the imported functions. To find the real imported function address, simply work your way through the original IAT until you find the named function that you want to hook, and then write the hook address in the corresponding entry in the real IAT, which the program is using. By taking this extra step, the hooking code will always work no matter where it's called.

Listing 12-2 shows *HookImportedFunctionsByName*, the function I wrote to take care of your hooking needs. Table 12-3 shows the parameters to *HookImported-FunctionsByName* and describes each one. Because I wanted to make the hooking as generic as possible, I went to the trouble of allowing you to hook multiple functions imported from the same DLL at the same time. As its name implies, the *HookImportedFunctionsByName* function will hook only those functions imported by name. In Chapter 14, I'll discuss how to hook functions imported by ordinal value as part of the LIMODS utility.

Table 12-3 *HookImportedFunctionsByName* Parameter Descriptions

Parameter	Description
hModule	The module in which the imports will be hooked.
szImportMod	The name of the module whose functions are imported.
uiCount	The number of functions to hook. This parameter is the size of the *paHookArray* and *paOrigFuncs* arrays.
paHookArray	The array of function descriptor structures that list which functions to hook. The array doesn't have to be in *szFunc* name order (though it's wise to keep the array sorted in function name order, because I might implement better searching in the future). Also, if a particular *pProc* is *NULL*, *HookImportedFunctionsByName* skips that item. The structure for each element in *paHookArray* is simply the name of the function to hook and a pointer to the new hook procedure. Because you might want to hook or unhook functions at will, *HookImportedFunctionsByName* returns all the original imported function addresses.
paOrigFuncs	The array of original addresses hooked by *HookImportedFunctions-ByName*. If a function wasn't hooked, that item index will be *NULL*.
pdwHooked	Returns the number of functions hooked out of *paHookArray*.

```
BOOL BUGSUTIL_DLLINTERFACE __stdcall
        HookImportedFunctionsByName ( HMODULE          hModule    ,
                                      LPCSTR           szImportMod ,
                                      UINT             uiCount    ,
                                      LPHOOKFUNCDESCA  paHookArray ,
                                      PROC *           paOrigFuncs ,
                                      LPDWORD          pdwHooked   )
{
    // Assert the parameters.
    ASSERT ( FALSE == IsBadReadPtr ( hModule                    ,
                                     sizeof ( IMAGE_DOS_HEADER ) ) ) ;
    ASSERT ( FALSE == IsBadStringPtr ( szImportMod , MAX_PATH ) ) ;
    ASSERT ( 0 != uiCount ) ;
    ASSERT ( NULL != paHookArray ) ;
    ASSERT ( FALSE == IsBadReadPtr ( paHookArray ,
                                     sizeof (HOOKFUNCDESC) * uiCount ));

    // In debug builds, perform deep validation of paHookArray.
#ifdef _DEBUG
    if ( NULL != paOrigFuncs )
    {
        ASSERT ( FALSE == IsBadWritePtr ( paOrigFuncs ,
                                          sizeof ( PROC ) * uiCount ) );

    }
    if ( NULL != pdwHooked )
    {
        ASSERT ( FALSE == IsBadWritePtr ( pdwHooked , sizeof ( UINT )));
    }

    // Check each item in the hook array.
    {
        for ( UINT i = 0 ; i < uiCount ; i++ )
        {
            ASSERT ( NULL != paHookArray[ i ].szFunc  ) ;
            ASSERT ( '\0' != *paHookArray[ i ].szFunc ) ;
            // If the function address isn't NULL, it is validated.
            if ( NULL != paHookArray[ i ].pProc )
            {
                ASSERT ( FALSE == IsBadCodePtr ( paHookArray[i].pProc));
            }
        }
    }
#endif
```

Listing 12-2 HookImportedFunctionsByName *from HOOKIMPORTEDFUNCTIONSBYNAME.CPP*

```
// Perform the error checking for the parameters.
if ( ( 0    == uiCount    )                              ||
     ( NULL == szImportMod )                             ||
     ( TRUE == IsBadReadPtr ( paHookArray ,
                         sizeof ( HOOKFUNCDESC ) * uiCount ) ))
{
    SetLastErrorEx ( ERROR_INVALID_PARAMETER , SLE_ERROR ) ;
    return ( FALSE ) ;
}
if ( ( NULL != paOrigFuncs )                             &&
     ( TRUE == IsBadWritePtr ( paOrigFuncs ,
                         sizeof ( PROC ) * uiCount ) ) )
{
    SetLastErrorEx ( ERROR_INVALID_PARAMETER , SLE_ERROR ) ;
    return ( FALSE ) ;
}
if ( ( NULL != pdwHooked )                               &&
     ( TRUE == IsBadWritePtr ( pdwHooked , sizeof ( UINT ) ) ) )
{
    SetLastErrorEx ( ERROR_INVALID_PARAMETER , SLE_ERROR ) ;
    return ( FALSE ) ;
}

// Is this a system DLL above the 2-GB line, which Windows 98 won't
// let you patch?
if ( ( FALSE == IsNT ( ) ) && ( (DWORD)hModule >= 0x80000000 ) )
{
    SetLastErrorEx ( ERROR_INVALID_HANDLE , SLE_ERROR ) ;
    return ( FALSE ) ;
}


// TODO TODO
// Should each item in the hook array be checked in release builds?

if ( NULL != paOrigFuncs )
{
    // Set all the values in paOrigFuncs to NULL.
    memset ( paOrigFuncs , NULL , sizeof ( PROC ) * uiCount ) ;
}
if ( NULL != pdwHooked )
{
    // Set the number of functions hooked to 0.
    *pdwHooked = 0 ;
}
```

(continued)

Listing 12-2 *continued*

```
// Get the specific import descriptor.
PIMAGE_IMPORT_DESCRIPTOR pImportDesc =
                GetNamedImportDescriptor ( hModule , szImportMod );
if ( NULL == pImportDesc )
{
    // The requested module wasn't imported. Don't return an error.
    return ( TRUE ) ;
}


// Get the original thunk information for this DLL. I can't use
// the thunk information stored in pImportDesc->FirstThunk
// because the loader has already changed that array to fix up
// all the imports. The original thunk gives me access to the
// function names.
PIMAGE_THUNK_DATA pOrigThunk =
                MakePtr ( PIMAGE_THUNK_DATA          ,
                          hModule                    ,
                          pImportDesc->OriginalFirstThunk  ) ;
// Get the array the pImportDesc->FirstThunk points to because
// I'll do the actual bashing and hooking there.
PIMAGE_THUNK_DATA pRealThunk = MakePtr ( PIMAGE_THUNK_DATA   ,
                                         hModule             ,
                                         pImportDesc->FirstThunk  );


// Loop through and find the functions to hook.
while ( NULL != pOrigThunk->u1.Function )
{
    // Look only at functions that are imported by name, not those
    // that are imported by ordinal value.
    if (  IMAGE_ORDINAL_FLAG !=
                ( pOrigThunk->u1.Ordinal & IMAGE_ORDINAL_FLAG ))
    {
        // Look at the name of this imported function.
        PIMAGE_IMPORT_BY_NAME pByName ;

        pByName = MakePtr ( PIMAGE_IMPORT_BY_NAME   ,
                            hModule                 ,
                            pOrigThunk->u1.AddressOfData  ) ;

        // If the name starts with NULL, skip it.
        if ( '\0' == pByName->Name[ 0 ] )
        {
            continue ;
        }
```

```
// Determines whether I hook the function
BOOL bDoHook = FALSE ;

// TODO TODO
// Might want to consider bsearch here.

// See whether the imported function name is in the hook
// array. Consider requiring paHookArray to be sorted by
// function name so that bsearch can be used, which
// will make the lookup faster. However, the size of
// uiCount coming into this function should be rather
// small, so it's OK to search the entire paHookArray for
// each function imported by szImportMod.
for ( UINT i = 0 ; i < uiCount ; i++ )
{
    if ( ( paHookArray[i].szFunc[0] ==
                                    pByName->Name[0] ) &&
        ( 0 == strcmpi ( paHookArray[i].szFunc ,
                        (char*)pByName->Name   )  )    )
    {
        // If the function address is NULL, exit now;
        // otherwise, go ahead and hook the function.
        if ( NULL != paHookArray[ i ].pProc )
        {
            bDoHook = TRUE ;
        }
        break ;
    }
}

if ( TRUE == bDoHook )
{
    // I found a function to hook. Now I need to change
    // the memory protection to writable before I overwrite
    // the function pointer. Note that I'm now writing into
    // the real thunk area!

    MEMORY_BASIC_INFORMATION mbi_thunk ;

    VirtualQuery ( pRealThunk                         ,
                &mbi_thunk                            ,
                sizeof ( MEMORY_BASIC_INFORMATION ) ) ;

    if ( FALSE == VirtualProtect ( mbi_thunk.BaseAddress ,
                                mbi_thunk.RegionSize   ,
                                PAGE_READWRITE         ,
                                &mbi_thunk.Protect     ))
```

(continued)

Listing 12-2 *continued*

```
            {
                ASSERT ( !"VirtualProtect failed!" ) ;
                SetLastErrorEx ( ERROR_INVALID_HANDLE , SLE_ERROR );
                return ( FALSE ) ;
            }

            // Save the original address if requested.
            if ( NULL != paOrigFuncs )
            {
                paOrigFuncs[i] = (PROC)pRealThunk->u1.Function ;
            }

            // Microsoft has two different definitions of the
            // PIMAGE_THUNK_DATA fields as they are moving to
            // support Win64. The W2K RC2 Platform SDK is the
            // latest header, so I'll use that one and force the
            // Visual C++ 6 Service Pack 3 headers to deal with it.

            // Hook the function.
            DWORD * pTemp = (DWORD*)&pRealThunk->u1.Function ;
            *pTemp = (DWORD)(paHookArray[i].pProc);

            DWORD dwOldProtect ;

            // Change the protection back to what it was before I
            // overwrote the function pointer.
            VERIFY ( VirtualProtect ( mbi_thunk.BaseAddress ,
                                      mbi_thunk.RegionSize ,
                                      mbi_thunk.Protect ,
                                      &dwOldProtect    ) ) ;

            if ( NULL != pdwHooked )
            {
                // Increment the total number of functions hooked.
                *pdwHooked += 1 ;
            }
        }
    }
    // Increment both tables.
    pOrigThunk++ ;
    pRealThunk++ ;
    }

    // All OK, Jumpmaster!
    SetLastError ( ERROR_SUCCESS ) ;
    return ( TRUE ) ;
}
```

HookImportedFunctionsByName shouldn't be difficult for you to follow. After doing the proactive debugging practice of validating every parameter thoroughly, I call the helper function *GetNamedImportDescriptor* to find the *IMAGE_IMPORT-_DESCRIPTOR* for the requested module. After getting the pointers to the original and real IATs, I loop through the original IAT looking at each function imported by name to see whether it's in the *paHookArray* list. If the function is in the hook list, I simply set the real IAT's memory to *PAGE_READWRITE* so that the hooked address can be written safely, write the hook into the entry for the real function, and reset the memory protection to its original setting. The unit test function for *HookImported-FunctionsByName* is included with the BUGSLAYERUTIL.DLL source code on the companion CD, so feel free to use it to step through the code if you don't quite follow what's going on.

Now that you have an idea of how to hook the imported functions, let's move on to implementing the rest of DeadlockDetection.

Implementation Highlights

One of my primary goals in implementing DeadlockDetection was to make the utility as data-driven and table-driven as possible. When you step back and look at what the DLL does in its hook processing, you'll see that the processing is almost identical for each function in Table 12-1. The hooked function gets called, determines whether its class of functions is being monitored, calls the real function, and (if logging is on for that class) logs the information and returns. I had to write a bunch of similar hook functions, and I wanted to make them as simple as possible. Complicated hook functions are a perfect breeding ground for bugs.

The best way to show this simplicity is to talk about writing a DeadDetExt DLL. A DeadDetExt DLL must have three exported functions. The first two, *DeadDet-ExtOpen* and *DeadDetExtClose*, are self-explanatory. The interesting function is *DeadDetProcessEvent*, which each hook function calls when there is information to write. *DeadDetProcessEvent* takes a single parameter, a pointer to a *DDEVENT-INFO* structure:

```
typedef struct tagDDEVENTINFO
{
    // The identifier that specifies what the rest of
    // this structure contains
    eFuncEnum    eFunc       ;
    // The pre-call or post-call indicator
    ePrePostEnum ePrePost    ;
    // The return address. This address helps in finding the calling
    // function.
    DWORD        dwAddr      ;
    // The thread ID of the calling thread
```

(continued)

```
DWORD         dwThreadId    ;
// The return value for post calls.
DWORD         dwRetValue    ;
// The parameter information. Cast this information to the appropriate
// structure, as described below, for the function. When accessing
// the parameters, treat them as read-only.
DWORD         dwParams      ;
} DDEVENTINFO , * LPDDEVENTINFO ;
```

The entire output for a single function that appears in Listing 12-1 comes from the information in the *DDEVENTINFO* structure. Although most of the fields in *DDEVENTINFO* are self-explanatory, the *dwParams* field needs special mention. The *dwParams* field is really a pointer to the parameters as they appear in memory.

In Chapter 6, I discussed how parameters are passed on the stack. Just to jog your memory, parameters for __*stdcall* functions are passed right to left and the stack grows from high memory to low memory. The *dwParams* field in the *DDEVENTINFO* structure points to the last parameter on the stack, so the structure lists the parameters in left-to-right order. I applied a little creative casting to make it easy to convert *dwParams*.

In DEADLOCKDETECTION.H, I provide *typedefs* that describe each intercepted function's parameter lists. For example, if *eFunc* were *eWaitForSingleObjectEx*, you would cast *dwParams* to *LPWAITFORSINGLEOBJECTEX_PARAMS* to get the parameters. To see all of this creative casting in action, check out the TEXTFILEDDEXT.DLL code included on the companion CD.

Although output processing is relatively easy, gathering the information can be difficult. I wanted DeadlockDetection to hook the synchronization functions in Table 12-1, but I didn't want the hook functions to change the behavior of the real functions. I also wanted to get the parameters and the return value and to write the hook functions in C/C++ easily. I spent quite a while with the debugger and the disassembler before I got it right.

Initially, I wrote all the hook functions so that they were just pass-through functions and called the real functions directly. This approach worked great. Then I put the parameters and the return value for the functions into local variables. Although getting the value returned from the real function was simple, I realized that I didn't have a clean way to get the return address with my C/C++ hook function. I needed the *DWORD* right before the current stack pointer. Unfortunately, in straight C/C++, the function prolog would've already done its magic by the time I could get control, so the stack pointer would've already moved away from where it needed to be.

You might think that the stack pointer is just offset by the number of local variables, but that isn't always the case. The Visual C++ compiler does a pretty good job of optimizing so that the stack pointer isn't in the same place with different optimization flags set. Although you might declare a variable as a local variable, the compiler can optimize the variable by storing it in a register so that it doesn't even appear on the stack.

I needed a guaranteed way to get the stack pointer no matter what optimizations were set. At this point, I started thinking naked (no, not me without clothes): why not declare the hook functions as *__declspec(naked)* and create my own prolog and epilog code? With this approach, I'd have complete control over ESP no matter what optimization settings were used. Additionally, getting the return address and parameters would be a snap because they are at ESP+04h and ESP+08h, respectively. Keep in mind that I'm not doing anything out of the ordinary with the prolog and epilog code, so I still perform the usual PUSH EBP and MOV EBP, ESP for the prolog and MOV ESP, EBP and POP EBP for the epilog.

Because each hook function was going to be declared as *__declspec(naked)*, I wrote a couple of macros to handle the prolog and epilog: *HOOKFN_PROLOG* and *HOOKFN_EPILOG*. I also went ahead and declared some common local variables that all hook functions would need in *HOOKFN_PROLOG*. These variables included the last error value, *dwLastError*, and the event information structure to pass to the DeadDetExt DLL, *stEvtInfo*. The *dwLastError* is yet another bit of state that I needed to preserve when intercepting functions.

The Windows API can return a special error code through *SetLastError* to provide more information if a function fails. This error code can be a real boon because it tells you why an API function failed. For example, if *GetLastError* returns 122, you know that the buffer parameter was too small. WINERROR.H contains all the error codes the operating system returns. The problem with hook functions is that they can reset the last error as part of their processing. This behavior can wreak havoc if your application relies on the last error.

If you call *CreateEvent* and want to see whether the returned handle was created or just opened, *CreateEvent* sets the last error to *ERROR_ALREADY_EXISTS* if it just opened the handle. Because the cardinal rule of intercepting functions is that you can't change the expected behavior of the function, I needed to call *GetLastError* immediately after the real function call so that my hook function could properly set the last error code that the real function returned. The general rule for a hook function is that you need to call *GetLastError* right after you call the real function and then call *SetLastError* as the last action before leaving the hook function.

At this point, I thought I was done except for testing. Unfortunately, my first test uncovered a bug: I wasn't preserving ESI and EDI across the hook call because the documentation on using the inline assembler explicitly stated that you didn't have to save them. After I fixed the ESI/EDI register problem, DeadlockDetection seemed to work fine. When I started doing register comparisons on before, during, and after cases, however, I noticed that I wasn't returning the values the real functions left in EBX, ECX, and EDX, and worse yet, in the flags registers. Although I didn't see any problems and the documentation said that those registers didn't need to be preserved, I still was concerned that my hook functions were changing the application state. I declared the *REGSTATE* structure to hold the register values after the real function call so that I could restore them when my hook function returned. To save and restore the registers, I created two additional macros, *REAL_FUNC_PRE_CALL* and *REAL_FUNC_POST_CALL*, which I placed around the real call the hook function makes.

After a little more testing, I found another problem: in release builds with full optimizations, I crashed inexplicably every so often. I finally tracked down those crashes and was able to attribute them to the effect of the optimizer on some of my hook functions. The optimizer was trying to be helpful but ended up doing more harm than good. I was very careful about the register usage in my hook functions and used only EAX or stack memory directly. Even though I was taking every precaution to preserve the registers, I found that the debug build code sequence

```
MOV DWORD PTR [EBP-018h] , 00000002h
MOV DWORD PTR [EBP-014h] , 00000002h
```

was being transformed by the optimizer into

```
PUSH    002h
POP     EBX
MOV     DWORD PTR [EBP-01Ch] , EBX
MOV     DWORD PTR [EBP-018h] , EBX
```

It's easy to see in the second snippet that the POP into EBX was trashing the register. To prevent the optimizer from stealing registers behind my back, I turned optimizations off for all hook function files by placing a

```
#pragma optimize("", off )
```

at the top of each file. Turning optimizations off also made debugging easier because the unoptimized code the compiler generates is very similar for both release and debug builds.

Listing 12-3 shows the final version of DD_FUNCS.H, which is the internal header file in which all the special hook function macros are declared. The comment at the top of the file has a sample hook function that explains how I used each of the special macros. I strongly encourage you to step through the SimpTest example that's part of the source code. Make sure that you watch an entire function call at the assembly-language level because that's the only way you'll see all the processing that takes place.

```
/*-------------------------------------------------------------------------
"Debugging Applications" (Microsoft Press)
Copyright (c) 1997-2000 John Robbins -- All rights reserved.
-------------------------------------------------------------------------
The prototypes for all the hook functions and the prolog/epilog code
-----------------------------------------------------------------------*/


#ifndef _DD_FUNCS_H
#define _DD_FUNCS_H

/*///////////////////////////////////////////////////////////////////////
    All the hook functions are __declspec(naked) functions, so I must
provide the prolog and epilog. I need to provide a custom prolog and
epilog for several reasons:
1. Functions written in C have no control over which registers are used
   or when the compiler saves the original registers. Not having control
   over the registers means that getting the return address is nearly
   impossible. For the DeadlockDetection project, the return address is
   critical.
2. I also wanted to hand the parameters to the extension DLL processing
   function without having to copy massive amounts of data on
   each function call.
3. Because almost all the hook functions behave the same way, I set up
   the common variables needed in all functions.
4. Hook functions can't change any of the return values, including
   the value from GetLastError. By doing my own prolog and epilog, I
   can make it much easier to return the correct value. Also,
   I need to restore the register values to the state they were in
   following the real function call.

A basic hook function looks like this:

HANDLE NAKEDDEF DD_OpenEventA ( DWORD   dwDesiredAccess ,
                                BOOL    bInheritHandle  ,
                                LPCSTR  lpName                    )
{
    // Any local variables for the function must be specified before
    // any other code.

    // HOOKFN_PROLOG must be specified right after the local variables.
    HOOKFN_PROLOG ( ) ;

    // Is the function type logging turned on?
    if ( TRUE == DoLogging ( DDOPT_EVENT ) )
    {
```

Listing 12-3 *DD_FUNCS.H* *(continued)*

Listing 12-3 *continued*

```
            // Use the FILL_EVENTINFO macro to fill the stEvtInfo variable
            // that's declared in the HOOKFN_PROLOG macro. All hook
            // functions automatically have certain local variables to help
            // standardize their code.
            FILL_EVENTINFO ( eOpenEventA ) ;

            // You *MUST* call the REAL_FUNC_PRE_CALL macro BEFORE calling
            // the real function or else ESI and EDI won't be saved across
            // invocations.
            REAL_FUNC_PRE_CALL ( ) ;

            // Call the real function. The return value, stored in EAX, is
            // stored as part of the REAL_FUNC_POST_CALL processing.
            OpenEventA ( dwDesiredAccess ,
                         bInheritHandle ,
                         lpName          ) ;

            // You *MUST* call the REAL_FUNC_POST_CALL macro AFTER calling
            // the real function. The register values and the last error
            // value are stored as part of REAL_FUNC_POST_CALL.
            REAL_FUNC_POST_CALL ( ) ;

            // Call the logging code to log the event.
            ProcessEvent ( &stEvtInfo ) ;
        }
        else
        {
            // See the comments above. The else clause handles the case
            // where the function isn't being logged.
            REAL_FUNC_PRE_CALL ( ) ;
            OpenEventA ( dwDesiredAccess ,
                         bInheritHandle ,
                         lpName          ) ;
            REAL_FUNC_POST_CALL ( ) ;
        }

    // The last macro in the function is HOOKFN_EPILOG. The parameter
    // is the number of function parameters, so the stack will get
    // cleaned up correctly. The HOOKFN_EPILOG macro also takes care of
    // setting all the registers to the same values that the real
    // function returned.
    HOOKFN_EPILOG ( 3 ) ;
}

///////////////////////////////////////////////////////////////////////*/
```

```
/*//////////////////////////////////////////////////////////////////////
    The register state structure. I use this structure to ensure that
ALL registers are returned exactly as they came from the real function.
Notice that EBP and ESP are handled as part of the prolog.
//////////////////////////////////////////////////////////////////////*/
typedef struct tag_REGSTATE
{
    DWORD    dwEAX ;
    DWORD    dwEBX ;
    DWORD    dwECX ;
    DWORD    dwEDX ;
    DWORD    dwEDI ;
    DWORD    dwESI ;
    DWORD    dwEFL ;
} REGSTATE , * PREGSTATE ;


/*//////////////////////////////////////////////////////////////////////
    The common prolog code for all DD_* functions
//////////////////////////////////////////////////////////////////////*/
#define HOOKFN_PROLOG()                                                  \
/* All hook functions automatically get the same three local    */\
/* variables.                                                    */\
DDEVENTINFO stEvtInfo   ;    /* The event information for the function*/\
DWORD       dwLastError ;    /* The last error value                  */\
REGSTATE    stRegState  ;    /* The register state to ensure that I   */\
                             /* restore the registers correctly       */\
{                                                                        \
__asm PUSH  EBP              /* Always save EBP explicitly.       */\
__asm MOV   EBP , ESP        /* Move the stack.                   */\
__asm MOV   EAX , ESP        /* Get the stack pointer to calculate the*/\
                             /* return address and the parameters.    */\
__asm SUB   ESP , __LOCAL_SIZE /* Save space for the local variables.*/\
__asm ADD   EAX , 04h + 04h /* Account for PUSH EBP and the        */\
                             /* return address.                       */\
                             /* Save start of parameters on the stack.*/\
__asm MOV   [stEvtInfo.dwParams] , EAX                                \
__asm SUB   EAX , 04h        /* Get back to the return address.   */\
__asm MOV   EAX , [EAX]       /* EAX now holds the return address. */\
                             /* Save the return address.          */\
__asm MOV   [stEvtInfo.dwAddr] , EAX                                  \
__asm MOV   dwLastError , 0 /* Initialize dwLastError.             */\
                             /* Initialize the event information. */\
__asm MOV   [stEvtInfo.eFunc] , eUNINITIALIZEDFE                      \
__asm MOV   [stRegState.dwEDI] , EDI /* Save the two registers that */\
__asm MOV   [stRegState.dwESI] , ESI /* need to be saved across     */\
```

(continued)

Listing 12-3 *continued*

```
                                        /* function calls.          */\
    }


/*//////////////////////////////////////////////////////////////////////
    The common epilog code for all DD_* functions. iNumParams is the
number of parameters to the function that is used to restore the
stack to the proper place after the hook call.
//////////////////////////////////////////////////////////////////////*/
#define HOOKFN_EPILOG(iNumParams)                                       \
{                                                                       \
SetLastError ( dwLastError ) ;        /* Set the real function's last  */\
                                      /* error value.                 */\
__asm ADD    ESP , __LOCAL_SIZE       /* Add back the local variables. */\
__asm MOV    EBX , [stRegState.dwEBX]/* Restore all the registers so   */\
__asm MOV    ECX , [stRegState.dwECX]/* that this call looks           */\
__asm MOV    EDX , [stRegState.dwEDX]/* identical to the intercepted   */\
__asm MOV    EDI , [stRegState.dwEDI]/* function.                      */\
__asm MOV    ESI , [stRegState.dwESI]                                   \
__asm MOV    EAX , [stRegState.dwEFL]                                   \
__asm SAHF                                                              \
__asm MOV    EAX , [stRegState.dwEAX]                                   \
__asm MOV    ESP , EBP                /* Put back ESP.                 */\
__asm POP    EBP                      /* Restore the saved EBP.        */\
__asm RET    iNumParams * 4           /* stdcall restore of the stack  */\
}


/*//////////////////////////////////////////////////////////////////////
    The REAL_FUNC_PRE_CALL macro needs to be placed IMMEDIATELY *BEFORE*
ANY call to the real function the hook function is handling. The macro
ensures that EDI and ESI are returned in the same condition they were
in when passed to the hook function.
//////////////////////////////////////////////////////////////////////*/
#define REAL_FUNC_PRE_CALL()                                            \
{                                                                       \
__asm MOV    EDI , [stRegState.dwEDI]   /* Restore the real EDI.     */\
__asm MOV    ESI , [stRegState.dwESI]   /* Restore the real ESI.     */\
}


/*//////////////////////////////////////////////////////////////////////
    The REAL_FUNC_POST_CALL macro needs to be placed IMMEDIATELY *AFTER*
ANY call to the real function the hook function is handling. All the
register values after the real call are saved so that the hook function
epilog can return the same register values as the real function call.
//////////////////////////////////////////////////////////////////////*/
#define REAL_FUNC_POST_CALL()                                           \
```

```
{                                                                \
__asm MOV   [stRegState.dwEAX] , EAX  /* Save the EAX value.        */\
__asm MOV   [stRegState.dwEBX] , EBX  /* Save the EBX value.        */\
__asm MOV   [stRegState.dwECX] , ECX  /* Save the ECX value.        */\
__asm MOV   [stRegState.dwEDX] , EDX  /* Save the EDX value.        */\
__asm MOV   [stRegState.dwEDI] , EDI  /* Save the EDI value.        */\
__asm MOV   [stRegState.dwESI] , ESI  /* Save the ESI value.        */\
__asm XOR   EAX , EAX                  /* Zero out EAX.              */\
__asm LAHF                             /* Load the flag values into AH.*/\
__asm MOV   [stRegState.dwEFL] , EAX  /* Save the flag values.      */\
}                                                                \
dwLastError = GetLastError ( ) ;      /* Save the last error value. */\
{                                                                \
__asm MOV   EAX , [stRegState.dwEAX]  /* Restore EAX to its original */\
                                      /* value.                     */\
                                      /* Set the return value for   */\
                                      /* the information.           */\
__asm MOV   [stEvtInfo.dwRetValue] , EAX                          \
}

/*/////////////////////////////////////////////////////////////////////
    A convenient macro to fill out the event information structure
/////////////////////////////////////////////////////////////////////*/
#define FILL_EVENTINFO(eFn)                             \
    stEvtInfo.eFunc      = eFn       ;                  \
    stEvtInfo.ePrePost   = ePostCall ;                  \
    stEvtInfo.dwThreadId = GetCurrentThreadId ( )

/*/////////////////////////////////////////////////////////////////////
    The declaration for all DD_* definitions
/////////////////////////////////////////////////////////////////////*/
#define NAKEDDEF __declspec(naked)

/*/////////////////////////////////////////////////////////////////////
BIG NOTE BIG NOTE BIG NOTE BIG NOTE
All the following prototypes look like cdecl functions. They are
not--they are all stdcall! The custom prolog and epilog ensure that
the correct calling convention is used!
/////////////////////////////////////////////////////////////////////*/

/////////////////////////////////////////////////////////////////////
// The mandatory functions that have to be intercepted to make the
// system work
HMODULE DD_LoadLibraryA ( LPCSTR lpLibFileName ) ;
HMODULE DD_LoadLibraryW ( LPCWSTR lpLibFileName ) ;
```

(continued)

Listing 12-3 *continued*

```
HMODULE DD_LoadLibraryExA ( LPCSTR  lpLibFileName ,
                            HANDLE  hFile          ,
                            DWORD   dwFlags          ) ;
HMODULE DD_LoadLibraryExW ( LPCWSTR lpLibFileName ,
                            HANDLE  hFile          ,
                            DWORD   dwFlags          ) ;


VOID DD_ExitProcess ( UINT uExitCode ) ;

FARPROC DD_GetProcAddress ( HMODULE hModule , LPCSTR lpProcName ) ;

//////////////////////////////////////////////////////////////////////////
// The thread-specific functions
HANDLE DD_CreateThread (LPSECURITY_ATTRIBUTES  lpThreadAttributes ,
                        DWORD                  dwStackSize        ,
                        LPTHREAD_START_ROUTINE lpStartAddress     ,
                        LPVOID                 lpParameter        ,
                        DWORD                  dwCreationFlags    ,
                        LPDWORD                lpThreadId           ) ;
VOID DD_ExitThread ( DWORD dwExitCode ) ;
DWORD DD_SuspendThread ( HANDLE hThread ) ;
DWORD DD_ResumeThread ( HANDLE hThread ) ;
BOOL DD_TerminateThread ( HANDLE hThread , DWORD dwExitCode ) ;

//////////////////////////////////////////////////////////////////////////
// Waiting and special functions
DWORD DD_WaitForSingleObject ( HANDLE hHandle        ,
                               DWORD  dwMilliseconds  ) ;
DWORD DD_WaitForSingleObjectEx ( HANDLE hHandle      ,
                                 DWORD  dwMilliseconds ,
                                 BOOL   bAlertable      ) ;
DWORD DD_WaitForMultipleObjects( DWORD          nCount         ,
                                 CONST HANDLE * lpHandles      ,
                                 BOOL           bWaitAll       ,
                                 DWORD          dwMilliseconds   ) ;
DWORD DD_WaitForMultipleObjectsEx( DWORD          nCount       ,
                                   CONST HANDLE * lpHandles    ,
                                   BOOL           bWaitAll     ,
                                   DWORD          dwMilliseconds ,
                                   BOOL           bAlertable     ) ;
DWORD DD_MsgWaitForMultipleObjects ( DWORD   nCount        ,
                                     LPHANDLE pHandles      ,
                                     BOOL    fWaitAll       ,
                                     DWORD   dwMilliseconds ,
                                     DWORD   dwWakeMask       ) ;
```

```
DWORD DD_MsgWaitForMultipleObjectsEx ( DWORD    nCount        ,
                                        LPHANDLE pHandles      ,
                                        DWORD    dwMilliseconds ,
                                        DWORD    dwWakeMask    ,
                                        DWORD    dwFlags       ) ;
DWORD DD_SignalObjectAndWait ( HANDLE hObjectToSignal ,
                               HANDLE hObjectToWaitOn ,
                               DWORD  dwMilliseconds  ,
                               BOOL   bAlertable      ) ;
BOOL DD_CloseHandle ( HANDLE hObject ) ;

/////////////////////////////////////////////////////////////////////////////
// Critical-section functions
VOID DD_InitializeCriticalSection(LPCRITICAL_SECTION lpCriticalSection);
BOOL DD_InitializeCriticalSectionAndSpinCount (
                               LPCRITICAL_SECTION lpCriticalSection,
                               DWORD              dwSpinCount   );
VOID DD_DeleteCriticalSection(LPCRITICAL_SECTION lpCriticalSection ) ;
VOID DD_EnterCriticalSection ( LPCRITICAL_SECTION lpCriticalSection ) ;
VOID DD_LeaveCriticalSection ( LPCRITICAL_SECTION lpCriticalSection ) ;
DWORD DD_SetCriticalSectionSpinCount (
                               LPCRITICAL_SECTION lpCriticalSection,
                               DWORD              dwSpinCount   );
BOOL DD_TryEnterCriticalSection ( LPCRITICAL_SECTION lpCriticalSection);

/////////////////////////////////////////////////////////////////////////////
// Mutex functions
HANDLE DD_CreateMutexA ( LPSECURITY_ATTRIBUTES lpMutexAttributes ,
                         BOOL                  bInitialOwner    ,
                         LPCSTR                lpName           ) ;
HANDLE DD_CreateMutexW ( LPSECURITY_ATTRIBUTES lpMutexAttributes ,
                         BOOL                  bInitialOwner    ,
                         LPCWSTR               lpName           ) ;
HANDLE DD_OpenMutexA ( DWORD  dwDesiredAccess ,
                       BOOL   bInheritHandle  ,
                       LPCSTR lpName          ) ;
HANDLE DD_OpenMutexW ( DWORD   dwDesiredAccess ,
                       BOOL    bInheritHandle  ,
                       LPCWSTR lpName          ) ;
BOOL DD_ReleaseMutex ( HANDLE hMutex ) ;

/////////////////////////////////////////////////////////////////////////////
// Semaphore functions
HANDLE
```

(continued)

Listing 12-3 *continued*

```
       DD_CreateSemaphoreA ( LPSECURITY_ATTRIBUTES lpSemaphoreAttributes ,
                             LONG                  lInitialCount         ,
                             LONG                  lMaximumCount         ,
                             LPCSTR                lpName                );
HANDLE
       DD_CreateSemaphoreW ( LPSECURITY_ATTRIBUTES lpSemaphoreAttributes ,
                             LONG                  lInitialCount         ,
                             LONG                  lMaximumCount         ,
                             LPCWSTR               lpName                );
HANDLE DD_OpenSemaphoreA ( DWORD   dwDesiredAccess ,
                           BOOL    bInheritHandle  ,
                           LPCSTR  lpName          ) ;
HANDLE DD_OpenSemaphoreW ( DWORD   dwDesiredAccess ,
                           BOOL    bInheritHandle  ,
                           LPCWSTR lpName          ) ;
BOOL DD_ReleaseSemaphore ( HANDLE hSemaphore      ,
                           LONG   lReleaseCount    ,
                           LPLONG lpPreviousCount ) ;


///////////////////////////////////////////////////////////////////////
// Event functions
HANDLE DD_CreateEventA ( LPSECURITY_ATTRIBUTES lpEventAttributes ,
                         BOOL                  bManualReset      ,
                         BOOL                  bInitialState     ,
                         LPCSTR                lpName            ) ;
HANDLE DD_CreateEventW ( LPSECURITY_ATTRIBUTES lpEventAttributes ,
                         BOOL                  bManualReset      ,
                         BOOL                  bInitialState     ,
                         LPCWSTR               lpName            ) ;
HANDLE DD_OpenEventA ( DWORD   dwDesiredAccess ,
                       BOOL    bInheritHandle  ,
                       LPCSTR  lpName          ) ;
HANDLE DD_OpenEventW ( DWORD   dwDesiredAccess ,
                       BOOL    bInheritHandle  ,
                       LPCWSTR lpName          ) ;
BOOL DD_PulseEvent ( HANDLE hEvent ) ;
BOOL DD_ResetEvent ( HANDLE hEvent ) ;
BOOL DD_SetEvent ( HANDLE hEvent ) ;

#endif  // _DD_FUNCS_H
```

I want to mention several other minor points about DeadlockDetection. The first is that DeadlockDetection is always active in your application, even if you suspend DeadlockDetection logging. Instead of hooking and unhooking dynamically, I leave the functions hooked and look at some internal flags to determine how the hook should behave. Keeping all functions hooked makes it easier to toggle different function logging at run time, but it adds some overhead to your application. I felt that allowing hooking and unhooking on the fly would have led to more errors in the DeadlockDetection code.

Second, DeadlockDetection hooks the functions out of a DLL when brought into your program through *LoadLibrary*. However, it can gain control only after that DLL's *DllMain* has executed, so if any synchronization objects are created or used during *DllMain*, DeadlockDetection can miss them.

Third, DeadlockDetection also hooks *GetProcAddress* and *ExitProcess*. The *GetProcAddress* hooking is there in case your program, or a third-party control you might be deadlocking against, calls *GetProcAddress* to find a synchronization method at run time.

I hook *ExitProcess* because when the application is ending, I need to unhook and shut down DeadlockDetection so that it doesn't crash or hang your program. Because there's no way to control the unload order of DLLs during program termination, you can easily get into situations in which a DLL that DeadlockDetection relies on, such as DeadDetExt, has been unloaded before DeadlockDetection itself. Fortunately, very few developers are doing major multithreaded control after the application calls *ExitProcess*.

Finally, several test programs are included with DeadlockDetection on the companion CD. All of them are included in the main DeadlockDetection workspace, and all link against DEADLOCKDETECTION.DLL, so you can use them to see how DeadlockDetection operates.

WHAT'S NEXT FOR DEADLOCKDETECTION?

DeadlockDetection is a fairly complete utility, and I've used it successfully to track down quite a few multithreaded deadlocks. As always, however, I encourage you to look for ways that you can extend DeadlockDetection to make it more useful. Here are some of my ideas for enhancements to DeadlockDetection:

■   Create a stand-alone application to manipulate the DEADLOCK-DETECTION.INI file. Your program could be even nicer if it allowed you to set the DeadDetExt DLL and validated that the selected DeadDetExt DLL exported the correct functions.

■   You could optimize the hook functions better if they weren't doing any logging. In that case, not all the register values need to be copied.

■   Right now, DeadlockDetection just skips hooking a couple of DLLs that it knows about. A mechanism for specifying on a program-by-program basis which DLLs to skip would be nifty.

DEBUGGING WAR STORY

Uncommitted Transactions with Pooled COM Objects

The Battle

My good friend Peter Ierardi told me about an interesting multithreading bug he encountered. He was working on a large DCOM project that used a multithreaded DCOM service to coordinate database transactions. The DCOM service managed the transactions by creating a pool of database-centric in-process COM objects, which were used to write data into and read data from his relational database management system (RDBMS). The component-to-component communication took place through Microsoft Message Queue Server (MSMQ). Even though there were explicit, transactional commits, the data didn't seem to be written to the database. The DCOM service would retry three to five times, and the data would finally appear, as if by magic. Obviously, the excessive retries were taking a toll on the application's performance, and the fact that the data wasn't being written to the database was cause for alarm.

The Outcome

After some heavy debugging sessions, Peter found that the DCOM service was performing the reads and write on separate, nonsynchronized threads. The read occurred before a separate instance of the database COM object had written the data. This behavior wasn't evident during debugging sessions because the debugger was forcing the proper timing and synchronization. He eventually uncovered the problem through appropriate labeling of object instances in the Event Log.

The Lesson

The big lesson Peter said he learned from this bug was that in a large-scale distributed application such as the one he was working in, you can't assume that the debug environment will accurately represent the release environment. He solved the problem by adding appropriate synchronization code and wrapping the component-to-component communications, which originally went through MSMQ individually, into the same transaction along with the database writes such that the messages would be sent only upon transactional commits.

What was happening in Peter's bug was that the MSMQ reads/writes, not surprisingly, were cycling much faster than the database reads/writes. Even though Peter and his team had walked through and planned all the multithreading carefully, they were still bitten by some initial misunderstanding about how much faster certain operations outside their project would take in the real world.

SUMMARY

Multithreaded programming is difficult and the area in which you'll encounter some of the hardest bugs you'll ever have to solve. This chapter presented tips and techniques that should help you avoid deadlocks from the beginning of your project. As I stressed early in the chapter, in multithreaded programming, up-front planning is vital, and you must make sure to allot your team enough time and resources to plan multithreaded applications carefully and correctly. Once you're faced with the inevitable multithreaded deadlocks, however, there's no need to panic: this chapter also covered DeadlockDetection, a utility that will allow you to figure out which threads deadlocked on which synchronization object

Finally—and, I can't stress this point enough—if you're doing multithreaded programming, you must be developing, running, and testing your projects on multiprocessor computers. If you're not, you probably shouldn't be doing multithreaded programming because you're leaving yourself open to some extremely serious bugs.

Chapter 13

Automated Testing

In Chapter 3, I talked about unit tests and explained why unit testing is such a vital part of producing high-quality code. For those of us who work mostly on an application's internal logic, unit tests can be fairly simple. Look at the files in SourceCode\BugslayerUtil\Tests on the companion CD, and you'll see all the unit tests I used to develop BUGSLAYERUTIL.DLL. All those tests are console applications that do their jobs admirably.

Unfortunately, testing user interface (UI) code is more difficult. In this chapter, I'll present a utility I wrote, Tester, that will help you automate some of your UI testing. Although not as extensive as a full-blown commercial regression-testing tool, Tester is sophisticated enough to let you run your applications through their unit testing paces. Not only that, but Tester is much easier to use and less expensive than a commercial system.

THE BANE OF UNIT TESTING: USER INTERFACES

I'm firmly convinced that Microsoft Windows developers get their carpal tunnel syndrome not from typing their source code but from hitting the same keystroke combinations over and over to test their applications. After the 5,000th time you type "Alt+F, O," your wrists are locked tighter than rebar in concrete. Without a tool to automate the tasks involved in accessing the different features of your applications, you generally have to follow some sort of script to ensure that you're doing sufficient unit testing. Testing with scripts is totally boring—and the boredom that results leaves plenty of room for human error.

Automating your unit tests will mean that you don't have to type so much and that you can quickly verify the state of your code. Unfortunately, the Recorder application that used to ship with Windows 3 and 3.1 doesn't come with any of the 32-bit operating systems. For those of you newer to Windows, Recorder wrote your mouse and keyboard interactions to a file so that you could play them back as if they were physical mouse and keyboard events. Although several third-party products that will automate your application and a whole lot more (such as completely validate every pixel in a screen comparison and maintain databases of which tests ran when) are available, I wanted something that was lightweight and geared toward development engineers. Thus, the idea for my Tester application was born.

When I started thinking about creating an automation utility, I spent some time considering exactly what I'd expect from such a tool. At first, I thought about developing a utility akin to the old Recorder application. Back in the days of Windows 3, I had a complete set of REC files to drive my tests. However, the big problem with Recorder was that it didn't provide a way to do conditional tests. If my application signaled an error during the test, Recorder just went along its merry way, playing back the recorded keystrokes and mouse clicks, completely oblivious to my application's distress. One time I wiped out half my operating system with Recorder because I was testing a WINFILE.EXE extension, and when my extension had a problem, Recorder played the delete files sequence all over the System directory. My new automation tool definitely had to have an *if...then...else* construct.

To incorporate conditional constructs into my tests, I obviously needed to use some sort of language. Developing my own testing language would've been an intriguing intellectual exercise, but I soon concluded that I was more interested in writing a useful debugging tool than in designing a language and dealing with YACC and FLEX. It took all of two seconds to realize that I should write Tester as a COM object—that way, developers could use my utility and still write tests in their language of choice, and I could concentrate on programming the utility's regression-testing features instead of designing a new language. My personal testing languages of choice are scripting languages, such as Microsoft Visual Basic, Scripting Edition (VBScript) and Java Script (JScript), because the testing scripts don't require compiling. The different Windows Scripting Host (WSH) scripting engine implementations have a few limitations, however, which I'll point out later in the chapter. For now, let's talk about the requirements that guided my creation of Tester.

TESTER REQUIREMENTS

I wanted to keep Tester focused on doing one thing and doing it well: automating the keystrokes sent to your application so that you can unit test faster. If you've ever explored commercial regression-testing tools, you've undoubtedly seen what a wild ride they can involve, from simply controlling a window on the screen to validating all sorts of complicated and weird data of the most obscure window properties possible. I wanted to concentrate on the developer's needs during unit testing and keep Tester simple to use.

Here are the main requirements for Tester:

1. Tester can be controlled through any language that supports COM.

2. Given an input string of keystrokes, in the same format used by the Visual Basic *SendKeys* function, Tester can play the keystrokes to the active window.

3. Tester can find any top-level or child window by its caption or class.

4. Given any arbitrary *HWND*, Tester can get all the window's properties.

5. Tester must notify the user's script of specific window creation or destruction so that the script can handle potential error conditions or do advanced window handling.

6. Tester scripts can be shared with anyone on the development team.

7. Tester doesn't limit developers from extending the code in any direction they need for their shops' requirements.

As you can see from this requirements list, Tester does nothing to help you with mouse input. Although recording mouse input through a journal hook is relatively easy, if you do choose this method, don't forget about one small but critical detail: the screen resolution in which you record the mouse input is the only resolution in which the mouse input can be played back. Not many shops can live with this restriction. I can assure you that not everyone in the average development shop uses the same screen resolution. If you resolve your mouse-input problem with a hard-coded screen resolution, the scripts are basically worthless if you want to share them among your team. Another problem is that the script breaks easily if you move a control in the UI even a pixel or two. Unless you record your scripts only after the UI is frozen, a recorded script is far too fragile. The catch-22 is that if you wait until the UI is frozen, you're not doing adequate testing.

Tester probably isn't a general solution for your 20-person QA department. My intention was to build a tool that you and I, as development engineers, could use to automate our unit testing. To that end, I think Tester fits the bill. I used Tester quite a bit to help develop WDBG, the graphical user interface (GUI) debugger I developed as part of Chapter 4. The best part of using Tester with WDBG was that I saved myself thousands of keystrokes—this far into the book, I can still move my wrists!

USING TESTER

Using Tester is relatively simple. You just create a couple Tester objects, either start or find your application's main window, play some keystrokes to your application, check the results, and end. Listing 13-1 shows a sample VBScript test that starts NOTEPAD.EXE, enters a few lines of text, and closes Notepad.

```
' A minimal VBScript Tester example. It just starts Notepad, enters a
' few lines of text, and closes Notepad.

' Get the system and input objects.
Dim tSystem
Dim tInput
Dim tWin
Set tSystem = WScript.CreateObject ( "Tester.TSystem" )
Set tInput = WScript.CreateObject ( "Tester.TInput" )

' Start Notepad.
tSystem.Execute "NOTEPAD.EXE"

' Wait 200 milliseconds.
tSystem.Pause 200

' Try to find Notepad's main window.
Set tWin = tSystem.FindTopWindowByTitle ( "Untitled - Notepad" )
If ( tWin Is Nothing ) Then
    MsgBox "Unable to find Notepad!"
    WScript.Quit
End If

' Ensure that Notepad is in the foreground.
tWin.SetForegroundTWindow

' Type something.
tInput.PlayKeys "Be all you can be!~~~"
' Play it again, Sam.
tInput.PlayKeys "Put on your boots and parachutes....~~~"
' Third time's the charm.
tInput.PlayKeys "Silver wings upon their chests.....~~~"

' Wait 1 second.
tSystem.Pause 1000

' End Notepad.
tInput.PlayKeys "%FX"
tSystem.Pause 50
tInput.PlayKeys "{TAB}~"

' Script is done!
```

Listing 13-1 *Using common Tester objects*

Listing 13-1 shows the three objects Tester uses most often. The *TSystem* object allows you to find top-level windows, start applications, and pause the testing. The *TWindow* object, which is returned by *FindTopWindowByTitle* in Listing 13-1, is the main workhorse. It is a wrapper around an *HWND* and has all sorts of properties that tell you everything about the window. Additionally, *TWindow* allows you to enumerate all the child windows that belong to a particular parent. The last object in Listing 13-1 is the *TInput* object, which supports the single method *PlayKeys* to funnel keystrokes to the window that has the focus.

Listing 13-2 shows the *TNotify* object used in a VBScript test. When developing automation scripts, one of the most difficult cases you'll need to handle is when an unexpected window, such as an *ASSERT* message box, pops up. The *TNotify* object makes it a snap to provide an emergency handler for such events. The simple script in Listing 13-2 just watches for any windows with "Notepad" in their captions. Although you might not use the *TNotify* class much, when you do need it, you really need it.

```
' A VBScript test to show the window notification handlers

' Constants for the TNotify.AddNotification routine. If I were
' using Visual Basic 6, I'd define these constants with Enums.
Const antDestroyWindow    = 1
Const antCreateWindow     = 2
Const antCreateAndDestroy = 3

Const ansExactMatch       = 0
Const ansBeginMatch       = 1
Const ansAnyLocMatch      = 2

' Get the system and input objects.

Dim tSystem
Dim tInput
Set tSystem = WScript.CreateObject ( "Tester.TSystem" )
Set tInput = WScript.CreateObject ( "Tester.TInput" )


' The TNotify object variable
Dim Notifier

' Create the TNotify object.
Set Notifier = _
      WScript.CreateObject ( "Tester.TNotify"        , _
                             "NotepadNotification_"       )
```

Listing 13-2 *Using* TNotify *in VBScript*   *(continued)*

Listing 13-2 *continued*

```
' Add the notifications that I want. For this demonstration, I want both
' window destroy and window create notifications. See the TNotify source
' code for all the possible notification combinations.
Notifier.AddNotification  antCreateAndDestroy , _
                          ansAnyLocMatch       , _
                          "Notepad"

' Start Notepad.
tSystem.Execute "NOTEPAD.EXE"

' Pause for half a second.
tSystem.Pause 500

' Because Visual Basic isn't thread-safe, I set up the notification
' scheme to use a timer. However, the message can get blocked because
' all the processing is forced to a single thread. This function lets
' you manually check the window create and window destroy conditions.
Notifier.CheckNotification

' The message box in the NotepadNotification_CreateWindow event
' procedure blocks, so the code to end Notepad won't execute until the
' message box is cleared.
tInput.PlayKeys "%FX"
tSystem.Pause 50
tInput.PlayKeys "{TAB}~"

' Again, check notifications.
Notifier.CheckNotification

' Give TNotify a chance to intercept the window destroy message.
tSystem.Pause 100

' Disconnect the notifications. If you don't do this in WSH, the class
' terminate never gets called so the notification is still active in the
' notification table.
WScript.DisconnectObject Notifier

Set Notifier = Nothing


Sub NotepadNotificationCreateWindow ( tWin )
    MsgBox ( "Notepad was created!" )
End Sub


Sub NotepadNotificationDestroyWindow ( )
    MsgBox ( "Notepad has gone away...." )
End Sub
```

You need to call the *TNotify CheckNotification* method every once in a while. (I'll explain the reasons you need to call this method in the section "Implementing Tester" later in the chapter.) Periodically calling the *CheckNotification* method ensures that the notification messages can get through given that you might not have a message loop in your language of choice. The code in Listing 13-2 shows how to use a message box in the notification event procedures, though you probably don't want to use message boxes in your real scripts because they can cause problems by unexpectedly changing the window with the focus.

Also keep in mind that I allow you to set only a limited number of notifications—five—so you shouldn't use *TNotify* for general scripting tasks such as waiting for the File Save dialog box to appear. *TNotify* should be used only for unexpected windows. Depending on how you set up your notification handlers and how they search for the specified text in the window caption, you can easily receive notifications for windows that you might not be interested in. You're most likely to receive unwanted notifications when you use a generic string such as "Notepad" and you specify that the string can appear anywhere in the window caption. To avoid notifications you don't want, you should be as specific as possible with your notifications when calling the *TNotify AddNotification* method. Your *CreateWindow* event procedures should also look at the *TWindow* passed in so that you can verify that it's the window you're interested in. For *DestroyWindow* event procedures that handle generic notifications, you should search the open windows to ensure that the window you're interested in no longer exists.

Included with the source code on the companion CD are two other samples that you might want to look at to see how you can use Tester. The first sample, NPAD_TEST.VBS, is a more complete VBScript test and has some reusable routines. The other sample, TT (or Tester Tester), is the main unit test for Tester, and you can access it with the TESTER.VBG project group file. TT is a Visual Basic–based application, and it should give you an idea of how to use Tester with Visual Basic. Additionally, these two samples show the *TWindows* object, which is a collection that contains *TWindow* objects.

Although I'm partial to using VBScript for my unit tests, I realize that getting it to work correctly can be a challenge. VBScript variables are untyped and there's no magic VBScript editor, such as the editor in Visual Basic, so you're back to the old run-and-crash style of debugging. The main reason I like using VBScript is that I don't need to rely on compiling my tests. If you have a flexible build environment—one in which you can easily build other binaries in addition to your main application—you might want to consider using Visual Basic so that you can build your tests as you build your application. Of course, Tester doesn't limit you to the easiest-to-use testing languages—if you're more comfortable in C or the Microsoft Macro Assembler (MASM), you're welcome to use those languages instead.

Although using the objects in Tester is fairly simple, the real work is planning your tests. You should keep your tests as focused and simple as possible. When I first started automating my unit tests in my early development days, I tried to force my tests to do too much. Now I write each script to test just a single operation. A good example of a single-operation test is to limit the script just to sending the keystrokes to open a file. You can chain the scripts together in various ways to maximize script reuse. Once you have the script to open a file, you can use it in three different tests: a test to see whether you can open a valid file, a test to open an invalid file, and a test to open a corrupt file. As in normal development, you should avoid any hard-coded strings if possible. Not only will this make internationalizing your script a piece of cake, but it will also help when you change your menu system and accelerators for the hundredth time.

Another detail to consider when you're designing your Tester scripts is how you'll be able to verify that the script actually worked. If you're bored and have the time, I guess you could just sit there and watch the scripts run to see whether you get the same results on each run. Probably a better idea is to log states and key points in your script so that you can compare the output to previous runs automatically. If you use the CSCRIPT.EXE WSH executable, you can use *WScript.Echo* and redirect the output to a file. After the script finishes, you can run a difference utility (such as WinDiff) on the output; if the utility turns up any differences, you can check to see that the script executed correctly. Keep in mind that you'll want to normalize the information you log and keep the information free of run-specific details. For example, if you're writing an application that downloads stock quotes, you won't want to include the last price-update time in the logging output.

What about debugging your Tester scripts? Because Tester doesn't have its own integrated debugger, as Visual Basic does, you need to be careful that you don't stop your debugger on a *TInput PlayKeys* method call. If the debugger does stop there, the keystrokes will obviously go to the wrong window. To work around this potential problem, I generally force the window to which I'm sending keystrokes to the top of the z-order by calling the *TWindow SetForegroundTWindow* method before each *PlayKeys* call. This way, I can break on the *SetForegroundTWindow* call, check the state of the application, and still get the keystrokes to the correct window.

IMPLEMENTING TESTER

Now that you have an idea of how to use Tester, I want to go over some of the high points of its implementation. I first started to implement Tester using C++ and the Active Template Library (ATL), but then I realized that Visual Basic was a far better choice. Much of what I was going to implement in Tester is simple, and I just wanted to get the job done quickly. I ended up using Visual Basic, though as you'll see later in this section, I sometimes needed to take some odd twists and turns to make it work.

The first object I started implementing was *TInput*, which is responsible for all the input that you need to send to another window. Initially, I thought the keyboard input was going to be simple—I thought I'd just wrap the Visual Basic *SendKeys* statement. This approach worked fine when I sent some keys to Notepad, but when I tried to send keys to Microsoft Outlook 2000 I noticed that some didn't get through. I never did get the *SendKeys* statement to work, so I had to implement my own function, which I call *PlayKeys*. In the course of researching what I needed to include in my function, I noticed that Microsoft Windows 98 and Microsoft Windows 2000 have a neat new function: *SendInput*. For those of you who need to support Windows NT 4, Service Pack 3 and higher also implement the *SendInput* function. *SendInput* is part of Microsoft Active Accessibility (MSAA) and replaces all the previous low-level event functions, such as *keybd_event*. *SendInput* handles keyboard, mouse, and hardware events. It also places all the input information in the keyboard or mouse input stream as a contiguous unit, ensuring that your input isn't interspersed with any extraneous user input. This functionality was especially attractive for Tester. A quick test proved that *SendInput* also worked when sending input to Outlook 2000.

Once I knew how to send the keystrokes properly, I needed to develop the keystroke input format. Because the Visual Basic *SendKeys* statement already provides a nice input format, I thought I'd duplicate it for my *PlayKeys* function. I used everything but the repeat key code. There's nothing too thrilling about the parsing code—if you want to see it, look in the SourceCode\Tester\TInputHlp directory on the companion CD. When I started working on the *TInput* object, I was still intending to write Tester in C++. I wrote all the parsing code in a C++ dynamic-link library (DLL). The Visual Basic *TInput PlayKeys* method is just a wrapper to call the DLL.

The *TWindow*, *TWindows*, and *TSystem* objects are straightforward, and you should be able to understand them just by reading their source code. I implemented those three classes in Visual Basic; they're just wrappers around some Windows application programming interface (API) functions. I ran into some interesting obstacles in the *TNotify* class. When I first started thinking about what it would take to determine whether a window with a specific caption was created or destroyed, I didn't expect that creating such a class would be too hard. I discovered that not only was the job moderately difficult, but also that the window creation notifications can't be made foolproof without heroic effort.

My first idea was to implement a systemwide computer-based training (CBT) hook. The SDK documentation seemed to say that a CBT hook was the best method for determining when windows are created and destroyed. I whipped up a quick sample but soon hit a snag. When my hook got the *HCBT_CREATEWND* notification, I couldn't retrieve the window caption consistently. After I thought about the problem a bit, it started to make sense; the CBT hook is probably called as part of the *WM_CREATE* processing, and very few windows have set their captions at that point.

The only windows I could get reliably with the *HCBT_CREATEWND* notification were dialog boxes. The window destruction surveillance always worked with the CBT hook.

After looking through all the other types of hooks, I extended my quick sample to try them all. As I suspected, just watching *WM_CREATE* wasn't going to tell me the caption reliably. A friend suggested that I watch just the *WM_SETTEXT* messages. Eventually, to set the caption in a title bar, almost every window will use a *WM_SETTEXT* message. Of course, if you're doing your own nonclient painting and bit blitting, you won't use the *WM_SETTEXT* message. One interesting behavior I did notice was that some programs, Microsoft Internet Explorer in particular, post *WM_SETTEXT* messages with the same text many times consecutively.

Having figured out that I needed to watch *WM_SETTEXT* messages, I took a harder look at the different hooks I could use. In the end, the call window procedure hook (*WH_CALLWNDPROCRET*) was the best choice. It allows me to watch *WM_CREATE* and *WM_SETTEXT* messages easily. I can also watch *WM_DESTROY* messages. At first, I expected to have some trouble with *WM_DESTROY* because I thought that the window caption might have been deallocated by the time this message showed up. Fortunately, the window caption is valid until the *WM_NCDESTROY* message is received.

After considering the pros and cons of handling *WM_SETTEXT* messages only for windows that didn't yet have a caption, I decided to just go ahead and process all *WM_SETTEXT* messages. The alternative would've involved writing a state machine to keep track of created windows and the times they get their captions set, and this solution sounded error prone and difficult to implement. The drawback to handling all *WM_SETTEXT* messages would be that you could receive multiple creation notifications for the same window. For example, if you set a *TNotify* handler for windows that contained "Notepad" anywhere in their caption, you'd get a notification when NOTEPAD.EXE launched, but you'd also get a notification every time NOTEPAD.EXE opened a new file. In the end, I felt it was better to accept a less-than-optimal implementation rather than spend days and days debugging the "correct" solution. Also, writing the hook was only about a quarter of the implementation of the final *TNotify* class; the other three-quarters addressed the problem of how to let the user know that the window was created or destroyed.

I made the decision to implement Tester in Visual Basic before I wrote the *TNotify* class. Earlier, I mentioned that using *TNotify* isn't completely hands-off and that you have to call the *CheckNotification* method every once in a while. The reason you have to call *CheckNotification* periodically is that Visual Basic can't be multithreaded, and I needed a way to check whether a window was created or destroyed and still use the same thread in which the rest of Tester was running.

After sketching out some ideas about the notification mechanisms, I narrowed down the implementation needs to the following basic requirements:

- The *WH_CALLWNDPROCRET* hook has to be systemwide, so it must be implemented in its own DLL.

- The Tester DLL obviously can't be that DLL because I don't want to drag the entire Visual Basic Tester DLL and, in turn, MSVBM60.DLL into each address space on the user's computer. This condition means that the hook DLL probably has to set a flag or something that the Tester DLL can read to know that a condition is met.

- Tester can't be multithreaded, so I need to do all the processing in the same thread.

The first ramification of the basic requirements is that the hook function had to be written in C. Because the hook function is loaded into all address spaces, the hook DLL itself couldn't call any functions in the TESTER.DLL written in Visual Basic. Consequently, my Visual Basic code would need to check the results of the hook-generated data periodically.

If you ever developed 16-bit Windows applications, you know that finding a way to get some background processing done in a single-threaded, nonpreemptive environment was the perfect job for the *SetTimer* API function. With *SetTimer*, you could get the background processing capabilities yet still keep your application single-threaded. Consequently, I set up a timer notification as part of the *TNotify* class to determine when windows I needed to monitor were created or destroyed.

What made the *TNotify* background processing interesting was that the timer procedure solution seemed like the answer, but in reality, it only almost works in the *TNotify* case. Depending on the length of the script and on whether your language of choice implements a message loop, the *WM_TIMER* message might not get through, so you'll need to call the *CheckNotification* method, which checks the hook data as well. In an attempt to make the checking automatic, I tried to set up the *TSystem.Pause* method to call *DoEvents* for the amount of time specified. Unfortunately, using *DoEvents* in *TSystem.Pause* was a major performance drag on the scripts, so I settled on just asking users to call the *CheckNotification* function every once in a while.

All these implementation details might seem confusing, but you'll be surprised at how little code it really takes to implement Tester. Listing 13-3 shows the hook function code from TNOTIFYHLP.CPP. On the Tester side, TNOTIFY.BAS is the module in which the timer procedure resides, and the actual class is implemented in TNOTIFY.CLS. The *TNotify* class has a couple of hidden methods and properties that the *TNotify* module can access to get the events fired and to determine what types of notifications the user wants. The interesting part of the hook code is the globally shared data segment, .HOOKDATA, which holds the array of notification data. When looking at the code, keep in mind that the notification data is global but all the rest of the data is on a per-process basis.

```
/*-------------------------------------------------------------------------
"Debugging Applications" (Microsoft Press)
Copyright (c) 1997-2000 John Robbins -- All rights reserved.
-------------------------------------------------------------------------
The main file for TNotifyHlp.dll
-----------------------------------------------------------------------*/
#include <tchar.h>
#include <windows.h>
#include "TNotifyHlp.h"


/*/////////////////////////////////////////////////////////////////////
                    File Scope Defines and Constants
/////////////////////////////////////////////////////////////////////*/
// The maximum number of notification slots
static const int TOTAL_NOTIFY_SLOTS = 5 ;
// The mutex name
static const LPCTSTR k_MUTEX_NAME  = _T ( "TNotifyHlp_Mutex" ) ;
// The longest amount of time I'll wait on the mutex
static const int k_WAITLIMIT = 5000 ;

// I have my own trace here because I don't want to drag
// BugslayerUtil.DLL into each address space.
#ifdef _DEBUG
#define TRACE    ::OutputDebugString
#else
#define TRACE    (void)0
#endif


/*/////////////////////////////////////////////////////////////////////
                        File Scope Typedefs
/////////////////////////////////////////////////////////////////////*/
// The structure for an individual window to look for
typedef struct tag_TNOTIFYITEM
{
    // The PID for the process that created this item
    DWORD   dwOwnerPID  ;
    // The notification type
    int     iNotifyType ;
    // The search parameter
    int     iSearchType ;
    // The handle to the HWND being created
    HWND    hWndCreate  ;
    // The destroy Boolean
    BOOL    bDestroy    ;
```

Listing 13-3 *TNOTIFYHLP.CPP*

```
    // The title string
    TCHAR   szTitle [ MAX_PATH ] ;
} TNOTIFYITEM , * PTNOTIFYITEM ;

/*///////////////////////////////////////////////////////////////////////
                    File Scope Global Variables
///////////////////////////////////////////////////////////////////////*/
// This data is **NOT** shared across processes, so each process gets
// its own copy.

// The HINSTANCE for this module. Setting global system hooks requires
// a DLL.
static HINSTANCE g_hInst = NULL ;

// The mutex that protects the g_NotifyData table
static HANDLE g_hMutex = NULL ;

// The hook handle. I don't keep this handle in the shared section because
// multiple instances could set the hook when running multiple scripts.
static HHOOK g_hHook = NULL ;

// The number of items added by this process. This number lets me know
// how to handle the hook.
static int  g_iThisProcessItems = 0 ;

/*///////////////////////////////////////////////////////////////////////
                    File Scope Function Prototypes
///////////////////////////////////////////////////////////////////////*/
// Our happy hook
LRESULT CALLBACK CallWndRetProcHook ( int     nCode ,
                                      WPARAM wParam ,
                                      LPARAM lParam ) ;


// The internal check function
static LONG __stdcall CheckNotifyItem ( HANDLE hItem , BOOL bCreate ) ;

/*///////////////////////////////////////////////////////////////////////
                    Funky Shared Data
                    Across All Hook Instances
///////////////////////////////////////////////////////////////////////*/
#pragma data_seg ( ".HOOKDATA" )
// The notification items table
static TNOTIFYITEM g_shared_NotifyData [ TOTAL_NOTIFY_SLOTS ] =
    {
        { 0 , 0 , 0 , NULL , 0 , '\0' } ,
        { 0 , 0 , 0 , NULL , 0 , '\0' } ,
        { 0 , 0 , 0 , NULL , 0 , '\0' } ,
```

(continued)

373

Listing 13-3 *continued*

```
        { 0 , 0 , 0 , NULL , 0 , '\0' } ,
        { 0 , 0 , 0 , NULL , 0 , '\0' }
    } ;
// The master count
static int g_shared_iUsedSlots = 0 ;
#pragma data_seg ( )


/*////////////////////////////////////////////////////////////////////////
                    EXTERNAL IMPLEMENTATION STARTS HERE
/////////////////////////////////////////////////////////////////////////*/

extern "C" BOOL WINAPI DllMain ( HINSTANCE hInst      ,
                                 DWORD     dwReason    ,
                                 LPVOID    /*lpReserved*/ )
{
#ifdef _DEBUG
    BOOL bCHRet ;
#endif

    BOOL bRet = TRUE ;
    switch ( dwReason )
    {
        case DLL_PROCESS_ATTACH :
            // Set the global module instance.
            g_hInst = hInst ;
            // I don't need the thread notifications.
            DisableThreadLibraryCalls ( g_hInst ) ;
            // Create the mutex for this process.  The mutex is created
            // here but isn't owned yet.
            g_hMutex = CreateMutex ( NULL , FALSE , k_MUTEX_NAME ) ;
            if ( NULL == g_hMutex )
            {
                TRACE ( _T ( "Unable to create the mutex!\n" ) ) ;
                // If I can't create the mutex, I can't continue, so
                // fail the DLL load.
                bRet = FALSE ;
            }
            break ;
        case DLL_PROCESS_DETACH :

            // Check to see whether this process has any items in the
            // notification array. If it does, remove them to avoid
            // leaving orphaned items.
            if ( 0 != g_iThisProcessItems )
```

```
        {
            DWORD dwProcID = GetCurrentProcessId ( ) ;
            // I don't need to grab the mutex here because only a
            // single thread will ever call with the
            // DLL_PROCESS_DETACH reason.

            // Loop through and take a gander.
            for ( int i = 0 ; i < TOTAL_NOTIFY_SLOTS ; i++ )
            {
                if ( g_shared_NotifyData[i].dwOwnerPID == dwProcID )
                {
#ifdef _DEBUG
                    TCHAR szBuff[ 50 ] ;
                    wsprintf ( szBuff ,
                        _T( "DLL_PROCESS_DETACH removing : #%d\n" ),
                            i ) ;
                    TRACE ( szBuff ) ;
#endif

                    // Get rid of it.
                    RemoveNotifyTitle ( ( HANDLE)i ) ;
                }
            }
        }

        // Close the mutex handle.
#ifdef _DEBUG
        bCHRet =
#endif
        CloseHandle ( g_hMutex ) ;
#ifdef _DEBUG
        if ( FALSE == bCHRet )
        {
            TRACE ( "!!!!!!!!!!!!!!!!!!!!!!!!!!!\n" ) ;
            TRACE ( "CloseHandle(g_hMutex) "
                    "failed!!!!!!!!!!!!!!!!!!!!!\n" ) ;
            TRACE ( "!!!!!!!!!!!!!!!!!!!!!!!!!!!\n" ) ;
        }
#endif
        break ;
    default                :
        break ;
    }
    return ( bRet ) ;
}
```

(continued)

Listing 13-3 *continued*

```
HANDLE TNOTIFYHLP_DLLINTERFACE __stdcall
    AddNotifyTitle ( int      iNotifyType ,
                     int      iSearchType ,
                     LPCTSTR szString     )
{
    // Ensure that the notify type range is correct.
    if ( ( iNotifyType < ANTN_DESTROYWINDOW     ) ||
         ( iNotifyType > ANTN_CREATEANDDESTROY  )   )
    {
        TRACE ( "AddNotify Title : iNotifyType is out of range!\n" ) ;
        return ( INVALID_HANDLE_VALUE ) ;
    }
    // Ensure that the search type range is correct.
    if ( ( iSearchType < ANTS_EXACTMATCH   ) ||
         ( iSearchType > ANTS_ANYLOCMATCH )   )
    {
        TRACE ( "AddNotify Title : iSearchType is out of range!\n" ) ;
        return ( INVALID_HANDLE_VALUE ) ;
    }
    // Ensure that the string is valid.
    if ( TRUE == IsBadStringPtr ( szString , MAX_PATH ) )
    {
        TRACE ( "AddNotify Title : szString is invalid!\n" ) ;
        return ( INVALID_HANDLE_VALUE ) ;
    }

    // Wait to acquire the mutex.
    DWORD dwRet = WaitForSingleObject ( g_hMutex , k_WAITLIMIT ) ;
    if ( WAIT_TIMEOUT == dwRet )
    {
        TRACE ( _T( "AddNotifyTitle : Wait on mutex timed out!!\n" ) ) ;
        return ( INVALID_HANDLE_VALUE ) ;
    }

    // If the slots are used up, abort now.
    if ( TOTAL_NOTIFY_SLOTS == g_shared_iUsedSlots )
    {
        ReleaseMutex ( g_hMutex ) ;
        return ( INVALID_HANDLE_VALUE ) ;
    }

    // Find the first free slot.
    for ( int i = 0 ; i < TOTAL_NOTIFY_SLOTS ; i++ )
```

```
    {
        if ( _T ( '\0' ) == g_shared_NotifyData[ i ].szTitle[ 0 ] )
        {
            break ;
        }
    }


    // Add this data.
    g_shared_NotifyData[ i ].dwOwnerPID  = GetCurrentProcessId ( ) ;
    g_shared_NotifyData[ i ].iNotifyType = iNotifyType ;
    g_shared_NotifyData[ i ].iSearchType = iSearchType ;
    lstrcpy ( g_shared_NotifyData[ i ].szTitle , szString ) ;


    // Bump up the master count.
    g_shared_iUsedSlots++ ;


    // Bump up the count for this process.
    g_iThisProcessItems++ ;


    TRACE ( "AddNotifyTitle - Added a new item!\n" ) ;


    ReleaseMutex ( g_hMutex ) ;


    // If this is the first notification request, enable the hook.
    if ( NULL == g_hHook )
    {
        g_hHook = SetWindowsHookEx ( WH_CALLWNDPROCRET  ,
                                     CallWndRetProcHook ,
                                     g_hInst            ,
                                     0                  ) ;
#ifdef _DEBUG
        if ( NULL == g_hHook )
        {
            char szBuff[ 50 ] ;
            wsprintf ( szBuff ,
                       _T ( "SetWindowsHookEx failed!!!! (0x%08X)\n" ) ,
                       GetLastError ( ) ) ;
            TRACE ( szBuff ) ;
        }
#endif
    }


    return ( (HANDLE)i ) ;


}
```

(continued)

Listing 13-3 *continued*

```
void TNOTIFYHLP_DLLINTERFACE __stdcall
    RemoveNotifyTitle ( HANDLE hItem )
{
    // Check the value.
    int i = (int)hItem ;
    if ( ( i < 0 ) || ( i > TOTAL_NOTIFY_SLOTS ) )
    {
        TRACE ( _T ( "RemoveNotifyTitle : Invalid handle!\n" ) ) ;
        return ;
    }

    // Get the mutex.
    DWORD dwRet = WaitForSingleObject ( g_hMutex , k_WAITLIMIT ) ;
    if ( WAIT_TIMEOUT == dwRet )
    {
        TRACE ( _T ( "RemoveNotifyTitle : Wait on mutex timed out!\n" ) );
        return ;
    }

    if ( 0 == g_shared_iUsedSlots )
    {
        TRACE ( _T ( "RemoveNotifyTitle : Attempting to remove when "
                     "no notification handles are set!\n" ) ) ;
        ReleaseMutex ( g_hMutex ) ;
        return ;
    }

    // Before removing anything, make sure this index points to a
    // NotifyData entry that contains a valid value. If I
    // didn't check, you could call this function with the same value
    // over and over, which would mess up the used-slots counts.
    if ( 0 == g_shared_NotifyData[ i ].dwOwnerPID )
    {
        TRACE ( "RemoveNotifyTitle : Attempting to double remove!\n" ) ;
        ReleaseMutex ( g_hMutex ) ;
        return ;
    }

    // Remove this item from the array.
    g_shared_NotifyData[ i ].dwOwnerPID   = 0 ;
    g_shared_NotifyData[ i ].iNotifyType  = 0 ;
    g_shared_NotifyData[ i ].hWndCreate   = NULL ;
    g_shared_NotifyData[ i ].bDestroy     = FALSE ;
    g_shared_NotifyData[ i ].iSearchType  = 0 ;
    g_shared_NotifyData[ i ].szTitle[ 0 ] = _T ( '\0' ) ;
```

```
    // Bump down the master item count.
    g_shared_iUsedSlots-- ;

    // Bump down this process's item count.
    g_iThisProcessItems-- ;

    TRACE ( _T ( "RemoveNotifyTitle - Removed an item!\n" ) ) ;

    ReleaseMutex ( g_hMutex ) ;

    // If this is the last item for this process, unhook this process's
    // hook.
    if ( ( 0 == g_iThisProcessItems ) && ( NULL != g_hHook ) )
    {
        if ( FALSE == UnhookWindowsHookEx ( g_hHook ) )
        {
            TRACE ( _T ( "UnhookWindowsHookEx failed!\n" ) ) ;
        }
        g_hHook = NULL ;
    }

}

HWND TNOTIFYHLP_DLLINTERFACE __stdcall
    CheckNotifyCreateTitle ( HANDLE hItem )
{
    return ( (HWND)CheckNotifyItem ( hItem , TRUE ) ) ;
}

BOOL TNOTIFYHLP_DLLINTERFACE __stdcall
    CheckNotifyDestroyTitle ( HANDLE hItem )
{
    return ( (BOOL)CheckNotifyItem ( hItem , FALSE ) ) ;
}

/*///////////////////////////////////////////////////////////////////////
                INTERNAL IMPLEMENTATION STARTS HERE
///////////////////////////////////////////////////////////////////////*/

static LONG __stdcall CheckNotifyItem ( HANDLE hItem , BOOL bCreate )
{
    // Check the value.
    int i = (int)hItem ;
    if ( ( i < 0 ) || ( i > TOTAL_NOTIFY_SLOTS ) )
```

(continued)

Listing 13-3 *continued*

```
    {
        TRACE ( _T ( "CheckNotifyItem : Invalid handle!\n" ) ) ;
        return ( NULL ) ;
    }

    LONG lRet = 0 ;

    // Get the mutex.
    DWORD dwRet = WaitForSingleObject ( g_hMutex , k_WAITLIMIT ) ;
    if ( WAIT_TIMEOUT == dwRet )
    {
        TRACE ( _T ( "CheckNotifyItem : Wait on mutex timed out!\n" ) ) ;
        return ( NULL ) ;
    }

    // If all slots are empty, there's nothing to do.
    if ( 0 == g_shared_iUsedSlots )
    {
        ReleaseMutex ( g_hMutex ) ;
        return ( NULL ) ;
    }

    // Check the item requested.
    if ( TRUE == bCreate )
    {
        // If the HWND value isn't NULL, return that value and NULL it
        // out in the table.
        if ( NULL != g_shared_NotifyData[ i ].hWndCreate )
        {
            lRet = (LONG)g_shared_NotifyData[ i ].hWndCreate ;
            g_shared_NotifyData[ i ].hWndCreate = NULL ;
        }
    }
    else
    {
        if ( FALSE != g_shared_NotifyData[ i ].bDestroy )
        {
            lRet = TRUE ;
            g_shared_NotifyData[ i ].bDestroy = FALSE ;
        }
    }

    ReleaseMutex ( g_hMutex ) ;

    return ( lRet ) ;
}
```

```
static void __stdcall CheckTableMatch ( int      iNotifyType ,
                                        HWND     hWnd        ,
                                        LPCTSTR  szTitle     )
{
    // Grab the mutex.
    DWORD dwRet = WaitForSingleObject ( g_hMutex , k_WAITLIMIT ) ;
    if ( WAIT_TIMEOUT == dwRet )
    {
        TRACE ( _T ( "CheckTableMatch : Wait on mutex timed out!\n" ) ) ;
        return ;
    }

    // The table shouldn't be empty, but never assume anything.
    if ( 0 == g_shared_iUsedSlots )
    {
        ReleaseMutex ( g_hMutex ) ;
        TRACE ( _T ( "CheckTableMatch called on an empty table!\n" ) ) ;
        return ;
    }


    // Search through the table.
    for ( int i = 0 ; i < TOTAL_NOTIFY_SLOTS ; i++ )
    {
        // Does this entry have something in it, and does the type of
        // notification match?
        if ( ( _T ( '\0' ) != g_shared_NotifyData[ i ].szTitle[ 0 ] ) &&
             ( g_shared_NotifyData[ i ].iNotifyType & iNotifyType   ) )
        {
            BOOL bMatch = FALSE ;
            // Perform the match.
            switch ( g_shared_NotifyData[ i ].iSearchType )
            {
                case ANTS_EXACTMATCH   :
                    // This is simple.
                    if ( 0 == lstrcmp ( g_shared_NotifyData[i].szTitle ,
                                        szTitle                        ) )
                    {
                        bMatch = TRUE ;
                    }
                    break ;
                case ANTS_BEGINMATCH   :
                    if ( 0 ==
```

(continued)

Listing 13-3 *continued*

```
                            _tcsnccmp ( g_shared_NotifyData[i].szTitle ,
                                         szTitle                        ,
                                strlen(g_shared_NotifyData[i].szTitle) ) )
                {
                    bMatch = TRUE ;
                }
                break ;
            case ANTS_ANYLOCMATCH    :
                if ( NULL != _tcsstr ( szTitle                          ,
                                      g_shared_NotifyData[i].szTitle ) )
                {
                    bMatch = TRUE ;
                }
                break ;
            default                  :
                TRACE ( _T ( "CheckTableMatch invalid "\
                                "search type!!!\n" ) ) ;
                ReleaseMutex ( g_hMutex ) ;
                return ;
                break ;
        }
        // Tell them, Johnny. Do we have a match?
        if ( TRUE == bMatch )
        {
            // If this is a destroy notification, stick "1" in the
            // table.
            if ( ANTN_DESTROYWINDOW == iNotifyType )
            {
                g_shared_NotifyData[ i ].bDestroy = TRUE ;
            }
            else
            {
                // Otherwise, stick the HWND in the table.
                g_shared_NotifyData[ i ].hWndCreate = hWnd ;
            }
        }
    }
    }
    ReleaseMutex ( g_hMutex ) ;
}

LRESULT CALLBACK CallWndRetProcHook ( int     nCode  ,
                                      WPARAM wParam ,
                                      LPARAM lParam  )
{
```

```
// Buffer for storing the window title
TCHAR szBuff[ MAX_PATH ] ;

// Always pass the message to the next hook before I do any
// processing. This way I don't forget and I can do my processing
// in peace.
LRESULT lRet = CallNextHookEx ( g_hHook , nCode , wParam , lParam ) ;

// The docs say never to mess around with a negative code, so I
// don't.
if ( nCode < 0 )
{
    return ( lRet ) ;
}

// Get the message structure. Why are there three (or more)
// different message structures?  What's wrong with consistently
// using the stock ole MSG for all message/proc hooks?
PCWPRETSTRUCT pMsg = (PCWPRETSTRUCT)lParam ;

// No caption, no work to do
LONG lStyle = GetWindowLong ( pMsg->hwnd , GWL_STYLE ) ;
if ( WS_CAPTION != ( lStyle & WS_CAPTION ) )
{
    return ( lRet ) ;
}

// The WM_DESTROY messages are copacetic for both dialog boxes and
// normal windows. Just get the caption and check for a match.
if ( WM_DESTROY == pMsg->message )
{
    if ( 0 != GetWindowText ( pMsg->hwnd , szBuff , MAX_PATH ) )
    {
        CheckTableMatch ( ANTN_DESTROYWINDOW , pMsg->hwnd , szBuff ) ;
    }
    return ( lRet ) ;
}

// Window creation isn't as clean as window destruction.

// Get the window class. If it is a true dialog box, the
// WM_INITDIALOG is all I need.
if ( 0 == GetClassName ( pMsg->hwnd , szBuff , MAX_PATH ) )
{
```

(continued)

Listing 13-3 *continued*

```
#ifdef _DEBUG
        TCHAR szBuff[ 50 ] ;
        wsprintf ( szBuff                                            ,
                    _T ( "GetClassName failed for HWND : 0x%08X\n" ) ,
                    pMsg->hwnd                                      ) ;
        TRACE ( szBuff ) ;
#endif
        // There's not much point in going on.
        return ( lRet ) ;
    }
    if ( 0 == lstrcmpi ( szBuff , _T ( "#32770" ) ) )
    {
        // The only message I need to check is WM_INITDIALOG.
        if ( WM_INITDIALOG == pMsg->message )
        {
            // Get the caption of the dialog box.
            if ( 0 != GetWindowText ( pMsg->hwnd , szBuff , MAX_PATH ) )
            {
                CheckTableMatch ( ANTN_CREATEWINDOW ,
                                  pMsg->hwnd         ,
                                  szBuff            ) ;
            }
        }
        return ( lRet ) ;
    }
    // That took care of true dialog boxes. Start figuring out what to do
    // for actual windows.

    if ( WM_CREATE == pMsg->message )
    {
        // Very few windows set the title in WM_CREATE.
        // However, a few do and they don't use WM_SETTEXT, so I have
        // to check.
        if ( 0 != GetWindowText ( pMsg->hwnd , szBuff , MAX_PATH ) )
        {
            CheckTableMatch ( ANTN_CREATEWINDOW ,
                              pMsg->hwnd         ,
                              szBuff            ) ;
        }
    }
    else if ( WM_SETTEXT == pMsg->message )
    {
        // I always default to WM_SETTEXT because that's how captions
        // get set. Unfortunately, some applications, such as Internet
```

```
    // Explorer, seem to call WM_SETTEXT a bunch of times with the
    // same title. To keep this hook simple, I just report
    // the WM_SETTEXT instead of maintaining all sorts of weird,
    // hard-to-debug data structures that keep track of the windows
    // that called WM_SETTEXT previously.
    if ( NULL != pMsg->lParam )
    {
        CheckTableMatch ( ANTN_CREATEWINDOW     ,
                          pMsg->hwnd            ,
                          (LPCTSTR)pMsg->lParam ) ;
    }
}

return ( lRet ) ;
}
```

Although the *TNotify* implementation was a brainteaser in some ways, I was pleased at how few troubles I experienced implementing it. If you do want to extend the hook code, be aware that debugging systemwide hooks isn't a simple endeavor. Although you can debug systemwide hooks with the Microsoft Visual C++ debugger, I've never tried it. I just use SoftICE. The other way you can debug systemwide hooks is to resort to *printf*-style debugging. Using DBGVIEW, you can watch all the *OutputDebugString* calls to see the state of your hook.

I did experience one annoying problem when developing Tester that appeared only on Windows 98. All my test code worked just fine on Windows NT 4 and Windows 2000, but on Windows 98 I couldn't get the *TWindows* collection filled. I was checking whether the *HWND* passed into the *Add* method was valid with *IsWindow*. A quick read of the documentation said that *IsWindow* returns a *BOOL*. My mistake was assuming that *BOOL* was *TRUE* for positive and *FALSE* for negative. I also like to use the positive form of conditionals, so I was using *1 = IsWindow(hWndT)*, which obviously didn't work. As you can guess, the different operating systems don't return the same value. It was a small problem, but I thought you could learn from it.

WHAT'S NEXT FOR TESTER?

As I mentioned earlier, Tester does one thing well: playing keystrokes. As with all the utilities in this book, you're welcome to find ways to improve Tester if you're so inclined. Here are some possible enhancements you might pursue:

■   Add wrapper classes such as *TListBox*, *TTreeControl*, and *TRadioButton* so that you can check various states and verify that control items contain the proper data. With these classes, you can start validating controls and writing more complicated scripts.

- Add a recorder application so that you can record keystrokes. Try to make the recorder extensible so that if you do add additional wrapper classes, you can take advantage of them with the recorder application to generate better scripts.

- Explore ways to add mouse input to Tester. You might be able to record the mouse placement as a percentage of screen offsets. The only problem would be that you might miss a control you need to click on when you change resolutions. Another idea would be to first add all the wrapper classes and then use only the *Click* method for the wrapper classes for clicks. The problem here is that you'd need to ensure that you have all types of windows wrapped with specific tester controls.

SUMMARY

Performing UI unit tests can be a challenge. This chapter introduced a simple utility, Tester, that will automate your testing by playing keystrokes to your application. Although not as complete as a commercial regression-testing tool, Tester will certainly save wear-and-tear on your wrists.

I hope that Tester shows you how valuable tools that automate your application can be. If your application is complex enough, I'd recommend investing in a commercial regression-testing tool so that you can speed up your unit testing. If you spend a little time planning how you're going to use the regression-testing tool, you can grow a system in which your developers are contributing regression scripts that the QA department can then roll into the master QA automated testing scripts. If you play your cards right, your main QA suites will almost appear to write themselves.

Chapter 14

Limiting
OutputDebugString Calls

Have you ever heard the saying, "Too much of a good thing can kill you"? That phrase has often come to mind when I've had to search through 2 megabytes of trace statements looking for a single line to indicate what went wrong with my program—or worse yet, after I've dozed off waiting for the debugger to process the trace statements inside a loop that has 10,000 iterations. I'm willing to bet that you've suffered from trace statement glut as well and that you've been as annoyed by it as I have. I don't mean to seem overly critical of trace statements. As I said in Chapter 3, trace statements used correctly with assertions are great: they let you debug your application without the debugger. But too many trace statements spell trouble.

Having too many trace statements is especially bad in real-world team development. Everyone sprinkles in a few, and yours are lost in the morass as soon as you check in your code. Because trace statements quickly lose their effectiveness if they are overused, you stop adding them to your code—and thus lose some capability to debug your problems easily.

Wouldn't it be nice if you could use a ton of trace statements but only see the ones that came out of the source files you're interested in—no matter which modules they came from? The good news is that I've developed a utility that let's you do just that for both Microsoft Visual C++ and compiled Microsoft Visual Basic. After presenting my solution, I'll talk about some of the scrapes and bruises I earned implementing LIMODS (Limit OutputDebugStrings). Armed with LIMODS, you'll be in a better position to add as many trace statements to your applications as you like to help you debug your problems faster, without worrying that you've added too many. Go ahead—wallow in trace statement excess to your heart's content!

ALSO-RAN SOLUTIONS

I wish I could say that the idea for LIMODS came to me fully formed in a dream and wrote itself. In reality, the road to "discovering" a solution to the problem of easily limiting trace statements included quite a few twists and turns. My initial thought was to recommend conditional compilation so that each source file had a *#define* associated with it. To see the trace statements for a particular file or set of files, you'd just need to set the *#define* and compile. Although the conditional compilation technique would work, I certainly didn't want to recompile every time I turned trace statements on or off in a source file. From what I've seen, developers often use the conditional compilation approach in the real world, but I preferred something more automatic than chugging through different compiles just for different trace statements.

Another possible solution involved unique trace macros. In an effort to solve the too-many-traces problem across a huge development team, I tried this approach. Each subteam received a unique trace macro for its particular section of the project. The Microsoft Foundation Class (MFC) library uses a similar approach with the internal tracing that's turned on with MFC's TRACER.EXE program. MFC's internal trace statements check a global flag variable, and if the bit assigned to a subsystem is active, the trace statements appear in the Output window. On my large team, the unique-macro approach worked for a while but started breaking down because the MFC wizards themselves generated *TRACE* macros and the developers were forgetting to use their unique macros. I tried to combat this problem by undefining *TRACE* in the source files to force the developers to use the correct macros, but I found it quite annoying to have to fix wizard-generated and third-party code. Another problem with the unique-macro approach is that it's not that extensible. You generally have to spend a good bit of time up front porting the trace macros from project to project. It also becomes a pain to maintain these macros when the program's architecture changes and when code is moved from one subsystem to another. Moreover, the unique-macro approach doesn't work with Visual Basic.

After realizing that starting from the source code side wasn't working, I tried to step back and think about the problem from an entirely different perspective. I realized that what I really needed was a way to associate a call to a tracing function with the particular source file it came from. I also needed a way to decide whether or not the tracing function call was to go through. Finally, I needed a way to toggle trace statement output from both source files and modules. When I summarized the problem this way, I had my "Eureka!" moment (though thankfully I didn't jump up naked out of the tub and run through the streets).

You might recognize the problems described in the preceding paragraph from other chapters—throughout the book, I've solved each of them independently. To build a system that limits trace statements, I just needed to tie the individual solutions together. As you'll see when I get to the section "Implementing LIMODS" later in this chapter, I was able to achieve the elusive dream of code reuse and nerdvana.

LIMODS REQUIREMENTS

As I've done in presenting the other utilities in this book, I'll start with the requirements I set out for myself in writing LIMODS before I talk about its usage and implementation. As you can see from the following list, simplicity was a key requirement. The simpler a development tool is to use, the more likely developers are to use it.

- To use LIMODS, the user should have to make only minimal source code changes. Ideally, I wanted LIMODS to require only a single-line change to a user's program.

- LIMODS keeps out of the way and automatically takes care of initializing itself so that users don't have to do any work other than just include LIMODS in their projects.

- LIMODS has a simple user interface that lets users quickly and easily pick the source files from which they want to see trace statements.

Before I jump into the implementation of LIMODS, I want to explain how you use it. Understanding LIMODS usage will make implementing it that much easier.

USING LIMODS

Before reading any further, you need to install LIMODS. All the source code for LIMODS is on the book's companion CD, and you'll need to compile the entire LIMODS project. After compiling, copy the LIMODS settings file, LIMODS.INI, to your %SYSTEMROOT% or Windows directory. By default, LIMODS will place its data files (LOM) in the same directory in which each loaded module resides when LIMODS is active. If you set the LOMDirectory in the [LIMODS] section of LIMODS.INI, GENLIMODS.EXE will place all generated LOM files in one directory. I use this setting because I prefer to have all the LOM files sent to one location instead of scattered all over my hard drive. After taking care of the settings file, you need to put the binary files—LIMODSDLL.DLL, BUGSLAYERUTIL.DLL, GENLIMODS.EXE, and LIMODS.EXE—in a directory specified by your PATH environment variable.

Living with MFC

If you want to use LIMODS with an application that uses either MFC42D.DLL or MFC42UD.DLL, you'll need to take an extra step to install it. Unfortunately, there must be at least 1,001 versions of those two very important DLLs. LIMODS must know which ordinal value corresponds to the exported *AfxTrace* function from each of the MFC DLLs. Although you'd think that *AfxTrace* would always have the same ordinal value regardless of which DLL it's in, it doesn't. The distributed LIMODS.INI holds the information for MFC42(U)D.DLL that's used with Visual C++ 5 with no service packs, Visual C++ 6 with no service packs, Visual C++ 6 with Service Pack 1 (SP1), Visual C++ 6 with Service Pack 2 (SP2), and Visual C++ 6 with Service Pack 3 (SP3).

If you're using a version of Visual C++ different from the ones listed in LIMODS.INI (including any subsequent service pack releases), you'll need to do some additional work to ensure that LIMODS gets the right export out of MFC42D.DLL and MFC42UD.DLL. You can find the version information for %SYSTEMROOT%\-System32\MFC42(U)D.DLL by right-clicking on it in Windows Explorer and selecting Properties from the pop-up menu. Click the Version tab in the Properties dialog box; the first item, File Version, is the number you want. For example, the version of MFC42D.DLL that Visual C++ 6.0 SP3 uses is 6.00.8447.0.

Next change to the \MFC\SRC\Intel directory in your Visual C++ installation. There you'll find the DEF files used to link MFC. Each DEF file name corresponds to a binary file name. For example, MFC42D.DEF is the matching DEF file for MFC42D.DLL. Open the appropriate DEF file, and for MFC42D.DLL, search for the text *?AfxTrace-@@YAXPBDZZ*. For MFC42UD.DLL, search for the text *?AfxTrace@@YAXPBGZZ*. The important line will look like this:

```
?AfxTrace@@YAXPBDZZ @ 1179 NONAME
```

The number after the @ sign is the ordinal value of the exported *AfxTrace* function. Remember this number—you'll need to enter this ordinal value into the LIMODS.INI file.

Open your copy of LIMODS.INI. For MFC42D.DLL, look for the section [MFC42D.DLL Hack-O-Rama]. For MFC42UD.DLL, the section is [MFC42UD.DLL Hack-O-Rama]. The section for MFC42D.DLL will look like the following, and it's nearly identical to the section for MFC42UD.DLL:

```
[MFC42D.DLL Hack-O-Rama]
VerCount=3
; VC 6.0 SP3
Ver0=6.00.8447.0,1179
; VC 6.0 SP1 and SP2.
Ver1=6.00.8267.0,1179
; VC 6.0 NO SERVICE PACKS
Ver2=6.00.8168.0,1179
```

The Ver*n* lines show the version number and ordinal value information. The first number is the MFC file version number, and the second number is the *AfxTrace* ordinal value.

Add your MFC file version and *AfxTrace* ordinal value as the next line in the [MFC42D.DLL Hack-O-Rama] or [MFC42UD.DLL Hack-O-Rama] section. For example, if you're working with Visual C++ 5 with no service packs, you'd add the line *Ver3=4.21.7022,1253* to the preceding sample for MFC42D.DLL. You'd also need to increment the right-hand side of *VerCount*. For MFC42UD.DLL in Visual C++ 5 with no service pack, the line would be *Ver3=4.21.7022,1256*.

If you modify the MFC source code and build your own private MFC42(U)D.DLL, you can check the ordinal value information in the same way as I described earlier. I'd suggest, however, that you never change the MFC source code and create your own MFC version—unless, of course, you feel like manually updating every MFC bug fix into your version of the source files.

LIMODS validates the MFC file version when MFC42(U)D.DLL is loaded into memory. If you don't have the corresponding file version in LIMODS.INI, you'll get an error message in the Output window, accompanied by a few beeps. If you compile and run the LIMODS test program in the \SoureCode\LIMODS\TestLIMODS directory on the companion CD, you'll quickly find out whether you configured LIMODS correctly.

Calling LIMODS from Your Code

After all the hoops you had to jump through to ensure that you're using the correct MFC DLL, you might find it almost a letdown when I tell you that for C/C++ programs, the following line of code is the only one you need to add to your program to get LIMODS working:

```
LoadLibrary ( "LIMODSDLL.DLL" ) ;
```

LIMODSDLL.DLL works all its magic in its *DllMain*, so you don't need to call any other functions. I figure adding one line of code isn't too much to ask to reap the benefits of LIMODS.

If you're developing in Visual Basic, getting LIMODS to work in your code is a little more complicated—but not by much. First you'll need to copy LIMODS.CLS and INDESIGNMOD.BAS out of the \SourceCode\LIMODS\VB directory from the companion CD and add them to your project. Then you'll need to create a global instance of the *clsLIMODS* class, shown in Listing 14-1. I'd recommend naming the global instance variable something like *cLIMODS*. The *clsLIMODS* class has only one method; it's named (surprise) *Trace*, and it takes the same input as the *Debug.Print* method. There's no way to intercept the internal *Debug.Print* object, so you must compile your application for LIMODS to work. When you run from the Visual Basic integrated development environment (IDE), the *clsLIMODS Trace* method will resolve to a *Debug.Print* call, so you'll still be able to see trace statement output in the Immediate window.

You'll also need to define the conditional compilation option LIMODS=−1 in your project so that you get the appropriate class functions when you compile. If you don't define the conditional compilation, you get the empty versions. By using the conditional compilation, you won't have to pay the full overhead for LIMODS when you don't need it, although you'll still get the empty function overhead. To avoid the cost of the empty functions, you'll need to wrap all your calls to the *clsLIMODS* object in conditional compilation.

```
VERSION 1.0 CLASS
BEGIN
  MultiUse = -1  'True
  Persistable = 0  'NotPersistable
  DataBindingBehavior = 0  'vbNone
  DataSourceBehavior  = 0  'vbNone
  MTSTransactionMode  = 0  'NotAnMTSObject
END
Attribute VB_Name = "clsLIMODS"
Attribute VB_GlobalNameSpace = False
Attribute VB_Creatable = True
Attribute VB_PredeclaredId = False
Attribute VB_Exposed = False
'''''''''''''''''''''''''''''''''''''''''''''''''''''''''''''''''''''''
' Copyright (c) 1997-2000 John Robbins -- All rights reserved.
' "Debugging Applications" (Microsoft Press)
'''''''''''''''''''''''''''''''''''''''''''''''''''''''''''''''''''''''
' The LIMODS helper class for Visual Basic development
' 1. Include this class file in your Visual Basic project. Create a
'    global instance of this class in your project. (I'd name the global
'    instance variable "cLIMODS".)
' 2. Just call cLIMODS.Trace to direct trace statements through here.
' 3. LIMODS is active only with compiled Visual Basic. If you run this
'    class under the Visual Basic IDE debugger, your trace statements
'    will be sent through the regular Debug.Print trace statement.
'''''''''''''''''''''''''''''''''''''''''''''''''''''''''''''''''''''''


Option Explicit

Private Declare Function LoadLibrary Lib "kernel32" _
        Alias "LoadLibraryA" _
        (ByVal lpLibFileName As String) As Long
Private Declare Sub OutputDebugString Lib "kernel32" _
        Alias "OutputDebugStringA" _
        (ByVal lpOutputString As String)
Private Declare Function GetModuleFileName Lib "kernel32" _
        Alias "GetModuleFileNameA" _
        (ByVal hModule As Long, _
         ByVal lpFileName As String, _
         ByVal nSize As Long) As Long
Private Declare Function GetModuleHandle Lib "kernel32" _
        Alias "GetModuleHandleA" _
        (ByVal lpModuleName As String) As Long
```

Listing 14-1 *LIMODS.CLS*

```
Private m_IsInIDE As Boolean

#If LIMODS Then
Private Sub Class_Initialize()
    Dim bIsInIDE As Boolean

    bIsInIDE = InDesign()
    ' If bIsInIDE is False, the main module isn't the Visual Basic IDE,
    ' so I can load LIMODSDLL.DLL.
    If (False = bIsInIDE) Then
        LoadLibrary "LIMODSDLL.DLL"
        m_IsInIDE = False
    Else
        m_IsInIDE = True
    End If
End Sub
#End If

#If LIMODS Then
Public Sub Trace(sOut As Variant)
    If (True = m_IsInIDE) Then
        Debug.Print sOut
    Else
        Dim s As String
        s = sOut
        OutputDebugString s
    End If
End Sub
#Else    ' LIMODS is *not* conditionally defined.
Public Sub Trace(sOut As Variant)
End Sub
#End If
```

Selecting Which Source Files to Trace From

All the LOM files for modules compiled with debug symbols will be generated the first time you run with LIMODSDLL.DLL loaded, so you'll experience a slight pause in your application as they're being processed. LIMODS keeps the LOM files up to date as your modules change, so you don't have to worry about tracking these changes manually. If you prefer, you can generate the LOM files as part of your normal build process by using GENLIMODS.EXE. Just run GENLIMODS.EXE without any command-line parameters to see a description of its use.

After the LOM files are loaded, simply run LIMODS.EXE and select which source files from which modules you want to view. Figure 14-1 shows LIMODS.EXE in action. Select the check box next to the source files from which you want to see trace statements.

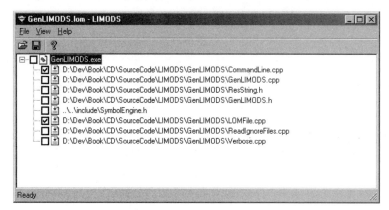

Figure 14-1 *LIMODS.EXE in action*

IMPLEMENTING LIMODS

The LIMODS implementation turned out to be quite interesting. I had to do some finagling to get the DBGHELP.DLL symbol engine to work, but the really interesting parts involved writing __*cdecl* import hook functions and hooking imports by ordinal value.

Determining Source Code Ranges

You probably won't be surprised to find out that I'm using my old friend DBGHELP.DLL yet again. (I introduced this DLL in Chapter 4.) With the source file and line number functions in the DBGHELP.DLL symbol engine, I figured that I could find the first and last addresses (what I call the *address range*) that correspond to a particular source file. Armed with the address range, I could hook *OutputDebugString* using the techniques I discussed in Chapter 12 and look at the return address to see whether it's in a source file the user wants to allow trace statements from. Although this approach was simple in theory, the actual implementation had me going around my elbow to get the information the way I needed it.

There's no specific application programming interface (API) function that enumerates the source file address ranges, but I figured I could make do with the symbol enumeration function *SymEnumerateSymbols*. I'd use *SymEnumerateSymbols* to retrieve the first symbol, and in my symbol enumeration function, I'd move back to the start of the source file with *SymGetLinePrev* and then walk to the end of the source file with *SymGetLineNext*. Using *SymEnumerateSymbols* worked great on my simple test cases, but when I ran it against GENLIMODS.EXE, I noticed that the source ranges didn't jibe with what the disassembly showed. I seemed to be missing entire sections of the source file.

When I manually calculated the ranges, they came out looking like those listed in Table 14-1. The issue was that the *SymGetLineNext* and *SymGetLinePrev* functions enumerate only the contiguous ranges. As you can see in Table 14-1, source files with inline functions occur between the first part of GENLIMODS.CPP and the second part. I quickly realized that this isn't a bug but rather just how the compiler operates. The misunderstanding was on my part; I was focusing on the source file when I really needed to be thinking about the ranges first.

Table 14-1   **GENLIMODS.EXE SAMPLE ADDRESS RANGES**

Start	*End*	*Source File*
0x00401900	0x00401A8A	COMMANDLINE.CPP
0x00401D00	0x00402F1F	GENLIMODS.CPP
0x00403450	0x00403774	RESSTRING.H
0x004037C0	0x004037DD	GENLIMODS.H
0x00403D60	0x004040F9	SYMBOLENGINE.H
0x00404690	0x004046AC	GENLIMODS.CPP
0x00407080	0x0040852E	LOMFILE.CPP
0x00409D50	0x0040A532	READIGNOREFILES.CPP
0x0040C800	0x0040C894	VERBOSE.CPP

LOM Files Explained

The LOM files GENLIMODS.EXE generates are just INI files, as you can see in Listing 14-2. The first section of the code is where I keep the main module information, which includes the name, load address, and date and timestamp of the module used to build the LOM file. When LIMODSDLL.DLL looks at the module in memory, it checks the module against the LOM file; if the module's date and timestamp is different from the LOM file's date and timestamp, LIMODSDLL.DLL has GENLIMODS.EXE generate a new LOM file for the module. I store the base address of the module so that if the image loader relocates the module, LIMODSDLL.DLL can recalculate the address ranges on the fly. LIMODSDLL.DLL will also let you know through calls to *OutputDebugString* that a module has been relocated.

```
[Module Info]
DateTimeStamp=380b75e8
BaseAddress=400000
ModuleName=LIMODS.exe
[Ranges]
RangeCount=11
Range0=0x004017D0|0x00401C8E|0|D:\Book\SourceCode\LIMODS\About.cpp
Range1=0x00401EF0|0x00402313|0|D:\Book\SourceCode\LIMODS\BigIcon.CPP
Range2=0x00402430|0x00402A5E|0|D:\Book\SourceCode\LIMODS\LIMODS.cpp
Range3=0x00402D60|0x00403727|1|D:\Book\SourceCode\LIMODS\LIMODSDoc.cpp
Range4=0x004044B0|0x0040480D|0|D:\Book\SourceCode\LIMODS\LIMODSOptions.cpp
Range5=0x00404950|0x00405823|0|D:\Book\SourceCode\LIMODS\LIMODSView.cpp
Range6=0x00405D70|0x00405DB0|0|D:\Book\SourceCode\LIMODS\LIMODSDoc.h
Range7=0x00406150|0x00407521|0|D:\Book\SourceCode\LIMODS\LOMFile.cpp
Range8=0x00408D00|0x004090FF|0|D:\Book\SourceCode\LIMODS\MainFrm.cpp
Range9=0x00409270|0x00409516|0|D:\Book\SourceCode\LIMODS\OptionsDialog.cpp
Range10=0x0040A0A0|0x0040A140|0|appmodul.cpp
[Sources]
Source0=0|D:\Book\SourceCode\LIMODS\About.cpp
Source1=0|D:\Book\SourceCode\LIMODS\BigIcon.CPP
Source2=0|D:\Book\SourceCode\LIMODS\LIMODS.cpp
Source3=1|D:\Book\SourceCode\LIMODS\LIMODSDoc.cpp
Source4=0|D:\Book\SourceCode\LIMODS\LIMODSOptions.cpp
Source5=0|D:\Book\SourceCode\LIMODS\LIMODSView.cpp
Source6=0|D:\Book\SourceCode\LIMODS\LIMODSDoc.h
Source7=0|D:\Book\SourceCode\LIMODS\LOMFile.cpp
Source8=0|D:\Book\SourceCode\LIMODS\MainFrm.cpp
Source9=0|D:\Book\SourceCode\LIMODS\OptionsDialog.cpp
Source10=0|appmodul.cpp
SourceCount=11
```

Listing 14-2 *A sample LOM file*

The format of the [Ranges] section defines the address ranges for the source files and is primarily what LIMODSDLL.DLL uses to determine what trace statements to show and when to show them. In order, the fields are start address, end address, the show trace Boolean value, and the source file name. LIMODS.EXE uses the [Sources] section to show the source file names in its tree view control. I used the INI file format originally to make initial testing easier and had it hidden by an accessor class in LOMFILE.H and LOMFILE.CPP. As I kept working on LIMODS as a whole, I found the performance acceptable, so I never changed to a different format.

Excluding Source Files from LOM Files

GENLIMODS.EXE offers an exclusion capability to limit the source files in the resulting LOM file to the ones that include trace statements. Although you might find it interesting to see that you have half the Standard Template Library (STL) in the generated code, those files contain no trace statements and they just cause LIMODSDLL.DLL to take up more memory and process slowly. GENLIMODS.EXE looks for two files that Visual C++ uses to exclude files from its dependency checking: SYSINCL.DAT and the optional, user-supplied MSVCINCL.DAT. SYSINCL.DAT is just a list of files that appear in your <VC Dir>\Include and <VC Dir>\MFC\Include directories. MSVCINCL.DAT can contain any list of headers you don't want dependency checking used on. In addition to those files, GENLIMODS.EXE looks for a LIMODSINCL.DAT in your PATH directories for any extra files you want to exclude. For example, if you don't want to see the C run-time library files in your LOM files, you can include them in LIMODSINCL.DAT. On the companion CD in the \SourceCode\LIMODS directory is a version of LIMODSINCL.DAT that will exclude all the C run-time library source files.

What LIMODSDLL.DLL Hooks

When LIMODSDLL.DLL starts, it intercepts the key imported tracing functions in all process modules. For this version of LIMODS, those functions are *OutputDebugStringA* and *OutputDebugStringW* from KERNEL32.DLL, *DiagOutputA* and *DiagOutputW* from BUGSLAYERUTIL.DLL, *_CrtDbgReport* from MSVCRTD.DLL, and *AfxTrace* from MFC42(U)D.DLL. In addition, I hooked the *LoadLibrary* family of functions so that I'd know when additional modules are loaded into the address space.

For LIMODS to work with Visual Basic, I also needed to hook *GetProcAddress* so that I could return the appropriate function when MSVBVM60.DLL tries to get *OutputDebugStringA*. I talked about hooking functions in Chapter 12, and you might've thought that I'd exhausted this topic. As it turned out, hooking *DiagOutputA*, *DiagOutputW*, and the *AfxTrace* functions posed some unique challenges. For one thing, these functions are *__cdecl* functions instead of the *__stdcall* functions I showed how to hook in Chapter 12. Also, *AfxTrace* is exported by ordinal value.

Handling __*cdecl* Hooks

As you saw in Chapter 12, *__stdcall* functions are easy to hook because the function itself cleans up the stack; the caller cleans up the stacks of *__cdecl* functions. The *DiagOutputA*, *DiagOutputW*, and *AfxTrace* functions also have variable-length parameters, so intercepting them is that much more difficult. The act of hooking is the same as with *__stdcall* exported functions, but the *__cdecl* hook function processing has to be different. In LIMODSDLL.DLL, I wanted the hook function to grab the return address and determine whether it's an address range from which the user wants to see trace statements. After checking the source, I'll either let the trace function execute or ignore the trace function and return to the caller. With *__stdcall* functions, this processing is all very simple. I can just call the trace function directly and return right from my hook function to the caller because I clean up the stack from the hook

```
VOID NAKEDDEF LIMODS_DiagOutputA ( void )

{
    // Holds the return address of the caller
    DWORD_PTR dwRet ;
    // Holds the saved ESI so that Visual C++ 6 debug builds work. (The
    // chkesp function inserted with the /GZ switch uses ESI.)
    DWORD_PTR dwESI ;

    __asm PUSH   EBP                    /* Set up the standard frame.       */
    __asm MOV    EBP , ESP
    __asm SUB    ESP , __LOCAL_SIZE    /* Save room for the local          */
                                        /* variables.                       */
    __asm MOV    EAX , EBP             /* EBP points to the original stack.*/
    __asm ADD    EAX , 4               /* Account for PUSH EBP.            */
    __asm MOV    EAX , [EAX]           /* Get the return address.          */
    __asm MOV    [dwRet] , EAX         /* Save the return address.         */
    __asm MOV    [dwESI] , ESI         /* Save ESI so chkesp in debug      */
                                        /* builds works.                    */

    // Call the function that determines whether this address is one to
    // show. The return value is in EAX after this call and is checked
    // below. A return of TRUE means execute the trace function. A return
    // of FALSE means skip the trace function.
    CheckIfAddressIsOn ( dwRet ) ;

    __asm MOV    ESI , [dwESI]         /* Restore ESI.                     */
    __asm ADD    ESP , __LOCAL_SIZE    /* Take away local variable space.  */
    __asm MOV    ESP, EBP              /* Restore the standard frame.      */
    __asm POP    EBP

    // Here's where the fun begins! The preceding four lines of asm code
    // restored the stack to exactly what it looked like coming into
    // this function, so I'm now prepared to jump to the trace function.
    // pReadDiagOutputA holds the trace function address that I got
    // during initialization.
    __asm TEST   EAX , EAX             /* Test EAX for 0.                  */
    __asm JZ     lblDiagOutputA        /* If 0, just return.               */
    __asm JMP    pReadDiagOutputA      /* Do it! THE JUMP WILL RETURN TO   */
                                        /* THE CALLER, NOT TO THIS FUNCTION.*/
lblDiagOutputA:

                                        /* Skipped the TRACE! Just return   */
    __asm RET                          /* to the caller.                   */
}
```

Listing 14-3 *A __cdecl hook function with macros expanded* function. With __*cdecl* functions, I have to get the stack back to the original state and then jump to (not call) the trace function if I need to execute it.

Listing 14-3 shows a hook function, with macros expanded, that takes care of *DiagOutputA* from BUGSLAYERUTIL.DLL. To make it easier to reuse common assembly-language routines, such as __*cdecl* prolog code, I define several assembly-language macros in LIMODSDLL.CPP for use in my hook functions. I strongly encourage you to step through the macros in the Visual C++ debugger's Disassembly window so that you can watch each instruction in action.

Hooking Functions Exported by Ordinal Value

I have to be honest and say that I almost didn't support hooking functions exported by ordinal value because the endeavor is so error prone, especially because different versions of the MFC DLLs use different ordinal values. Once you get past these version problems, however, the process of hooking by ordinal value is almost identical to hooking by name. Compare the *HookOrdinalExport* function, shown in Listing 14-4, with the *HookImportedFunctionsByName* function shown in Chapter 12 and you'll see that both functions perform many of the same operations.

```
BOOL BUGSUTIL_DLLINTERFACE __stdcall
                    HookOrdinalExport ( HMODULE  hModule       ,
                                        LPCTSTR  szImportMod ,
                                        DWORD    dwOrdinal   ,
                                        PROC     pHookFunc   ,
                                        PROC *   ppOrigAddr   )
{
    // Assert the parameters.
    ASSERT ( NULL != hModule ) ;
    ASSERT ( FALSE == IsBadStringPtr ( szImportMod , MAX_PATH ) ) ;
    ASSERT ( 0 != dwOrdinal ) ;
    ASSERT ( FALSE == IsBadCodePtr ( pHookFunc ) ) ;

    // Perform the error checking for the parameters.
    if ( ( NULL  == hModule                              ) ||
         ( TRUE  == IsBadStringPtr ( szImportMod , MAX_PATH ) ) ||
         ( 0     == dwOrdinal                            ) ||
         ( TRUE  == IsBadCodePtr ( pHookFunc )           )  )
    {
        SetLastErrorEx ( ERROR_INVALID_PARAMETER , SLE_ERROR ) ;
        return ( FALSE ) ;
    }

    if ( NULL != ppOrigAddr )
```

Listing 14-4 *The* HookOrdinalExport *function*   *(continued)*

Listing 14-4 *continued*

```
{
    ASSERT ( FALSE ==
                IsBadWritePtr ( ppOrigAddr , sizeof ( PROC ) ) ) ;
    if ( TRUE == IsBadWritePtr ( ppOrigAddr , sizeof ( PROC ) ) )
    {
        SetLastErrorEx ( ERROR_INVALID_PARAMETER , SLE_ERROR ) ;
        return ( FALSE ) ;
    }
}

// Get the specific import descriptor.
PIMAGE_IMPORT_DESCRIPTOR pImportDesc =
                GetNamedImportDescriptor ( hModule , szImportMod ) ;

if ( NULL == pImportDesc )
{
    // The requested module wasn't imported. Don't return an error.
    return ( TRUE ) ;
}

// Get the original thunk information for this DLL. I can't use
// the thunk information stored in pImportDesc->FirstThunk
// because the loader has already changed that array to fix up
// all the imports. The original thunk gives me access to the
// function names.
PIMAGE_THUNK_DATA pOrigThunk =
                MakePtr ( PIMAGE_THUNK_DATA          ,
                          hModule                    ,
                          pImportDesc->OriginalFirstThunk  ) ;
// Get the array that pImportDesc->FirstThunk points to because I'll
// do the actual hooking there.
PIMAGE_THUNK_DATA pRealThunk = MakePtr ( PIMAGE_THUNK_DATA      ,
                                         hModule                ,
                                         pImportDesc->FirstThunk  );

// The flag is going to be set from the thunk, so make it
// easier to look up.
DWORD dwCompareOrdinal = IMAGE_ORDINAL_FLAG | dwOrdinal ;

// Loop through and find the function to hook.
while ( NULL != pOrigThunk->u1.Function )
{
    // Look only at functions that are imported by ordinal value,
    // not those that are imported by name.
```

```
if ( IMAGE_ORDINAL_FLAG ==
              ( pOrigThunk->u1.Ordinal & IMAGE_ORDINAL_FLAG ))
{
    // Did I find the function to hook?
    if ( dwCompareOrdinal == pOrigThunk->u1.Ordinal )
    {
        // I found the function to hook. Now I need to change
        // the memory protection to writable before I overwrite
        // the function pointer. Note that I'm now writing into
        // the real thunk area!
        MEMORY_BASIC_INFORMATION mbi_thunk ;

        VirtualQuery ( pRealThunk                            ,
                       &mbi_thunk                            ,
                       sizeof ( MEMORY_BASIC_INFORMATION ) ) ;

        if ( FALSE == VirtualProtect ( mbi_thunk.BaseAddress ,
                                       mbi_thunk.RegionSize  ,
                                       PAGE_READWRITE        ,
                                       &mbi_thunk.Protect    ))
        {
            ASSERT ( !"VirtualProtect failed!" ) ;
            // There's nothing I can do but fail the function.
            SetLastErrorEx ( ERROR_INVALID_PARAMETER ,
                             SLE_ERROR               ) ;
            return ( FALSE ) ;
        }

        // Save the original address if requested.
        if ( NULL != ppOrigAddr )
        {
            *ppOrigAddr = (PROC)pRealThunk->u1.Function ;
        }


        // Microsoft has two different definitions of the
        // PIMAGE_THUNK_DATA fields as they are moving to
        // support Win64. The W2K RC2 Platform SDK is the
        // latest header, so I'll use that one and force the
        // Visual C++ 6 Service Pack 3 headers to deal with it.

        // Hook the function.
        DWORD * pTemp = (DWORD*)&pRealThunk->u1.Function ;
        *pTemp = (DWORD)(pHookFunc) ;

        DWORD dwOldProtect ;
```

(continued)

401

Listing 14-4 *continued*

```
                    // Change the protection back to what it was before I
                    // overwrote the function pointer.
                    VERIFY ( VirtualProtect ( mbi_thunk.BaseAddress ,
                                              mbi_thunk.RegionSize ,
                                              mbi_thunk.Protect     ,
                                              &dwOldProtect      ) ) ;
                    // Life is good.
                    SetLastError ( ERROR_SUCCESS ) ;
                    return ( TRUE ) ;
                }
            }
            // Increment both tables.
            pOrigThunk++ ;
            pRealThunk++ ;
        }

    // Nothing was hooked. Technically, this isn't an error. It just
    // means that the module is imported but the function isn't.
    SetLastError ( ERROR_SUCCESS ) ;
    return ( FALSE ) ;
}
```

If I had tried to handle *AfxTrace* without hooking it, I would've had to do some stack walking on each call to get back to the real caller of *OutputDebugString*. The extra work on each call would've been slow compared with hooking *AfxTrace* directly. Also, if I had ignored *AfxTrace*, LIMODS would be basically useless for MFC programmers. In the end, I opted for making LIMODS as complete as possible, even though I had to double-check the MFC DLL versions.

General Implementation Issues

Once I got past hooking the ordinal value exports, I didn't have too many problems implementing LIMODS as a whole. One interesting feature I implemented in LIMODS.EXE was the autochecking behavior of its tree view control. When you check or uncheck the root node of the tree view (the module name), the tree view automatically checks or unchecks all the child nodes (the source files). To make the autochecking work, I had to implement check-toggling notification. Refer to LIMODSVIEW.CPP on the companion CD to see how I implemented everything.

The biggest problem I had with the implementation of LIMODS was with STL. I realize that engineers much, much smarter than I wrote STL, but still I was unprepared for how impenetrable the Visual C++ STL code is. Just deciphering compilation errors took me quite a while; and I absolutely dreaded stepping into the code to see why things failed or how something worked. As I recommend in Chapter 2,

I use level 4-compiler warnings and treat all warnings as errors, so I would appreciate it if the STL code would compile at warning-level 4 without errors and if the Microsoft compiler would stop producing the C4786 warning, "'identifier' : identifier was truncated to '255' characters in the debug information," with STL templates for any class that has more than two characters in the class name.

The secret to shutting off the C4786 warning is to disable the warning through the *#pragma warning* directive before including any STL headers. This *#pragma warning* technique also works best if you include STL headers only in the main precompiled header and disable the warning in the precompiled header once and for all. Even though I had to tweak the build a little, I saved some time by using STL instead of implementing my own growable arrays and map classes.

As for the last problem I ran into, I can't tell whether it was a bug in the compiler or a misunderstanding on my part. In LIMODSDLL.DLL, I use a static array of *HOOKFUNCDESC* to hold the real function pointers for *DiagOutputA* and *DiagOutputW* from BUGSLAYERUTIL.DLL. In the hook functions, I use the real function pointer out of the structure as the destination for the jump. The problem was that referencing the second item in the array would produce an invalid reference. The inline assembler source line

```
JMP g_stBugslayerUtilRealFuncs[0].pProc
```

would generate the assembly-language code

```
JMP g_stBugslayerUtilRealFuncs+4h
```

which was correct. However, the source line that referenced the second item in the structure,

```
JMP g_stBugslayerUtilRealFuncs[1].pProc
```

would generate

```
JMP g_stBugslayerUtilRealFuncs+5h
```

when I thought it should generate

```
JMP g_stBugslayerUtilRealFuncs+0Ch
```

Consequently, the generated code was jumping off into never-never land. I worked around the problem by using

```
JMP g_stBugslayerUtilRealFuncs[0x8].pProc
```

as the reference. This is an isolated problem and shouldn't cause trouble for anyone, but it could affect you if you want to add your own special trace functions to LIMODSDLL.DLL. If you do add your own functions, use the BUGSLAYERUTIL.DLL tables as an example to follow.

WHAT'S NEXT FOR LIMODS?

I'm happy with how LIMODS version 1.1 turned out, but there's always room for improvement. I challenge you to add the following features and to come up with completely new ones.

■   LIMODS.EXE looks at one LOM file at a time. What would be very nice is if LIMODS.EXE could support multiple LOM files using a LOP (LIMODS project) file so that you could look at and manipulate an entire project's LOM files. Also, you don't need to stick with the checkable tree control interface that I used; you might find better ways for users to work with the project data when implementing multiple LOMs.

■   With LIMODS.EXE 1.1, you have to specify the files from which you want to see trace statements before you run your application, and the list remains fixed for the length of the run. LIMODS would be even more useful with some sort of communication channel between the running instances of LIMODSDLL.DLL and LIMODS.EXE so that saving a LOM file would automatically update all instances of LIMODSDLL.DLL that have hooked that module.

■   Design a better icon for LIMODS. My artistic ability extends to being able to name two of the three primary colors. The icon on LIMODS.EXE is supposed to be a funnel (just in case you had trouble identifying it).

SUMMARY

This chapter presented some of the issues involved with limiting trace statements and explained why, until LIMODS, controlling trace statements across large development teams has been difficult. The key requirement for LIMODS was to make it simple to use. To that end, LIMODS requires only a single-line source change for Visual C++ programs and just slightly more lines for Visual Basic programs.

LIMODS has been a long time in the making. I had the original idea for LIMODS five years ago but until now hadn't figured out a way to make the utility as nonintrusive as possible—and easy to use. With LIMODS, you can now use trace statements all you want. LIMODS lets you have your cake and eat it too—without gaining an ounce!

Chapter 15

The Debug
C Run-Time Library

I've written a magazine column on debugging for several years, and I get many, many questions about memory corruption and memory leaks. If developers would just stop using memory in their programs, they wouldn't have so many problems. Right. And if we'd all stop breathing, we'd never have any trouble with our lungs. Memory is the elixir of life for your C and C++ programs, and if you want to do more about memory corruption and memory leaks than just wish they would go away, you need to be proactive about handling them. The first step you need to take is to learn how to use the Microsoft debug C run-time library.

Microsoft Visual Basic programs have an easy life because Visual Basic doesn't require you to allocate memory directly, so you don't have to worry as much about memory problems. Java advocates have been smug in telling us that in Java you never need to worry about memory because the vaunted Java Virtual Machine garbage collector will handle all your memory woes. Of course, I find it quite amusing that the bestselling tools for Java programmers are memory trackers and performance monitors that tell you how much slower your application runs because of the garbage collector.

Developers working in C and C++ get to have all the fun of wrangling memory. C and C++ offer all sorts of programming freedom, but they also provide the opportunity to do much more than just shoot yourself in the foot; you can blow off your whole leg when you make even a small mistake. Fortunately, the C run-time (CRT) library developers heard our cries of anguish and, starting with Microsoft Visual C++ 4, have built in a wonderful feature: the debug CRT (DCRT) library.

Oddly enough, many C and C++ developers don't seem to realize that the DCRT library exists. The reason the library is something of a mystery is that by default much of it is turned off. Once you get the proper flags switched on, however, you'll find out what you've been missing. In this chapter, I'll introduce the DCRT library and build two extensions, MemDumperValidator and MemStress, that will provide you with even more functionality while you're using the library.

FEATURES OF THE DEBUG C RUN-TIME LIBRARY

The main claim to fame for the DCRT library is its wonderful heap memory tracking support. All the memory allocated through standard C/C++ memory allocation functions, such as *new*, *malloc*, and *calloc*, can be tracked in debug builds. The tracking checks for memory underwrites, in which your program writes past the beginning of a block of memory, and memory overwrites, in which your program writes past the end of a block of memory. The tracking also monitors and reports memory leaks in your application. If you've been writing Microsoft Foundation Class (MFC) library programs, you've probably noticed the memory leak reports when your application ends; those leak reports come from the DCRT library. MFC partially turns on the DCRT library for you automatically.

Another neat feature of the DCRT library is the reporting subsystem, which you and I would call trace, through its *_RPTn* and *RPTFn* macros and assertion support. I introduced the DCRT library assertion support in Chapter 3 and explained some of the issues associated with using it. As I mentioned, the DCRT library assertions are good, but they destroy the last error value and therefore cause debug and release builds to behave differently. For your assertions, I strongly recommend that you use the *SUPERASSERT* assertion code that's part of BUGSLAYERUTIL.DLL.

Another nice feature of the DCRT library is that its source code is included with the compiler. Table 15-1 lists all the files that make up the DCRT library. If you elected

Table 15-1 DEBUG C RUN-TIME LIBRARY SOURCE FILES

Source File	Description
DBGDEL.CPP	The debug global *delete* operator.
DBGHEAP.C	All the debug heap-handling functions.
DBGHOOK.C	The stub memory allocation hook function.
DBGINT.H	The internal debug headers and functions.
DBGNEW.CPP	The debug global *new* operator.
DBGRPT.C	The debug reporting functions.
CRTDBG.H	The header file you include. This file is in the standard include directory.

to install the CRT library source code when you installed Microsoft Visual Studio, which I highly recommend doing, you can find all the CRT and DCRT library source code in the <VC Directory>\CRT\SRC directory.

USING THE DEBUG C RUN-TIME LIBRARY

The first step in using the DCRT library is to include it and turn it on so that you can start benefiting from the memory tracking as early in your project as possible. In your main precompiled header file (or whatever header file all the source files in your project will include), add the following line before any *#include* directive:

```
#define _CRTDBG_MAP_ALLOC
```

After the rest of your header files, include CRTDBG.H. Defining *_CRTDBG_MAP_ALLOC* will redirect normal calls to memory allocation and deallocation functions to special versions that record the source file and line number for each allocation or deallocation.

The second step you need to take is to turn on the DCRT library heap code. As I mentioned at the beginning of this chapter, by default, most of the features of the DCRT library are turned off. The documentation states that most of the features are turned off to keep the code small and to increase execution speed. Although size and speed might be important for a release build, the whole point of a debug build is to find bugs! The increased size and reduced speed of debug builds is inconsequential. So don't hesitate to turn on all the features you think will help you. The *_CrtSetDbgFlag* function takes a set of flags, shown in Table 15-2, that can be OR'd together to turn on various options in the DCRT library.

After building your application with the appropriate *#include*s and *#define*s, and calling *_CrtSetDbgFlag*, you now have the DCRT library, with its slew of functions that help you control and report on memory usage, fully available. You can call these functions at any time. Many of them lend themselves to being used in assertions, so you can sprinkle them around freely and catch your memory problems close to the source.

One of the most useful DCRT library functions is *_CrtCheckMemory*. This function walks through all the memory you've allocated and checks to see whether you have any underwrites or overwrites and whether you've used any previously freed blocks. This one function alone makes the entire DCRT library worth using.

Another set of functions allows you to easily check the validity of any piece of memory. The *_CrtIsValidHeapPointer*, *_CrtIsMemoryBlock*, and *_CrtIsValidPointer* functions are perfect for use as debugging parameter validation functions. These functions, combined with *_CrtCheckMemory*, offer excellent memory checking features.

Table 15-2 DEBUG C RUN-TIME LIBRARY FLAGS

Flag	Description
_CRTDBG_ALLOC_MEM_DF	Turn on the debug heap allocations and use the memory block identifiers. This is the only flag that's on by default.
_CRTDBG_CHECK_ALWAYS_DF	Check and validate all memory on each allocation and deallocation request. Turning on this flag catches any underwrites and overwrites as close to when they happen as possible.
_CRTDBG_CHECK_CRT_DF	Include _CRT_BLOCK memory allocations in all leak detection and state differences. In general, unless you're having a problem with the CRT library functions, you shouldn't turn on this flag. If you do, you'll get CRT library memory allocation reports. Because the CRT library must keep some memory allocated until the true end of the program, which is after the leaked memory reporting, you'll see a large number of false positive leak reports on that memory.
_CRTDBG_DELAY_FREE_MEM_DF	Instead of truly freeing memory, keep the block allocated and in the internal heap list. The blocks are filled with the value 0xDD, so you know the memory is freed when you're looking at it in the debugger. By not freeing the memory, this flag allows you to test your program under memory stress conditions. Additionally, the DCRT library will check that you don't access the deallocated block again by ensuring that all values in the block remain 0xDD. You should always turn on this flag, but keep in mind that your program's memory requirements can easily double because the deallocated memory isn't reclaimed by the heap.
_CRTDBG_LEAK_CHECK_DF	Check for memory leaks at the end of the program. Turning on this extremely useful flag is mandatory.

Another neat feature of the DCRT library is the memory state functions: _CrtMemCheckpoint_, _CrtMemDifference_, and _CrtMemDumpStatistics_. These functions make it easy to do before-and-after comparisons of the heap to see whether anything is amiss. For example, if you're using a common library in a team environment, you can take before-and-after snapshots of the heap when you call the library to see whether there are any leaks or to see how much memory the operation uses.

The icing on the memory-checking cake is that the DCRT library allows you to hook into the memory allocation code stream so that you can see each allocation and deallocation function call. If the allocation hook returns *TRUE*, the allocation is allowed to continue. If the allocation hook returns *FALSE*, the allocation fails. When I first discovered this functionality, my immediate thought was that, with a small amount of work, I could have a means to test code in some really nasty boundary conditions that would otherwise be very difficult to duplicate. You can see the result of this brainstorm in MemStress, a feature of BUGSLAYERUTIL.DLL that allows you to force allocation failures in your programs, which I'll present later in the chapter.

The cherry on top of the icing on the memory-checking cake is that the DCRT library also allows you to hook the memory dump functions and to enumerate client blocks (your allocated memory). You can replace the default memory dump functions with custom dump functions that know all about your data. Now, instead of seeing the cryptic dumped memory you get as the default (which besides being hard to decipher isn't that helpful), you can see exactly what the memory block contains and format it exactly as you want. MFC has the *Dump* function for this purpose, but it works only with *CObject*-derived classes. If you're like me, you don't spend your entire coding life in MFC and you need dumping functions that are more generic to accommodate different types of code.

The client block enumeration feature, as the name implies, allows you to enumerate the memory blocks you've allocated. This excellent feature gives you the power to create some interesting utilities. For example, in the MemDumperValidator functions in BUGSLAYERUTIL.DLL, I call the dumping hooks from the client block enumerator so that the enumeration can dump and validate many types of allocated memory in one operation. This extensible validation is critical in that it allows you to do deep validations instead of the surface checks of underwrites and overwrites. By deep validation, I mean an algorithm that knows the data formats in the memory block and walks those formats making sure that each data element is correct.

CHOOSING THE RIGHT C RUN-TIME LIBRARY FOR YOUR APPLICATION

Some of the confusion surrounding the use of the CRT libraries in Microsoft Windows development revolves around figuring out which library to use. There are six versions of the library, and they fall into two main categories: debug (DCRT) and release (CRT). In each category is a single-threaded static library, a multithreaded static library, and a multithreaded dynamic-link library (DLL).

The static versions of the CRT libraries link the library functions directly into your application and are the default versions used for non-MFC-wizard-generated applications. The advantage of using the static versions is that you won't have to ship a CRT library DLL with your product. The disadvantage is that the size of your binary files grows tremendously and your application's working set is much larger. The two static CRT library variants, single-threaded and multithreaded, are self-explanatory. If you're building a DLL and want to use a static CRT library, you should link only with a multithreaded version—if you don't, multithreaded applications can't use your DLL because the single-threaded static CRT libraries aren't thread-safe.

The DLL versions of the CRT libraries, named MSVCRT(D).DLL, allow you to import the CRT libraries' functions. The upside of using these DLLs is that your binary's size is drastically smaller, thus reducing your application's working set. Because other applications are loading the same CRT library DLLs, the operating system can share the page tables for the DLLs' code sections across processes and the entire system will run faster. The downside to using the DLL versions is that you might need to distribute another DLL with your application.

For your applications, it's extremely important that you choose one version of the CRT library to use across all binaries that load into your main program's address space. If you have some DLLs using the static CRT library and others using the DLL CRT library, not only are you making your address space larger with duplicated code, but you're also running the risk of introducing one of the most insidious memory bugs there is—a bug that could take months to track down. If you allocate heap memory out of one DLL and attempt to deallocate that heap memory in another DLL that uses a different version of the CRT library, you can easily crash because the deallocating DLL doesn't know where the allocated memory came from. Don't assume that heap memory is heap memory—having different versions of the CRT library running at the same time means that you have multiple versions of heap memory tracking code.

I almost always use the DLL versions of the CRT libraries, and I suggest that you do the same. The benefit of shrinking the working set and having smaller main binaries overrides any other considerations. In only a few instances—for example, when I'm developing games, where I'm guaranteed never to need multithreading and where performance is supercritical—do I even consider using the single-threaded static versions to avoid the overhead of the multithreaded locking mechanisms.

I've set up BUGSLAYERUTIL.DLL to use the DLL versions of the CRT libraries. The two extensions I demonstrate in this chapter, MemDumperValidator and MemStress, are also in BUGSLAYERUTIL.DLL. These extensions expect you to be using the DLL versions. If you want to use the extensions in your application but not the DLL versions, however, it's trivial to pull out the source files, MEMDUMPERVALIDATOR.CPP, MEMDUMPERVALIDATOR.H, MEMSTRESS.CPP, MEMSTRESSCONSTANTS.H, and MEMSTRESS.H; change the function linkage specified; and drop them into your application.

I want to mention one additional detail about using BUGSLAYERUTIL.DLL in your projects. You might experience a slowdown in your application depending on how you allocate memory. As part of the MemDumperValidator extension, I turn on all the appropriate flags, including *_CRTDBG_CHECK_ALWAYS_DF*, in the DCRT library to allow full memory tracking and validation. The *_CRTDBG_CHECK_ALWAYS_DF* flag tells the DCRT library to walk through and validate each piece of heap memory each time you allocate or deallocate heap memory. If you're doing thousands of small allocations in your application, you'll see the slowdown. If the amount of slowdown is unacceptable, you have two choices. Your first option is to turn off the flag, through a call to *_CrtSetDbgFlag*, before you start doing all the small allocations. Your other option is to check your algorithm and see whether you need to do all those small allocations, because even without debug heap checking, many small allocations are extremely slow.

USING MEMDUMPERVALIDATOR

The MemDumperValidator extension makes memory debugging much easier. By default, the DCRT library reports memory leaks and validates that memory blocks haven't experienced overwrite or underwrite corruption. Both those reports can be very useful, but when the memory leak report looks something like the following, it can get difficult to figure out exactly which type of memory leaked:

```
Detected memory leaks
Dumping objects ->
c:\vc\INCLUDE\crtdbg.h(552) : {596} normal block at 0x008CD5B0,
    24 bytes long.
 Data: < k      w k > 90 6B 8C 00 B0 DD 8C 00 00 00 80 77 90 6B 8C 00
Object dump complete.
```

As I mentioned earlier, having more than just the default memory validation helps—having deep memory validation can help you catch some wild writes that you might not otherwise catch. The extra information in MemDumperValidator's leak report and the additional validations the extension supplies provide you with more information when you're debugging. And the more information you have when you debug, the faster you can debug.

The MemDumperValidator extension takes advantage of the DCRT library block identifier capabilities so that it can associate a block type with a set of functions that know something about what the block contains. Each block allocated through the DCRT library is assigned an identifier. The different identifiers are listed in Table 15-3. The block types are a parameter to DCRT library functions that allocate memory: *_nh_malloc_dbg* (*new*), *_malloc_dbg* (*malloc*), *_calloc_dbg* (*calloc*), and *_realloc_dbg* (*realloc*).

Table 15-3   **MEMORY BLOCK IDENTIFIERS**

Block Identifier	Description
_NORMAL_BLOCK	A normal call to *new*, *malloc*, or *calloc* creates a Normal block. Defining *_CRTDBG_MAP_ALLOC* causes all heap allocation to default to Normal blocks and associates the source file and line number that allocated the block with the memory block.
_CRT_BLOCK	The memory blocks allocated internally by many run-time library functions are marked as CRT blocks so that they can be handled separately. As a result, you're able to exclude them from leak detection and other memory validation operations. Your application must never allocate, reallocate, or free any block of type CRT.

_CLIENT_BLOCK	If you want your application to do special tracking on a type of memory, you can call the debug allocation functions and pass a special Client value as a parameter. You can track sub-types of Client blocks by putting a 16-bit value into the upper 16 bits of the Client block value, as shown here:
	
	```#define CLIENT_BLOCK_VALUE(x) \```
	``` (_CLIENT_BLOCK|(x<<16))```
	``` ⋮```
	```_heap_alloc_dbg (10 ,```
	``` CLIENT_BLOCK_VALUE(0xA),```
	``` __FILE__ ,```
	``` __LINE__) ;```
	
	The application can supply a hook function, through *_CrtSetDumpClient*, for dumping memory registered as Client blocks. The hook will be called whenever a DCRT library function needs to dump a Client block. The *_CrtDoForAllClientObjects* function also allows you to enumerate the Client blocks currently allocated.
	
	MFC uses a Client block identifier for all *CObject*-derived classes. MemDumperValidator also uses the Client hook.

_FREE_BLOCK	Calling a memory deallocation routine normally removes the memory from the debug heap lists. If you set the *_CRTDBG_DELAY_FREE_MEM_DF* flag with *_CrtSetDbgFlag*, however, the memory isn't freed but left allocated and filled with 0xDD.
_IGNORE_BLOCK	If you temporarily toggle off DCRT library tracking, any allocations made after the tracking is turned off will be marked as Ignore blocks.

After you set up a class or a C data type to use the MemDumperValidator extension, the DCRT library will call MemDumperValidator when it wants to dump a block. The extension will look at the block value, and if it sees a matching dumping function, it will call the function to dump the memory. The validation portion goes through the same process when called by the DCRT library except that it calls the matching validation function on the memory block.

Describing MemDumperValidator is the easy part—getting it to work is a little more difficult. Listing 15-1 shows MEMDUMPERVALIDATOR.H, which takes care of much of the initialization for you. By including BUGSLAYERUTIL.H in your program, you'll automatically include MEMDUMPERVALIDATOR.H.

```
/*--------------------------------------------------------------------
"Debugging Applications" (Microsoft Press)
Copyright (c) 1997-2000 John Robbins -- All rights reserved.
--------------------------------------------------------------------*/

#ifndef _MEMDUMPERVALIDATOR_H
#define _MEMDUMPERVALIDATOR_H

// Don't include this file directly; include BUGSLAYER.H
// instead.
#ifndef _BUGSLAYERUTIL_H
#error "Include BUGSLAYERUTIL.H instead of this file directly!"
#endif  // _BUGSLAYERUTIL_H

// Include the header that sets up CRTDBG.H.
#include "MSJDBG.h"

#ifdef __cplusplus
extern "C" {
#endif      // __cplusplus

// This library can be used only in _debug builds.
#ifdef _DEBUG

////////////////////////////////////////////////////////////////////
// The typedefs for the dumper and validator functions
////////////////////////////////////////////////////////////////////
// The memory dumper function. This function's only parameter is a
// pointer to the block of memory. This function can output the memory
// data for the block in any way it chooses, but to be consistent, it
// should use the same reporting mechanism the rest of the DCRT
// library uses.
```

Listing 15-1 *MEMDUMPERVALIDATOR.H* (continued)

Listing 15-1 *continued*

```
typedef void (*PFNMEMDUMPER)(const void *) ;
// The validator function. This function's first parameter is the memory
// block to validate, and the second parameter is the context
// information passed to the ValidateAllBlocks function.
typedef void (*PFNMEMVALIDATOR)(const void * , const void *) ;


/////////////////////////////////////////////////////////////////////
// Useful macros
/////////////////////////////////////////////////////////////////////
// The macro used to set a Client block subtype value. Using this macro
// is the only approved means of setting the value of the dwValue field
// in the DVINFO structure below.
#define CLIENT_BLOCK_VALUE(x) (_CLIENT_BLOCK|(x<<16))
// A macro to pick out the subtype
#define CLIENT_BLOCK_SUBTYPE(x) ((x >> 16) & 0xFFFF)


/////////////////////////////////////////////////////////////////////
// The header used to initialize the dumper and validator for a specific
// Client block subtype
/////////////////////////////////////////////////////////////////////
typedef struct tag_DVINFO
{
    // The subtype value for the Client blocks. This value must be set
    // with the CLIENT_BLOCK_VALUE macro above. See the AddClientDV
    // function to find out how to have the extension assign this
    // number.
    unsigned long   dwValue     ;
    // The pointer to the dumper function
    PFNMEMDUMPER    pfnDump     ;
    // The pointer to the dumper function
    PFNMEMVALIDATOR pfnValidate ;
} DVINFO , * LPDVINFO ;


/*-------------------------------------------------------------------
FUNCTION        :   AddClientDV
DISCUSSION      :
    Adds a Client block dumper and validator to the list. If the
dwValue field in the DVINFO structure is 0, the next value in
the list is assigned. The value returned must always be passed to
_malloc_dbg as the subtype value of the Client block.
    If the subtype value is set with CLIENT_BLOCK_VALUE, a macro can be
used for the value passed to _malloc_dbg.
    Notice that there's no corresponding remove function. Why run the
risk of introducing bugs in debugging code? Performance is a nonissue
when it comes to finding errors.
```

```
PARAMETERS    :
   lpDVInfo - The pointer to the DVINFO structure
RETURNS       :
   1 - The client block dumper and validator were properly added.
   0 - The client block dumper and validator couldn't be added.
------------------------------------------------------------------------*/

   int BUGSUTIL_DLLINTERFACE __stdcall AddClientDV (LPDVINFO lpDVInfo);


/*------------------------------------------------------------------------
FUNCTION       :   ValidateAllBlocks
DISCUSSION     :
   Checks all the memory allocated out of the local heap. Also goes
through all Client blocks and calls the special validator function for
the different subtypes.
   It's probably best to call this function with the VALIDATEALLBLOCKS
macro below.
PARAMETERS     :
   pContext - The context information that will be passed to each
              validator function
RETURNS        :
   None
------------------------------------------------------------------------*/

   void BUGSUTIL_DLLINTERFACE __stdcall
                                 ValidateAllBlocks ( void * pContext ) ;


#ifdef __cplusplus
///////////////////////////////////////////////////////////////////////
// Helper C++ class macros
///////////////////////////////////////////////////////////////////////
// Declare this macro in your class just as you would an MFC macro.
#define DECLARE_MEMDEBUG(classname)                               \
public  :                                                         \
   static DVINFO  m_stDVInfo ;                                    \
   static void ClassDumper ( const void * pData ) ;               \
   static void ClassValidator ( const void * pData ,             \
                                const void * pContext )      ;\
   static void * operator new ( size_t nSize )                   \
   {                                                              \
      if ( 0 == m_stDVInfo.dwValue )                             \
      {                                                           \
          m_stDVInfo.pfnDump     = classname::ClassDumper ;      \
          m_stDVInfo.pfnValidate = classname::ClassValidator ;   \
          AddClientDV ( &m_stDVInfo ) ;                          \
      }                                                           \
```

(continued)

Listing 15-1 *continued*

```
        return ( _malloc_dbg ( nSize                        \
                               (int)m_stDVInfo.dwValue ,     \
                               __FILE__                  ,   \
                               __LINE__                ) ) ; \
    }                                                        \
    static void * operator new ( size_t nSize         ,      \
                                 char * lpszFileName ,        \
                                 int    nLine        )        \
    {                                                        \
        if ( 0 == m_stDVInfo.dwValue )                        \
        {                                                    \
            m_stDVInfo.pfnDump     = classname::ClassDumper ;  \
            m_stDVInfo.pfnValidate = classname::ClassValidator ; \
            AddClientDV ( &m_stDVInfo ) ;                     \
        }                                                    \
        return ( _malloc_dbg ( nSize                    ,    \
                               (int)m_stDVInfo.dwValue , \
                               lpszFileName             ,    \
                               nLine                ) ) ;    \
    }                                                        \
    static void operator delete ( void * pData )             \
    {                                                        \
        _free_dbg ( pData , (int)m_stDVInfo.dwValue ) ;      \
    }

// Declare this macro at the top of your CPP file.
#define IMPLEMENT_MEMDEBUG(classname)                         \
    DVINFO  classname::m_stDVInfo = { 0 , 0 , 0 }

// The macro for memory debugging allocations. If DEBUG_NEW is defined,
// it can be used.
#ifdef DEBUG_NEW
#define MEMDEBUG_NEW DEBUG_NEW
#else
#define MEMDEBUG_NEW new ( __FILE__ , __LINE__ )
#endif

#endif      // __cplusplus defined

////////////////////////////////////////////////////////////////////
// Helper C macros
////////////////////////////////////////////////////////////////////

// Use this macro for C-style allocations. The only problem
// with C is that you need to drag around a DVINFO structure.
#define INITIALIZE_MEMDEBUG(lpDVInfo , pfnD , pfnV )          \
```

```
    {                                                               \
        ASSERT ( FALSE == IsBadWritePtr ( lpDVInfo ,                \
                                    sizeof ( DVINFO ) ) ) ;         \
        ((LPDVINFO)lpDVInfo)->dwValue = 0 ;                         \
        ((LPDVINFO)lpDVInfo)->pfnDump = pfnD ;                      \
        ((LPDVINFO)lpDVInfo)->pfnValidate = pfnV ;                  \
        AddClientDV ( lpDVInfo ) ;                                  \
    }

// The macros that map the C-style allocations. It might be easier if
// you use macros to wrap these so that you don't have to remember which
// DVINFO block value to drag around with each memory usage function.
#define MEMDEBUG_MALLOC(lpDVInfo , nSize)                    \
            _malloc_dbg ( nSize                 ,            \
                            ((LPDVINFO)lpDVInfo)->dwValue ,  \
                            __FILE__            ,            \
                            __LINE__            )
#define MEMDEBUG_REALLOC(lpDVInfo , pBlock , nSize)          \
            _realloc_dbg( pBlock                ,            \
                            nSize               ,            \
                            ((LPDVINFO)lpDVInfo)->dwValue ,  \
                            __FILE__            ,            \
                            __LINE__            )
#define MEMDEBUG_EXPAND(lpDVInfo , pBlock , nSize )          \
            _expand_dbg( pBlock                 ,            \
                            nSize               ,            \
                            ((LPDVINFO)lpDVInfo)->dwValue ,  \
                            __FILE__            ,            \
                            __LINE__            )
#define MEMDEBUG_FREE(lpDVInfo , pBlock)                     \
            _free_dbg ( pBlock              ,                \
                            ((LPDVINFO)lpDVInfo)->dwValue )
#define MEMDEBUG_MSIZE(lpDVInfo , pBlock)  \
            _msize_dbg ( pBlock , ((LPDVINFO)lpDVInfo)->dwValue )

// Macro to call ValidateAllBlocks
#define VALIDATEALLBLOCKS(x)    ValidateAllBlocks ( x )


#else       // _DEBUG is not defined.


#ifdef __cplusplus
#define DECLARE_MEMDEBUG(classname)
#define IMPLEMENT_MEMDEBUG(classname)
#define MEMDEBUG_NEW new
#endif      // __cplusplus
```

(continued)

Listing 15-1 *continued*

```
#define INITIALIZE_MEMDEBUG(lpDVInfo , pfnD , pfnV )

#define MEMDEBUG_MALLOC(lpDVInfo , nSize) \
                    malloc ( nSize )
#define MEMDEBUG_REALLOC(lpDVInfo , pBlock , nSize) \
                    realloc ( pBlock , nSize )
#define MEMDEBUG_EXPAND(lpDVInfo , pBlock , nSize)  \
                    _expand ( pBlock , nSize )
#define MEMDEBUG_FREE(lpDVInfo , pBlock) \
                    free ( pBlock )
#define MEMDEBUG_MSIZE(lpDVInfo , pBlock) \
                    _msize ( pBlock )

#define VALIDATEALLBLOCKS(x)

#endif      // _DEBUG

#ifdef __cplusplus
}
#endif      // __cplusplus

#endif      // _MEMDUMPERVALIDATOR_H
```

Using MemDumperValidator with C++

Fortunately, setting up a C++ class so that MemDumperValidator can handle it is a relatively simple operation. In the declaration of the C++ class, just specify the *DECLARE_MEMDEBUG* macro with the class name as the parameter. This macro is a little like some of the "magic" MFC macros in that it expands into a couple of data and method declarations. If you're following along in Listing 15-1, you'll notice three inline functions: *new*, *delete*, and *new* with source file and line number information. If any of these three operators are defined in your class, you'll need to extract the code from the extension operators and place it in your class's operators.

In the implementation file for your C++ class, you need to use the *IMPLE-MENT_MEMDEBUG* macro, again with your class name as the parameter. This macro sets up a static variable for your class. The *DECLARE_MEMDEBUG* and *IMPLE-MENT_MEMDEBUG* macros expand only in debug builds, so they don't need to have conditional compilation used around them.

After you've specified both macros in the correct place, you'll need to implement only the two methods that will do the actual dumping and validating for your class. The prototypes for those methods are shown on the next page. Obviously, you'll want to use conditional compilation around them so that they aren't compiled into release builds.

```
static void ClassDumper ( const void * pData ) ;
static void ClassValidator ( const void * pData,
                             const void * pContext  ) ;
```

For both methods, the *pData* parameter is the memory block that points to an instance of the class. All you need to do to get to a usable pointer is to cast the value in *pData* to the class type. Whatever you do when you're dumping or validating, treat the value in *pData* as super read-only or you could easily introduce as many bugs into your code as you meant to eliminate. For the *ClassValidator* method, the second parameter, *pContext*, is the context parameter you passed to the original call to the *ValidateAllBlocks* function. I'll talk more about the *ValidateAllBlocks* function in the "Deep Validations" section later in this chapter.

I have only two recommendations for implementing the *ClassDumper* method. First, stick to the *_RPTn* and *_RPTFn* macros from the DCRT library so that your formatted output will be dumped in the same place as the rest of the DCRT library output. Second, end your output with a carriage return/line feed combination because the DCRT library macros don't do any formatting for you.

Setting up a dumper and a validator for a C++ class seems almost trivial. But what about those C data structures that you'd like to dump cleanly at long last? Unfortunately, handling them takes a little more work.

Using MemDumperValidator with C

You might be wondering why I even bothered to support C. The answer is simple: there's still quite a bit of C code out there in many products you and I are using. And believe it or not, some of these applications and modules use memory too.

The first step you need to take to use MemDumperValidator in a C application is to declare a *DVINFO* structure for each different type of memory you want to dump and validate. The C++ macros automatically declare dumper and validator methods for you, but in C, you have to do some work. Keep in mind that all the macros I talk about here require a pointer to the specific *DVINFO* structures.

The prototypes for the C dumper and validator functions are the same as the C++ methods except that the *static* keyword isn't used. As with declaring the unique memory block *DVINFO* structures, for convenience, you might want to consider placing all the C memory dumping and validation function implementations in a combined file.

Before you can start allocating, dumping, or validating memory in a C application, you must tell the MemDumperValidator extension about the Client block subtype and the dumper and validator functions for it. You pass all this information to the MemDumperValidator extension by using the *INITIALIZE_MEMDEBUG* macro, which takes the assigned *DVINFO* structure, the dump function, and the validation function as parameters. You'll need to execute the macro before you allocate any memory blocks of this type.

Finally—and this is the area in which C++ memory handling is far better than C memory handling—to allocate, free, reallocate, expand, or get the size of a block, you must use an entire set of macros that pass the block value through to the underlying memory function. For example, if your *DVINFO* structure is *stdvBlockInfo*, you need to allocate your C blocks with the following code:

```
MEMDEBUG_MALLOC ( &stdvBlockInfo , sizeof ( x ) ) ;
```

At the bottom of Listing 15-1, you'll see all the different macros for the C memory functions. Remembering the *DVINFO* structure for every type of allocation isn't impossible but it isn't practical either, so you might want to set up wrapper macros to handle the different *DVINFO* structures for you; all you'll need to pass to your wrapper macros are the normal parameters to the memory functions.

Deep Validations

Although the dumping portion of the MemDumperValidator extension is unquestionably useful, you might be wondering why you need the validation method, even if it does allow you to do deep validation of the memory block. In many cases, the validation function might even be an empty function if all the class holds is a couple string variables. Even so, the validation function can be invaluable because it gives you some excellent debugging capabilities. One of the reasons I started using deep validation was to provide a second level of data validation on a set of base classes that I had developed. Although a validation function shouldn't replace good old-fashioned parameter and input checking, it can give you another layer of assurance that your data is correct. Deep validations can also be a second line of defense against wild writes.

The neatest use of the validation function is for double-checking complex data structures after operations have been performed on them. For example, one time I had a relatively complex situation in which two separate self-referential data structures both used the same allocated objects because of space considerations. After filling in the data structures with a large set of data, I used the validation function to look at the individual blocks from the heap and check that they were referentially correct. I could've written a bunch of code to walk each data structure, but I knew that any code I wrote would be an open target for bugs. By using the validation function, I could bounce through the allocated blocks using code that I'd already tested, and I could check the data structures from different positions because the memory was in the order of allocation, not in sorted order.

Although setting up allocations is more difficult in C than in C++, using the memory validation function is the same in both languages. All you need to do is call the *VALIDATEALLBLOCKS* macro. This macro expands in debug builds to a call to the *ValidateAllBlocks* routine. The parameter required is any value that you want to pass on through to the validation functions that you registered with the library. I've used this parameter in the past to determine the depth of the validation that the function will perform. Keep in mind that *ValidateAllBlocks* passes this value to every registered validation routine, so you might need to coordinate the values across your team.

To see the MemDumperValidator functions in action, check out the Dump program shown in Listing 15-2. Dump is a stripped-down program that shows what you need in order to use the extension. Although I didn't provide a code example, the MemDumperValidator extension works well with MFC because MFC will call any previously registered client dump hook functions. With MemDumperValidator, you get the best of both worlds!

```
/*-------------------------------------------------------------------------
"Debugging Applications" (Microsoft Press)
Copyright (c) 1997-2000 John Robbins -- All rights reserved.
--------------------------------------------------------------------------*/
#include <stdio.h>
#include <stdlib.h>
#include <memory.h>
#include <string.h>
#include <iostream.h>
#include "BugslayerUtil.h"

class TestClass
{
public:
    TestClass ( void )
    {
        strcpy ( m_szData , "TestClass constructor data!" ) ;
    }
    ~TestClass ( void )
    {
        m_szData[ 0 ] = '\0' ;
    }

    // The declaration of the memory debugging stuff for C++ classes
    DECLARE_MEMDEBUG ( TestClass ) ;

private    :
    char m_szData[ 100 ] ;

} ;

// This macro sets up the static DVINFO structure.
IMPLEMENT_MEMDEBUG ( TestClass ) ;
```

Listing 15-2 *DUMP.CPP*

Listing 15-2 *continued*

```
// The methods you must implement to dump and
// validate
#ifdef _DEBUG
void TestClass::ClassDumper ( const void * pData )
{
    TestClass * pClass = (TestClass*)pData ;
    _RPT1 ( _CRT_WARN ,
            " TestClass::ClassDumper : %s\n" ,
            pClass->m_szData ) ;
}
void TestClass::ClassValidator ( const void * pData  ,
                                 const void *        )
{
    // Validate the data here.
    TestClass * pClass = (TestClass*)pData ;
    _RPT1 ( _CRT_WARN
            " TestClass::ClassValidator : %s\n" ,
            pClass->m_szData                ) ;
}
#endif

typedef struct tag_SimpleStruct
{
    char szName[ 256 ] ;
    char szRank[ 256 ] ;
} SimpleStruct ;

// The dumper and validator for simple string data memory
void DumperOne ( const void * pData )
{
    _RPT1 ( _CRT_WARN , " Data is : %s\n" , pData ) ;
}

void ValidatorOne ( const void * pData , const void * pContext )
{
    // Validate the string data here.
    _RPT2 ( _CRT_WARN ,
            " Validator called with : %s : 0x%08X\n" ,
            pData , pContext ) ;
}

// The dumper and validator for the structure allocations
void DumperTwo ( const void * pData )
```

```
{
    _RPT2 ( _CRT_WARN                          ,
            " Data is Name : %s\n"
            "          Rank : %s\n"           ,
            ((SimpleStruct*)pData)->szName   ,
            ((SimpleStruct*)pData)->szRank   ) ;
}

void ValidatorTwo ( const void * pData , const void * pContext )
{
    // Validate any structures here.
    _RPT2 ( _CRT_WARN                          ,
            "  Validator called with :\n"
            "   Data is Name : %s\n"
            "           Rank : %s\n"          ,
            ((SimpleStruct*)pData)->szName   ,
            ((SimpleStruct*)pData)->szRank   ) ;
}

// Unfortunately, the C functions need to drag around their own
// DVINFO structures. In the real world, you'd define these structures
// as extern references and wrap the MEMDEBUG macros with your own
// macros.
static DVINFO g_dvOne ;
static DVINFO g_dvTwo ;

void main ( void )
{
    cout << "At start of main\n" ;

    // The memory debugging initialization for type one.
    INITIALIZE_MEMDEBUG ( &g_dvOne , DumperOne , ValidatorOne )  ;
    // The memory debugging initialization for type two.
    INITIALIZE_MEMDEBUG ( &g_dvTwo , DumperTwo , ValidatorTwo )  ;

    // Allocate the class with the MEMDEBUG new.
    TestClass * pstClass ;
    //pstClass = MEMDEBUG_NEW TestClass ;
    pstClass = new TestClass ;

    // Allocate the two C types.
    char * p = (char*)MEMDEBUG_MALLOC ( &g_dvOne , 10 ) ;
    strcpy ( p , "VC VC" ) ;

    SimpleStruct * pSt =
            (SimpleStruct*)MEMDEBUG_MALLOC ( &g_dvTwo ,
                                              sizeof ( SimpleStruct ) ) ;
```

(continued)

423

Listing 15-2 *continued*

```
    strcpy ( pSt->szName , "Pam" ) ;
    strcpy ( pSt->szRank , "CINC" ) ;

    // Validate all the blocks in the list.
    VALIDATEALLBLOCKS ( NULL ) ;

    cout << "At end of main\n" ;

    // Every block will get dumped as part of the memory leak checking.

}
```

IMPLEMENTING MEMDUMPERVALIDATOR

Implementing the MemDumperValidator functions was generally straightforward. The first unexpected problem I had to deal with was that the DCRT library doesn't document a way for the hook functions to get the memory block value. The hook functions are passed only a pointer to the user data, not the whole memory block the DCRT library allocates. Fortunately, with the DCRT library source code, I was able to see exactly how the library allocates memory blocks. Memory blocks are all allocated as a *_CrtMemBlockHeader* structure defined in the DBGINT.H file.

Also in the DBGINT.H file are macros to get at the *_CrtMemBlockHeader* from a user data pointer and to get at the user data from a *_CrtMemBlockHeader* pointer. I copied the *_CrtMemBlockHeader* structure and access macros into a header file, CRTDBG_INTERNALS.H (shown in Listing 15-3), so that I could get at the header information. Although relying on a copy of a structure definition when the definition might change isn't a good practice, it works in this case because the DCRT library *_CrtMemBlockHeader* structure hasn't changed between Visual C++ 4 and Visual C++ 6. That doesn't mean that this structure won't change in a future version of Visual C++. If you're using the MemDumperValidator extension, you need to quickly check each service pack and major release of the compiler to see whether the internal structures have changed.

If you'd feel more comfortable with using DBGINT.H directly, you can replace the structure definition in CRTDBG_INTERNALS.H with *#include DBGINT.H*. You'll also need to add the <VC Directory>\CRT\SRC to both your master INCLUDE environment variable and the Include Files on the Directories tab of the Visual C++ Options dialog box. Because not everyone installs the CRT library source code and because many developers could have missed the mention in any README.TXT file I included, I decided it would be easier if I just included the structure definition directly.

```
/*-----------------------------------------------------------------
"Debugging Applications" (Microsoft Press)
Copyright (c) 1997-2000 John Robbins -- All rights reserved.
-----------------------------------------------------------------*/

#ifndef _CRTDBG_INTERNALS_H
#define _CRTDBG_INTERNALS_H

#define nNoMansLandSize 4

typedef struct _CrtMemBlockHeader
{
    struct _CrtMemBlockHeader * pBlockHeaderNext       ;
    struct _CrtMemBlockHeader * pBlockHeaderPrev       ;
    char *                      szFileName             ;
    int                         nLine                  ;
    size_t                      nDataSize              ;
    int                         nBlockUse              ;
    long                        lRequest               ;
    unsigned char               gap[nNoMansLandSize]   ;
    /* followed by:
     *  unsigned char           data[nDataSize];
     *  unsigned char           anotherGap[nNoMansLandSize];
     */
} _CrtMemBlockHeader;

#define pbData(pblock) ((unsigned char *) \
                                ((_CrtMemBlockHeader *)pblock + 1))
#define pHdr(pbData) (((_CrtMemBlockHeader *)pbData)-1)

#endif      // _CRTDBG_INTERNALS_H
```

Listing 15-3 *CRTDBG_INTERNALS.H*

You can also use the *_CrtMemBlockHeader* structure definition to get more information from the *_CrtMemState* structures returned by *_CrtMemCheckpoint* because the first item in the structure is a pointer to a *_CrtMemBlockHeader*. I hope a future version of the DCRT library gives us real access functions to get the memory block information.

As you look through the source code in MEMDUMPERVALIDATOR.CPP, part of the BUGSLAYERUTIL.DLL project on the companion CD, you might notice that I use straight Windows application programming interface (API) heap functions from the *HeapCreate* family for internal memory management. The reason I use these API functions is that the dump and hook functions you use with the DCRT library will cause reentrancy if you use routines from the standard library. Keep in mind that I'm not talking about multithreaded reentrancy. If my hook code allocates memory with a call to *malloc*, my hook would be reentered because the hooks are called on every memory allocation.

Initialization and Termination in C++

After I finished implementing MemDumperValidator and started to test it, I was pleased that the extension worked as planned. However, as I was pondering all the ways that a program can allocate heap memory, I started to break out in a cold sweat. Were static constructors that possibly allocate memory going to give me any problems? As I looked at my initial code for MemDumperValidator, I discovered a glaring hole in my logic.

Although most developers don't do it much, in some cases, memory is allocated before an application's entry point. The problem with my approach in MemDumper-Validator was that I needed to ensure that the appropriate flags to *_CrtSetDbgFlag* are set before any allocations take place.

The last thing I wanted to do with MemDumperValidator was force you to remember to call some goofy initialization function before you could use the library. It's bad enough that you have to drag around your *DVINFO* structures for C programming. I wanted to make MemDumperValidator as automatic as possible so that more developers would use it—without any hassle.

Fortunately, my cold sweat didn't last too long because I remembered the *#pragma init_seg* directive, which can be used to control the initialization and destruction order of statically declared values. You can pass one of several options to the *#pragma init_seg* directive: *compiler*, *lib*, *user*, *section name*, and *funcname*. The first three are the important ones.

The *compiler* option is reserved for the Microsoft compiler, and any objects specified for this group are constructed first and destructed last. Those marked as *lib* are constructed next and destructed before the *compiler*-marked group, and those marked *user* are constructed last and terminated first.

Because the code in MemDumperValidator needs to be initialized before your code, I could just specify *lib* as the directive to *#pragma init_seg* and be done with it. However, if you're creating libraries and marking them as *lib* segments (as you should) and want to use my code, you still need to initialize my code before your code. To handle this contingency, I set the *#pragma init_seg* directive as *compiler*. Although you should always follow the rules when it comes to proper segment initializations, using the *compiler* option with debug code is safe enough.

Because the initialization idea works only with C++ code, MemDumperValidator uses a special static class, named *AutoMatic*, that simply calls the *_CrtSetDbgFlag* function. I need to go to all this trouble because it's the only way to set the DCRT flags before any other library's initialization. Additionally, as you'll see in a moment, to get around some limitations in the DCRT library memory leak checking, I need to do some special processing on the class destruction. Even though the MemDumper-Validator has only a C interface, I can take advantage of C++ to get the extension up and running so that it's ready when you call it.

Where Have All the Leak Reports Gone?

I survived my bout of anxiety over initialization issues and finally got the Mem-DumperValidator extension running. I was happy with how it all worked—except that when the program terminated I never saw the nicely formatted output from my dumping functions if I had memory leaks. The memory dumps were just the old standard DCRT library dumps. I tracked down the "missing" leak reports and was surprised to see that the DCRT library termination functions call *_CrtSetDumpClient* with a parameter of *NULL*, thus clearing out my dump hook before calling *_CrtDumpMemoryLeaks*. I was distressed by this behavior until it dawned on me that I just had to do the final memory leak checking myself. Fortunately, I had the perfect place to do it.

COMMON DEBUGGING QUESTION

Why do I need the C debug run-time library if I'm using an error detection tool like BoundsChecker?

Error detection tools such as Compuware NuMega's BoundsChecker and Rational Software's Purify automatically handle memory underwrites, memory overwrites, and memory leaks. If you use one of these tools, you might think that using the DCRT library isn't worth your time and effort. Technically, that's true, but to ensure that you find all your memory problems, you need to run your application under your error detection tool every time anyone on the team runs a debug build of the application. "Anyone" includes you, your fellow developers, and if you followed my advice from Chapter 2, even your quality engineers. I just don't see everyone being that vigilant.

Using the DCRT library is like having good fire or theft insurance. You hope you'll never need to use the insurance, but if you do, it can be a lifesaver. Any time you can validate data in your application, you should. The DCRT library doesn't impose a drastic performance hit, and it can unearth some outstanding bugs. You should always use it—even if you have all the tools in the world.

Because I was already using the *#pragma init_seg(compiler)* directive to get the *AutoMatic* class initialized before your code and to call the destructor after your code, I just needed to do the leak checking there and then turn off the *_CRTDBG-_LEAK_CHECK_DF* flag so that the DCRT library didn't do its own reporting. The only caveat with using this approach is that you need to make sure that the CRT library of your choice comes before BUGSLAYERUTIL.LIB if you link with the /NODEFAULTLIB switch. When you link against BUGSLAYERUTIL.LIB, the CRT libraries can't depend on their *#pragma init_seg(compiler)* directive to ensure that their data gets initialized first and destroyed last, so you need to enforce the correct ordering yourself.

If you think about it, having the DCRT library clear out any dump hooks installed makes sense. If your dump hook were using any CRT library functions, such as *printf*, it could crash the termination of your program because the library is in the middle of shutting down when *_CrtDumpMemoryLeaks* is called. If you follow the rules and always link with the DCRT library before any other libraries, you'll be fine because the MemDumperValidator functions are shut down before the DCRT library shuts down. To avoid problems, use the *_RPTn* and *_RPTFn* macros only in your dumper functions anyway, because *_CrtDumpMemoryLeaks* uses only these macros.

USING MEMSTRESS

Now it's time to add a little stress to your life. Believe it or not, stress can be a good thing. Unfortunately, stressing Microsoft Win32 applications is much harder these days than it used to be. In the days of 16-bit Windows—and still today for the 16-bit subsystem on Windows 98—we could run our programs through their paces with STRESS.EXE, a neat program that comes with the SDK. STRESS.EXE allowed you to torment your application in all sorts of nasty ways, such as eating up disk space, gobbling up the graphics device interface (GDI) heap, and using up file handles. It even had a cool icon: an elephant walking a tightrope.

To stress your Win32 applications, you can hook into the DCRT library's allocation system and control whether allocations succeed or fail. The MemStress extension gives you a means to stress your C and C++ memory allocation. (I'll leave it up to you to write the disk-eating code.) To make MemStress easy to use, I wrote a Visual Basic front end that lets you specify exactly what conditions you'd like to fail.

The MemStress extension lets you force allocation failures based on various criteria: all allocations, on every *n* allocations, after *x* bytes are allocated, on requests over *y* bytes, on all allocations out of a source file, and on a specific line in a source file. In addition, you can have the MemStress extension prompt you with a message box on each allocation asking whether you want this particular allocation to fail, and you can also set the DCRT library flags you'd like in effect for your program. The MemStressDemo program is a sample MFC program on the companion CD that allows you to experiment with setting different options from the MemStress user interface (UI) and see the results.

Using the MemStress extension is relatively simple. In your code, include BUGSLAYERUTIL.H and call the *MEMSTRESSINIT* macro with the name of your program. To stop the memory allocation hooking, use the *MEMSTRESSTERMINATE* macro. You can start and stop the hook as many times as you want when running your program.

After you've compiled your program, start the MemStress UI, click the Add Program button, and type the same name that you specified in the *MEMSTRESSINIT* macro. After you've selected the failure options you want, press the Save Settings For This Program button to save the settings into MEMSTRESS.INI. Now you can run your program and see how it behaves when it fails memory allocations.

You'll probably want to be very selective about using the MemStress extension. For example, if you specify that you want all allocations over 100 bytes to fail and you have the *MEMSTRESSINIT* macro in your MFC application's *InitInstance* function, you'll likely take down MFC because it will be unable to initialize. You'll have the best results with the MemStress extension if you limit its use to key areas in your code so that you can test them in isolation.

Most of the implementation of MemStress is in the reading and processing of the MEMSTRESS.INI file, in which all the settings for individual programs are stored. From the DCRT library perspective, the important function is the call to *_CrtSetAllocHook* during the MemStress initialization because this call sets the hook function, *AllocationHook*, as the allocation hook. If the allocation hook function returns *TRUE*, the allocation request is allowed to continue. By returning *FALSE*, the allocation hook can have the DCRT library fail the allocation request. The allocation hook has only one hard requirement from the DCRT library: if the type of block, as specified by the *nBlockUse* parameter, is marked as a *_CRT_BLOCK*, the hook function must return *TRUE* to allow the allocation to take place.

The allocation hook gets called on every type of allocation function. The different types, as specified in the first parameter to the hook, are *_HOOK_ALLOC*, *_HOOK_REALLOC*, and *_HOOK_FREE*. In my *AllocationHook* function, if the type is *_HOOK_FREE*, I skip all the code that determines whether the memory request should pass or fail. For *_HOOK_ALLOC* and *_HOOK_REALLOC* types, my *AllocationHook* function performs a series of *if* statements to determine whether any of the failure conditions are met. If a failure condition is met, I return *FALSE*.

An Interesting Stress Problem

Everything worked great in MemStress on my initial console sample program, and I was feeling fine. As I finished off the MFC-based MemStressDemo program, I noticed a compelling problem. If I elected to have MemStress ask me with a message box whether I wanted allocations to fail, I would hear a series of beeps and MemStressDemo would stop working. I was able to duplicate the problem every time—and to duplicate the serious stress the problem was causing me because I didn't see what the issue could be.

After a few runs, I finally got a message box to show up. Instead of being in the center of the screen, the message box was down in the lower right-hand corner. When message boxes start moving off the lower right-hand corner of the screen, you can be pretty sure that you're stuck in a situation in which calling the *MessageBox* API function somehow became reentrant. I suspected that my allocation hook was getting called in the middle of my call to *MessageBox*. I confirmed my hypothesis by setting a breakpoint on the first instruction of *AllocationHook* just before I stepped over the *MessageBox* call. Sure enough, the debugger stopped on the breakpoint.

I looked up the stack and saw that a direct call to the *MessageBox* API function was somehow going through MFC code. As I poked through the code looking at what was happening, I saw that I was in the *_AfxActivationWndProc* function on a line that was calling *CWnd::FromHandle*, which causes memory allocations so that MFC can create a *CObject*. I was a little stumped about how I got in there, but a comment in the code indicated that *_AfxActivationWndProc* is used to handle activation and make gray dialog boxes. MFC uses a computer-based training (CBT) hook to catch window creations in the process space. When a new window is created—in my case, a simple message box—MFC subclasses the window with its own window procedure.

When I understood all the issues, my personal stress level really shot up because I wasn't sure how to handle the situation. Because the reentrancy was on the same thread, I couldn't use a synchronization object such as a semaphore because that would have deadlocked the thread. After contemplating the problem a bit, I concluded that what I needed was a recursion flag that told me when *AllocationHook* was being reentered—but it had to be on a per-thread basis. I already had a critical section protecting against multiple-thread reentrancy in *AllocationHook*.

When I stated the problem this way, I realized that all I needed was a variable in thread local storage that I would access at the beginning of *AllocationHook*. If the value was greater than 0, *AllocationHook* was being reentered as part of the *MessageBox* processing and I just needed to bail out of the function. I implemented a quick dynamic thread local storage solution and my anxiety dropped considerably because everything started working as planned.

SUMMARY

The debug C run-time library has many wonderful features—provided you turn them on in your application. Because using memory is a fact of life in our C and C++ programs, we need all the help we can get solving the problems we invariably have with memory. This chapter covered the high points of the DCRT library and presented two utilities I wrote, MemDumperValidator and MemStress, that will help you get more information about the memory your application uses and allow you to better test your application under stressful conditions.

The extensibility of the DCRT library is pretty amazing. If you've been in this business for more than a year or two, you've probably written something like it in the past. I hope I was able to give you some sense of the power of the DCRT library. I encourage you to devise other utilities and helper code that will ease your memory debugging chores.

Part IV

Appendixes

Reading Dr. Watson Log Files

Dr. Watson should really be named Dr. Jekyll and Mr. Hyde. In Dr. Jekyll mode, you get the information about a crash on a user's machine and can easily find where the crash occurred and fix it quickly. In Mr. Hyde mode, all you get is another set of numbers that don't tell you anything. In this appendix, I'll explain how to read Dr. Watson logs so that you can see less of Mr. Hyde and more of Dr. Jekyll.

I'll walk you through a complete Dr. Watson log in the following pages, explaining all the pertinent information as we go. (Relevant information in a particular section appears in boldface type.) The crash log in this appendix is for an early version of WDBG.EXE, the debugger I wrote in Chapter 4.

Now that you've read this book, nothing in the Dr. Watson log should come as a big surprise. The log here is from Microsoft Windows 2000, but a log produced by Microsoft Windows NT 4 would be identical. The Microsoft Windows 98 Dr. Watson logs are similar in core information to the one shown in this appendix, and once you understand how to read the Windows 2000 version of the log, you'll know enough to be able to read a Windows 98 log. I'll cover the information unique to Windows 98 at the end of this appendix.

WINDOWS 2000 DR. WATSON LOG

Here's the first section of the Dr. Watson log from Windows 2000:

```
Microsoft (R) Windows 2000 (TM) Version 5.00 DrWtsn32
Copyright (C) 1985-1999 Microsoft Corp. All rights reserved.



Application exception occurred:
        App:  (pid=252)
        When: 9/4/1999 @ 16:43:56.173
        Exception number: c0000005 (access violation)
```

The header information tells you what caused the crash—in this case, an application exception. The exception numbers for some crashes might not get translated into a human-readable description, such as "access violation" for exception number 0xC0000005. You can see all the possible exception number values by searching for *STATUS_* in WINNT.H. The crash values are documented as *EXCEPTION_* values returned by the *GetExceptionCode* function, but the real values are in all the *STATUS_* *#defines*. Once you translate back into the *EXCEPTION_* value, you can look up the description for the crash in the *GetExceptionCode* documentation.

The System Information section should be self-explanatory:

```
*----> System Information <----*
        Computer Name: PLATO
        User Name: John
        Number of Processors: 1
        Processor Type: x86 Family 6 Model 6 Stepping 10
        Windows 2000 Version: 5.0
        Current Build: 2128
        Service Pack: None
        Current Type: Uniprocessor Free
        Registered Organization: Enter your company name here
        Registered Owner: John Robbins
```

The Task List section looks like this:

```
*----> Task List <----*
    0 Idle.exe
    8 System.exe
  132 smss.exe
  160 csrss.exe
  156 winlogon.exe
  208 services.exe
  220 lsass.exe
  364 svchost.exe
  424 svchost.exe
  472 spoolsv.exe
  504 MWMDMSVC.exe
  528 MWSSW32.exe
  576 regsvc.exe
  592 MSTask.exe
  836 Explorer.exe
  904 tp4mon.exe
  912 tphkmgr.exe
  920 4nt.exe
  940 taskmgr.exe
  956 tponscr.exe
  268 msdev.exe
  252 WDBG.exe
  828 NOTEPAD.exe
  416 drwtsn32.exe
    0 _Total.exe
```

The Task List section shows the processes that were running at the time of the crash. Unfortunately, Windows 2000 doesn't show the version information, so you'll have to ask the user for the file versions of all the processes in this section. The numbers down the left-hand side are the decimal process IDs (PIDs) at the time of the crash. The numbers are worthless after the fact.

This list contains all the modules loaded into the address space at the time of the crash:

```
(00400000 - 0042D000) D:\Dev\Book\CD\SourceCode\Output\WDBG.pdb
(77F80000 - 77FF9000) E:\WINNT\symbols\dll\ntdll.dbg
(60000000 - 6001A000) D:\Dev\Book\CD\SourceCode\Output\BugslayerUtil.pdb
(77E80000 - 77F35000) E:\WINNT\symbols\dll\kernel32.dbg
(77E10000 - 77E74000) E:\WINNT\symbols\dll\user32.dbg
(77F40000 - 77F7C000) E:\WINNT\symbols\dll\gdi32.dbg
(72950000 - 72967000) E:\WINNT\symbols\dll\dbghelp.dbg
(78000000 - 78046000)
(77DB0000 - 77E07000) E:\WINNT\symbols\dll\advapi32.dbg
(77D30000 - 77DA2000) E:\WINNT\symbols\dll\rpcrt4.dbg
(10200000 - 10264000)
(63100000 - 63108000) D:\Dev\Book\CD\SourceCode\Output\LocalAssist.pdb
(62000000 - 6202B000) D:\Dev\Book\CD\SourceCode\Output\i386CPUHelp.pdb
(63000000 - 63010000) D:\Dev\Book\CD\SourceCode\Output\LocalDebug.pdb
(5F400000 - 5F4E5000)
(77B30000 - 77BBA000) E:\WINNT\symbols\dll\comctl32.dbg
(775A0000 - 777DE000) E:\WINNT\symbols\dll\shell32.dbg
(77C50000 - 77C9A000) E:\WINNT\symbols\dll\shlwapi.dbg
(76B20000 - 76B5E000) E:\WINNT\symbols\dll\comdlg32.dbg
(77A30000 - 77B24000) E:\WINNT\symbols\dll\ole32.dbg
(77990000 - 77A24000) E:\WINNT\symbols\dll\oleaut32.dbg
(77CA0000 - 77D25000)
(77850000 - 7788B000)
(770B0000 - 770D3000)
(6B6E0000 - 6B6FC000) E:\WINNT\symbols\dll\msdbi.dbg
(68ED0000 - 68EDB000) E:\WINNT\symbols\dll\psapi.dbg
```

The numbers are in the format (load address - maximum address) for each module. This section would be more useful if Dr. Watson showed the actual names of the modules loaded into the address space. Unfortunately, as you can see by the names to the right of the numbers, the only information shown is the location where Dr. Watson loaded the debugging symbols for that module. The blank entries mean that no debugging information was loaded for the module.

To figure out what modules were loaded, you have to guess. As I've mentioned several times in this book, it's vital for you to know where your dynamic-link libraries (DLLs) load into the process address space. You can probably recognize your DLLs just from the load addresses. To find the information for the other DLLs on the user's machine, you could write a small utility that would run through the DLLs on the user's system and report their names, load addresses, and sizes.

The following output is the beginning of the three-part thread state. (You'll notice that I removed the code bytes from beside the disassembly addresses and wrapped the register display so that it would fit on the page.)

```
State Dump for Thread Id 0x2fc

eax=00000000 ebx=7ffdf000 ecx=008c67c0 edx=0000033c esi=00134c78
edi=0012fd74
eip=0040bd2d esp=0012fb98 ebp=0012fbc4 iopl=0    nv up ei pl nz na pe nc
cs=001b  ss=0023  ds=0023  es=0023  fs=003b  gs=0000
efl=00000202


function: CWDBGProjDoc::HandleBreakpoint
        0040bd11  push    esi
        0040bd12  push    edi
        0040bd13  mov     eax,0xcccccccc
        0040bd18  mov     [ebp+0xe0],eax          ss:00b4d19a=????????
        0040bd1b  mov     [ebp+0xe4],eax          ss:00b4d19a=????????
        0040bd1e  mov     [ebp+0xe8],eax          ss:00b4d19a=????????
        0040bd21  mov     [ebp+0xec],eax          ss:00b4d19a=????????
        0040bd24  mov     [ebp+0xf0],eax          ss:00b4d19a=????????
        0040bd27  mov     [ebp+0xe0],ecx          ss:00b4d19a=????????
        0040bd2a  mov     eax,[ebp+0xc]           ss:00b4d19a=????????
FAULT ->0040bd2d  mov     ecx,[eax+0x4]           ds:00a1d5d6=????????
        0040bd30  cmp dword ptr [ecx],0x80000003 ds:008c67c0=0041b714
        0040bd36  jz CArray<COneShotBP,COneShotBP>::SetSize+0x25d (0041485d)
        0040bd38  mov     esi,esp
        0040bd3a  push    0x382
        0040bd3f  push    0x420030
        0040bd44  push    0x420064
        0040bd49  push    0x0
        0040bd4b  call    dword ptr [_imp__DiagAssertA (00423ad4)]
        0040bd51  cmp     esi,esp
        0040bd53  call    _chkesp (00416b5a)
        0040bd58  test    eax,eax
```

Dr. Watson displays the state information for each thread running in a process at the time it crashed. The thread states contain all the information you need to determine how and why the system crashed.

The register portion shows what all the registers contained at the time of the crash. The important register to look at is EIP, the instruction pointer. The example

I show has symbols, so you can see which function this thread was executing when the crash occurred—most Dr. Watson logs won't have symbol information. Of course, it's not a problem if Dr. Watson doesn't give you the function name. Using CrashFinder from Chapter 8, simply load up the CrashFinder project for your application, press Ctrl+F, and enter the EIP for the thread in the Find dialog box.

This thread happened to be the thread that crashed. The only indicator is the FAULT-> pointer in the middle of the disassembly. I've seen a Dr. Watson log or two that didn't display the FAULT-> pointer. If you don't see this pointer in a log, run through each thread state and enter each EIP address into CrashFinder to figure out where the thread was sitting at the time of the crash.

The disassembly should look familiar to you if you remember what you read in Chapter 6. The only new elements are the values after the instructions. The Dr. Watson disassembler attempts to look up the effective address of the memory reference for the instruction so that you can see what value the instruction was manipulating. The addresses that start with *ss* indicate that the memory was a stack segment reference; *ds* indicates a data segment reference.

The only effective address in the disassembly that's guaranteed to be correct is the one at the instruction pointer. The others might be incorrect because the value the instruction refers to could have been changed. For example, let's say that the first instruction disassembled in the thread state had a memory reference at EBX. If the crash instruction occurred 10 instructions later, one of the intervening instructions could easily have changed EBX. When Dr. Watson does its disassembly, however, it uses the value *currently* in EBX—that is, the one at the time of the crash—to do the effective address translation. For this reason, the effective address shown in the disassembly could be incorrect. Carefully check whether any instructions could change the register values before you believe what you see in the effective address display.

Using your newfound assembly-language skills, you should be able to figure out that this thread crashed because the instruction at 0x0040BD2D, MOV ECX , [EAX+0x4] was trying to access a *NULL* pointer in EAX. If you look at the instruction on the line just above this one, MOV EAX , [EBP+0xC], the light bulb should go on in your head that positive offsets from EBP are probably parameter references. An offset of 0xC from EBP means that the instruction referenced the second parameter to the function. Your first debugging hypothesis for this crash should be that the function failed because an invalid parameter was passed in the second parameter. (I hope this paragraph has convinced you how important it is to know enough assembly language to read a Dr. Watson log!)

Here's the second part of the thread state: the Stack Back Trace. (Notice that I wrapped the function names so that everything would fit on the page.)

```
*----> Stack Back Trace <----*

FramePtr ReturnAd Param#1  Param#2  Param#3  Param#4  Function Name
0012FBC4 0040BCB5 0000033C 00000000 80000003 008C67C0
                                          !CWDBGProjDoc::HandleBreakpoint
0012FBE0 00405A9C 0000033C 010DFC0C 008C68B0 0012FCF4
                                          !CWDBGProjDoc::HandleExceptionEvent
0012FBF4 5F42F3AC 0000033C 010DFC0C 0012FD74 00134C78
                                          !CDocNotifyWnd::HandleExceptionEvent
0012FCF4 5F42ECE8 00000502 0000033C 010DFC0C 0012FD10 !Ordinal4118
0012FD14 5F42C889 00000502 0000033C 010DFC0C 77F86618 !Ordinal5076
0012FD88 5F42CD25 008C68B0 000602A4 00000502 0000033C !Ordinal1045
0012FDB4 5F4905FD 000602A4 00000502 0000033C 010DFC0C !Ordinal1192
0012FDE4 77E135F8 000602A4 00000502 0000033C 010DFC0C !Ordinal1193
0012FE04 77E15FE8 5F4905B3 000602A4 00000502 0000033C
                                          user32!UserCallWinProc
0012FE20 77E1600E 004A9B70 00000502 0000033C 010DFC0C
                         user32!DispatchClientMessage (FPO: Non-FPO [5,1,0])
0012FE48 77F9D8B7 0012FE58 00000018 004A9B70 00000502
                               user32!__fnDWORD (FPO: Non-FPO [1,4,0])
0012FE68 77E15FB5 77E17BD9 00422250 00000000 00000000
                           ntdll!KiUserCallbackDispatcher  (FPO: [0,0,0])
0012FE90 5F4396F8 00422250 00000000 00000000 00000000
                         user32!DispatchClientMessage (FPO: Non-FPO [5,1,0])
0012FEB8 5F438E1D 77F86618 77F81A9B 7FFDF000 00000001 !Ordinal4239
0012FEDC 5F439AD4 00422218 0012FF08 5F43366E 77F86618 !Ordinal4409
0012FEE8 5F43366E 77F86618 77F81A9B 7FFDF000 00422218 !Ordinal4408
0012FF08 00417028 00400000 00000000 00133A73 00000001 !Ordinal1190
0012FF20 00416E53 00400000 00000000 00133A73 00000001 !WinMain
0012FFC0 77E9BC52 77F86618 77F81A9B 7FFDF000 C0000005 !WinMainCRTStartup
0012FFF0 00000000 00416CA0 00000000 000000C8 00000100
                         kernel32!BaseProcessStart (FPO: Non-FPO [1,8,3])
```

Although my example Dr. Watson log has symbols, your user's log probably won't. The ReturnAd column lists the return addresses of functions on the call stack. If your user's log doesn't have symbols, all you need to do is load each address in the ReturnAd column into CrashFinder to find out the sequence of function calls leading up to the crash.

The Param# columns show a function's first four possible parameters on the stack. With highly optimized release builds and no symbols, the values are probably incorrect. However, you can still use them as a starting point for hand-walking your code.

The function names are shown in <module>!<function> format. Those functions shown as Ordinal# are ordinal exports. If you don't have the source code for the DLL that does the exports by ordinal, you're mostly out of luck. However, because you do have the source code for the Microsoft Foundation Class (MFC) library, you can look up MFC ordinal values. In the WDBG program, I know that MFC42D.DLL is loaded at 0x5F400000, so I can look up those ordinals because all MFC functions are exported by ordinal value through a linker definition (DEF) file.

The one prerequisite for converting MFC ordinal values to functions is that you must be certain of the version of the MFC DLL on the machine that crashed. On my machine, named \\PLATO, I had MFC42D.DLL from Visual C++ 6 Service Pack 3. If you're unsure of the version of MFC on the user's machine, you'll either have to ask for it or beg for it—I'll let you choose the method you're most comfortable with.

Follow these simple steps to turn ordinal values into functions:

1. Open the <Visual C++ directory>\MFC\SRC\Intel directory.

2. Select the appropriate DEF file for the MFC file you want to look up. For example, MFC42D.DLL's DEF file is MFC42D.DEF.

3. Search for the ordinal number. To find Ordinal4118 from the preceding stack, I'd search the MFC42D.DEF file for 4118. The line with 4118 is "?OnWndMsg@CWnd@@MAEHIIJPAJ@Z @ 4118 NONAME."

4. The name to the left of "@ 4118 NONAME" is the decorated function name exported at that ordinal value. To undecorate the name, use the UNDNAME.EXE program that comes with the Platform SDK. For 4118, the function is *CWnd::OnWndMsg*.

The third part and final part of the thread state is the Raw Stack Dump:

```
*----> Raw Stack Dump <----*
0012fb98 74 fd 12 00 78 4c 13 00-00 f0 fd 7f c0 67 8c 00 t...xL.......g..
0012fba8 cc cc cc cc cc cc cc cc-cc cc cc cc cc cc cc cc ................
0012fbb8 e8 fc 12 00 2e 8a 41 00-ff ff ff ff e0 fb 12 00 ......A.........
0012fbc8 b5 bc 40 00 3c 03 00 00-00 00 00 00 03 00 00 80 ..@.<...........
0012fbd8 c0 67 8c 00 cc cc cc cc-f4 fb 12 00 9c 5a 40 00 .g...........Z@.
0012fbe8 3c 03 00 00 0c fc 0d 01-b0 68 8c 00 f4 fc 12 00 <........h......
0012fbf8 ac f3 42 5f 3c 03 00 00-0c fc 0d 01 74 fd 12 00 ..B_<.......t...
0012fc08 78 4c 13 00 00 f0 fd 7f-09 00 00 00 b0 68 8c 00 xL...........h..
0012fc18 04 00 00 00 00 00 00 00-00 00 8c 00 50 00 8c 00 ............P...
0012fc28 50 00 8c 00 01 00 00 00-ae 05 12 00 70 2d 00 00 P...........p-..
0012fc38 01 00 00 00 fa 00 00 00-8c fc 12 00 8b 48 fb 77 .............H.w
0012fc48 00 00 8c 00 00 00 9f 01-01 00 00 00 80 fc 12 00 ................
0012fc58 7c fc 12 00 84 fc 12 00-00 00 00 00 00 00 00 00 |...............
0012fc68 00 00 8c 00 00 00 8c 00-90 fc 12 00 d5 19 49 5f ..............I_
0012fc78 04 00 00 00 18 66 f8 77-9b 1a f8 77 a4 fc 12 00 .....f.w...w....
0012fc88 d5 19 49 5f 04 00 00 00-18 66 f8 77 9b 1a f8 77 ..I_.....f.w...w
0012fc98 00 f0 fd 7f 48 e1 4c 5f-48 4d 13 00 cc fc 12 00 ....H.L_HM......
0012fca8 45 16 49 5f cc fc 12 00-d5 19 49 5f d4 fc 12 00 E.I_......I_....
0012fcb8 d8 fc 12 00 d5 19 49 5f-04 00 00 00 18 66 f8 77 ......I_.....f.w
0012fcc8 50 22 42 00 00 00 00 00-0a 00 00 00 00 a5 41 00 P"B...........A.
```

I rarely look at this information. If I'm really stuck on a crash, however, I might start looking at the information to see whether I can guess at local variable values. The two return addresses I can correlate with the preceding stack walk are shown in boldface.

WINDOWS 98 DR. WATSON LOG

The one area in which Windows 98 beats Windows 2000 for debugging is with its Dr. Watson logs. The Windows 98 logs contain far more information, especially about the processes running on the system and the version information for each module. With the information you get from a Windows 98 Dr. Watson log, you'll have a much easier time setting up a duplicate machine to test against.

Much of the crash information logged is the same in Windows 2000 and Windows 98—you just get a whole lot more of it in Windows 98. For example, the Windows 98 Dr. Watson log disassembles each location in the call stack. I'll show only the Details section for a Windows 98 crash because I want to explain some of the extra information you'll see.

Here's the start of the Details section:

```
*----> Details <----*

Command line: "g:\Dev\Book\CD\SourceCode\Output\WDBG.exe"

Trap 0e 0000 - Invalid page fault
eax=00000000 ebx=0065fba6 ecx=00b938b0 edx=fffdc1a5 esi=005301c0
edi=0065fae4
eip=0040bd2d esp=0065f908 ebp=0065f934  -- -- -- nv up EI pl nz na PE nc
cs=0167 ss=016f ds=016f es=016f fs=38d7 gs=382f
WDBG.EXE:.text+0xad2d:
>0167:0040bd2d 8b4804                        mov      ecx,dword ptr [eax+04]
```

This section shows the full command line and the fault, which is the same as an exception on Windows 2000. After the fault come the usual registers followed by the instruction that caused the crash.

Here Windows 98 is showing some of its 16-bit heritage. These are all the segment registers showing the selector values. For more information, see the Intel processor manuals.

```
    sel  type base      lim/bot
    ---- ---- --------- --------
cs  0167 r-x- 00000000  ffffffff
ss  016f rw-e 00000000  0000d7a0
ds  016f rw-e 00000000  0000d7a0
es  016f rw-e 00000000  0000d7a0
fs  38d7 rw-- 81630798  00000037
gs  382f rw-- 00657000  0000ffff
```

```
stack base:    00560000
TIB limits:    0065b000 - 00660000
```

The exception record is a dump of the first field in the *EXCEPTION_POINTERS* structure when the Dr. Watson debugger is notified of the exception:

```
-- exception record --

   Exception Code: c0000005 (access violation)
Exception Address: 0040bd2d (WDBG.EXE:.text+0xad2d)
   Exception Info: 00000000
                   ffffffff
```

The disassembly shows the current state of the thread. An asterisk delineates the current instruction. (Notice that I removed the code bytes from the disassembly so that it would fit on the page.)

```
WDBG.EXE:.text+0xad2d:
>0167:0040bd2d   mov   ecx,dword ptr [eax+04]

  0167:0040bd11   push  esi
  0167:0040bd12   push  edi
  0167:0040bd13   mov   eax,cccccccc
  0167:0040bd18   mov   dword ptr [ebp-20],eax
  0167:0040bd1b   mov   dword ptr [ebp-1c],eax
  0167:0040bd1e   mov   dword ptr [ebp-18],eax
  0167:0040bd21   mov   dword ptr [ebp-14],eax
  0167:0040bd24   mov   dword ptr [ebp-10],eax
  0167:0040bd27   mov   dword ptr [ebp-20],ecx
  0167:0040bd2a   mov   eax,dword ptr [ebp+0c]
WDBG.EXE:.text+0xad2d:
*0167:0040bd2d   mov   ecx,dword ptr [eax+04]
  0167:0040bd30   cmp   dword ptr [ecx],80000003
  0167:0040bd36   jz    0040bd5d = WDBG.EXE:.text+0xad5d
  0167:0040bd38   mov   esi,esp
  0167:0040bd3a   push  00000382
  0167:0040bd3f   push  00420030
  0167:0040bd44   push  00420064
  0167:0040bd49   push  +00
  0167:0040bd4b   call  dword ptr [00423ad4] -> BUGSLAYERUTIL.DLL!DiagAssertA
  0167:0040bd51   cmp   esi,esp
  0167:0040bd53   call  00416b5a = MSVCRTD.DLL!_chkesp
```

Appendix B

Resources for Windows Developers

As I pointed out in Chapter 1, being a good developer is a prerequisite for being a good debugger. The best debuggers also have a solid skill set and, most important, can draw on a broad range of knowledge to help them solve any debugging problem they encounter. Having a solid grasp of the language, the technologies involved, the operating system, and the CPU can make the difference between solving a debugging problem in minutes and spending days in the debugger wondering what's going on.

My motivation for putting together this list of resources is that developers continually ask me what resources I use to learn about Microsoft Windows development. Please keep in mind that the books, tools, and Web sites in this appendix don't comprise an exhaustive list by any means, and you might even disagree with some of my recommendations. All the items I list are suggestions—except for one. The one item you absolutely must have for Windows development is a subscription to the Microsoft Developer Network (MSDN) CDs. If you don't have access to these CDs, there's no way you can do serious, professional Windows development. Microsoft has come out with MSDN Online, but the MSDN CDs are the only place that some information appears. For more information on subscribing to MSDN, see *msdn.microsoft.com/ subscriptions*.

BOOKS

I've referred to the following books time and time again during my career as a software developer and debugger. I strongly recommend them to you.

Software Development

- *Code Complete* by Steve McConnell (Microsoft Press, 1993)
  This is simply the best book on software construction that I've ever read.
  Every developer should own a copy and read it cover to cover every year.
  After reading it annually for six years, I'm still learning things from this book!

- *Rapid Development* by Steve McConnell (Microsoft Press, 1996)
  This book taught me how to manage teams and schedule projects.

- *Debugging the Development Process* by Steve Maguire (Microsoft Press, 1994)
  This book is a great introduction to the way Microsoft develops software.
  Obviously, since Microsoft is the most successful software company on
  the planet, they must be doing something right. You can learn a great deal
  from this book.

- *Dynamics of Software Development* by Jim McCarthy (Microsoft Press, 1995)
  This book is a very interesting look at software development from the
  perspective of a manager with a track record for shipping great products.
  The rules Jim proposes are excellent because they all come from actual
  experience; he's not just some academic theorizing.

Languages

- *The C Programming Language* by Brian W. Kernighan and Dennis Ritchie
  (2nd ed., Prentice Hall, 1988)
  This book is the definitive guide to C programming and the best-written
  technical book I've ever read.

- *Learning C++* by Neill Graham (McGraw-Hill, 1991)
  I used this book to learn C++. Unlike other C++ doorstop books, *Learning C++* is short, sweet, and to the point.

- *Advanced Microsoft Visual Basic 6.0* by The Mandelbrot Set (2nd ed.,
  Microsoft Press, 1998)
  An excellent book on Visual Basic that goes into many real-world issues.
  The first chapter, "On Error GoTo Hell," by Peet Morris, and the sixth
  chapter, "Staying in Control," by Mark Pearce, are must-reads for all Visual
  Basic programmers. Although the chapter on hiring developers is good,
  I'm still not sure what is has to do with advanced Visual Basic.

- *C++ Programmer's Guide to the Standard Template Library* by Mark Nelson
  (IDG Books, 1995)
  I have a severe love-hate relationship with the Standard Template Library.
  Fortunately, Mark's book does a great job of providing samples and
  explaining the finer points of using this library.

Debugging and Testing

■ *The Practice of Programming* by Brian Kernighan and Rob Pike (Addison-Wesley, 1999)
This book is a wonderful discussion of developing, debugging, and testing.

■ *Writing Solid Code* by Steve Maguire (Microsoft Press, 1993)
Although it focuses mainly on C programming, this book contains excellent advice on interface definitions and avoiding nasty problems in the language.

■ *Managing the Testing Process* by Rex Black (Microsoft Press, 1999)
To develop better, you need to know how to test better. This excellent book will change the way you develop and the way you interact with your QA teams.

■ *How Debuggers Work* by Jonathan B. Rosenberg (John Wiley & Sons, 1996)
This book is an excellent introduction to how debuggers work and to the issues you need to consider when designing a debugger.

Windows and Windows Technologies

■ *Programming Windows* by Charles Petzold (5th ed., Microsoft Press, 1999)
This one book will teach you everything you need to know about how Windows programs work at the most fundamental level. People could solve many of the problems they ask me about if they only had a better understanding of how message handling, graphics device interface (GDI), and other subjects work at the SDK level.

■ *Programming Applications for Microsoft Windows* by Jeffrey Richter (4th ed., Microsoft Press, 1999)
This book covers all the unique aspects of Microsoft Win32 development. The chapters on DLLs, threads, synchronization, and structured exception handling are the best descriptions available and all relate directly to debugging your problems more quickly and efficiently.

■ *Programming Windows with MFC* by Jeff Prosise (2nd ed., Microsoft Press, 1999)
This book is the definitive guide to programming with the Microsoft Foundation Class (MFC) library. If you're using MFC, you must have this book.

■ *Windows++* by Paul Dilascia (Addison-Wesley, 1992)
Unlike other design books, which have only toy examples, this book produces a strong and viable C++ class library for Windows. I learn best by example, and this book taught me how to think in terms of objects.

- *Essential COM* by Don Box (Addison-Wesley, 1998)
  In the Disassembly window ("unambiguous mode"), a Component Object Model (COM) interface is just a pointer to an array of pointers, so COM should be easy to understand. COM is so much more than just a pointer and is so fundamental to programming life, however, that you must understand how it works if you expect to stand a chance of correctly implementing and debugging your code. Don's book will give you a great start along the path of COM enlightenment.

- *Inside Windows NT* by David A. Solomon (2nd ed., Microsoft Press, 1998)
  The book is the official "big picture" view of the Windows NT kernel. Although more directly applicable for device driver writers, this book will help you make sense out of how the different parts of the operating system fit together in Windows NT.

- *Windows 95 System Programming Secrets* by Matt Pietrek (IDG Books, 1995)
  Matt's book is out of print, but you should really try to find a copy. Debugging anything more than a simple access violation on Windows 95 and Windows 98 is an exercise in extreme frustration mainly because Windows 95 and Windows 98 are hybrid 16-bit/32-bit operating systems. Much of the information in the book, such as the Portable Executable (PE) file format chapter, applies to Windows 2000 as well.

- *ATL Internals* by Brent Rector and Chris Sells (Addison-Wesley, 1999)
  The Active Template Library (ATL) makes the smallest and fastest COM objects around. To take full advantage of ATL, you have to have this book.

The CPU and Hardware

- *Structured Computer Organization* by Andrew S. Tanenbaum (4th ed., Prentice-Hall, 1998)
  An excellent introduction to computer architecture, this book is filled with information that I use to debug problems daily. The book has some typos and technical errors, but if you can get past that you'll be glad you read it.

- Intel CPU reference manuals
  Intel makes available, for free, the CPU manuals for their processors. If you're doing serious debugging, these manuals are extremely helpful and informative. You can download the Adobe PDF files from Intel's Literature Center at *developer.intel.com/design/litcentr/index.htm*. Intel also provides the manuals in book form if you prefer having hard copies.

- *The Indispensable PC Hardware Book* by Hans-Peter Messmer (3rd ed., Addison-Wesley, 1997)
  This book is the best discussion of PC hardware around. When you need to interact with hardware, this book is an invaluable resource.

TOOLS

Keep in mind that when it comes to software tools, I'm not a biased observer. As you can see from my biography, I worked at NuMega for four years, and I was a member of the teams that developed some of the leading tools in the marketplace. I use those tools all the time. The list of tool vendors here is for your reference and not an implied endorsement of any company or product. The tools listed are geared toward debugging and automated testing.

- Compuware NuMega (*www.numega.com*)

  - BoundsChecker
    Automatic run-time error detection and diagnosis for Visual C++, Borland Delphi, and Borland C++ Builder programs for all Windows operating systems

  - TrueTime
    Automatic performance analysis for Visual C++, Visual Basic, and Java programs for all Windows operating systems

  - TrueCoverage
    Automatic code-coverage analysis for Visual C++, Visual Basic, and Java programs for all Windows operating systems

  - CodeReview
    Automatic source code analysis for Visual Basic programs for all Windows operating systems

  - SmartCheck
    Automatic run-time error detection and diagnosis for Visual Basic programs for all Windows operating systems

  - FailSafe
    Automatic error handling and recovery for Visual Basic programs for all Windows operating systems

❑   JCheck
   Visual thread and event analysis for Java programs for all Windows operating systems

❑   SoftICE
   Advanced Windows debugger for debugging both user-mode and kernel-mode programs for all Windows operating systems

■   Rational Software (*www.rational.com*)

❑   Purify
   Automatic run-time error detection and diagnosis for Visual C++ programs on Windows NT and Windows 2000 only

❑   PureCoverage
   Automatic code-coverage analysis for Visual C++, Visual Basic, and Java programs for Windows NT and Windows 2000 only

❑   Quantify
   Automatic performance analysis for Visual C++, Visual Basic, and Java programs for Windows NT and Windows 2000 only

❑   Rational Robot
   Regression-testing tool for all Windows operating systems

❑   Visual Test
   Regression-testing tool for all Windows operating systems

■   Mutek Software (*www.mutek.com*)

❑   BugTrapper
   Error trapping and postmortem debugging for Visual C++ and Visual Basic on all Windows operating systems

WEB SITES

These are the only three development sites I have in my Microsoft Internet Explorer Favorites folder:

■   MSDN Online (*msdn.microsoft.com*)
   MSDN is the first place to start for Windows information. MSDN Online can be accessed at this address, as well as through the Microsoft-endorsed magazines *Microsoft Systems Journal* (MSJ) and *Microsoft Internet Developer* (MIND). Keep in mind that MSDN is partly a marketing organization, so sometimes a little hype creeps into various pieces.

■ Sysinternals (*www.sysinternals.com/*)
Mark Russinovich and Bryce Cogswell have some of the best debugging utilities around: Regmon, Filemon, DebugView, HandleEx, and many more. Many utilities come with full source code, and all are free! I check Mark and Bryce's site at least once a week so that I can keep my competitive edge.

■ MVPS.org (*www.mvps.org*)
This is the Web site for the Most Valuable Professional (MVP) newsgroup contributors. MVPs are developers and users who are experts in a particular area and assist in the various newsgroups with answering questions about Microsoft technologies and products. This site has great FAQs and links. I always read the newsgroup postings of Felix Kasza, Tomas Restrepo, and Karl E. Peterson.

Here are some other sites you might be interested in perusing:

■ CodeGuru (*www.codeguru.com*)
Primarily a Visual C++ information site

■ Experts Exchange (*www.experts-exchange.com*)
A technical information exchange site that covers many Windows topics

■ Dr. Dobb's Journal Microprocessor Resources (*www.x86.org*)
Everything you ever wanted to know about the x86 family of processors

■ Various mailing list archives (*discuss.microsoft.com/archives*)
Archives of some useful mailing lists, such as ATL and DCOM

Index

Note: Italicized page references indicate figures, tables, or program listings.

Index

N

naked calling convention, 191, *192*
NEG instruction, 197
/NODEFAULTLIB switch, 39
NOP instruction, 181–82
NOT instruction, 197

O

/O1 and /O2 switches, 38–39
OMAP format, 126
OnDebugBreak function, 119, *119–22*, 124
one-shot breakpoints, 119
OnIdle function, 328
OnOK method, 119
OnWndMsg function, 441
OpenDeadlockDetection function, 335
OpenProcess function, 113
/ORDER switch, 39
OR instruction, 197
OutputDebugStringA function, 397
OUTPUT_DEBUG_STRING_EVENT debug
    event, *101,* 113
OutputDebugString function, 61, 68, 113,
    168, 171, 337–38, 385, 394, 395.
    See also LIMODS (Limit
    OutputDebugStrings) utility
OutputDebugStringW function, 397

P

page faults, 38–39, 181
parameter access, 186–87
p-code
    history lesson, 226–27
    introduced, 226
    ramifications of using, 227–29
PDB format. *See* Program Database (PDB)
    format
/PDBTYPE:CON switch, 40
performance, poor, 5–6
performance tools, 19
planning, bugs and, 7

PlayKeys method, 365, 368, 369
pointer manipulation instructions, 199
POPAD instruction, 183–84
POP instruction, 182–83
PostThreadMessage function, 123
#pragma init_seg directive, 426, 428
#pragma warning directive, 32–33
PrintDlg API function, 221
PRINTDLG structure, 221
procedure call and return instructions,
    190–91
process bugs and solutions, 6–11
PROCESS_INFORMATION structure, 169–70
processor. *See CPU entries*
ProcessTrace function, 312, *312–16,*
    316, 319
Program Database (PDB) format, 31, 124,
    125–26
programming language books, 446
prolog, 184, 185
/P switch, 37
PulseModuleNotification function, 142
Purify (Rational Software), 427
PUSHAD instruction, 183–84
PUSH instruction, 182–83

Q

quality, bugs and, 9–11
quick break keys, 95–96

R

RaiseException API function, 258
ReadProcessMemory function, 96, 102,
    112, 113
REBASE.EXE utility, 34–36, *35*
rebasing DLLs, 34–36, *35*
Red Time, 25–26
registers, 177–79, *177, 178, 179,* 223
RegisterServiceCtrlHandler API
    function, 299
Registers window, 178–79, *178, 179*

Index

JOHN ROBBINS

John is an independent contractor and a developer based in New Hampshire. He lives with his wife, Pam, and the world-famous debugging cat, Pearl. He is also a contributing editor for *Microsoft Systems Journal*, where he writes the popular "Bugslayer" column. In his column, he discusses issues related to debugging, performance tuning, and team development. Additionally, he offers debugging seminars to companies throughout the world through David Solomon Expert Seminars (*www.solsem.com*). He is also a frequent speaker at developer conferences, including WinDev and WinSummit. John can be reached at *www.jprobbins.com*.

John was one of the first engineers at NuMega Technologies (now Compuware NuMega), where he was a key player in designing, developing, and managing many of the most-used and award-winning developer tools in the C/C++, Microsoft Visual Basic, and Java marketplace today. He worked on BoundsChecker (versions 3, 4, and 5), TrueTime (versions 1.0 and 1.1), TrueCoverage (version 1.0), SoftICE (version 3.24), and a product that hasn't been announced. He was also the only developer at NuMega with a couch in his office.

Prior to stumbling into software development in his late 20s, John was a paratrooper and Green Beret in the United States Army. Since he no longer gets the same adrenaline high that he used to jumping out of airplanes in the middle of the night onto an unlit, postage-stamp-size drop zone, with a full combat load, he rides motorcycles at high rates of speed—much to his wife's chagrin.

The manuscript for this book was prepared using Microsoft Word 2000. Pages were composed by Microsoft Press using Adobe PageMaker 6.52 for Windows, with text in Garamond and display type in Helvetica Black. Composed pages were delivered to the printer as electronic prepress files.

Cover Graphic Designer

Girvin | Strategic Branding & Design

Cover Illustrator

Glenn Mitsui

Interior Graphic Artist

Rob Nance

Principal Compositor

Dan Latimer

Principal Proofreader/Copy Editor

Roger LeBlanc

Indexer

Hugh Maddocks

Best practices
for real-world software development

Now you can apply the industry's best software engineering practices to your own development projects with the BEST PRACTICES series from Microsoft Press. Written by some of the most knowledgeable and articulate practitioners in the business, these award-winning books take a pragmatic approach to managing the people, processes, and principles of software development. Use them to learn how to:

- Get high-pressure development schedules under control

- Energize software teams to work effectively
- Communicate delivery and quality expectations across the team and to management
- Keep costs down
- Deliver the best possible product to customers

Packed with practical, field-tested tools and tactics, BEST PRACTICES books offer candid accounts of what works and what doesn't, straight from the real-world experiences of the leading software vendors. Get them—and you get the inside track to everyday software excellence.

Code Complete		Debugging the Development Process		Dynamics of Software Development		Managing the Testing Process		Rapid Development		Writing Solid Code		Software Project Survival Guide	
ISBN: 1-55615-484-4		ISBN: 1-55615-650-2		ISBN: 1-55615-823-8		ISBN: 0-7356-0584-X		ISBN: 1-55615-900-5		ISBN: 1-55615-551-4		ISBN: 1-57231-6217	
U.S.A.	$35.00	U.S.A.	$24.95	U.S.A.	$24.95	U.S.A.	$39.99	U.S.A.	$35.00	U.S.A.	$24.95	U.S.A.	$24.99
UK	£22.99	UK	£16.99	UK	£16.99	UK	£25.99	UK	£22.99	UK	£16.99	UK	£16.99
Canada	$44.95	Canada	$32.95	Canada	$33.95	[V.A.T. included] Canada $59.99		Canada	$46.95	Canada	$32.95	Canada	$34.99

Microsoft Press® products are available worldwide wherever quality computer books are sold. For more information, contact your book or computer retailer, software reseller, or local Microsoft® Sales Office, or visit our Web site at mspress.microsoft.com. To locate your nearest source for Microsoft Press products, or to order directly, call 1-800-MSPRESS in the U.S. (in Canada, call 1-800-268-2222).

Prices and availability dates are subject to change.

mspress.microsoft.com

MICROSOFT LICENSE AGREEMENT
Book Companion CD

IMPORTANT—READ CAREFULLY: This Microsoft End-User License Agreement ("EULA") is a legal agreement between you (either an individual or an entity) and Microsoft Corporation for the Microsoft product identified above, which includes computer software and may include associated media, printed materials, and "online" or electronic documentation ("SOFTWARE PRODUCT"). Any component included within the SOFTWARE PRODUCT that is accompanied by a separate End-User License Agreement shall be governed by such agreement and not the terms set forth below. By installing, copying, or otherwise using the SOFTWARE PRODUCT, you agree to be bound by the terms of this EULA. If you do not agree to the terms of this EULA, you are not authorized to install, copy, or otherwise use the SOFTWARE PRODUCT; you may, however, return the SOFTWARE PRODUCT, along with all printed materials and other items that form a part of the Microsoft product that includes the SOFTWARE PRODUCT, to the place you obtained them for a full refund.

SOFTWARE PRODUCT LICENSE

The SOFTWARE PRODUCT is protected by United States copyright laws and international copyright treaties, as well as other intellectual property laws and treaties. The SOFTWARE PRODUCT is licensed, not sold.

1. **GRANT OF LICENSE.** This EULA grants you the following rights:

    a. **Software Product.** You may install and use one copy of the SOFTWARE PRODUCT on a single computer. The primary user of the computer on which the SOFTWARE PRODUCT is installed may make a second copy for his or her exclusive use on a portable computer.

    b. **Storage/Network Use.** You may also store or install a copy of the SOFTWARE PRODUCT on a storage device, such as a network server, used only to install or run the SOFTWARE PRODUCT on your other computers over an internal network; however, you must acquire and dedicate a license for each separate computer on which the SOFTWARE PRODUCT is installed or run from the storage device. A license for the SOFTWARE PRODUCT may not be shared or used concurrently on different computers.

    c. **License Pak.** If you have acquired this EULA in a Microsoft License Pak, you may make the number of additional copies of the computer software portion of the SOFTWARE PRODUCT authorized on the printed copy of this EULA, and you may use each copy in the manner specified above. You are also entitled to make a corresponding number of secondary copies for portable computer use as specified above.

    d. **Sample Code.** Solely with respect to portions, if any, of the SOFTWARE PRODUCT that are identified within the SOFTWARE PRODUCT as sample code (the "SAMPLE CODE"):

    i. **Use and Modification.** Microsoft grants you the right to use and modify the source code version of the SAMPLE CODE, *provided* you comply with subsection (d)(iii) below. You may not distribute the SAMPLE CODE, or any modified version of the SAMPLE CODE, in source code form.

    ii. **Redistributable Files.** Provided you comply with subsection (d)(iii) below, Microsoft grants you a nonexclusive, royalty-free right to reproduce and distribute the object code version of the SAMPLE CODE and of any modified SAMPLE CODE, other than SAMPLE CODE, or any modified version thereof, designated as not redistributable in the Readme file that forms a part of the SOFTWARE PRODUCT (the "Non-Redistributable Sample Code"). All SAMPLE CODE other than the Non-Redistributable Sample Code is collectively referred to as the "REDISTRIBUTABLES."

    iii. **Redistribution Requirements.** If you redistribute the REDISTRIBUTABLES, you agree to: (i) distribute the REDISTRIBUTABLES in object code form only in conjunction with and as a part of your software application product; (ii) not use Microsoft's name, logo, or trademarks to market your software application product; (iii) include a valid copyright notice on your software application product; (iv) indemnify, hold harmless, and defend Microsoft from and against any claims or lawsuits, including attorney's fees, that arise or result from the use or distribution of your software application product; and (v) not permit further distribution of the REDISTRIBUTABLES by your end user. Contact Microsoft for the applicable royalties due and other licensing terms for all other uses and/or distribution of the REDISTRIBUTABLES.

2. **DESCRIPTION OF OTHER RIGHTS AND LIMITATIONS.**

    • **Limitations on Reverse Engineering, Decompilation, and Disassembly.** You may not reverse engineer, decompile, or disassemble the SOFTWARE PRODUCT, except and only to the extent that such activity is expressly permitted by applicable law notwithstanding this limitation.

    • **Separation of Components.** The SOFTWARE PRODUCT is licensed as a single product. Its component parts may not be separated for use on more than one computer.

    • **Rental.** You may not rent, lease, or lend the SOFTWARE PRODUCT.

    • **Support Services.** Microsoft may, but is not obligated to, provide you with support services related to the SOFTWARE PRODUCT ("Support Services"). Use of Support Services is governed by the Microsoft policies and programs described in the user manual, in "online" documentation, and/or in other Microsoft-provided materials. Any supplemental software code provided to you as part of the Support Services shall be considered part of the SOFTWARE PRODUCT and subject to the terms and conditions of this EULA. With respect to technical information you provide to Microsoft as part of the Support Services, Microsoft may use such information for its business purposes, including for product support and development. Microsoft will not utilize such technical information in a form that personally identifies you.

- **Software Transfer.** You may permanently transfer all of your rights under this EULA, provided you retain no copies, you transfer all of the SOFTWARE PRODUCT (including all component parts, the media and printed materials, any upgrades, this EULA, and, if applicable, the Certificate of Authenticity), **and** the recipient agrees to the terms of this EULA.

- **Termination.** Without prejudice to any other rights, Microsoft may terminate this EULA if you fail to comply with the terms and conditions of this EULA. In such event, you must destroy all copies of the SOFTWARE PRODUCT and all of its component parts.

3. **COPYRIGHT.** All title and copyrights in and to the SOFTWARE PRODUCT (including but not limited to any images, photographs, animations, video, audio, music, text, SAMPLE CODE, REDISTRIBUTABLES, and "applets" incorporated into the SOFTWARE PRODUCT) and any copies of the SOFTWARE PRODUCT are owned by Microsoft or its suppliers. The SOFTWARE PRODUCT is protected by copyright laws and international treaty provisions. Therefore, you must treat the SOFTWARE PRODUCT like any other copyrighted material **except** that you may install the SOFTWARE PRODUCT on a single computer provided you keep the original solely for backup or archival purposes. You may not copy the printed materials accompanying the SOFTWARE PRODUCT.

4. **U.S. GOVERNMENT RESTRICTED RIGHTS.** The SOFTWARE PRODUCT and documentation are provided with RESTRICTED RIGHTS. Use, duplication, or disclosure by the Government is subject to restrictions as set forth in subparagraph (c)(1)(ii) of the Rights in Technical Data and Computer Software clause at DFARS 252.227-7013 or subparagraphs (c)(1) and (2) of the Commercial Computer Software—Restricted Rights at 48 CFR 52.227-19, as applicable. Manufacturer is Microsoft Corporation/One Microsoft Way/Redmond, WA 98052-6399.

5. **EXPORT RESTRICTIONS.** You agree that you will not export or re-export the SOFTWARE PRODUCT, any part thereof, or any process or service that is the direct product of the SOFTWARE PRODUCT (the foregoing collectively referred to as the "Restricted Components"), to any country, person, entity, or end user subject to U.S. export restrictions. You specifically agree not to export or re-export any of the Restricted Components (i) to any country to which the U.S. has embargoed or restricted the export of goods or services, which currently include, but are not necessarily limited to, Cuba, Iran, Iraq, Libya, North Korea, Sudan, and Syria, or to any national of any such country, wherever located, who intends to transmit or transport the Restricted Components back to such country; (ii) to any end user who you know or have reason to know will utilize the Restricted Components in the design, development, or production of nuclear, chemical, or biological weapons; or (iii) to any end user who has been prohibited from participating in U.S. export transactions by any federal agency of the U.S. government. You warrant and represent that neither the BXA nor any other U.S. federal agency has suspended, revoked, or denied your export privileges.

DISCLAIMER OF WARRANTY

NO WARRANTIES OR CONDITIONS. MICROSOFT EXPRESSLY DISCLAIMS ANY WARRANTY OR CONDITION FOR THE SOFTWARE PRODUCT. THE SOFTWARE PRODUCT AND ANY RELATED DOCUMENTATION ARE PROVIDED "AS IS" WITHOUT WARRANTY OR CONDITION OF ANY KIND, EITHER EXPRESS OR IMPLIED, INCLUDING, WITHOUT LIMITATION, THE IMPLIED WARRANTIES OF MERCHANTABILITY, FITNESS FOR A PARTICULAR PURPOSE, OR NONINFRINGEMENT. THE ENTIRE RISK ARISING OUT OF USE OR PERFORMANCE OF THE SOFTWARE PRODUCT REMAINS WITH YOU.

LIMITATION OF LIABILITY. TO THE MAXIMUM EXTENT PERMITTED BY APPLICABLE LAW, IN NO EVENT SHALL MICROSOFT OR ITS SUPPLIERS BE LIABLE FOR ANY SPECIAL, INCIDENTAL, INDIRECT, OR CONSEQUENTIAL DAMAGES WHATSOEVER (INCLUDING, WITHOUT LIMITATION, DAMAGES FOR LOSS OF BUSINESS PROFITS, BUSINESS INTERRUPTION, LOSS OF BUSINESS INFORMATION, OR ANY OTHER PECUNIARY LOSS) ARISING OUT OF THE USE OF OR INABILITY TO USE THE SOFTWARE PRODUCT OR THE PROVISION OF OR FAILURE TO PROVIDE SUPPORT SERVICES, EVEN IF MICROSOFT HAS BEEN ADVISED OF THE POSSIBILITY OF SUCH DAMAGES. IN ANY CASE, MICROSOFT'S ENTIRE LIABILITY UNDER ANY PROVISION OF THIS EULA SHALL BE LIMITED TO THE GREATER OF THE AMOUNT ACTUALLY PAID BY YOU FOR THE SOFTWARE PRODUCT OR US$5.00; PROVIDED, HOWEVER, IF YOU HAVE ENTERED INTO A MICROSOFT SUPPORT SERVICES AGREEMENT, MICROSOFT'S ENTIRE LIABILITY REGARDING SUPPORT SERVICES SHALL BE GOVERNED BY THE TERMS OF THAT AGREEMENT. BECAUSE SOME STATES AND JURISDICTIONS DO NOT ALLOW THE EXCLUSION OR LIMITATION OF LIABILITY, THE ABOVE LIMITATION MAY NOT APPLY TO YOU.

MISCELLANEOUS

This EULA is governed by the laws of the State of Washington USA, except and only to the extent that applicable law mandates governing law of a different jurisdiction.

Should you have any questions concerning this EULA, or if you desire to contact Microsoft for any reason, please contact the Microsoft subsidiary serving your country, or write: Microsoft Sales Information Center/One Microsoft Way/Redmond, WA 98052-6399.

Breakpoint Syntax Format

{[function],[source file],[binary module]}[operation]
The part in braces is called the *context*; the commas are not optional.

Element	Description
Function	The optional name of the function to break in, which can include full function prototype
Source file	The optional source file name to break in, which can include complete path
Binary module	The optional binary module to break in, which can include complete path
Operation	The mandatory breakpoint type: location, global expression, global location, or Windows message

Location Breakpoints

All location breakpoints are manually set in the Breakpoints dialog box, Location tab, Break At edit control

Location Type	Description	Display in Breakpoints Dialog Box
Source line	Click the Insert/Remove breakpoint button when the cursor is on the line of source code you want to break on.	at '{,TEST.CPP,}.20'
First instruction of a function	Enter the name of your function. If the debugger is running, it might prompt you for the proper function with the Resolve Ambiguity dialog box.	at 'CDialog::OnOK'
Any address	Enter the hexadecimal number for the address you want to break at.	at '0x417013'
Break on exported system function (symbols loaded for module)	Enter the context information and fill in the binary module information. For the exported function, enter the name preceded by an underscore and followed by an @ sign and the number of parameters multiplied by 4.	at '{,,KERNEL32.DLL}_LoadLibraryA@4'
Break on exported system function (symbols not loaded for module)	Enter the context information, fill in the binary module information, and enter the exported name.	at '{,,KERNEL32.DLL}LoadLibraryA'

Location Breakpoint Modifiers

After setting a regular location breakpoint, you can modify how you want to break on that location. To set a condition, select the location breakpoint in the Breakpoints dialog box and click the Condition button to bring up the Breakpoint Condition dialog box.

Modifier Type	Description	Display in Breakpoints Dialog Box
Skip count	Skip the breakpoint a specific number of times. In the Enter The Number Of Times To Skip Before Stopping edit control, enter the number of times to skip the breakpoint. If you want to see how many times a breakpoint was hit before a crash in a loop, set the skip count to a number higher than the maximum iterations. When the loop crashes, bring up the Breakpoints dialog box and the number of skips will show after the breakpoint in the bottom of the dialog box.	at '{,WINMAIN.CPP,}.24, skip five times(5)'
Break when conditional expression is true	Enter your expression to evaluate in the Enter The Expression To Be Evaluated edit control. Your expression can't contain function calls or macro values. You can use all C-style comparison operators. To check string values, check each individual character value with logical-AND operators.	at '{,WINMAIN.CPP,}.24' when 'i==3'
Break when variable changes	Enter the variable in the Enter The Expression To Be Evaluated edit control. Enter the number of elements in the Enter The Number Of Elements To Watch In An Array Or Structure edit control. The element size is based on the size of the variable entered. Only data writes that change the variable will cause the break.	at '{,WINMAIN.CPP,}.24' when 'szBuff' (length:5) changes

Global Expression and Conditional Breakpoints

Global expression and conditional breakpoints are set in the Breakpoints dialog box, Data tab, Enter The Expression To Be Evaluated edit control. These breakpoints use the Intel CPU debug registers. Although there are four registers, you'll probably be able to set only two breakpoints that use them. With both global breakpoints, you'll be better off if you use the hexadecimal address of the memory you want to watch and cast it to either a short, word, or double word. Although the debugger might accept your breakpoint, it might not be able to use a debug register and thus will force your process to single-step each assembly-language instruction to check the memory address.

Modifier Type	Description	Display in Breakpoints Dialog Box
Global expression	The breakpoint that triggers when the memory at a specific location changes.	at '*(char*)0x4287C8'
Global conditional	The breakpoint to use if you want to check a memory location to see when a specific value is written to that location. This breakpoint is notoriously difficult to get the debugger to accept.	at '*(char*)0x4287C8=='G''

Message Breakpoints

Message breakpoints are much more useful when you're doing straight SDK programming. With Microsoft Foundation Class (MFC) library programming, setting a message breakpoint on the one *AfxWndProc* for all windows in your program can be very frustrating. You might be better off using a location breakpoint with a conditional expression modifier. For example, to break on the *WM_PAINT* message for a particular class, the expression would be "{,WINCORE.CPP.}.1584 when (this==0x0012EFE74)&&(message==0xF)".

Expression and Watch Window Pseudoregisters

Pseudoregister	Description
@ERR	Last error value; the same value returned by the *GetLastError* API function
@TIB	Thread information block for the current thread; necessary because the debugger doesn't handle the "FS:0" format
@CLK	Undocumented clock register; usable only in the Watch window
@EAX, @EBX, @ECX, @EDX, @ESI, @EDI, @EIP, @ESP, @EBP, @EFL	Intel CPU registers
@CS, @DS, @ES, @SS, @FS, @GS	Intel CPU segment registers
@ST0, @ST1, @ST2, @ST3, @ST4, @ST5, @ST6, @ST7	Intel CPU floating-point registers

Formatting Symbols for Watch Window Variables

Symbol	Format Description	Sample	Displays
d, i	Signed decimal integer	(int)0xF000F065,d	-268373915
u	Unsigned decimal integer	0x0065,u	101
o	Unsigned octal integer	0xF065,o	0170145
x, X	Hexadecimal integer	61541,X	0x0000F065
l, h	Long or short prefix for d, i, u, o, x, X	0x00406042,hx	0x0c22
f	Signed floating-point	3./2.,f	1.500000
e	Signed scientific notation	3./2,e	1.500000e+000
g	Signed floating-point or signed scientific notation, whichever is shorter	3./2,g	1.5
c	Single character	0x0065,c	'e'
s	String	szHiWorld,s	"Hello world"
su	Unicode string	szWHiWorld,su	"Hello world"
st	Unicode string or ANSI string, depending on Unicode Strings setting in AUTOEXP.DAT		
hr	*HRESULT* or Win32 error code	0x00000000,hr	S_OK
wm	Windows message numbers	0x0010,wm	WM_CLOSE

Formatting Symbols for Watch Window Memory Dumps

Symbol	Format Description	Sample	Displays
ma	64 ASCII characters	0x0012ffac,ma	0x0012ffac .4...0...".0W&.......1W&.0.:W..1 ....".1.JO&.1.2."..1...0y....1
m	16 bytes in hexadecimal followed by 16 ASCII characters	0x0012ffac,m	0x0012ffac b3 34 cb 00 84 30 94 80 ff 22 8a 30 57 26 00 00 .4...0...".0W&..
mb	16 bytes in hexadecimal followed by 16 ASCII characters	0x0012ffac,mb	0x0012ffac b3 34 cb 00 84 30 94 80 ff 22 8a 30 57 26 00 00 .4...0...".0W&..
mw	8 words	0x0012ffac,mw	0x0012ffac 34b3 00cb 3084 8094 22ff 308a 2657 0000
md	4 double words	0x0012ffac,md	0x0012ffac 00cb34b3 80943084 308a22ff 00002657
mq	4 quadwords	0x0012ffac,mq	0x0012ffac 8094308400cb34b3 00002657308a22ff
mu	2-byte characters (Unicode)	0x0012ffac,mu	0x0012ffac 34b3 00cb 3084 8094 22ff 308a 2657 0000 ?.?????.
# (undocumented)	Expands a pointer to a memory location to the specified number of values	pCharArray,10	Expanded array of 10 characters using +/- expanders

Instruction Format

Basic Format	[prefix] instruction [operands]
Single-instruction operands	XXX source
Two-instruction operands	XXX destination, source

General-Purpose Registers

32-Bit Register	16-Bit Access	Low-Byte Access (bits 0–7)	High-Byte Access (bits 8–15)	Special Uses
EAX	AX	AL	AH	Integer function return values are stored here.
EBX	BX	BL	BH	
ECX	CX	CL	CH	Loop instruction counters use this register for counting.
EDX	DX	DL	DH	The high 32 bits of 64-bit values are stored here.
ESI	SI			In memory move or compare instructions, the source address is stored here.
EDI	DI			In memory move or compare instructions, the destination is stored here.
ESP	SP			The stack pointer. This register is changed implicitly when calling functions, returning from functions, making room on the stack for local variables, and cleaning up the stack.
EBP	BP			Base/frame pointer. This register holds the stack frame for a procedure.

Memory Addressing

Addressing Example	Description and How to Find the Value
[0040129Ah]	Global variable. Look up the value in the Memory window.
[EAX]	Dereferencing pointer stored in a register. Look at the number in the register and use that number in the Memory window.
[EAX+EBX*2]	Use the Register window Effective Address display to see the value.

Variable Access

Type	Description
Global variable	Global variables are located at absolute memory addresses, such as [0040129Ah].
Function parameter	In standard stack frames, parameters are positive offsets from the EBP register, such as [EBP+8h].
Local variables	In standard stack frames, local variables are negative offsets from the EBP register, such as [EBP-4h].

Common Assembly-Language Instructions

Instruction	Description
ADD	Addition. Adds the source to the destination and stores the result in the destination operand.
AND	Logical-AND. Performs a bitwise AND operation on the destination and source and stores the result in the destination.
CALL	Calls a procedure.
CMP	Compare. Compares by subtracting the destination operand from the source operand.
CMPS	Compare strings. Compares the memory pointed to by the EDI and ESI registers.
DEC	Subtracts 1 from the destination operand.
DIV	Unsigned division. Divides the value in the EAX register by the source operand. The quotient is stored in EAX, and the remainder in EDX.
IDIV	Signed division. Divides the value in the EAX register by the source operand. The quotient is stored in EAX, and the remainder in EDX.
IMUL	Signed multiplication. Multiplies the value in EAX by the source operand. The result is stored in EDX:EAX.
INC	Increment. Adds 1 to the destination operand.
INT 3	Breakpoint interrupt

Common Assembly-Language Instructions (continued)

Instruction	Description*
JA	Jump if above; CY = 0 and ZR = 0
JB	Jump if below; CY = 1
JBE	Jump if below or equal; CY = 1 or ZR = 1
JC	Jump if carry; CY = 1
JE	Jump if equal; ZR = 1
JG	Jump if greater than; ZR = 0 and PL = OV
JGE	Jump if greater than or equal; PL = OV
JL	Jump if less than; PL <> OV
JLE	Jump if less than or equal; ZR = 1 or PL <> OV
JMP	Jump to an absolute address
JNC	Jump if no carry; CY = 0
JNE	Jump if not equal; ZR = 0
JNZ	Jump if not 0; ZR = 0
JZ	Jump if 0; ZR = 1
LEA	Load effective address. Loads the destination with the address of the source operand.
LEAVE	Restore the CPU state when leaving the function. Does the same as MOV ESP, EBP POP EBP
LOCK	Assert LOCK# signal prefix. This is not an instruction but a prefix to other instructions. LOCK tells the CPU that the memory accessed by the following instruction needs to be an atomic operation so that the CPU can lock the memory bus.
LOOP	Loop a number of times as specified in ECX.
MOV	Move a value from a register to memory or from memory to a register.
MOVS	Move data from string to string. Moves the memory at the address in ESI to the memory address in EDI.
MOVSX	Move with sign-extend. Sign extends a smaller-size value into a bigger-size value.
MOVZX	Move with zero-extend. Zero extends a smaller-size value into a bigger-size value.
MUL	Unsigned multiplication. Multiplies the value in EAX by the source operand. The result is stored in EDX:EAX.
NEG	Two's complement negation. Subtracts the operand from 0.
NOT	One's complement negation. Performs a bitwise operation that turns each binary 1 into a 0 and each 0 into a 1.
OR	Logical-OR. Performs a bitwise inclusive OR operation on the destination and source operands and stores the result in the destination.
POP	Pop a value from the stack
POPAD	Pop all general-purpose registers
PUSH	Push a word or a double word onto the stack
PUSHAD	Push all general-purpose registers
REP	Repeat for count in ECX. A common prefix to STOS.
REPE	Repeat while equal or ECX count is not 0. A common prefix to CMPS.
REPNE	Repeat while not equal or ECX count is not 0. A common prefix to SCAS.
RET	Return from a procedure. RET can be followed by a fixed number, which is the number of bytes to remove from the stack before returning the caller.
SCAS	Scan string. Compares the memory at the address in EDI with the value in EAX.
SHL	Shift left, multiply by 2
SHR	Shift right, divide by 2
STOS	Store string. Stores the value in EAX into the memory at the address in EDI.
SUB	Subtracts the source from the destination operand and stores the value in the destination operand.
TEST	Logical compare. Performs a bitwise logical-AND of the operands and sets the flags accordingly.
XOR	Logical-OR (exclusive). Primarily used to clear a register, such as XOR EAX, EAX.

* In the jump instructions, CY = Carry Flag, ZR = Zero Flag, PL = Sign Flag, and OV = Overflow Flag.

OWNER REGISTRATION CARD

Register Today!

0-7356-0886-5

Return the bottom portion of this card to register today.

Debugging Applications

FIRST NAME   MIDDLE INITIAL   LAST NAME

INSTITUTION OR COMPANY NAME

ADDRESS

CITY   STATE   ZIP

(   )

E-MAIL ADDRESS   PHONE NUMBER

U.S. and Canada addresses only. Fill in information above and mail postage-free.
Please mail only the bottom half of this page.

For information about Microsoft Press®
products, visit our Web site at
mspress.microsoft.com

Microsoft